THE COMPLETE
SEA KAYAKER'S
HANDBOOK
SECOND EDITION

THE COMPLETE
SEA KAYAKER'S
HANDBOOK
SECOND EDITION

SHELLEY JOHNSON

McGraw Hill

New York Chicago San Francisco Lisbon London Madrid Mexico City
Milan New Delhi San Juan Seoul Singapore Sydney Toronto

The McGraw·Hill Companies

3 4 5 6 7 8 9 10 11 12 13 14 15   DOC/DOC   1 9 8 7 6 5 4

ISBN   978-0-07-174711-0
MHID   0-07-174711-7

Library of Congress Cataloging-in-Publication Data

Johnson, Shelley, 1954-
       The complete sea kayaker's handbook / Shelley Johnson. — 2nd ed.
              p.   cm.
       Includes index.
       ISBN-13: 978-0-07-174711-0
       ISBN-10: 0-07-174711-7
       1. Sea kayaking.   I. Title.

   GV788.5.J62   2011
   797.1'224—dc22   2010040420

Interior design by Irving Perkins
Interior illustrations by Christopher Hoyt

Photos by Jim Dugan except as noted: Ocean Kayak, pages 2 (upper and lower left), 23, 90, 91, 257; Joel Rogers, pages 2, 277 (left); Wilderness Systems, pages 2 (lower right), 22; Doug Hayward, pages 3, 6, 45, 49, 69, 96, 113, 134, 136, 140, 147, 149 (top), 180 (right); Current Designs, pages 14, 15, 27, 33, 34, 275; Courtesy Provincial Archives of British Columbia, page 17; America's Coastlines Collection, National Marine Fisheries Service, page 18 (top); Superior Kayaks, page 32; Eddyline Kayaks, 38; Francis Zera, page 42; Cliff Leight, pages 43, 268, 269; Bob Foote and Karen Knight, page 127 (left); United States Forest Service, pages 127 (right), 128 (top); Mark Theobald/kayakdiving .com, page 129; Shelley Johnson, pages 139, 180 (left), 184, 277 (right); Nancy Weal, page 150; Outside Images, pages 173, 196, 276; NOAA, page 188; Eldridge Tide and Pilot Book, page 186; Nigel Calder, pages 190 (top), 191 (top); Bill Brogdon, pages 202, 203; Jonathan Hanson, page 240; Corbis Images, page 272.

McGraw-Hill books are available at special quantity discounts to use as premiums and sales promotions or for use in corporate training programs. To contact a representative, please e-mail us at bulksales@mcgraw-hill.com.

This book is printed on acid-free paper.

Contents

Acknowledgments

For this new edition, I was fortunate to work with many of the same people who were so helpful the first time around in 2001. Molly Mulhern has been a constant source of support and positive influence as senior editor. Jim Dugan was again a joy to work with during photo shoots and during the computer photo editing and selection (this step has certainly changed since 2001). Cheryl Levin once again served as the primary model and graciously lugged boats one minute and then assumed a precise yoga pose for the camera the very next. Thanks to Ed Eaton for the loan of cartop equipment and then agreeing to show how it's used for the camera; Stuart Lee of Accent Paddles for an hour-long discussion on the minutia of paddle design and materials; Vaughan Smith for the loan of paddles and accessories that I always seem to need the night before a photo shoot; and the crew in the paddlesports department of Maine Sport for helping move boats around and covering for staff stolen from the sales floor and put in front of a camera. Kayakers are good people.

This book is the result of years of goofing around in boats, fielding questions from students and prospective kayak gear buyers, and pestering everyone from kayak designers to meteorologists with my own nagging questions. I've reaped more than my share of help from fellow paddlers, industry colleagues, and friends. In particular I'd like to thank the following people:

Vaughan Smith for his unerring eye for technique explanations and a very sharp blue pencil; Lee Moyer for his patient and exhaustive explanations of boat design and the engineering reality behind it; Derek Hutchinson and Brian Henry for their good-natured support; Kevin Bedford for his insightful feedback during the original manuscript development; Stuart and Marianne Smith of Maine Sport Outfitters and their staff for allowing me to paw through merchandise, grab customers for photos, and clutter their lawn with gear; Matthew Levin, Cheryl Levin, Vaughan Smith, and Ben Fuller, who served as superb models for kayaking techniques during photo shoots (and cheerfully jumped in and out of chilly water on a cold, raw day); all the manufacturers and individuals who provided photos and samples—Current Designs, Necky Kayaks, Eddyline Kayaks, Ocean Kayak, Wilderness Systems, Accent Paddles, Kokatat, MTI, Paddle Boy Designs, Seattle Sports, Stearns Manufacturing, Thule, Mark and Celeste Rogers of Superior Kayaks, Cheri Nylen and Janet Zeller of the American Canoe Association, Mark Theobold, Tamsin Venn of Atlantic Coastal Kayaker, and Karen Knight.

Preface

Ten years have passed since the original edition of *The Complete Sea Kayaker's Handbook* was published. During those ten years, the sport of kayaking has undergone some meaningful adjustments and adapted to shifts in lifestyle and economic realities. But the act of putting paddle to water with only the human body for power is elegantly simple and will never change. Instead, our ability to find the time and place for these pursuits and wring every ounce of enjoyment from them mark a notable shift in the paddling world. The past ten years have seen the development of new materials, boat designs, and even where and how kayaks are sold.

The aging of the paddling population has driven the need for lighter-weight materials, smaller and more manageable boats, tools for cartop loading and carrying kayaks, and much more comfortable seats and practical cockpit designs. The ready availability of information and shopping via the Web have created a heightened price consciousness among many consumers. This has often driven the sale of kayak equipment from the local enthusiast's shop into the larger chain stores and outlets as kayaks became "commoditized." Although this has brought kayaking to the masses, the important safety and local paddling information that was usually included with each kayak sale was often lost.

The most noticeable change in kayak designs is the huge growth in the popularity of recreational boats of less than fourteen feet. With the plethora of these small and wide kayak designs, more people now have access to and are willing to try out kayaking. These user-friendly and accommodating boats coupled with ever furiously paced lifestyles that leave little time for recreation now mean that kayaking is often done only in small chunks of time and in local waters not likely to be defined as "the sea." This is a good thing in that it gets more people outside and on the water. Yet it is somewhat troubling that there is often little regard for safety and good technique by these new paddlers and the stores that support their purchases, the thought apparently being, How much could it really matter for an hour on the local pond? But these boats don't always stay on the local pond, and several fatal accidents over the past few years have proven the inadvisability of taking a recreational kayak to sea.

This book will give you a deeper understanding of why it matters and explain how to become a good and safe paddler. You may never go to sea, but these same skills and understanding of how to move a small boat from place to place will allow you to relax and enjoy the process at a deeper level—and maybe whet your appetite to try a bit more.

Over the years, there have been many exciting and heartening developments in the world of sea kayaking: a burgeoning and well-supported network of water trails; concern about and protection of public access to bodies of water; increased interest in the history of our waterways and how they were tied to one another and to the life of local populations; and, thankfully, no decrease in the fierce love and protection that most kayakers feel for the places they paddle and explore.

Little has changed about how and why we paddle and the questions that most novice paddlers ask. I am still challenged by the need for hard and fast formulas for how long, how wide, how stable, how cold, and how thick when helping others make choices. And I still refuse to take shortcuts when explaining these things to the reader, believing that others must have the same questions I had when I was starting out.

As to the *why*, I think we will always need a way to escape to a place where we lower our guard and let the rhythms, sounds, and challenges of nature come in. A kayak is a great way to get there.

Introduction

Sea kayaking is a sport that engages both mind and body. It offers the simple pleasures of gliding peacefully through a quiet cove and the complex demands of responding to the interactions between hull and sea. It's an activity that rewards the miles of rhythmic, repetitious movement with sudden and unexpected delights, then confronts you with the intellectual exercise of navigating in fog. You'll never tire of this sport.

Sea kayaking is as hard to define as it is easy to enjoy. Its origins are as ancient as the hunting expeditions that plied brutal, arctic waters, but its current development includes high-tech boats of ultralight Kevlar and satellite navigation systems. Sea kayaking even defies the limitations of its own name by embracing freshwater rivers, ponds, and streams as comfortably as it settles into a wave trough on the open ocean.

My interest in sea kayaking grew from a need to get onto the water in a way that was affordable and wouldn't limit me to high-adrenaline moments only. I happily abandoned my whitewater boat and embraced this long, sleek kayak that promised to take me almost anywhere but back into the realm of rock-dodging whitewater (been there, done that). More than twenty years and several long, sleek boats later, the sport of sea kayaking continues to fascinate and sustain me. And I am still just as puzzled and fascinated by the breadth of what it has to offer. That is the very core of sea kayaking: simple, yet demanding; easy, but difficult to master; a placid pond, and a breaking wave face.

This book takes much the same approach to the sport as my own over the years. We'll gather information, only to poke and prod it, and question its very right to exist. Each section will start with information that makes no assumption of past knowledge. It will nurture your interest in getting started and answer some of those questions in a straightforward manner. But we won't stop there. We're going to explore the theory—even controversy—behind some of these simple explanations and pull at all those little loose threads until we figure things out. I want every reader to experience the joy of newfound information, whether you're just starting out or whether you feel confident enough in your skills to be instructing others.

As you read through the book, feel comfortable to bail out when you have enough information for your needs at that moment. This is a book to come back to. As you mature as a paddler, the information you need will mature, and you'll find it all here. There are sidebars offering contrary opinions, formulas from the technicians, and plenty of support from those who haven't lost their "beginner's mind." Every step of the way, I'll urge you to test your new knowledge on the water: don't just take my word for it!

May your copy of this book be dog-eared, water stained, and enjoyed for many years.

THE COMPLETE
SEA KAYAKER'S
HANDBOOK
SECOND EDITION

1

Getting Ready

MAKING A DECISION AMID A SEA OF OPTIONS

Sea kayaking offers so many ways to explore our world that one of your most important decisions will have to be made before you even slide into the cockpit of your boat. You'll need to consider what you want from your sea kayaking experience. Are you looking forward to sitting alone in a quiet marsh at sunset to watch the returning shorebirds? Facing a challenging coastline of rocks and pounding surf? Or spending an afternoon of tidal pool exploring and then having an island picnic with your family? Wherever your imagination leads you, you'll need the skills and the proper equipment to get you there and back.

Focus on what your goals might be by asking yourself a few basic questions. Your answers to the following questions will guide your equipment purchases, selection of an instructional program, and plans for kayak outings. As you become a more proficient sea kayaker, your answers to these questions may change. That's OK: sea kayaking is a sport that will grow with you.

- What do I want to be able to do right away?
- What will I primarily use my boat for? Do I plan to go most often on day trips from home or on longer, overnight excursions?
- Where will I do most of my paddling? Will I be kayaking on inland lakes, on one of the Great Lakes, or along the coastline?
- What would I love to do (maybe it's just a fantasy at this point) once I become more skilled?
- What sport or hobby (scuba diving, fly-fishing, photography, etc.) do I do now that sea kayaking can enhance?
- If I'm purchasing another round of equipment, what do the new pieces need to do differently or better?
- If I have been paddling for a while, what skills do I still lack or need to work on?

As you read this book, bear in mind your answers to these questions, focusing on how each new piece of information can help you clarify and reach your paddling goals.

Sea kayaking encompasses a broad range of boat uses, skills, and interests.

INSTRUCTION

I'm a real believer in the value of instructional programs. By giving you a solid base of information and skills you can build upon at your own pace, they're the most efficient way to learn a new sport. You won't have to unlearn bad techniques or habits, and starting out with a more skilled and knowledgeable paddler at your side is reassuring.

Many instructional programs are available to a novice sea kayaker. You can choose from two-hour indoor pool sessions to fourteen-day courses on a remote island. There's nothing wrong with checking out the sport in a two-hour sampler, but you'll need at least a full day of instruction to cover some of the basic skills for paddling and safety. It's important for you to have a chance to view and then practice reentry skills under supervision, and to get some helpful guidance on your paddling strokes before heading out on your own. You should then consider enrolling in programs to take you beyond the basic skills.

Most sea kayaking instructors in the United States are certified by either the American Canoe Association (ACA) or the British Canoe Union (BCU), but don't use certification as a criteria for selecting an instructor—some of the best instructors aren't certified. These two organizations run instructional programs for all levels of skill, and they certify instructors at various proficiency levels. They differ primarily in their emphasis on different aspects of sea kayaking skills. The BCU has traditionally emphasized seamanship skills and the ability of its instructors to control groups safely in a wide variety of sea conditions. The ACA has traditionally emphasized modeling perfected paddling skills and developing instructors' teaching skills. Both organizations clearly outline course contents and clearly define the levels of proficiency required of their instructors. Similar certification programs are available through the Canadian Recreational Canoe Association (CRCA).

If you have the opportunity, try to get instruction through a variety of organiza-

An instructional program is the best place to start.

tions or from an instructor familiar with different styles. The ACA and U.S. chapters of the BCU have recently become closer in style and content, making their differences less pronounced. For example, in response to requests by students for seamanship and rough-water skills, the ACA has broadened its offerings. And, because the U.S. market demands a kinder, gentler approach to instruction, many BCU instructors have modified their teaching styles to be more reassuring to novice paddlers.

When you begin looking for an instructional program, ask the following questions.

- What is the instructor-to-student ratio? Anything exceeding a 1:6 ratio is too low, limiting your access to the instructor and the amount you can learn in a day.
- Will you get a chance to observe and practice ways to get back into your boat after a capsize (solo and assisted)? If not, when and how can you get this experience?
- What training or certifications do the instructors have? Ask for specifics. Being told they are BCU- or ACA-"trained" is not sufficient since anyone could claim that after a single class. (Ask if they hold instructor certification.)
- If the instructor has chosen to not be involved in a certifying organization, how long has he or she been teaching? Ask local paddling clubs for recommendations.
- Are there concerns about cold-water temperatures? If so, will you be pro-

vided with a wet suit or dry suit, or will you need to rent or provide your own?
- Will different models of kayaks be available in the class to fit different-sized people?
- Do you need to bring a lunch, snacks, or water bottle?
- Do you need to carry in your kayak everything you need for the day? If so, will waterproof bags be provided?
- Where will the class be held? Will you have a chance to paddle on any open water, or will the entire class be held in a small pond or in a pool?
- Who determines a class cancellation because of bad weather? Must you reschedule or will you receive a refund?
- Are there any incentives with boat purchases? (Often, paddlesports dealers offer some sort of instructional package for those buying a boat.)
- If you have a disability, what adaptations will be made to the equipment? When will these be done?
- Do you get a discount on the class fee for using your own boat?
- If a boat is provided, can you specify a particular model?
- After your first class, will other courses or methods of instruction be suggested?

Your first day of sea kayaking instruction should cover a variety of techniques that will help you feel more comfortable in your kayak. You'll learn how to get into and out of the boat at a shoreline or low dock, and how to exit when you capsize (these techniques are discussed in chapters 4, 5, and 6). You're going to get wet, so be prepared. Secure your glasses with a retainer strap, be prepared for the water temperature, and keep a spare set of clothes and a towel someplace dry. If this is your first time in a kayak, don't worry: you won't be the only one. If possible, talk to your instructor before the class starts to let him or her know what you hope to gain from the instruction. That's also a good time to air any fears or questions you have about getting started. Find out from the instructor how boats will be assigned; you want to ensure you get a boat that's a proper fit for you.

A good beginner's class won't make assumptions about prior skills: all you'll need is an open mind and a willingness to try something new. Certain movements and physical demands may seem awkward at first. You may even carry over a few bad habits from past canoeing days. Let them go. Trust the instructor to show and then lead you through proper paddling techniques.

Your first day of instruction should include practicing a *wet exit*, which means exiting the boat after you've flipped upside down (see page 131). Although it's actually easy, many beginners are fearful of this step in their instruction. They have visions of being trapped or of panicking underwater. Don't hesitate to voice these concerns if you have them, and ask your instructor to spot you through your first wet exit.

If you're reluctant to try a wet exit, take the opposite approach: start *in* the water with your kayak beside you (wear a life vest for flotation). Crawl around on the boat, turn the boat over and stick your head up inside,

and try hanging upside down in the cockpit. Kayaking is a *water*sport, so you might as well enjoy getting wet and playing in the water with your kayak. You'll become so comfortable that a wet exit won't even register on the anxiety radar.

GUIDED TOURS

Many people are introduced to kayaking through guided tours. They might have signed on for a short harbor tour by kayak while on vacation or been talked into tagging along for a full day of exploring by a friend. Guided tours are a fun introduction to the sport, but bear in mind their purpose isn't to help you with paddling technique or answer equipment questions. Instead, kayak tours focus on the sights and scenery along the way. That's not to say that you won't get pointers from a helpful guide, but the focus is different from an instructional program. Some

A guided tour is a great way to sample the sport.

longer wilderness tours may include a day of instruction before setting out or require that you show some basic paddling skills before registering. For more information on guide services, see pages 280–81.

FITNESS AND STRETCHING

Although you can start kayaking without any preliminary physical training, your body will appreciate a few good stretches and some strength-building exercises. These stretches and exercises are good habits to get into regardless of the frequency of your paddle outings. If you are an infrequent paddler, they may save you from a "weekend warrior" injury or soreness; if you paddle regularly, you should incorporate these into your weekly plans throughout the seasons. Anything that builds strength and flexibility is to your advantage.

Stretches should be done both before and after kayaking. Before you begin paddling, take a few moments to gradually warm your muscles. This can be a round of jumping jacks, "air paddling," or a spirited game of Frisbee on the beach. The goal is to get your blood pumping and the muscles warm. Once your muscles are warm, they will stretch more easily and there is less chance of a muscle strain. After paddling, a regimen of stretching is helpful to ease tired muscles and prevent soreness.

Stretches should be gradual and held for twenty to thirty seconds before being released. Don't bob or try to push your mus-

cles into position. Your movements should be fluid and slow. Consider incorporating some of your favorite stretches from other sports or poses from other practices such as yoga, Pilates, or Tai Chi. Be consistent and unhurried to get the best results.

During a day of paddling, be sure to take breaks that allow you to stretch and move muscles and joints in ways different from paddling motions. Shake your legs and hands and move around inside the cockpit. Point, flex, and rotate your feet, and scrunch up your toes. Too often, paddlers stay locked in a paddling position inside the cockpit and forget to move their lower body around or even remove their hands from the paddle. If your boat has a rudder, drop the blade so you can alternately press on the pedals to stretch out your legs. Find a quiet piece of water or have someone stabilize your boat so you can pull your legs up into a "cannonball" position to

Hugging your boat is a good lower back and hamstring stretch. Your boat will appreciate it, too!

ease some strain, or even hang your legs over either side of the boat.

Hamstrings

The backs of your legs will often get tight as you sit in your boat for long periods. I can feel my hamstrings bunch up if I don't have a chance to shake my legs out after a long time in my boat. To stretch these muscles, sit in your boat and lean forward to hug the deck. Hold this stretched position and then gradually ease off. Do this stretch several times, keeping your movements slow and controlled. At first, do this stretch while your boat is grounded; as your balance improves, you can do this while afloat.

While on land: Use the Downward Facing Dog yoga pose to stretch hamstrings, lower back, and calf muscles. Slowly press your heels to the ground and press your body back onto your hands and feet with legs and arms straight (see photo). Your body should form an inverted "V" as you breathe deeply and slowly while holding this pose.

The lunge pose (see photos below and on page 8) is another great stretch for hamstrings, quadriceps, and calves. Place yourself in a lunge position with the right leg forward with knee bent and left leg extended behind you. Then with your hands remaining in contact with the ground, slowly rise and press the back foot down (you may need to shorten your stride as you rise). You should feel this stretch first in the quadriceps of the extended (back) leg. And then as you rise, the hamstring in the forward leg will stretch as your calf muscles stretch in the back leg. Hold this for twenty seconds and then repeat with left leg forward. Anytime you use a lunge position, be careful to ensure that your front knee does not move forward of your foot and strain the connective tissue of the knee joint.

The Downward Facing Dog yoga pose stretches large muscle groups in the hamstrings, lower back, shoulders, and even the upper arms, wrists, and ankles. It is also a way to focus prior to an outing or to unwind following a long day of paddling.

This lunge position stretches the groin and quadriceps of the extended leg and the hamstring of the forward leg. To protect the knee, do not let the forward knee extend beyond the forward foot.

You can check for this by never allowing the lower leg bones (or shin) to exceed an angle that is perpendicular to the floor.

One last stretch for the hamstrings is a version of the "keyhole" stretch (see photo). While on your back, lift both legs and cross your right leg over the left. Holding on to the back of the left leg, gently bring both legs toward your left shoulder and hold the

Lift the body slowly, keeping your feet flat and hands reaching as low as possible. You may need to shorten your stride to do this. This move will stretch the hamstrings and calves of both legs.

This modification of the keyhole stretch is gentler to the knees and still gives you a great stretch for hamstrings, glutes, and lower back.

stretch for twenty seconds. Repeat this with leg positions swapped. This is a particularly good stretch after a day of paddling.

To strengthen hamstrings and quadriceps, practice walking lunges—picking up the back foot and lifting it to waist level before placing it forward for the next lunge. Be very careful to not stress your knees, and go only as low as you feel comfortable. Always make sure your forward knee does not extend over the front foot. This walking lunge is also good for your balance and the small muscles that stabilize the ankle and foot.

Torso and Lower Back

You will depend on your torso to drive many of your paddling strokes, so it's a good idea to start working on torso flexibility and

While still in your boat, stretch your back numerous times over the course of the day. While paddling, avoid slumping, and make sure your seatback is adjusted for the best support and comfort. An inflatable lumbar pad can ease back strain while paddling.

strength. There are numerous stretches and strength-building exercises for the torso. Any regimen that includes building core strength and flexibility will help you as a kayaker.

One of my favorite torso stretches is done in the boat. Hold your paddle straight out in front of you and swing your torso as far around to one side as you can. Drop the forward blade so that it touches the side of the boat, then push out with your upper hand; hold for at least twenty seconds and then change to the other side. (If you prefer, you can do this same stretch on land. Sit on the ground with your legs straight out in front of you and use the paddle as leverage off your foot on either side instead of using the boat for leverage.)

While on land: A variety of stretches will ease some of the back stiffness you may feel after a long day of paddling and also increase your range of torso rotation. Many yoga poses can be used to stretch the lower back and shoulders. My favorite, the Child's Pose, is easily done before and after paddling (though one wag at a local launch site suggested I was giving thanks for my safe return to land when I got out of my boat to assume this position alongside the boat ramp!).

Here's an easy stretch for the spine that can be done before or after any paddling activity. Stand with your feet about shoulder-width apart and your knees slightly bent. Now allow your upper body to dangle down toward the ground (this will also stretch your hamstrings). Hold this position for about ten seconds and then begin to gradually straighten. As you raise your upper body, imagine each vertebra falling into place on top of the one below. Do this very slowly

until you're completely upright. Then raise your head.

Cat-Cow Stretch. Get onto your knees and hands (see photos) and arch your back into a rounded position like a "mad cat." Engage your core muscles in the abdominal region while you do this stretch for maximum effectiveness. After holding the arched position

The "mad cat" portion of this stretch extends the back and shoulder muscles while engaging the core muscles in the abdomen.

The second portion of this stretch opens up the chest by rolling the shoulders back while stretching the hamstring and glutes. It is important to continue to keep the core abdominal muscles engaged.

for ten seconds, curve your spine in the other direction by lifting your buttocks and head. Make sure your shoulders are rolled back and the sternum opened in the "cow" part of this stretch. Continue to engage the core muscles of the abdomen during this phase. This Cat-Cow Stretch may feel a bit silly, but it is a great stretch for the back and hips.

Spine Twist. Lie down on the ground or floor and roll onto your left side with both arms stretched out in front of you and your knees bent (see photos). Now slowly lift your right arm, keeping it straight as it traces a half circle to finish straight out behind you and relaxed on the ground. This will twist your spine and the joint of the right shoulder. Do this very slowly and make sure the right shoulder is dropped away from your ear. (If you have had any shoulder rotation injuries or problems, take this very slowly and do not push beyond what is comfortable.) Hold this position for twenty seconds and then move first the top leg and then the bottom leg to roll over onto your right side. Repeat the exercise by tracing a half circle with the left arm and holding for twenty seconds.

To strengthen the torso, you want to concentrate on abdominals and the internal and external obliques. There are numerous "crunches" to choose from. Using good technique is key to getting the most from these exercises. When doing crunches, concentrate on isolating and working the different muscles of the abdomen and sides, letting them lift your upper torso off the floor rather than bending forward or pulling up with your hands laced behind your head. It isn't how

Start this stretch with arms closed (perpendicular to your centerline) and the legs forming a "seated" position while on your side. Make sure your hips and legs are evenly stacked.

Begin to open the chest by tracing a circle with your upper hand. Make sure the upper arm is straight up and perpendicular to your centerline.

The final position of this stretch opens up the chest while stretching the shoulders, abdominal area, and neck. This stretch should be done for each side.

far off the floor you raise your upper body but how well you engage the muscles in the abdomen and sides so they gain strength.

Other areas for strength training include these key muscles: latissimus dorsi, trapezius, and rhomboids. Strengthening these muscles will help with shoulder stabilization and good posture. Many traditional strength-training regimens include these exercises: seated row, straight arm pull-down, pull-ups, and one-arm row. Many Pilates exercises work these areas with an emphasis on dropping the shoulder blades and rolling the shoulders back to open up the sternum and chest.

Torso exercises can be enhanced by performing them on a balance, or stability, ball. This ups the ante by requiring you to move slowly and become aware of your balance on the ball while isolating and exercising these upper-body muscles. In fact, regularly using a balance ball for workouts is a great challenge and will bring noticeable results.

Shoulders

Whitewater kayakers and surf paddlers are usually well aware of the dangers of shoulder injury. Most of these injuries occur from a moment of poor technique or alignment that was unforgiving and resulted in a shoulder dislocation or similar injury. Trust me, these injuries are very painful and will haunt you forever. So the shoulder joint deserves care and protection while paddling even if you are not faced with rough water. (Proper paddling technique and alignment are discussed on page 95.)

Exercises and stretches that accentuate rolling the shoulders back and dropping the shoulder blades are useful and will help instill the habit of maintaining this alignment while paddling. Here's a simple exercise that engages the rhomboids and strengthens this area and instills good habits. While standing or seated, hold your arms out and position your forearm at a 90-degree angle to the upper arm. This will look as though you're forming a "goalpost." Now draw your shoulder blades together and hold for a count of ten. Do not simply swing your arms back;

External rotations of the shoulder must be done carefully so the shoulder joint is protected at all times. Keep your elbow tucked tightly into your rib cage, and start without a weight until you are clear about the proper alignment. Keep hips and legs stacked evenly.

Slowly lift the weight, keeping the elbow tucked into your side. Keep the forearm and wrist aligned and straight. Do not go beyond a comfortable stretch with the weight lifted above the elbow. Slowly lower and repeat.

instead, concentrate on moving your shoulder blades lower while pulling them together. Imagine a pencil placed along your spine between the shoulder blades, and then imagine trying to hold it in place with this move.

One exercise that is particularly good at building strength in the muscles around the shoulder (or rotator cuff) and helps to stabilize this joint uses a controlled external rotation of the joint. This is often done with a small weight. You can add this to your routine once you are sure you have the proper technique. If done poorly, external rotations can do more harm than good, so pay attention to your alignment and move slowly. Lie on your side and slowly raise your arm, keeping your elbow locked to your side. Slowly lower and then begin again for a total of five reps per side (see photos on page 11).

You may also choose to use a resistance band to work your shoulder muscles and help stabilize the joint. While standing, hold the band between two fists with your forearms out from your body and elbows locked against your sides. Slowly pull both fists against the band by opening out to the side and away from your center. You can regulate the resistance in the band by how much slack you allow between your hands. Make sure you are using good posture and alignment and have your shoulders dropped away from your ears and rolled back.

Wrist and Hand

Too often, kayakers strain their wrists and forearms by holding their paddles in a death grip. You may not even realize you're doing this until an ache prompts you to relax. I have to remind novice paddlers to wiggle their fingers and occasionally take their hands off the paddles for a break.

To stretch your wrists and move the tendons through a full range of motion, use one hand to gently pull the fingers of the other hand back, and then slowly release. Stretch your wrists in the other direction by gently pulling the fingertips toward the inside of the forearm and holding before releasing. Now do this with the fingers gently curled. Never force the wrist to bend; instead, help it through its range of motion with gentle pressure from the other hand.

The key to preventing wrist problems is to use a correct grip on your paddle that protects the alignment of the wrist. This is discussed in detail on pages 110–12. Having had two carpal tunnel release surgeries, I am particularly aware of wrist alignment and stresses to that area. My problems did not arise from paddling, but this activity has heightened my awareness of the fragility of the wrist joint and its tendons and connective tissue. I can assure you that any joint or muscle pain is trying to tell you something, and you should always pay attention to its messages.

Ankles

While seated on the ground, grab your left ankle with your right hand and pull back on the ball of your foot with your left hand. Holding this stretched position, slowly rotate your foot to the right and to the left, and then point it. Stretching against resistance offered by your hand enhances this stretch. Repeat with the other foot, reversing the instructions.

After a long day in your boat, a good ankle stretch provides support while you work the kinks out.

Your ankles might cramp when you've been in your boat for long periods. When you exit, be careful because you may be clumsy as you step out of your cockpit and take your first few steps after sitting for several hours. The algae and seaweed in many landing spots make footing treacherous. If you're faced with seaweed-covered rocks, walk between the rocks where you can wedge your foot in a stable position, and use your paddle as a cane if necessary.

Strengthening Exercises

Many of you do some form of strength training through a scheduled workout at home or the gym. Include exercises that target some specific paddling muscles, such as biceps, triceps, forearms, torso, and lower back. Since all paddling requires strong wrists, you might also consider strengthening your wrists by squeezing putty or a tennis ball for a few minutes several times a week.

COMMON QUESTIONS

When you're thinking about starting a new sport, you'll likely have questions about that sport. Maybe you need reassurance that you can really do this activity, or there's some basic issue that needs explaining. Get these out of the way so they don't nag at you and become stumbling blocks. Here are some common questions that sea kayaking students ask.

1. *Will I be able to get out of the boat if it capsizes?* It's only natural to be concerned about your first wet exit. After all, you're only being asked to hang upside down, underwater, in the dark!—three basic fears. Don't worry: after your first wet exit (see page 131), you'll wonder what all the fuss was about. If you're nervous, have your instructor spot you in shallow water, and try your first wet exit without your sprayskirt. Remember, if you can get into the boat on land, you can certainly exit the boat with gravity in your favor and water as a lubricant.
2. *Do I have to learn how to roll?* Not necessarily, but you'll miss out on some of the best experiences sea kayaking has to offer if you don't. Knowing how to roll (see pages 151–59) will allow you to relax and look for-

ward to challenges, and it's a way to learn to play in the seascapes you explore. Rolling is one of the ways to build confidence in your abilities as a kayaker. If you don't learn to roll, you'll never experience the heady feeling that accompanies a significant accomplishment. That said, you should know that many (I would say most) sea kayakers do not know how to roll or do not have a roll that's reliable in real conditions.

3. *Will I get seasick?* Seasickness seems less prevalent among kayakers than other boaters, though some folks are just more prone to seasickness, which can be debilitating. Simply paddling and looking ahead to a des-

tination seem to help. Avoid sitting still and wallowing in seas or fixating on the deck of your boat or compass. Let your partners know early if you're feeling queasy so you can plan a break on a nearby shore.

Many of the medications for seasickness may make you drowsy and affect your balance. If you choose to take these medications, inform your paddling partners of the medication and its possible side effects. For more on seasickness, see page 235.

4. *Do I have to know how to swim?* You'll be more relaxed and more confident in and around water if you know how to swim before you learn to kayak. When kayaking, you'll always be

wearing a life vest, so swimming skills are helpful but not required.

5. *Can I just paddle on lakes and ponds, or do I need access to the ocean?* Sea kayaks work just fine on lakes, ponds, reservoirs, and flatwater rivers. If you're primarily exploring small winding patches of water and have no need for storing gear, you might consider a small sit-on-top kayak or a recreational kayak. These shorter models are great for poking around these sorts of areas but may not have the length or features that make them suitable for open water or ocean.

6. *How expensive is this sport?* If you're purchasing new gear, you should plan on spending at least $1,800 to get started. You'll need more than just a boat and paddle. There will be essential pieces of safety gear (see pages 66–80), and you'll probably need some way to transport your kayak on your car. You won't regret spending extra money on high-quality gear, so your total may reach $5,000 before you're through! Purchasing used gear will probably save you a bit.

7. *Can I go by myself?* One of the joys of sea kayaking is the solitude and quiet of

Opposite and above: *Whatever slice of sea kayaking you choose to explore, be sure to develop the skills and the judgment you need to get you there and back.*

being on the water and exploring new places. But when you paddle by yourself, you're beyond the important safety net of other paddlers. You'll need all the skills and knowledge to take care of yourself with no help at all. As a novice, it's unwise to paddle alone until you have more experience in your kayak in a variety of conditions.

If you choose to go solo, you'll also have to be able to load and unload the kayak on and off your vehicle by yourself. For a discussion of these techniques, see pages 99–105.

THE DANGERS OF GOING TO SEA

The ocean is an exhilarating but challenging environment. It's fickle and can be stirred into a frenzy by strong winds, and in the right places, its gentle ebb and flow can turn frighteningly powerful. As a sea kayaker, you can choose which areas of this vast environment to explore, but never underestimate the challenges of taking a small boat on open water. If that water is cold, you must be even more conservative in your plans to ensure you're protected from the often devastating effects of immersion in cold water (see pages 80–85).

This book provides more than just warnings about the challenges of sea kayaking. We delve into techniques, gear, seamanship, and an understanding of this environment we've chosen to explore. As a kayaker, you'll find great satisfaction in completing a day of paddling that challenges your skills and knowledge and enhances them with newfound confidence and understanding.

Sea kayaking demands good judgment, but no instructor or book can endow you with that gift. What I can do here is provide the information and the tools you'll need to develop your own good judgment skills and make your own decisions about how and when to enjoy this fascinating environment.

2

Kayaks

Sea kayaks have an impressive pedigree dating back several thousand years. Today's kayak designs may show off their bloodlines in an angular shoulder or a graceful bow curve. Traditional hull designs speak clearly of what the kayak was used for and what materials were available for their construction. A sleek Greenland design was made for a hunting lifestyle, where maneuverability and acceleration were critical for the kayaker; a Russian-influenced baidarka was made to carry passengers and large loads of sea otter pelts as parties ventured farther and farther from their villages for trade.

The American in His Baidar engraving, which appeared in Krasheninnikov's *Opisanie* (1755), was the first published illustration of an Alaskan baidarka.

No one knows when the first kayaks were launched, since their biodegradable components of animal skins and thin wood frames have not survived the ravages of time. Kayaks were clearly an integral part of the lives of the people of both the northern Pacific and Greenland in the early 1700s when Russian and European explorers recorded their first observations. Anthropologists have estimated that Aleuts were paddling skin-covered decked boats several thousand years ago.

Numerous kayak designs met the needs of a coastal people dependent on the sea for food, fuel, and trade routes. Some have been conscientiously copied by traditional boatbuilders today, while others have morphed into the designs you'll find on any paddlesports shop floor. There's no one "traditional" kayak design, though the hard-chine and flat-

Eskimos in their kayaks, Nunivak Island, Alaska, in 1936.

deck Greenland designs are often mistakenly given this distinction by some paddlers. Instead, myriad designs arose from widely separated populations (in Greenland and

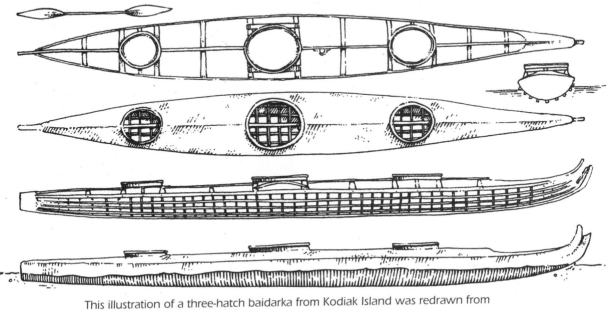

This illustration of a three-hatch baidarka from Kodiak Island was redrawn from Lisiansky's *Puteshestvie* (1812).

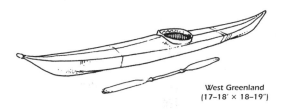

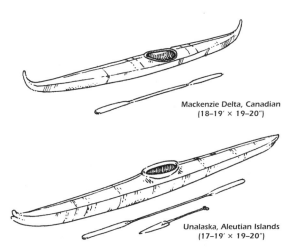

West Greenland
(17–18′ × 18–19″)

Mackenzie Delta, Canadian
(18–19′ × 19–20″)

Unalaska, Aleutian Islands
(17–19′ × 19–20″)

Kayak designs varied widely due to regional conditions, available materials, and the needs of paddlers.

what is now Alaska, British Columbia, and Northwest Territories), each with a variety of needs and raw materials at their disposal.

MAKING CHOICES

Single or double? Fiberglass or plastic? How long? Rudder or skeg? New or used? Blue or yellow?

Deciding which kayak to purchase can be daunting. Some of you will revel in the minutiae of product comparisons; stability curves and hydrostatic measurements will paper your walls as you approach decision-making time. Some of you will develop a budget that will drive your decisions, tallying numbers and trading off the cost of an accessory to get another feature on your dream boat (or vice versa). And some of you will fall in love with a shape or color, or maybe with the history of a particular design; your decision is made before a salesperson comes up with an opening line.

Whatever your strategy about purchasing equipment, it never hurts to be informed. Even if you don't consider hull design characteristics like chine or sheer in your final decision, understanding them makes you a more knowledgeable kayaker. So, I'm going to throw a lot of information your way from designers, opinionated industry folks, everyday paddlers, and my own take on this subject. This chapter isn't just about purchasing; it's about understanding the design, materials, and even the necessity for a particular piece of equipment.

As for those pressing decisions—remember your answers to the questions in chapter 1—use your answers and the information provided in this chapter to sort through some of the options.

NAMING THE PARTS

It's a good idea to learn the proper names of the parts of a kayak. I once saw an instructor yelling to a student to "grab the coaming." The only problem was the student didn't have a clue where she might find a coaming and began looking desperately for things

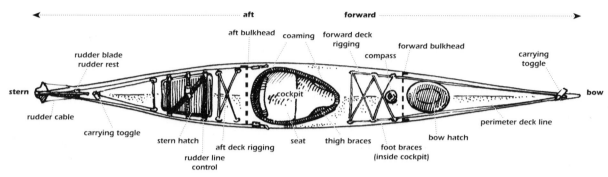

Get to know the names of all the parts and pieces of your sea kayak.

floating in the water. Learning the names of things is the first step in learning to "talk the talk." Sea kayaking has very little jargon, and most of that is related to boats in general. (Whitewater kayakers, on the other hand, have their own language and tribal rites. But then, they're less evolved than sea kayakers.)

The accompanying illustration shows a generic sea kayak with a rudder system. Not all sea kayaks will have all these features, but our version is typical of what you'll find at most retail stores. Refer to the illustration as we review the following terms.

- **carrying toggles:** loops of webbing or plastic handles at the bow and stern. Use these to lift your boat.
- **perimeter deck line:** line (or thin rope) running along the edges of the kayak. The perimeter deck lines are handy for grabbing, especially if you're in the water. Rudder control lines or painters may often double as perimeter deck lines on some models.
- **bow storage compartment:** a storage space in the forward part of the kayak. Often called the *bow hatch*,

though technically the hatch is the opening, not the compartment. The lids on the storage compartments are called hatch covers.
- **bulkhead:** a watertight wall that separates storage compartments and the cockpit. Most sea kayaks have a bow bulkhead and a stern bulkhead. Some models have a third bulkhead to create a small day hatch accessible from the cockpit.
- **compass:** the small navigation aid we're familiar with, only mounted on the forward deck of the kayak. The deck-mounted compass functions the same way as a handheld compass but is designed to be read at a glance while you're paddling. Compasses may be permanently mounted to the deck or clipped across the deck rigging for easy removal.
- **forward deck rigging:** pieces of bungee cord, straps, or line that cross the forward deck; used to secure items such as charts, water bottle, or safety gear.
- **cockpit:** the space in which the paddler sits.

- **foot braces:** pedals inside the cockpit on which you rest your feet while paddling (they're adjustable for leg length). Foot braces often double as rudder control pedals. They push along sliding tracks, moving the rudder blade from side to side.
- **thigh braces:** contoured sections at the forward end of the cockpit opening that help fit the boat to your upper legs, providing better control. Thigh braces are often custom-padded with foam to fit your body shape. Thus, when you move your knee or upper leg, the kayak moves with it.
- **coaming:** the edge around the cockpit opening. The lip shape of the coaming provides a place to attach the sprayskirt.
- **seat:** where the paddler sits. Seats are usually tilted for comfort and provide back support with a padded band or solid seatback. Seat bases are usually not movable, but seatbacks can usually be adjusted.
- **rudder lines:** lines that control the lifting and dropping of the rudder blade. These can be operated from the cockpit. Rudder cables that run from the rudder assembly to sliding foot brace tracks control the side-to-side movement of the rudder blade.
- **stern deck rigging:** pieces of bungee cord, straps, or line that cross the rear deck used to secure items such as a spare paddle, safety gear, or camping supplies.
- **stern storage compartment:** storage compartment in the rear of the boat.

Stern storage compartments usually have larger openings than bow compartments, because the stern deck is usually broader and flatter than the bow deck. Often called a *stern hatch*.
- **rudder:** a flat blade that can be dropped into the water at the stern and controlled by foot pedals in the cockpit. The rudder system provides directional control in certain conditions. When not in use, most rudder blades rest on the stern deck, usually held in place by a rudder rest, or chock. (A retractable skeg may be used instead of a rudder. These are both discussed on pages 45–46.)

This chapter, indeed the entire book, is primarily concerned with sea kayaks, or touring kayaks. Sea kayaks allow you to travel open water out of reach of land and carry gear to support these travels, whether for a day or several weeks. Open-water travel means your kayak must be seaworthy and capable of contending with waves and wind. In the event of a capsize, your kayak must allow for a reentry of the paddler and removal of water from the boat. So we will distinguish, sometimes arbitrarily, between sea kayaks and recreational kayaks. Recreational kayaks are shorter and often have large, open cockpits. They are great for cruising lakes, ponds, and even protected harbors under calm conditions. But they are not appropriate for extended open-water travel or exposure to many conditions found at sea. A capsized paddler would find it difficult, if not impossible, to reenter and remove the water from some recreational kayaks' large and open cockpits.

SINGLE OR DOUBLE?

Some of you will be faced with deciding between a single kayak or a double kayak. You want to be able to carry small children or a large dog in a center cockpit; you and your paddling partner have very disparate skill levels, and a double kayak guarantees you won't stray too far apart; you and your partner plan to cover long distances and like the speed and storage of a large double; or you have budget concerns—a double is less expensive than two singles. Whatever issues you face, you should still use the questions in chapter 1 to begin the decision-making process.

In general, doubles are considerably faster than singles (obviously, if you compare the shortest, widest double out there with the sleekest, longest single, this may not be true). Think about it: you've got two paddlers to power what is roughly, in length, a single kayak-and-a-half. This is a promising recipe for covering some miles pretty quickly. And, doubles are very stable and seaworthy. However, they do require two paddlers who must get along reasonably well. And therein lies the rub.

Two paddlers who want to go in opposite directions or at very different speeds may not tear the kayak apart, but the relationship may

Doubles can cover the miles and offer lots of stability. You also need a stable relationship with your paddling partner.

get a bit frayed. So be sure both paddlers are clear about steering, trip pace, philosophy, and who paddles in which position. Doubles may be outfitted with rudder controls in the bow or stern cockpit, or even both, positions. For more on double kayak paddling skills, see page 126.

And the shorter length (less than 14 feet) of recreational kayaks makes extended travel in exposed conditions more work than it might be worth, and perhaps even dangerous.

Sit-on-top kayaks, which have no cockpit or enclosed deck, may fall into either category. Some designs are made for open-water travel and have ample storage, others clearly belong in the recreational category. Sit-on-top designs make reentry a snap and may be easier for paddlers who have difficulty getting in and out of a kayak cockpit.

Sit-on-top paddlers are more exposed to the weather than paddlers who sit in a cockpit, although this is not an issue in some regions or paddling seasons. Since paddlers should dress

Recreational kayaks (foreground) are shorter and lack bulkheads and other features needed for seaworthiness.

for water temperature, exposure to weather on a sit-on-top may be of less concern for a sea kayaker than a recreational boater.

KAYAK DESIGN

There is no absolute "right" kayak design. A given design is right for its intended use and to meet the needs of its paddler. Many kayak designers are firm believers in particular

Some things are just easier with a sit-on-top kayak.

characteristics and will argue convincingly that to stray from their design path will result in a bogus design. The kayak market, on the other hand, has no absolutes, so you'll see an incredible array of kayak designs. Some designs will be as pure as the driven snow; others will be the Heinz 57s of the kayak world; some will just be odd. But it's fun to pick out the different design characteristics and determine what a particular kayak might do best. A word of caution: design characteristics are a dependent group of factors. They interact and subtly change one another and make the whole design process more intriguing but less predictable. Discussing these factors in isolation is useful for understanding their effects on a given design, but it overlooks the complexities and subtleties of the end result.

First, we'll look at hull design characteristics, because the shape and size of the kayak hull define how the boat travels through the water and how it reacts to different conditions and paddlers. Then we'll consider other features that also define a boat's use and style like rudders, thigh braces, and deck shapes and contours. Finally, we'll try to determine which boat may be right for you. Bearing in mind your answers to the questions posed in chapter 1, we'll work out a strategy for purchasing a kayak, whether it's your first or fifteenth.

Length

There are two kinds of length: length overall (LOA) and the length at waterline (LWL). The overall length is just what it sounds like— the maximum distance of the boat from bow to stern. The waterline length, which is usually shorter and never longer than the overall length, is the distance between the *immersed* ends of the boat. Imagine floating your kayak in a rather scummy pond. When you lift it out, there is a line of pond scum that marks the waterline of your boat. If you measure the length of this waterline from bow to stern, you have the waterline length of your boat under those exact conditions. You see, waterline length is not an absolute. It will change with the load the boat is carrying or the water in which it sits at rest. A heavier load

will increase the waterline length. A boat in Great Salt Lake would have a shorter waterline length because it sits higher under these unusually buoyant conditions than that same boat sitting in your local pond. The overall length remains the same unless you manage to crunch one end of your boat.

In general, kayaks with longer waterline lengths will track better and be potentially faster or more efficient as they move through the water (see sidebar).

Most single sea kayaks have an overall length of 14 to 19 feet (4.3–5.8 m); double kayaks have an overall length of 16 to 22 feet (4.9–6.7 m).

Shape and Sheer

If you could look down the waterline length of the boat, you might notice whether the widest part is forward of the halfway point (a fish-form hull), behind the halfway point (a Swede-form hull), or at the halfway point (a symmetrical hull). This matters a great deal to the designer and will often be vociferously defended, though most sea kayaks are not extreme examples of any one form. A designer who favors the Swede-form will claim it's eas-

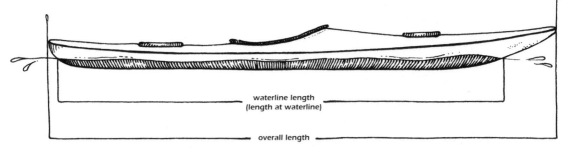

waterline length
(length at waterline)

overall length

The waterline length can be seen as the boat rests in the water. A boat's overall length is measured from one end to the other and is unaffected by any cargo load.

IT ISN'T SO SIMPLE

I've already given into temptation and said the expected: a longer boat will mean a potentially faster, or more efficient, boat. However, it isn't always that simple. There are two factors that affect the resistance of a hull as it moves through the water: the friction of its wetted surface and the wave action it creates. And, to complicate things, there may be other factors that can affect how easy a boat is to paddle and how fast it paddles (for example, stiffness).

When a hull moves through the water it creates a wave; the longer the boat, the longer the wave (called its wave of translation). The speed of this wave is directly proportional to the square root of the boat's waterline length (LWL; 1.34 times the square root of the LWL, to be exact). (There is disagreement as to whether this equation is even applicable to kayaks, since the constant was developed for boats of far different length-to-beam ratios.) The speed of this wave created by a boat is often called the hull speed (not to be confused with boat speed), which is the maximum speed a boat can attain before it rises up on its own bow wave. Think of hull speed as the speed at which adding more power doesn't add more speed because the drag on the boat is increasing rapidly.

So, the longer the boat, the longer the boat's wave of translation and the higher the calculated hull speed. So longer boats are potentially faster boats, but the paddler has to supply the power to attain the maximum speed, which is not always a realistic consideration for your typical touring kayaker. And we still have another factor to consider: the skin friction of the hull's wetted surface.

If you want to be exact, you must also consider the prismatic coefficient, the ratio of the immersed volume of the hull to the volume of a prism of the same length as the waterline length and a cross section equal to that of the largest cross section of the immersed part of the hull. Think of this as the distribution of the boat's volume below the waterline, or how "pointy" the ends are (or some say how hollow the waterline becomes at the ends). So the shape of the boat below the waterline must also be considered. Things only get more complicated since the wave action is a greater factor at higher speeds and the friction of the wetted surface is the bigger player at lower speeds. When you then consider that the paddler's weight and the boat's load of gear can greatly affect the outcome, you might just decide it's easier to buy a bicycle instead.

Few manufacturers really lose any sleep over these numbers (though their designers might). Sure, they care whether their boats are efficient, but mostly they care whether you like them and will buy them, and then recommend them to your friends. So, now you know.

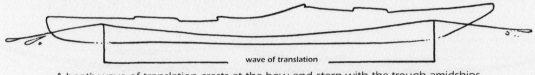

A boat's wave of translation crests at the bow and stern with the trough amidships.
Boats of different lengths and hull designs produce different waves of translation.

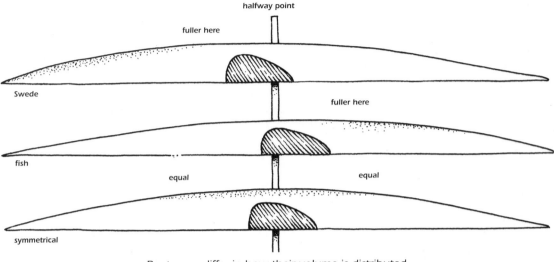

Boats may differ in how their volume is distributed.
These deck line tracings illustrate the subtleties.

ier to paddle since the widest part of the boat is behind the paddler. A designer who prefers a fish-form may argue that moving more volume forward creates a narrower stern and increases tracking ability. Proponents of symmetrical designs note that these designs are well balanced in the design style between a Swede- and fish-form.

Sheer is a term applied to the curvature above the waterline from the bow to the stern as you view the boat from the side. It's often applied to the sweep of the bow and, on occasion, to the stern and the cockpit coaming. The graceful rise of a bow, the surprising upturn at the stern on some designs, or even the curvature of a cockpit rim that accentuates a particu-

lar design may all claim use of the term *sheer*. The sheer line of a kayak can be viewed along the top edge of the hull or the corner of the deck and hull (where the seam is on composite boats). In some designers' eyes, a kayak without bow sheer lacks grace; other designers prefer little or no bow sheer, arguing that anything out of the water is wasted length.

Rocker

Rocker is the curvature of the keel from bow to stern as viewed from the side. A banana has a lot of rocker, a pencil does not. Rocker will create a greater disparity between the waterline length and the overall length and

The seam tape or channel on a composite kayak runs along the boat's sheer line. Accent tape is often used along a polyethylene kayak's sheer line to accentuate a graceful sweep.

DESIGNERS' VIEWS

A few years ago I was asked to write a feature article on kayak designs and their designers for *Canoe & Kayak* magazine. I suspected that I would hear some pretty strong opinions and disagreements among the designers interviewed. I was not disappointed!

All designers have their signature look, spotlighting design features that they care for deeply. Here are some comments from several kayak designers I interviewed.

Derek Hutchinson, P&H Kayaks Orion and Sirius, Current Designs Gulfstream, Slipstream, and other models: "I see the boats as lines and a series of cross sections." His consistent look is "a high foredeck, low rear, modified or full Swede-form, because if the widest part is in front of the kayak it will inhibit paddling."

Steve Scarborough, Dagger Meridian, Cortez, Sitka, and other models: "There is never a need for upturned ends on boats. We've handicapped ourselves with this notion . . . waterline length is as long as I can make it and still be aesthetically acceptable to the market. Get the bow on top of the water and it will go wherever it needs to go!"

Andy Singer, Wilderness Systems Tchaika, Poquito, Shenai, and others: "I tend to think like an artist or sculptor, which is what I am. I like curves rather than a boxy look. When I was a kid the only kayaks available were those homemade kits of plywood that were boxy. . . . I strive to make my boats neutral with no rudder dependency. . . . I like balance."

Brian Henry, founder and designer for Current Designs (Solstice, Storm, Extreme, and others): "My favorite designs are slightly fish-form with fine entry and exit points, minimal rocker for efficient cruising and a lively feel. I'm always paddling and thinking about what I would want or what someone I'm imagining would want."

Lee Moyer, founder and designer for Pacific Water Sports (Sea Otter, Skookumchuck, Chinook, and others): "Form always follows function. You've got to be sure that the boat meets the needs for which it was designed and functions properly. I prefer low ends and a strongly asymmetric hull with the cockpit significantly aft of center. . . . This gives the best hull efficiency, dry ride, and a neutral hull in terms of side wind control."

So, who's right? The short answer is—everyone. And all paddlers, novice to veteran, get to make choices about which boats they prefer that are every bit as personal as the design process that created them.

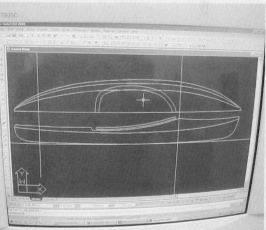

A kayak designer may use a computer program to view the lines on a design under development.

enhance maneuverability but retard tracking ability. A little bit of rocker may result in a playful, responsive boat; too much rocker and you end up with a whitewater boat.

Width

The beam of the boat is the boat's width at its widest point. Using the term *beam* is more exact since the width can travel all over the boat (for example, width at waterline), but the beam stays still. The beam of the boat is a common statistic and is readily available in any manufacturer's catalog. Unfortunately, only at its extremes does the beam tell you much about how a boat feels in the water. True, a narrower beam is often less stable than a wider beam, but putting your trust in the numbers to tell you how a boat feels in the water is misguided. You must also look at the cross section of the boat.

Cross Section

A boat's cross section will show you the shape of the hull. It may be rounded, have a pro-

nounced V shape, or be fairly flat. Kayak hull designs fall throughout the range of these shapes, as shown in the illustration below, and rarely appear in any pure form.

Imagine sitting on a log (round hull). Even if it's a wide log, you'll probably not be able to relax. Rounded kayak hulls may not be particularly reassuring, but they tend to be responsive and fast since there is little drag in their smooth, rounded shape. A perfectly flat hull will sit nicely in the water (think of a floating dock). You couldn't ask for a better platform for bird-watching or photography as long as you don't need to move through the water quickly. Now imagine that same floating dock if there were a little wave action. Soon the flat bottom of your hull would work against you by preventing waves from easily passing beneath you. It might come in handy to round a few edges and build in a wee bit of V to the hull. This would allow waves to pass underneath your boat and allow you to maneuver the boat more easily. You would lose some feeling of stability as the boat rocked back and forth with each passing wave, but you could easily adapt.

little rocker

a lot of rocker

Rocker is the curvature of the bottom from bow to stern. A lot of rocker allows quick spins and turns but would work against you when you're trying to maintain a course on open water.

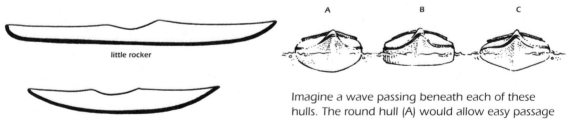

Imagine a wave passing beneath each of these hulls. The round hull (A) would allow easy passage but never feel reassuring; the flat bottom hull (B) would be rock solid in flat water but not very useful in seas; the shallow-V hull (C) is a good compromise between the two and can be seen in many of today's sea kayaks.

A CONTRARY OPINION

Lee Moyer doesn't believe in the concept of secondary stability. "Secondary stability is a real myth in this sport. No one can really define it. Some believe that all little tippy boats have good secondary stability. But that's not it at all, because this implies a property of the hull shape when in fact it is a property of volume. Imagine doing a sculling brace [see pages 119–21]. If someone were to reach under your kayak and gently lift it, you would have to support more of your weight with the paddle because you're higher out of the water. This is why low-volume boats are easier to play with. People call this good secondary stability, but it isn't! It is a function of the volume of the boat that determines how easy it is to lean, roll, and brace. If you partially flood the cockpit of a large, stable kayak, it will be easier to roll and brace, but you decreased all forms of stability. It isn't any characteristic of design other than volume. It's a myth."

This discussion of cross sections brings us to the notion of stability in your boat. Kayakers traditionally speak of two kinds of stability: initial and secondary. *Initial stability* is how solid and stable your boat feels as you sit upright and at rest in the water. The flatter the bottom and wider the boat, the greater the initial stability of the boat. Initial stability is a comment on the "tippiness" of a given boat. *Secondary stability*, sometimes called *reserve* or *ultimate* stability, is how stable the boat is as it nears capsizing. Think of secondary stability as how strongly the boat fights capsizing once it begins to tip toward its side or shoulder.

Stability is also affected by the paddler's center of gravity and how the boat is loaded. If you lower your seat, stability will increase since your center of gravity is lower. Just be sure you can still comfortably reach the water and paddle effectively. Uneven loading of your boat or placement of heavy objects on deck or toward the ends may decrease the stability. When paddling in rough seas, be sure that most of the weight is as close to the centerline and amidships as possible. For more on packing and boat trim, see pages 236–40.

You can see that many factors affect the stability of a given boat. Boat specifications, such as width, can be less important than weight distribution. Some men with wide shoulders who carry a lot of their weight high find a particular boat tippy, while women of the same weight who carry a lot of their weight low in the hips and thighs feel reassured in the same boat.

Try considering the boat's "footprint" in the water. Imagine taking your kayak and placing it in wet cement. The imprint it leaves would show you the shape of the boat underwater, not just the beam. Kayaks with identical beams may have decidedly different footprints depending on how quickly they taper from their beam. And they'll garner very different reviews. So don't put your faith in a beam measurement alone.

Chine and Flare

These two design features can affect a boat's stability and performance. Chine is the angle of intersection between the bottom and the side of the boat. If you look at the shoulders of a kayak, you'll notice that some designs make a sharp departure from the hull to the side, creating a square or angular shoulder (hard chine). Other designs may gradually round from the bottom to the side (soft chine), whereas many others fall between (moderate chine).

Paddlers typically find hard-chine boats more stable (given their width), though the transitions between a boat flat in the water and one on its side may be somewhat abrupt. However, a hard-chine boat is usually easy to hold on its shoulder and you can actually feel the boat "firm up" as you lean it with the barest of support strokes. A soft-chine boat has no transitions to speak of as you lean it on edge, because there is no easily delineated edge. While the transitions are smooth, the transition into a capsize is just as smooth! Moderate, or medium, chine falls somewhere in between.

Some kayaks appear to have multichine hulls. There is a series of flat planes as you move from the bottom to the side. However, this series of flat surfaces may approximate the smooth curve of a soft-chine boat. Thus, there may be no gain in stability typical of a hard-chine boat because it really isn't one.

What a hard-chine boat gains in stability may be traded for in speed. The angular departure from the hull increases the wetted surface and thus friction as the hull moves

The angular shoulder and abrupt departure from hull to side can be seen on the hard-chine model (left). The rounder shoulder on the soft-chine boat (right) is noticeably different.

through the water. However, this factor is usually insignificant for touring kayakers.

Flare can be built into the hull at various points. It may be used to "settle" a hard-chine shoulder or used to increase storage and buoyancy at either end of the boat. Often, the easiest place to see flare is at the bow on a design with a lot of bow sheer. Designers will often add a little lift to a bow design by adding some flare here. This adds a bit more storage space and makes for a drier ride.

Deck Profile

While sheer can usually be viewed by following the seam on a composite boat, the deck profile, or contour, is viewed along the centerline of the boat. Kayak decks may be flat, gently cambered, or decidedly peaked. The deck forward of the cockpit usually has more pronounced contours than the stern deck has. The volume and contour of the kayak above the waterline give it a profile that is affected by the wind (as does its sheer). Some forward decks present a high profile to the wind but may offer drier rides because their peaked contours shed water as the boat plows through waves. A peaked deck may also be more comfortable for paddlers with longer legs and larger feet. Other designs may present a lower forward deck profile to the wind but be a bit wetter for the paddler in rough seas. For more on the design of deck contours, see pages 49–50.

THE STUFF THEY'RE MADE OF

Modern kayaks are made of a wide range of materials. While use of animal skins is a rarity these days, treated fabrics are often stretched and sewn over wood frames to create tradi-

These deck profiles range from flat to decidedly peaked depending on the designer's intentions. A deck's profile affects windage, storage capacity, hatch design, and dryness of the ride in rough seas.

Kayak building programs offer students the chance to learn the skills involved in building a skin-on-frame boat and become intimately familiar with the resulting kayak.

Kayak kits allow paddlers with woodworking skills to construct elegant models that can be customized for their own purposes.

tional designs for modern paddlers. Usually, these designs are customized from the body measurements of each paddler, much in the way fledgling Inuit hunters built their own boats.

There are also kayak kits of lightweight plywood and epoxy coatings for the do-it-yourself paddlers, and wood strips for the aesthetically minded who have the woodworking skills to fashion their own boats. There are ingenious breakdown models for easy traveling between paddling routes, and inflatable kayaks that are simple alternatives. However, the bulk of today's kayaks fall into three categories of materials: cloth-and-resin (compos-

ite) kayaks, thermoformed plastic laminate kayaks, and rotomolded polyethylene kayaks.

Composite Kayaks

Composite kayaks are made from layers of cloth—fiberglass, Kevlar, graphite, and combinations of these fabrics—that are held together by resin. The resin of choice may be a vinylester, polyester, or some proprietary combination, but the result is the same: a compound that quickly cures into a hard shell of material. Composite kayaks are known for their excellent strength-to-weight ratio and the rigidity, and thus efficiency, of their final shape. In simple terms this means that you get a lot of strength for very little weight, and the boat is rigid, holding its shape as waves pass under it and paddlers crawl into and out of it.

It's easier to understand what is meant by a composite kayak if you understand how these boats are made. Making a composite boat requires skill and organization, but first you need a mold. Composite kayak molds are two pieces; the deck and the hull are built separately and then joined before the finishing touches like bulkheads, seats, and rudders are added. Kayak manufacturers keep a keen eye on their molds since they must be scrupulously clean and protected from nicks

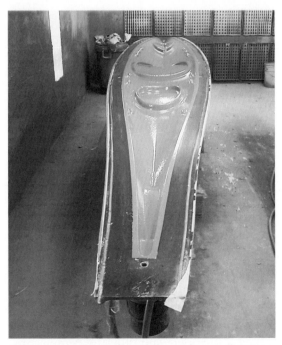

Gelcoat is sprayed into a half-kayak mold. The first defense against scratches and UV rays, gelcoat also lends the boat its color.

and abrasions. Each mold produces a particular model and may be used to make more than a thousand boats before being retired. Similar to seasoning a cast-iron skillet, a new mold may need to have a few boats made and pulled from it before it yields a smooth, top-quality boat.

Once the mold is ready, it's sprayed with gelcoat, which is the compound that gives the boat its color (clear gelcoat is also a possibility). The gelcoat protects the cloth and resin from ultraviolet rays and acts as the first line of defense against scratches and dings. There are dozens of gelcoat colors, but interestingly, they all show white when scratched—something to think about if you're fond of dark boat colors. When the gelcoat is dry and cured, approximately an hour later, it's ready for the cloth. Usually, large pieces of cloth are laid from one end of the mold to the other and then reinforcing pieces are put in place. This may be done in several steps when done by hand. Reinforcement may be added to the deck, around hatches and cockpit openings, and placed at the two ends of the boat and along the keel line. Each kayak model may have a different recipe of cloth pieces. Some form of stiffening material (usually a wafer-thin, dense foam mat) is also laid along the keel line and often in strips across the deck.

With the cloth in place, the mold is readied to receive the resin. This may be done by hand in open air or under vacuum pressure. The vacuum-bagging process of manufacture introduces the resin into a mold enclosed in a large nylon or vinyl bag that is then sealed and a vacuum is created. The bag holds the cloth in place and the resin is very quickly worked throughout the mold and smoothed out. Since vacuum-bagging minimizes the amount of resin used and forces the resin to saturate the cloth under high pressure (approximately 1 ton per square foot), this process has become the most popular, if more expensive, method of building composite kayaks. Once the resin has cured, usually in about twenty-four hours, the vacuum-bag is released and removed (the vacuum bag can be used more than once). Some manufacturers employ *infusion* techniques, which pull the resin across the mold under high pressure. This is a style of vacuum-bagging that can further minimize the amount of resin required as well as reduce fumes escaping into the work areas.

A hand layup technique applies resin to the cloth layers in a series of steps, pressing and smoothing the resin-saturated cloth during each step. The resin cures in about an hour during this process, and once all layers are formed, the kayak halves are ready to be joined.

The kayak half is removed from the mold and its edges trimmed and sanded (the deck half will have hatch openings cut). The two halves may be joined using layers of fiberglass seam tape and resin and then finished with a gelcoat color, or they may be joined with a plastic extrusion that has channels cut in either side to accept the two halves. Either method will use reinforcement on the inside of the seam, and marine sealant is used with the plastic channel as well.

Once the kayak halves are joined, the boat is stood on end to receive its *end pours*, thickened resin that is poured into both ends. These solid ends allow the fastening of hardware for rudder mounts and carrying toggles.

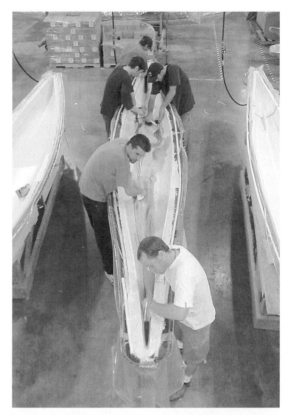

Many composite kayaks are made using vacuum bags, which compress the resin under high pressure as it is worked into the cloth laid in the mold.

Bulkheads can now be installed in the kayak. These watertight walls may be molded ABS plastic, Minicel foam, or fiberglass and resin and are set in position and sealed. Bulkheads are typically set forward of the foot brace tracks and behind the paddler's seat in single kayak models. This divides the kayak into three compartments: two for storage and one for the cockpit. In this way, the fore and aft compartments provide both flotation and watertight storage and only the center compartment can take on water in the event of a capsize.

METHODOLOGY OF COMPOSITE LAYUPS

Although vacuum-bagging has become a very common method for producing composite kayaks, some manufacturers have continued to use hand layup techniques. These manufacturers argue that this creates a stronger boat that is easier to repair. Vacuum-bagging fully cures resin and minimizes its amount, and hand layup proponents argue that cloth repairs (not gelcoat repairs) do not bond as readily or fully as they usually do on a kayak laid up by hand. Hand layup proponents also feel that they get better secondary bonding for stronger seams when the halves are joined.

Vacuum-bagging proponents note that their method is more controlled and uses less resin (a pretty nasty material) and does this in an enclosed system that is safer and cleaner. They also feel they have little chance of floating a piece of cloth in excess resin that can lead to air bubbles and delamination.

Both methods, when done well, create beautiful and functional boats. A thorough examination of the boat both inside and out will tell you if there are any sloppy spots or rough edges. Check the seams and slide in and out of the boat in shorts or rub your bare hand all along the inside of the cockpit to be sure everything is smooth. Rough composite finishes can irritate exposed skin and be very uncomfortable. If you're hoping to lessen the weight of a boat or build in added reinforcement, you should discuss this with the individual manufacturer. For both methods, manufacturers can customize their processes to some extent and may be able to accommodate special requests, though you might be faced with a longer wait for your dream boat.

After bulkhead installation, the remaining finishing touches are made to the kayak: seat, thigh braces, hatch covers, deck rigging, foot braces, rudder or skeg, carrying toggles, perimeter lines, and so forth. A composite kayak can be completed and ready for shipment in about five days.

Types of Cloth

A kayak manufacturer will often use several types of cloth and weave patterns to hit a targeted need for price, weight, strength, and interior finish. Different cloths will vary by weight and their resistance to abrasions and punctures. Weave will also determine the cloth's directional strength and its finished look.

Fiberglass cloth is by far the most common cloth used in kayaks. It's plentiful, not being patented to any particular supplier, and available in a wide variety of styles. Many of the cloths commonly referred to as fiberglass may actually be a blend of fiberglass and other fibers like polyester for increased strength.

In general, fiberglass cloth is fairly abrasion resistant and sufficiently rigid, and if you're reasonably handy, it's easy to repair. It can be punctured and its strands broken if you manage to slam into another kayak's rudder, dock piling bolt, or sharp rock edge (I've managed all three). However, even a puncture wound is not fatal to fiberglass. It can be field repaired with duct tape or epoxy putty, and then a new cloth patch repair can be done with only slightly noticeable results if you're good at this sort of thing. For more on repairs, see chapter 13.

Kevlar is the second most common cloth used in kayak manufacturing. It is lighter than fiberglass cloth and more puncture resistant (Kevlar cloth is used in bulletproof vests—and no, your Kevlar kayak is not bulletproof). It's more expensive than fiberglass cloth, and for every pound (0.45 kg) you save in boat weight, you add as much as $100 to the cost of your kayak when compared to its fiberglass cousin. The accompanying table shows a comparison of kayak costs, sizes, and materials. Five pounds may not sound like much weight to shave from a kayak, but if shaving that last 5 pounds (2.3 kg) allows you to heave it on top of your car by yourself, or saves you from that telltale back twinge the next morning, it's well worth the cost. A beautiful golden color, Kevlar will darken with age and even show "tan lines" after

Sea Kayaks at a Glance

Boats	Material	Price Range	Length (ft.) (m)	Weight (lb.) (kg)	Benefits	Drawbacks
single	polyethylene	$1,200–2,000	14–19 (4.3–5.8)	48–78 (21.8–35.4)	durable, least expensive	heavier; some flexing in material
single	thermoformed	$2,200–2,700	14–19 (4.3–5.8)	43–60 (19.5–27.2)	lighter than poly; look and feel of composite boat	still evolving; the best are very good, cheaper ones are bare bones
single	fiberglass	$2,600–3,100	14–19 (4.3–5.8)	48–57 (21.8–25.8)	light, sleek, efficient	more expensive; shows scratches and scrapes; may need repairs more often than polyethylene versions
single	Kevlar	$2,900–3,600	14–19 (4.3–5.8)	37–50 (16.8–22.7)	even lighter, more puncture resistant* than fiberglass	more expensive; repairs may be trickier; less abrasion resistant
double	polyethylene	$1,600–2,000	15–19 (4.6–5.8)	82–110 (37.2–49.9)	same as single	same as single
double	thermoformed	$2,600–3,000	15–18 (4.6–5.5)	60–75 (27.2–34)	same as single	same as single
double	fiberglass	$3,300–4,000	18–23 (5.5–7)	79–97 (35.8–44)	same as single	same as single
double	Kevlar	$3,700–4,600	18–23 (5.5–7)	70–84 (31.7–38.1)	same as single	same as single

* Except in special lightweight layups, which may be more fragile.

repeated UV exposure. You may choose to use a clear gelcoat to show off your golden boat. If you're really weight conscious, you can choose to use no gelcoat and knock a few more pounds off your kayak's weight. These "skincoat" boats don't have the protective coating of the gelcoat, so they are not as abrasion resistant and need added protection from UV rays. And, just for the record, a Kevlar boat is not 100 percent Kevlar. There will often be fiberglass cloth reinforcements in the ends or underneath the deck.

If you want the lightest composite kayak available, consider graphite. You'll pay dearly for the weight reduction (at least $800 more than its fiberglass cousin), and because graphite cloth is more brittle than other cloths, you'll need to baby the boat. To get a fully outfitted 17-foot (5.2 m) kayak that weighs as little as 30 pounds (14 kg) might be worth it. I just wanted to be sure you knew they existed!

If you choose to go the lightweight route (in Kevlar or graphite), you'll need to be more careful since these layups are more delicate. Lightweight Kevlar layups use less cloth (tough, expedition Kevlar layups are also available but without weight savings over fiberglass versions) and are thinner boats, so you'll need to be careful about dropping the boat, banging against sharp objects, and placing a heavy load (like you) on the deck.

Thermoformed Kayaks

In the 1970s the first rotomolded polyethylene kayaks hit the market. Their trajectory of sales proved to be one of the biggest game changers in the kayak world (more on rotomolded polyethylene boats in the next section, pages 39–40). However, many composite manufacturers were appalled at the shortcomings of the material while understanding the popularity of the price points. Plastic thermoforming had been around for a number of years and was even used to manufacture some of the small outfitting pieces on kayaks such as rudder blades, gear eyes, and jam cleats. In the late 1990s, Tom Derrer of Eddyline Kayaks introduced Carbonlite 2000, and an entirely new category of kayaks was born.

Thermoformed kayaks are created from sheets of layered plastic that are vacuum-formed over a kayak mold. The material has the glossy look of a composite boat and is significantly more rigid than its polyethylene cousins and less expensive than its composite counterparts. So one could say that thermoformed kayaks fall somewhere in between composite and rotomolded polyethylene kayaks in these discussions.

Thermoforming uses resin pellets that are extruded into sheets of varying thickness and size depending on the requirements of the finished product. These sheets can include layers of differing materials that are compatible, and therein lies the beauty of the thermoforming process. While more expensive than rotomolding, it allows more elegant and useful combinations of materials, which result in a finer product.

Typically, the outer layer of a thermoform sheet is some sort of modified acrylic. This material has a glossy finish with high UV resistance (acrylics are used on car finishes and in many waxes) and provides sun protection and preserves the exterior color of the kayak. Some manufacturers may add a second acrylic layer for special graphic effects such as pearlescence or a metallic finish. The substrate, or middle, of the thermoform sheet is considered the "muscle" of the material and is typically some form of high-impact ABS (acetyl-butyl-styrene). The final layer(s) of the sheet create the inside finish of the kayak.

Once a manufacturer has developed its proprietary recipe for thermoform sheets, the process is pretty simple. The sheet is clamped into a frame and then is moved into an oven, where the sheet is heated to a high temperature, generally between 350 and 400°F. At these temperatures, the sheet becomes rubbery and will stretch with ease. While the sheet is hot and flexible, the frame is removed from the oven and the sheet is placed over the mold. As the mold moves into the softened sheet, a vacuum is applied and the material is sucked down around the mold. This allows the sheet to take on the finer details of the kayak.

Unlike rotomolding. which puts material inside a female mold, thermoforming pulls a sheet over a male mold. The sheet stretches as it is pulled over the mold and remains thickest along its centerline. This is useful since most of the wear occurs along the centerline of a kayak, especially in the hull (see photo). There is also less chance of creating a kayak that is marred on its outer surface (what you show off to the world), since any blemish would be inherent in the surface of the sheet rather than created during the molding process. (That is, blemishes on the surface of a thermoform sheet are detectable prior to molding; inspecting a boat's outer surface is not possible during the rotomold-

The vacuum has been applied and the sheet now has the same shape as the mold.

ing process since the plastic is molten and spinning inside a female mold.)

Proponents of thermoformed kayaks point out that the plastic used in thermoforming is harder than other plastics, has better abrasion resistance, and does not "fuzz up" like polyethylene. In addition, it is lighter and has better UV resistance (UV inhibitors or stabilizers can be added to polyethylene powder; in thermoforming they are incorporated into the outer layer of the sheet). However, composite kayaks are still the longest lasting though most expensive.

One of the intriguing things about the materials used in thermoforming is that they can be combined with some composite layup materials to create an innovative blend of the two methods of manufacturing. This area is constantly being explored by leading manufacturers and will likely result in more blurring of the lines between materials and processes.

Thermoformed kayaks fall in between composites and rotomolded polyethylene kayaks in price, longevity, weight, and durability. The table on page 36 shows several examples for comparison of the three styles of manufacturing process.

Polyethylene Kayaks

It's hard to beat the durability and low cost of polyethylene, or plastic, kayaks. They make a great choice for those on a budget or purchasing for an entire family, outfitters and livery programs, kids, or folks who don't really expect to use their boats often or want to have a boat in place at their summer hideaway for general use. If your landing style is more demolition derby than delicate, or if you cannot bear the sound of your $2,700 investment screeching to a halt on a rocky ledge, you might be happier in a polyethylene boat. Polyethylene is a form of plastic that can take a lot of bangs and bumps. And, in the case of linear polyethylene, the most common form used in touring boats, it can be recycled when you're ready to retire your boat.

Polyethylene kayaks are manufactured using a rotomolding process. Plastic granules of a particular color are introduced into the kayak mold. These molds are usually two-piece and clamp together and then rotate and seesaw from end to end in a large oven to coat the mold with the now molten plastic. Rotomolding a 17-foot touring model takes about half an hour, and then the mold is cooled before opening. After initial cooling in the mold, the still hot, fledgling kayak is removed and placed in a cooling jig to hold its shape during further cooling. Cockpit and hatch openings are cut and trimmed, and the boat

Rotomolding can produce kayaks faster and less expensively than other methods. This technology continues to evolve as manufacturers strive to produce stiffer and lighter boats at affordable prices.

is outfitted with deck rigging, rudders, bulkheads, seat, and other finishing touches to complete the process. The entire process may take a full day, and the larger manufacturers may run three ovens or more at a time. The molds used for rotomolding are made of aluminum thin-wall casting and will last through the manufacture of thousands of boats.

Significant improvements in the rotomolding process since about 1990 have resulted in boats that are stiffer and more UV resistant and that can sport finer lines of design than the earlier models. So some of the bad rap you might have heard in the past about plastic boats has been addressed. However, polyethylene is still heavier than both composite and thermoformed layups and will flex more. This flexing of material may result in some loss of efficiency for you as a paddler. A polyethylene kayak is more likely to dent or develop ripples, which may also affect the efficiency of the boat as it moves through the water, so you need to be careful about how you transport and store these boats, especially in warm climates. I have seen a polyethylene boat on top of a car on a hot summer day deform under the sun's direct rays and then reform to its original shape as it cooled in the evening hours. For cartopping advice, see pages 99–105; for storage advice, see pages 286–88.

Weight can certainly be an issue when you move your boat around on land and on and off the top of a vehicle. But what about a boat's weight in the water? While it seems intuitive to assume that a heavier boat will be slower in the water, the final numbers are not quite what you would expect. You must also include the weight of the paddler and any gear when making comparisons between boat weight moving through the water.

For example, let's say we took a 150-pound (67.5 kg) paddler with 100 pounds (45 kg) of gear and put him in a 17-foot (5.2 m) fiberglass boat that weighs 52 pounds (23 kg). That's a total weight of 302 pounds (135.5 kg). Now let's take that same paddler and gear and put him in a polyethylene boat that weighs 63 pounds (28.4 kg), which yields 313 pounds (140.9 kg). The savings in boat weight alone (11 lb./5 kg) is actually a fairly small percentage of the overall weight package that is moving through the water.

Neo-Traditional Kayaks

If you've ever seen the translucent hull of a skin-on-frame kayak slicing through a sunlit wave, you were probably smitten with the beauty of that scene. These traditional

---

A FLEXIBLE VIEW OF RIGIDITY

While it's commonly argued that a rigid hull is more efficient, not wasting its energy in flexing, traditionalists offer a different view. They argue that the flexibility and responsiveness of skin-on-frame kayaks actually enhance efficiency and stability in the dynamic paddling conditions found at sea.

Skin-on-frame kayaks have a deserved reputation as being responsive and lively on the water. You can feel them stretch and compress as they travel over waves and even shudder when a wave hits the deck. Many argue that the flexing of the kayak's frame allows it to ride over waves and yield in a way that maintains the kayak's speed. Rigid boats muscle waves out of their way and waste precious energy, according to this argument.

Proponents of flexible hulls also feel that because their boats do not resist waves, they are more stable. The feeling is that flexing and shedding wave hits actually enhances a kayak's stability, while a rigid hull's fighting of the conditions lessens its stability. These are not easily quantified arguments but are often eloquently put and backed up by the believer's own sea experience. And ultimately, the interactions and feedback between paddler and kayak can affect how efficient and stable a given boat feels in the water. And therein lies the most valid point: if a given design or kayak material provides you with the paddling experience you enjoy, then it's the best choice for you.

IF I CAN DO IT, ANYONE CAN

I am not a boatbuilder. I am not even a woodworker. I have always thought of myself as lacking the patience and attention span to embark on such a project.

When my husband decided to sign up for Corey Freedman's baidarka-building class at the Center for Wooden Boats in Seattle, I said go for it—knock yourself out. Leave me out of it. (My few attempts at helping him on any kind of building project have ended badly.)

But I had to stop by the class a few times to see the boats taking shape. I had to talk to Michelle, who was building one herself and having a good time doing it. I had to try paddling a couple of the boats.

Now, I am a boatbuilder. I have sanded wood and routed wood and pegged wood and sawed wood and chiseled wood and tied lashings—with much more to come. As I write this, I am midway through building my own Aleutian kayak in Corey's shop. I hope that I will have finished by the time this reaches print.

The impetus for me to build one of these vessels came from paddling several of them. As Dennis Stuhaug [of *Canoe & Kayak* magazine] writes, they are beautiful on the water and wonderful to paddle —fast and true and alive. I also was drawn to the joy of having a boat that will fit me, my height, my weight, my strength, my paddling style.

I love learning about the other people building in Corey's shop. Next to me in the shop one day, a woman and her nine-year-old daughter were building two boats, a baidarka for the mother and a smaller Greenland-style kayak for the daughter. Another family—a husband and wife with a happy infant daughter—was building a triple baidarka, 22 feet long, to carry the entire family, which also includes a three-year-old son.

Now I find that I love the process of building the boat. I don't have a lot of free time, between work and family obligations, so I am picking off a day here and there to go to the shop and work on the boat. But when I am there, I don't think about the demands of the rest of my life. I can set the day aside to focus on what is immediately in front of me, on completing one step in the process. I am learning about wood, about its smell, how to handle it. I can see the blocks of wood start to look like a boat, as the bow piece and the tailpiece are fitted to the gunwales, as the deck beams are pegged and lashed into place.

I am looking forward to the day when I will put my boat, which I built, on the water and paddle out to explore my world. But I think I am getting much more than a new boat out of this experience.

Robin Stanton, managing editor, *Canoe & Kayak* magazine

designs just look right and appropriate on the water. And why shouldn't they? They represent designs and construction methods that were developed from materials at hand and for specific needs in a challenging marine environment.

Most owners of skin-on-frame kayaks built them themselves, often under the direction of a master builder. There are several schools throughout North America that teach and lead students through the sizing and construction of their own kayaks. Most of these courses last two weeks or more and are surprisingly inexpensive when you realize that you leave with a kayak that is the perfect fit and style for your own needs. See the Resources chapter for a listing of courses. However, these designs usually do not have the bulkheads, deck rigging, or rudders common to modern designs.

The framework for these kayaks is made of wood; its source and method of construction is specific to the master builder. Deck beams may be pegged in place or secured with bronze nails. Other elements of the wooden frame are commonly lashed together with nylon thread instead of sinew, and the skin is more likely to be nylon or polyester than seal skin coated with animal fat. Traditionalists may still place small pieces of bone as

Skin-on-frame kayaks are more flexible, and their thin outer covering allows paddlers to readily feel seas passing beneath the hull or striking on deck. Paddling a kayak you built with your own hands is immensely rewarding. Here, Robin Stanton enjoys the maiden voyage.

bearing surfaces in the frame to buffer the stresses and quiet the frame as it responds to the dynamics of ocean paddling.

The skin is stretched and sewn in place and then is usually coated with a urethane sealant to aid waterproofing and UV resistance, though paint may also be used, as well as a durable Hypalon coating on the hull. Fabrics differ in their response to a water environment and may tighten and sag with dampness and even continue to stretch for several years. However, fragility does not seem to be the problem you would expect. As one boatbuilder remarked, "You don't hear anyone worrying about the fragility of drum heads, do you?" Of course, the composite boat builder responded, "You do if they get wet!"

What you do hear a lot about is that building a skin-on-frame boat is very doable and results in a boat that is scaled to your exact measurements, paddling style, and temperament. In many cases, building the kayak was as important as the outcome. Participants have often remarked on their dawning understanding of the ingenuity and skill of an ancient culture even as their own personal satisfaction and confidence grew.

Folding Kayaks

If you plan to travel and want to carry your kayak with you to far-flung destinations, or if you find it impossible to store a boat, you should definitely consider folding kayaks.

A folding kayak can be checked through as airline baggage or backpacked to a destination. It can be reconstructed at the launch site and then stored in a closet when you return home.

Assembling a folding kayak

These ingenious designs pack into stow-able backpacks that can be checked through airlines or hoofed through the woods to a remote put-in. Folding kayaks also represent a piece of modern kayak history. They were the first to make a solo crossing of the Atlan-tic (Dr. Hannes Lindemann, 1956) and have stayed on in popularity that blossomed in the late 1940s and 1950s. Early models included beautifully crafted wooden frames and treated canvas skins that created boats stable enough for the whole family and an afternoon's picnic supplies.

Today, manufacturers may use wood frames or lightweight aluminum alloys. The skin may still be tried-and-true canvas or be a newer fabric like Cordura and sport a durable Hypalon bottom. Some models offer sailing rigs, and there are now even sleek, hard-chine models.

Inflatable Kayaks

Like folding kayaks, inflatables are packable and portable. You'll need to have a means of pumping them up at your put-in and main-taining their pressure if you're on a longer expedition. They are popular for flying off to island vacations since their open cockpit designs allow easy swimming and snorkel-ing. While many inflatable models are thin and bouncy, there are designs available that offer near-rigid hulls that are efficient to paddle.

DESIGN FEATURES

Design features represent all the finishing touches made to a kayak to complete what it has to offer you as a paddler. They range from the practical (bulkheads) to the aes-thetic (deck contour lines).

Touring kayaks are available in inflatable versions for easy storage and transport.

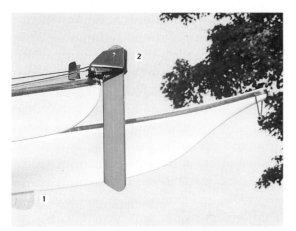

A skeg (1) can be dropped from the hull, and the range of the blade's drop can be controlled by the paddler. A rudder blade (2) is dropped from the stern and can be moved side to side using foot pedals.

Rudders Versus Skegs Versus Neither

Rudder systems and skegs provide directional control to a kayak. A rudder system allows a blade to be dropped from the stern and controlled by foot pedals inside the cockpit. A skeg is a blade dropped from the underside of the boat near the stern. This means you'll give up storage space in the stern hatch to the skeg box (housing). Dropping the skeg blade is usually done with a slide control or jam cleat alongside the cockpit, and the paddler can control the range of the blade's drop, but not any side-to-side movement. Dropping a rudder is an all-or-nothing proposition. The paddler can also control side-to-side movement of the rudder, which can be handy for steering but means your foot braces are only locked into position when you're not using the rudder. (However, there are a few exceptions: Prijon Kayaks and the Seal Line Smart

Track rudder systems allow you to use a rudder and still have locked-in rests for your feet.)

Rudders and skegs enhance the tracking ability of the kayak, though rudders also add a steering function. Some kayak designs, generally the more maneuverable ones, will not hold their course in certain wind or wave conditions. In these instances, dropping a rudder or skeg blade will improve the boat's tracking ability and help hold it on course. If a boat is moving forward through the water and is struck by a wind off, for instance, the right side of the bow (a bow quartering wind), there is a vector component pushing the boat sideways (see illustration page 163). But since the boat is moving forward, this lateral pressure also moves forward and begins to stack, or increase, at the bow on the downwind side. The bow now wants to swing into the wind, or weathercock. A rudder or skeg blade provides more lateral resistance, and the boat would be less able to weathercock.

You can use your paddling technique to keep the kayak on course (more on this in chapter 7), but doing battle with each stroke over a long crossing can be tiring. You can drop your skeg or rudder and paddle normally, but you're dependent on a mechanical feature to balance a design compromise under these conditions.

Some instructors often curse rudder or skeg systems and consider them the bane of learning proper paddling technique. Too many paddlers automatically drop their rudders as they pull away from their launch site, giving little thought to why they are doing this and what it says about their paddling ability or their boat's design. It's the sometimes mindless use of rudders and skegs that bothers some instructors, not rudders and skegs themselves. A paddler who is unable to control a boat in the wind without a rudder or skeg is heading for an accident, because rudders and skegs can jam and break.

All this rudder- and skeg-bashing aside, they are useful little creatures: dropping a rudder or skeg blade to help maintain a course in a loaded boat over several miles is a godsend; double kayaks are much easier to control with a rudder; and by steering with your feet, you can have your hands free to focus binoculars or a camera as you glide quietly by a feeding shorebird or sea otter.

Hatches and Bulkheads

Bulkheads divide a kayak into two or more compartments and serve as watertight walls between these sections. Bulkheads create flotation in the event of a capsize and provide watertight storage areas accessible through hatch openings on deck. These hatch openings need covers that are watertight, so careful attention to their design is important. There are numerous design styles for hatches and their placement on deck. Most single sea kayaks will have a bow hatch and a larger stern hatch; double kayaks will often have a bow hatch, a large center hatch, and a stern hatch. Some sea kayaks do not have bulkheads (or hatch covers) and must carry inflated flotation bags at the bow and stern to displace water in the event of a capsize. It's more difficult to remove water from these boats after a capsize since it can travel the length of the boat, and storage options

are limited. Many of the recreational models that can be used for weekend trips will have a stern bulkhead and hatch and carry a flotation bag in the forward portion of the boat.

One word of caution about bulkheads and hatches: while they are supposed to be watertight, don't assume that your gear will always be bone dry when stored in the hatches. Bulkhead sealants and hatch cover gaskets can crack and tear, and hatch covers can be left loose or lopsided by a careless paddler. And even in well-sealed compartments, condensation can occur. If there's anything that

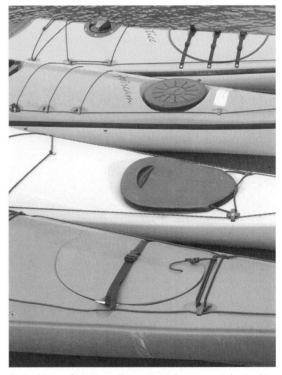

A deck's profile may dictate hatch cover style and the size of a storage compartment. Ensure hatch covers are properly secured and are tethered to the boat before setting out.

will ruin your trip if it turns up wet, put it in a dry bag before it goes in the hatch.

Seats, Thigh Braces, and Cockpit Comfort

There is no reason you should have to suffer in an uncomfortable cockpit. Seat styles range from the minimalist backband and foam slab to inflatable seats and adjustable back support (think of it as an air ride–equipped kayak). Choosing a comfortable seat and thigh brace design is almost as important as your choice of hull design. And, while you can't redesign your choice of hull, you can customize your cockpit area. You can purchase and retrofit seats and backbands and judiciously add padding throughout the cockpit to maximize your comfort and fit. So, if you're taken with a particular kayak design but find the seat uncomfortable, find a replacement seat or build your own out of foam padding. Unless you also wear a hair shirt while paddling,

don't even think of sitting in a cockpit that gouges or rubs you uncomfortably. Fix it! For more on customizing your kayak, see pages 96–97.

Your cockpit should not only be comfortable but also have an opening that you can readily exit if needed. Many designs sport small, round cockpit openings that proponents love for their snug fit and minimum exposure to wave hits and rough seas. Other paddlers may shudder at the thought of wedging into this style cockpit and prefer the longer cockpit openings that offer an easier exit and entry.

The depth of the cockpit should not be so great that you're swallowed whole and bump your elbows on either side. A too deep cockpit may also interfere with some rolling techniques that rely on finishing in a position flat on the back deck (this may also be affected by the seatback height as well). On the other hand, you don't want to be left with most of your upper body teetering out of the

This cockpit has been customized with shaped pieces of Minicel foam. These have been glued into place to provide the comfort and support required by the paddler.

cockpit or hips that simply can't be nudged into place. If you feel as if you're too high above the boat, you probably are, and you'll be keenly aware of this when you paddle the boat and try to remain stable. With the number of kayak designs on the market today, you shouldn't have any problem finding a boat that fits you properly and is comfortable.

Seatbacks that peer above the rear coaming may get in your way during some rolling maneuvers or reentry techniques. If you prefer this high back for the support it offers, be sure you can adapt to it during a reentry from the water. You'll also want to ensure that your

sprayskirt does not hang on any seatback edges as you lean forward to exit the boat.

Most paddlers find that a seat base with a slight upward lift to the front lip is the most comfortable. This design pushes the lower back deeper into the seatback or backband for improved support. It also raises the thighs into a more comfortable paddling position while supporting the back of the legs. Seat bases may be hung from the sides of the cockpit opening, be attached to the floor (sole) of the boat, or be separate units installed in the kayak by the original manufacturer or as a retrofit.

Kayak seats should offer a variety of adjustments for back height and seat base lift. They should always provide lower back support while still allowing the use of a sprayskirt and never impede the execution of a cockpit reentry from the rear deck.

If you make substantial changes to your seat base, you should always test it in the boat in the water. Often a change in a seat base means a change in your center of gravity. As you sit higher in your kayak, your center of gravity is also raised and may affect your stability. Before permanently installing a new seat base or seat design, check to see if it affects your stability. You may be able to adjust to small shifts in your center of gravity; a more decided one could leave you feeling unsettled in your boat and pack a challenge you don't need.

Thigh braces should allow you to relax your upper legs but quickly lock into a supportive position when needed. (For more on paddling position and posture, see pages 94–95.) Thigh braces contoured to fit the shape of the cockpit and your upper leg will be the most comfortable and supportive. Thigh braces should contact your legs somewhere between your knee and midthigh when you're in the correct paddling position. They should not pinch your skin or dig into the side of your kneecap. If there are no thigh braces, or only a flat surface attached to the coaming, consider creating your own. Without thigh braces, you won't have full lower body control of your boat. Both the seat and the entire cockpit can be customized with foam padding to get just the right fit (see pages 94–97).

Deck Rigging

The kayak manufacturer will usually provide deck rigging, carrying toggles, and all the up- and downhauls for the rudder or skeg system. If they are not provided, consider adding perimeter deck lines to your boat as well. These lines run around the perimeter of the boat and should be loose enough to get a hand underneath or to grab when needed. If you're in the water alongside of your boat, it will be far easier to grab a perimeter line than to hold on to a slippery boat hull while you get ready to reenter the boat.

Be sure that you have sufficient deck rigging to hold the items you'll need on the deck

Forward deck rigging can hold a chartcase and essential safety gear that must be reached from the cockpit or from the water. Be sure you can still read the compass.

of your boat, like a chart or GPS case, water bottle, bilge pump, paddle float, and spare paddle. It's easy and inexpensive to add additional deck rigging, though you don't want to encourage carrying a lot of extra stuff on deck that increases windage, makes the boat top-heavy, or interferes with your paddling strokes or reentry.

Deck Shape and Contour

The shape of your kayak's deck may not be as critical to performance as the hull, but it can hinder or enhance your time on the water. If you love the idea of learning rolling techniques that turn you into a human pretzel, then you should be eyeing a deck that is fairly flat both in front of and behind the cockpit. Otherwise, you're not going to be able to complete some of these techniques.

If you want a dry ride in rough conditions, consider a crowned forward deck that uses a flush-mounted hatch cover. This design spills water easily and has no protruding hatch edges that kick up spray in your face. Be sure that the deck height and crown don't cause you to scrape your knuckles across the deck during a forward or sweep stroke. If quietness on the water is important to you, look at a bow design that has a fine edge for slicing through a wave. If storage capacity is paramount, choose a boat that has fuller ends and a high deck to maximize your space. For more on deck profiles, see pages 30–31.

A kayak designer may develop signature deck configurations or add flourishes that are pleasing to the eye. There's nothing wrong with falling in love with a deck that sports a contour line to accent its sheer or whose color is deep and rich. Just remember to check under the hood as well.

A PRIMER FOR BUYING A SEA KAYAK

I hope you're now convinced that no single design does everything well. You can't have the most stable, most responsive, and most efficient boat all in one model regardless of what the manufacturer's brochure says. You'll always be trading design characteristics and balancing their end results to get a boat that is right for you. This is good news and bad news: you'll agonize over making your first choice, but it makes it easier to justify adding additional models to your fleet!

Just remember your answers to the questions posed in chapter 1. Choose a hull design and features that will allow you to do what you want to do with your kayak. A design with minimal storage capacity isn't going to be handy on long expeditions; a 21-foot (6.4 m) double kayak isn't going to be nimble enough to explore the winding saltwater marshes you're so fond of.

Unless you have your heart set on that sleek baby in the paddlesports shop window, take test-drives in the models that meet your needs. Some shops have demo models that you can try on a regular basis; others may have a single demo day event. If at all possible, try a kayak under conditions similar to your planned paddling environment. Too often, a test-drive is limited to a small patch of water where you do little more than paddle out a hundred yards, then turn around and head back in—hardly a thorough test of

A kayak demo day allows you to try many models but may not allow a test paddle that mimics the paddling conditions in your area. Try to use the same paddle and life vest while testing all the demo boats to avoid confounding the variables.

a kayak's abilities. Check with friends or local paddling clubs to see if they have a particular model in their fleet that you can try. Instructional programs will often provide a specific model on request for use in their classes.

Some of you will be tempted to gather information on every boat and then agonize over the data. Don't delay your choice while you engage in a two-year study of what's available. Get a boat, get on the water, and have a great time! If the relationship fails, it was good while it lasted. Sell that boat and get one that's more your type. Resale value on sea kayaks is excellent, or you can hang on to your original for family and friends.

Remember that your skill level will affect how a boat feels and performs in your hands.

While you don't want to buy a boat that is more than you can handle, one that packs some challenge is fun. A boat that you grow into as your skills sharpen will be more rewarding in the long run.

Since a boat doesn't magically appear at the water's edge when you're ready to go paddling, be sure you can move the boat around on land (you can use a kayak cart) and get the boat on and off of your car. Nothing should stand in the way of your actually using the boat. If you choose a folding or inflatable kayak, be sure you can get it ready to paddle by yourself.

Don't be shy about considering aesthetics. A boat you love to look at and show off on top of your car is a boat you'll use and enjoy.

BUYING AND SELLING USED EQUIPMENT

The used-equipment market for kayakers is a robust one, and the savvy buyer can save considerable money on a purchase. Knowing what to look for and what questions to ask can help you find a treasure and save you from getting stuck with someone else's junk or a piece of equipment with a short remaining shelf life.

Boats

The serial number on the boat will tell you the year of its manufacture (often the last two digits; for instance, "11" would indicate a kayak built in 2011), though that only narrows its age to a twelve-month range during which a lot of wear and tear could have occurred. You should be able to talk to the seller and ask about how and where the boat was used. Ask about any repairs that may have been done and what precipitated the need for them.

Composite Boats. Look carefully inside the boat for any signs of repair such as cloth patches or uneven resin drizzles, and check for milky spots, which indicate delamination. If you see fracture points (noticeable starbursts or spidering in the resin), test them with your finger for rough edges or any give, which indicates a weak spot in the boat and will require a significant repair. Small repairs and gelcoat patching are not necessarily a sign of a problem. If the repair was done well and the area seems solid and smooth, there's most likely no need for worry.

Polycarbonate, or Thermoformed, Boats. Check thoroughly as described for composite boats (above), and keep a keen eye out for any cracks in the material. Press down on any cracks to see if they have any give or seem to lengthen under pressure. These will need repairing. If you see any sign of a repair, check to make sure no cracks emanate from it. Such cracks indicate that the repair did not do its job, and you may now have not only additional repairs to this area but a growing weak spot on the boat.

Polyethylene Boats. First notice if the color seems deep and rich or chalky and faded. Older polyethylene boats did not contain many of the UV-inhibiting compounds (before the mid-1990s for most companies), and signs of fading coupled with an older serial number should be cause for concern unless the price is low and your planned use only occasional. Turn the boat over and sight down the keel line to check for any deformities or crooked lines. A boat that was pulled from the mold incorrectly or stored poorly over the long term may never resume or hold a correct shape. Push on the hull to see if it feels unusually thin or brittle, and look carefully for a high number of deep gouges or long curls of material from rough landings. Ask about the boat's storage and whether it has been treated regularly with UV-inhibitor coating such as wax or 303 Protectant (sunscreen for a boat).

All Boats. Look closely at all hatch gaskets and inner covers and the straps that seal the hatch covers in place. Significant fading suggests lots of age and possibly poor storage. Is the deck rigging solid and well anchored, or has it lost its flexibility? Do the rudder or skeg uphaul and downhaul lines (if present) look strong, and do they run freely and smoothly?

Check the bulkhead seals and make sure the wall is still solidly held in place. If you are unsure, consider dumping buckets of water into each storage compartment (in sequence) and in the cockpit and then seesawing the boat back and forth to detect leaks. Replacing sealant around a bulkhead is not a major repair, but any cracks or degradation of the actual bulkhead could be more challenging. Lower and raise any rudder or skeg and listen for gritty sounds, and try to detect any little catches that might point to a potential problem in these mechanisms. Look closely at the carrying toggles for fraying or any signs of abnormal wear around the cleat or the drill-through that holds the toggle cord.

Obviously, the best test for any boat is to paddle it or at least sit in it and adjust it to your needs. Many of the tests for new equipment apply here. Can you easily reach and adjust the foot braces, rudder or skeg, and seat? Are the thigh braces comfortable and intact? Thoroughly checking a used boat should not offend the buyer, and the more questions you ask, the more reassured you will be that some defect will not be detected at a later date.

Used Paddles and Other Accessories

Any item you purchase used should be viewed critically and thoroughly so all signs of wear or damage are noted. After all, this is *used* equipment! As long as you feel that the wear and tear is acceptable for the given price, there's no reason not to purchase used accessories. Just make sure you can repair any damage or wear points, and make note of the remaining life span versus the asking price. In particular, check life vests for faded fabric and any tears in the material. Both significantly decrease the remaining lifetime of this key piece of safety equipment. If possible, be sure the life vest will properly float you in the water before purchasing.

When purchasing used paddles, check the edges of the blades carefully. These are the points of greatest wear, and any splits or cracking in the material may be a problem. Normal use may wear the area down and create small chips in the laminate (for composite paddles), but large fractures or any separation of the layers point to a necessary repair in the near future. If you are considering a two-piece paddle, be sure to check the joint. Doing this should not be difficult, and the fit should feel neither gritty nor loose.

Used dry suits and other articles of paddling clothing may have lost some of their water repellency and should be checked by holding them under a faucet and even rubbing the wet cloth to see if spots form and grow. If water does not immediately bead up on the surface of the fabric, then the DWR (durable water repellency) coating may have worn off. The clothing can be re-treated (see pages 289–90), but the price of the treatment should be taken into account in determining your final price for the item. Note any cracking or tears in any latex gaskets that may be present, and check each zipper because salt corrosion can make these difficult to use.

Alternatives to Buying a Kayak

Often circumstances make you question the wisdom of purchasing a kayak. You may be planning a major shift in your lifestyle (a relocation, a baby, or a career change, for instance) that could radically change your needs for a particular kayak or how you would use a kayak. In situations like this, you might consider a leasing program with a local kayak store. If such a program is not available, ask if one could be designed that works for you and the store owners. Typically, a lease arrangement allows you to have a kayak to use for a season or a full year for a fee considerably less than the purchase price. And like a car lease, you may opt to purchase the kayak when your lease expires, or simply return the kayak to the store.

You may also find a local paddling or fitness club that can provide access to kayaks as part of your membership. Often members may sign out kayaks stored at water's edge for convenient use without the perils of ownership or commitment. Club programs and leases may not give you as wide a choice of styles or materials and may also limit your term or type of use (for instance, no overnight use in the case of some club programs), but if your circumstances do not make purchasing a realistic option, check out these alternatives.

3

Accessories and Clothing

PADDLES

Choosing a paddle can be every bit as demanding and important as choosing your kayak. You'll hold this one piece of equipment every time you go on the water. It's important that its balance, weight, length, blade shape, and aesthetics are all pleasing to you. Paddle prices may range from $40 to $495; the range in their design characteristics is just as broad. And scrimping on your paddle budget will come back to haunt you with every stroke.

The illustration shows a typical touring paddle and names its parts. You'll notice that the blades are asymmetrical—they are longer on the top edge than the bottom edge.

These blades are also "spooned," or concave on the side facing the paddler. The traditional Aleut and Greenland designs shown on page 57 are narrow and have symmetrical blade shapes that are not spooned. Instead, they may show a slight crown across the face of the blade. One of the first decisions you'll make in paddle choice is between these disparate styles.

Today's sea kayakers have overwhelmingly chosen the asymmetrical version that has its roots in European design and adaptations made by canoeists around the turn of the century. The popularity of this choice may be somewhat of a reflection on the market availability between the two styles. Greenland paddles are almost always made of wood

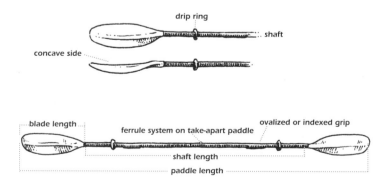

The most common touring paddles have asymmetrical blades that are spoon-shaped, or concave on one side. Most models can be taken apart for easy storage.

GREENLAND PADDLES

Traditional kayak paddles used by both Greenland and Aleut paddlers were narrow bladed and customized to the individual's size and needs. Made of wood, these paddles were wielded with great skill and used to execute a wide variety of rolls and braces essential to surviving in such a harsh environment. In arctic waters, a paddler's first wet exit might well be his last.

Greenland paddles, the general name given to these traditional wooden paddles, are available today, as are numerous plans and kits to make your own. The blades on a Greenland paddle are long and rarely exceed 4 inches (10 cm) in width. The loom, or shaft, is usually slightly oval for indexing to prevent it from readily rolling in your hand.

Advocates of these paddles argue that their style allows for an easy cruising stroke that can be efficiently maintained over many miles with less wear and tear to the body. The placement of the hands on the paddle is closer than that found on European style paddles with their larger, shorter blades, and the angle used in a forward stroke is lower and closer to the body.

The narrow blades will commonly zigzag through the water at certain speeds. This is because when a paddle is pulled through the water, the water against the power face (working face) of the blade moves outward, toward the edge of the blade, during the stroke. This water curls around each edge of the paddle blade and forms an eddy (or vortex) with its axis parallel to the blade edge. This is quite noticeable with the very narrow blades found on Greenland paddles because this vortex is large in relation to the width of these paddle blades. Some paddlers find this disturbing, while others claim this is advantageous. John Heath, an expert on traditional equipment and techniques, has argued that the narrow blades produce a "vortex shedding" phenomenon. The zigzag motion spreads the slip of the blade through the water over more time and distance. Thus for a given unit of time, the paddle has not moved as far aft in relation to the kayak during the stroke.

It's noticeably different to paddle with a Greenland paddle versus the more common large-bladed paddles found in most paddlesports shops. As with any wooden paddle, you can feel the increase in buoyancy as well as the zigzag motion specific to the narrow, slightly crowned blades. Greenland paddles seem easier to use when executing certain rolls. They will by no means guarantee a successful roll. But, the lift required during the blade sweep seems easier to produce with a Greenland paddle and success is more common.

Greenland paddles are normally sized by using a series of anthropomorphic measurements taken to determine the loom size and length, overall length, and width of the paddle blade. If you're building your own or having one custom-built for you, these measurements will most assuredly be taken. If you're sizing a Greenland paddle in a retail shop, you should be sure that the blade is no wider than your grip (certain techniques require a blade grip), or the distance between the web of your thumb and the second joint of your index finger. A reasonable length would be one that is no longer than the distance from the ground to your tips of your fingers with your arm fully extended upward. Your boat width and deck crown may also be factors on length since traditional measurements assume a narrow boat with a flat deck. The length of the loom is determined by measuring the distance from the outer edge of one index finger to another with the hands hung relaxed at your side. The maximum loom diameter is that of a circle formed by touching the thumb and index finger.

Even if you choose to paddle with another style, Greenland paddles are great fun to use while learning some of the more esoteric braces and rolls. They also teach us a lot about the traditions of sea kayaking and the people who were the first to travel and explore their arctic waters.

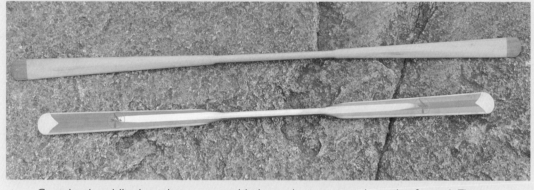

Greenland paddles have long, narrow blades and are commonly made of wood. They are typically one piece and unfeathered.

and may just as likely be homemade as purchased from a paddlesports shop. Asymmetrical touring paddles are readily available in a wide variety of materials and price points. Since the majority of the paddles you'll see and consider have evolved from these European designs, our discussion focuses on them.

Materials

Paddles are made from wood, fiberglass, aluminum, plastic, Kevlar, graphite, and various combinations of these materials. With the exception of a one-piece wood paddle, the paddle blades and shaft are separate pieces that may not even be of the same material. The choice of material determines the paddle's weight, balance, flexibility, cost, durability, and looks.

Plastic paddle blades are usually coupled with aluminum shafts to anchor the lower end of the cost scale. The least expensive of these plastic models offer only symmetrical blades that are flat and of a weight that you'd be hard pressed to deal with over a day of paddling. Because of their low cost, these paddles are popular with recreational kayaks and occasionally as a spare paddle for sea kayakers. But even spare paddles may have to be used.

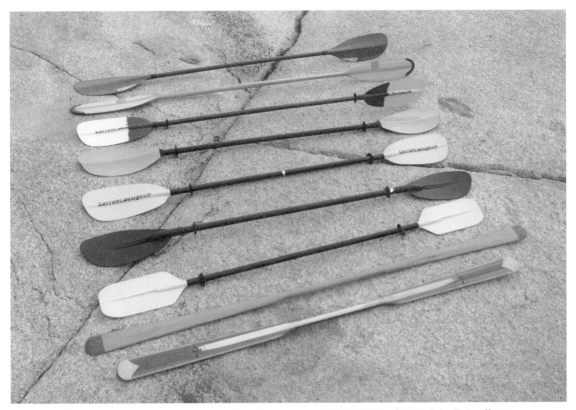

Paddles come in a wide variety of materials and combinations of materials. This affects their weight, flexibility, buoyancy, and cost.

Paddles can be made of cloth and resin, just like a composite kayak. Graphite paddles sit at the top of the cost scale but barely register in weight. These featherweights must be treated with the care you would extend to any object that costs several hundred dollars. They are more fragile than their fiberglass cousins because carbon fiber, a brittle material, is prone to chipping and nicking on the blade edges. The stiffness of this material has caused some paddlers to develop joint aches in their wrists, elbows, and shoulders. Many of the newer graphite shafts have more flexibility than the older versions and will absorb the shocks that used to be absorbed by a paddler's joints.

While slightly heavier than graphite paddles, fiberglass models nicely balance cost and durability and are available in a wide variety of blade shapes and colors. They also are among the most beautiful paddles (outside of wood ones), some with special weaves and resin colors that enhance their aesthetic and also provide directional flex and durability that are built into their designs.

In the past several years, designers have introduced innovative materials that combine fiberglass or carbon fiber strands with polymer construction. These blades are extremely durable and reasonably priced since they can be produced in mass quantities. They may be joined to a fiberglass or graphite shaft for lightweight versions or to an aluminum shaft for the economy model.

Wood has always been a popular material for paddles. It produces a paddle that tends to be quiet in the water and is naturally buoyant, warmer to the touch, and comparable in weight to the fiberglass paddles. Wood paddles come in a wide range of prices that reflect the quality of their workmanship and the type of wood used. To combat wear on the blade ends, which can lead to delamination, many manufacturers reinforce this area with a polycarbonate, epoxy, or even metal tip. Typically, for more protection, the blades are also covered with fiberglass, which is barely noticeable on the best wooden paddles.

Weight and Balance

Although overall paddle weight is a significant concern, the balance of the paddle should be considered as well. This is a very personal experience and one that is hard to quantify. If at all possible, try a field test with a paddle before you make a purchase, just as you would a kayak. If that's not possible, at least "air paddle" with your prospective purchase on the sales floor to get a feel for its balance. Holding a paddle stationary in your hands tells you little.

Often a paddle feels heavy in your hands but much lighter when you're using it in the water. This is because the paddle has more of its weight in the blades than in the shaft. Some designers even argue that more weight

in the blades is helpful during the forward stroke because it creates a kind of "flywheel" effect for the paddler.

However, the past ten years have seen a significant increase in the popularity of lightweight foam core blades. They are either fiberglass or carbon fiber (or some combination of a cloth and resin layup) and have a middle layer of foam. These blades are thicker than other styles and have little or no flexibility, although many paddlers feel that this offers increased stability as the blade moves through the water. The foam gives the blades great buoyancy. The blades also readily exit the water, which lends some snappiness to the stroke. The buoyancy does take some getting used to (as does a wood blade initially).

Grip and Shaft Size

Many manufacturers offer two or more shaft diameters, which allows you to find the grip and shaft diameter comfortable for your hand size. You should be able to close your hand easily around the paddle shaft in the grip areas. These grip areas are created in two ways. The shaft may be compressed to create an oval shape for hand placement, or the area may be built up, or indexed, for hand placement. Either way, this oval grip area is useful on a paddle. It not only gives you feedback about the orientation and hand position on the paddle, but it also allows you to grip the paddle in a less tiring way.

Bent-shaft paddles have become popular in the past ten years. This is probably due to the epidemic of creaky joints in an aging population that wants to maintain activity levels. These bent-shaft, or crankshaft, paddles can offer some relief to those with wrist problems because they minimize the bend

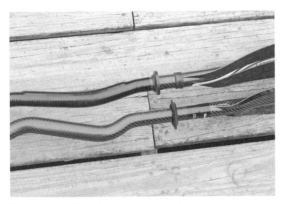

The angle of the bend in bent-shaft paddles varies across manufacturers. Often the grip area is larger because of the extra reinforcement needed here. Make sure the grip area is comfortable for your hand and protects your wrist alignment over the repetitive motions of the forward stroke.

required of the wrist joint during a forward stroke. (For more information on good wrist technique, see pages 112 and 260.)

Bent shafts come in neutral or forward angles. A forward angle bent shaft is normally used for additional power in whitewater or fitness paddling. The offset of the blade in relation to the shaft serves to set the blade in the water much like a caster aligns when rolling a piece of furniture. The neutral-bend shaft keeps the wrist aligned with the paddle shaft and will often ease the strain on wrists, especially those previously injured or weakened.

One warning about bent shafts: creating a bend in any paddle shaft requires additional strengthening at the bend to avoid easy breakage. This requirement adds weight and also decreases the flex at that point of the paddle. With the paddle shaft less able to

The neutral bend in some bent-shaft paddles helps protect the wrist alignment during all phases of the forward stroke. Good technique and mindfulness of your grip and alignment are key to preventing wrist injury and inflammation.

PREVENTING POTENTIAL WRIST PROBLEMS

The wrist joint is a complicated and often fragile joint, and many kayakers can experience discomfort and numbing pain if they don't properly care for their wrists and don't correct poor paddling techniques. The forward stroke is a repetitive motion; done incorrectly it can injure your wrist, causing everything from inflamed tendons to the neural pain of carpal tunnel problems. Your wrist should never move side to side and only slightly forward and back. Instead, it should remain aligned with your forearm and your grip should be relaxed. Maintaining a tight grip on the paddle shaft will cause injury and exacerbate any other technique problems. It is important to monitor your grip, wrist alignment, and fatigue in your hand and forearm over the course of a day's paddling. Small problems can quickly become large ones that can prevent you from paddling.

Bent-shaft paddles can ease the strain of some wrist injuries or weaknesses by minimizing the torque on the wrist joint. Good technique and a good paddle (lightweight with some flex in the shaft) will prevent almost all wrist problems. If you experience wrist pain, review your stroke techniques and have someone watch you to spot problems in alignment. Sometimes a challenging day of paddling will leave you sore; rest and icing the joint (ten minutes on, ten minutes off, repeated three times) will relieve some discomfort; gentle stretches before and after paddling will also help. If you continue to experience pain, see your medical practitioner.

absorb the shocks of each paddle stroke, your body may feel them, especially in the shoulders and elbows. So protecting one joint may lead to problems in others. Always review your forward stroke technique with careful attention to your wrist alignment and grip. Most problems can be corrected with adjustments to technique.

Blade Design

You'll be faced with making a decision between long, skinny blades and short, blunt blades and everything between. While a larger blade will accelerate your kayak more quickly, it takes little more than a broom handle to maintain that momentum in most situations. Many paddlers swear by narrow blades; they

feel they can paddle with a quicker cadence and less fatigue. Paddlers who use large blades like the solid bite they get of the water and feel reassured by a large blade during support strokes or rolls.

You also have to decide if you want your narrow or wide blade in a short, blunt package or an elongated one. Blade size is often given in square centimeters, but that doesn't tell you anything about the shape of that surface area. Shorter, blunt blades might feel snappier to paddlers using a high angle stroke, while an elongated blade might be more comforting to boaters with a slower cadence and lower angle to their stroke. Not surprisingly, the most popular blades are those that fall between: maybe this choice is a reasonable compromise, or maybe prospective buy-

POWER FACE AND BACK FACE

The blade face on the paddle that does the work during the forward stroke is called the power face; the other blade face is called the back face. The power face faces you during a forward stroke and is the concave blade face in spooned blade designs. Most of the time this is also the blade face that sports the manufacturer's name and logo.

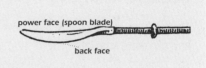

The power face, not the back face, does the work during the forward stroke.

Think of your blade faces as either power face or back face: paddle stroke descriptions use these terms regularly, since you need to define which is the working blade face for each stroke. These terms are used even with nonspoon blade designs, since paddlers still need to distinguish between the blade surfaces. By using the forward stroke as the reference point, this is easily done and avoids confusion.

ers and salespeople just feel overwhelmed by the nuances of all the choices.

Paddle blades can be incredibly complex, with subtle design features that affect the final feel in the water and the cost but are rarely discussed in detail. When you decide to buy, you will be faced with many choices, each espoused as "the best" (or at least "best deal"), and often there's only a minimal understanding of blade design from a given sales staff. But first let's talk about some real-life terms that apply to the blade and how it's made.

Spooned blades. A true spooned blade is just that: you can lift and hold water with it just like a soup spoon. A blade with a spoon shape can grab a nice chunk of water for a powerful catch. However, deeply spooned blades are not easily controlled as they move through the water. The water they grab has no place to go, and strokes with a heavily spooned

blade often feel erratic and fluttery in the hands of a novice paddler. Racers need blades that are spooned (or spooned dramatically in one section like a wing paddle) because they want the efficiency it gives them. Touring kayakers want some spoon but not too much.

Dihedral angle. If you look at the power face of a paddle blade on end, you will most likely see that the blade actually is made up of two angles that intersect along the centerline of the blade (the angle is rarely consistent along the entire length of the blade). Some paddles have a pronounced dihedral; others, such as whitewater paddles, have almost no dihedral. A pronounced dihedral lessens the efficiency of the stroke, but (and this is a big "but") it feels *easier* to move through the water. The low angle strokes of most touring paddlers benefit from a noticeable dihedral that spills water from the blade so that it slips through the water smoothly and without a great deal of effort. However, there is a trade-off in power and efficiency.

Spines. The spine of the blade can be pronounced or fairly flat depending on the materials used in its construction. A pronounced spine on the front, or power face, of the blade can dramatically affect how the blade moves through the water. A spine on the back face of the blade has a less dramatic effect on paddling efficiency but may produce noticeable noise. Spines are generally needed for strength and are more common in less expensive plastic paddles, where they add stiffness and durability.

Complex curves and angles that differ over the face of a paddle blade are meant to maximize the efficiency, quietness, and stiffness of a given blade. When choosing a blade, balance these factors with the cost and whether you like the feel of the blade design in the water.

Here are some general rules to follow for blade design choices:

- *How does the blade grab the water (or catch)?* You want a blade that will quickly catch water, entering it quietly without a telltale splash or plopping sound. A blade that feels like it wants to slip away from you at the catch of the stroke is not a good choice.
- *How does the blade move through the water?* You want a blade that does not flutter madly in your hands as you make your forward stroke. The blade should travel through the water with little turbulence and not so much buoyancy that you feel you must hold it down to complete the stroke.
- *How does the blade exit the water at the end of the stroke?* You want a blade that begins to rise at the end of the stroke and exits cleanly with a certain snappiness. A blade that struggles to exit the water as you finish your stroke will slow your rhythm and make the setup to the next stroke less efficient.

The true test of a paddle is using it on the water. See how it feels in your hands, and pay attention to the feedback it gives you as it moves through the water. Paddling a touring kayak is all about the repetitive motion of the forward stroke, so little annoyances may assume major significance over time.

Length

Blade design, the kayak's beam, your size, and your paddling style and conditions all affect your choice of paddle length. When you size a touring paddle, you're talking about overall lengths that may range from 210 to 260 centimeters.

The length of the blade plays a major role in determining this overall length since the object is to get the blade fully submerged in the water during the forward stroke. A short blade requires less overall length, a longer blade more overall length. Paddles with overall lengths that vary by as much as 10 centimeters may have identical shaft lengths. The blade design creates the difference.

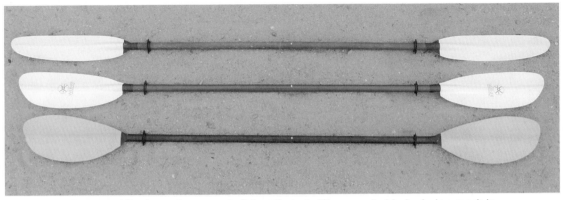

These paddles have the same shaft length, but differences in blade design result in different overall lengths ranging from 220 to 240 cm.

The beam of your kayak and the depth of its cockpit (these often go hand in hand) will also determine your proper paddle length. You must be able to comfortably reach the water and submerge the blade with each stroke. If the blade isn't fully submerged, it isn't doing any work, and you might as well cut off the dry parts to save weight! Thus, wider boats will need longer paddles than will narrower boats. Paddling a double kayak 26 inches (66 cm) wide with a deep, high-volume cockpit clearly requires a longer paddle than a sleek single with a 21.5-inch (55 cm) beam and low volume design.

Your own size will have some effect on your paddle length, though less than other factors. If you're dwarfed by your paddle length, it will be a struggle to move the paddle through the water. You'll have a long lever arm out there that you'll be fighting on each stroke.

If you have an unusually long torso, you must take this into account because your distance to the water is greater and may require a longer shaft. The wider your shoulders, the wider your hand placement on the paddle.

So factoring in your height, torso length, and shoulder width makes sense.

Your paddling style and the paddling conditions should definitely affect your choice of paddle length. If you're an aggressive, high-angle paddler (maybe you have a whitewater or racing background), you'll be happier with a short paddle length. If you're a Sunday driver who prefers easy cruising in quiet water, you'll be happier with a bit more length because your paddling angle will be lower. If your paddling conditions often include surfing or playing in rough water, consider a shorter length and a larger blade design for increased power and support.

One-Piece or Take-Apart Paddles?

One-piece paddles have the advantage of keeping it simple. Without the joint or ferrule system on a paddle, there's little that can give you a maintenance headache (see chapter 13 for repair and maintenance). Eliminating the ferrule also saves some weight. The downside of a one-piece paddle is that you'll

MAGIC FORMULAS

I need to claim two caveats on paddle length:

1. Bear in mind that a difference in overall paddle length of 5 centimeters is less than an inch (2.5 cm) on either end of the paddle. The accuracy of some manufacturers doesn't even fall within this range.
2. The most important factor for your choice of paddle length is what feels best for you. With this in mind, let's try to develop a scheme for making a choice.

The best strategy for determining your paddle length is to consider all the factors we've discussed, giving more weight to boat beam and blade size. While there is no hard and fast formula, consider this scheme as a starting point: if you're paddling a boat that is less than 23 inches (58 cm) in beam, start with a paddle length base of 230 cm; 23 to 25 inches (58–63 cm), use 235 to 240 cm; greater than 25 inches, use 240 to 245 cm. Now factor in the blade size. If you're serious about a wide blade (6.5 in./16.5 cm or more in blade width), drop 5 centimeters from your paddle length; medium-size blades (5.5–6.5 in./14–16.5 cm) require no adjustment; narrower blades (less than 5.5 in.), add 5 centimeters to your paddle length.

Now consider your size and paddling style. If you're at either extreme of these two factors, make an adjustment of plus or minus 2.5 centimeters for each factor. If you feel you're somewhere in the middle for size or style, make no adjustment for that factor. The final paddle length you come up with using this strategy will give you an idea about what lengths to try and test. Determine what feels best to you to make your choice.

I hesitate to include this scheme for paddle length determination; it's the equivalent of a political candidate giving an exact answer. But this question seems to cause so much agonizing on the part of both customers and salespeople, and a general answer wasn't getting the job done. So, give it a shot and see if it helps!

have a harder time stashing it in your car trunk or carrying it as a spare paddle on your stern deck. You'll also be locked in to either one feather angle setting or an unfeathered setting. A take-apart paddle usually gives you the choice of using the paddle unfeathered or feathered and makes storage easy. Three- and four-piece paddles are available for those who need to pack them for long-distance travel or fit them into a folding boat backpack.

Feathering and Other Weighty Matters

Get a roomful of kayaking instructors together and you'll find as many opinions on what feather angle is best as there are instruc-

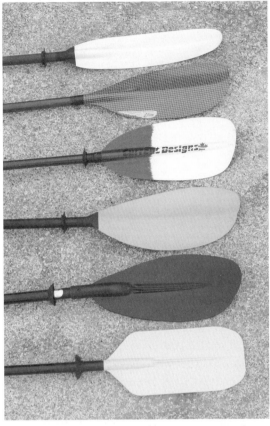

Blade designs vary widely. These are largely a function of personal preferences. All but the bottom blade are asymmetrical, though the degree of their asymmetry varies.

tors. Setting a feather angle on a paddle places the blades in positions offset to each other. An unfeathered paddle keeps the two blades in the same plane. The feather angle may range from 45 to 90 degrees in touring paddles, though most models fall in the 60- to 75-degree range.

Many paddles today offer unlimited feather angles and can be readily switched from one setting to another. Some offer only one unfeathered and one feathered angle setting.

Although many paddle joints are technological marvels, with dials and hidden cams, most paddlers tend to prefer one and only one feathered angle, so all those moving parts may not be needed. What is needed is your decision about what feather angle works best for you (there has been a decided trend in the lessening of these angles). Once you understand the nature of feathering and have a chance to try out several angles, you can decide if you need to customize your angle, reset it frequently, or live happily with the angle built into your paddle. Feathering and proper paddle grip are discussed in detail in chapter 5.

ESSENTIAL SAFETY GEAR

Some pieces of safety gear should be with you whenever you go paddling. The Brits call this their "kit"; I think of it as my "essentials bag." It includes my life vest, sprayskirt, deck compass, handheld compass, bilge pump, sponge, paddle float, rescue sling, signaling devices, waterproof flashlight, repair kit, first-aid kit, spare clothes, water bottle, energy bars, and spare paddle. This is the stuff that automatically gets thrown in for every trip. Sometimes it's overkill, but it's a good habit to get into because you aren't making a last-minute decision about what's important and what isn't. Just grab it and go.

Life Vests

Life vests, or personal flotation devices (PFDs), are essential sea kayaking gear. Yours should fit properly with a range of adjustments to allow for differences in clothing

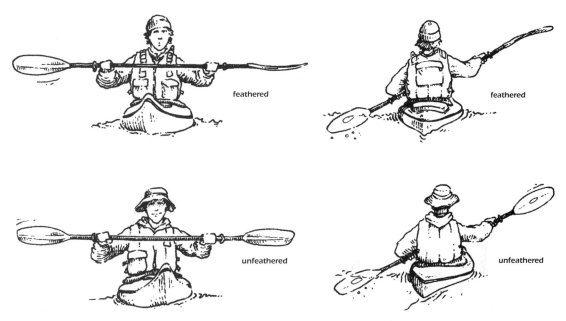

feathered

feathered

unfeathered

unfeathered

A feathered paddle (top) has blades in different planes; both blades are in the same plane on unfeathered paddles (bottom).

and be so comfortable that you won't hesitate to wear it zipped up anytime you're on the water. Paddling life vests are cut short so they won't ride up around your ears when you're seated in the boat (this is especially important for paddlers with short torsos).

When purchasing a new vest, test it in a seated position and take a few paddling strokes. It may surprise you by riding up in the back or front or chafing under your arms when you imitate your forward stroke. The foam in the vest should be soft and contoured to conform to your body, not leave you sandwiched rigidly between two slabs. Be sure you can comfortably lean forward while seated, as if you were checking the chart on your forward deck. Shoulder straps that adjust the height of the vest help hold the vest flat against the top of the shoulders

and collarbone and are essential for a paddler with a short torso.

Do not store your vest under the deck rigging when you go paddling: there's no way you'll be able to get your vest on and cinched while holding on to your boat and paddle if you capsize. Even trying to put on a vest while seated in your cockpit can be challenging when the conditions get rough. If it's a hot day, pour water over your head or practice hip snaps while holding a partner's boat, but don't forgo the life vest.

The large majority of life vests sold in paddlesports shops are U.S. Coast Guard–approved type 3 vests (Canadian Coast Guard requirements are very similar). These are for recreational use and keep you afloat but not necessarily face up if you're unconscious. Other vests are designed to do this (types 1 and

Keep your essentials bag packed and ready to go.

2) but are so bulky and cumbersome for paddling that few paddlers use them. If your vest doesn't come with reflective tape on the shoulders and back, it's a good idea to add some so it will be visible even if you're in the water.

Most paddling life vests have a pocket or two for small items like a handheld compass, some pencil flares, or an energy bar. You should attach a safety whistle (pealess) to the vest where it's accessible and will float close to your mouth if you're bobbing in the water.

Many paddlers attach the whistle to the zipper pull, but it may get in your way when reentering from the water or even unhelpfully unzip your vest during a reentry. Tying it around the shoulder or chest pocket tab is a reasonable choice.

The color of your life vest is important because your visibility on the water is determined by the visibility of your boat, paddle, and life vest. If you're separated from your boat and paddle, your vest will be all you're

COAST GUARD CERTIFICATION

Both the U.S. Coast Guard and the Canadian Coast Guard approve life vest models in their respective countries. The standards between the two countries are similar, though Canadian regulations permit only orange and yellow as the primary colors on life vests.

Life vest manufacturers have been moving toward developing more models with a contoured fit and adding a variety of bells and whistles for rescue and guide needs. The newer contoured styles often feature side-zip panels and over-the-head entry. The resulting vest is often more comfortable as it conforms to the individual body shape, especially for female paddlers. But U.S. Coast Guard regulations may result in these vests being classified as type 5 rather than the more common type 3 designation for kayaking vests. The reason lies in the results of the "don-time test."

A typical person must be able to put on a type 3 vest while out of the water (with no practice) within sixty seconds. If three randomly chosen test participants cannot do this, then the vest cannot be approved as a type 3 vest. (There are other benchmarks that type 3 vests must meet, such as flotation and impact rating.) Many vests that have become popular with sea kayakers are rated as type 5 vests because of these don-time tests or the presence of towlines and other rescue accoutrements. So, a type 5 rating is not necessarily a lower rating than a type 3 approval—it's just different.

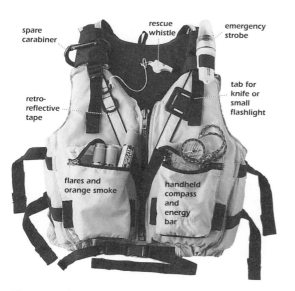

Your vest should be highly visible and adjustable for a snug fit. Signaling devices and small pieces of gear can be carried on or in your life vest.

left with. Yellow, lime, and orange are good choices, and red is OK though it's not as visible in low light or when backlit. Actually, mint green shows up very well on the water but hasn't been perfected in a life vest color, though it has for boats.

Sprayskirts

A kayak's sprayskirt seals you in the boat by attaching around your waist on one end and the cockpit coaming on the other. A sprayskirt may be a piece of safety equipment during challenging conditions or a simple convenience in benign conditions. In rough or cold conditions, a sprayskirt keeps you warm and keeps water from entering the cockpit and is invaluable during an Eskimo roll. In more placid conditions, a sprayskirt keeps sun off your legs and stops the slow torture of paddle drip in your lap. It's a rare sprayskirt that's completely waterproof, but it should keep out the major hits from waves and water over the side during a deep lean turn.

The most popular sprayskirts are made of nylon with taped seams. This construction is relatively inexpensive and keeps most of the water out without creating a cockpit sauna. Neoprene sprayskirts are warmer, drier, and typically have a better seal around the cockpit coaming. But a neoprene sprayskirt may be too hot during the warm paddling months unless you're surfing or playing in rough water. Nylon waist tunnels often use suspenders and a waist bungee to keep things in place; a neoprene skirt is usually held in place by the stretch of the neoprene across your ribs and belly. Sprayskirts are typically worn under the life vest, but models with suspenders may not be compatible with some paddling jacket designs that have sprayskirt tunnels and will need to be removed. Wearing a sprayskirt outside your life vest defeats the primary purpose of a sprayskirt, since doing so allows water to enter through the waist tunnel more easily.

Some skirts have small pockets that can be handy if you can get to them with your life vest on. A few designs provide mesh pockets on the sprayskirt deck, which are useful for a water bottle, sunscreen, or energy bar. Some neoprene designs also feature a rubberized band around their perimeter that helps hold the skirt in place even in very rough water. Some nylon skirts include a sticky "lip grip," which does much the same thing but not so aggressively. Often, it's difficult to keep

Sprayskirts come in a variety of styles and materials. The waist should fit over various layers of clothes, and the deck should fit snugly around the cockpit coaming. The grab loop should be easy to reach and allow you to peel the skirt away from the coaming with one hand.

a sprayskirt from slipping from the thick, molded coaming on polyethylene kayaks, and you may need a more aggressive fit. The deep, thinner edge to a composite kayak's coaming easily holds a sprayskirt in place.

You might also see "implosion bars" built into some touring designs. For the touring kayaker, this feature is less about preventing implosion from a mighty wave hit on your sprayskirt deck than it is about shedding water so it doesn't pool in your lap. Not a bad feature, though most paddlers look funny walking around in one of these (of course, any sprayskirt worn on land looks pretty odd). In general, sprayskirt designs are pretty basic, though some whitewater designs use plaids and other patterns.

Be sure that your sprayskirt fits your kayak. Sprayskirts come in several cockpit sizes, and there is usually a bit of room for adjustments. Convince yourself that you can pop the skirt from the cockpit coaming with a quick tug on the grab loop. (Wet exits are discussed on pages 131–33.) The grab loop should be firmly attached to the skirt and big enough that you can slide your entire hand through the loop. You do not want a grab loop that requires fine dexterity. When you pull on the grab loop, it should actually roll back the front lip of the sprayskirt; some only lift the deck material.

Your sprayskirt also needs to fit you properly. The waist adjustment should be comfortable and have enough range for use with a variety of clothing layers (the sprayskirt goes on under your life vest). Adjust the height of the waist tunnel so that, when you're seated in the boat, the skirt's deck sheds water instead of allowing it to pool. Be sure you can

lean forward without popping the back of the skirt from the coaming.

Bilge Pumps

You need some way to get water out of your boat, especially after a capsize and wet exit. A hand-operated bilge pump works pretty well, though you'll work hard to remove all the water if you've flooded your cockpit. Your bilge pump should have a float collar on it so it won't sink or even linger just below the water's surface. One disadvantage of a hand-held bilge pump is that you usually have to open the sprayskirt to use it, and it requires using both hands. In very rough conditions, it isn't easy to sit in a boat made unstable by water sloshing around the cockpit and actually work one of these things (other paddlers and additional pumps can help). You must also be careful to keep the sprayskirt tight around the bilge pump to keep water from reentering the cockpit with each wave hit. Despite these shortcomings, the handheld bilge pump is still the most effective tool for the money.

Many paddlers have installed foot-operated bilge pumps or electric pumps in their cockpits. Though some paddlers find this awkward, the foot-operated pump allows you to brace or paddle as you pump the boat dry. An electric pump will add weight and cost, but it requires no work on your part other than keeping the batteries charged and flipping a switch. A common feature of British-design boats is a bilge pump that pumps your boat dry through a hose mounted in the cockpit and an outlet on the boat's shoulder or deck; the pump handle is mounted on deck close to the cockpit. These more sophisticated hand pumps require maintenance to ensure that the outlets are clear and all the parts are functioning properly.

Don't forget a low-tech means of removing water—your sponge. A good boat sponge can sop up a surprising amount of water and is great for getting that last bit of slop out of the cockpit and hatches or cleaning gravel and other crud off the seat. A sponge, however, can't do the work of a bilge pump if the cockpit is flooded.

Paddle Floats, Sponsons, and Rescue Slings

These pieces of equipment are invaluable when you need to reenter your boat from the water without the aid of another paddler (these techniques are described on pages 133–37). A paddle float is an inflatable bladder that slips over a paddle blade to give you flotation, and thus support, while you reenter your boat from the water.

The best paddle floats offer ample flotation for even the heaviest paddlers and most awkward reentry. They should have two flotation chambers so you'll have a backup if one valve fails. There should also be some mechanism for fastening the paddle float in place to keep it from slipping off the blade, especially when it's inflated. Avoid metal hardware that corrodes rapidly in salt water, however.

Paddle floats are also helpful for stabilizing your boat while under way for a clothing change, pee break, or camera maintenance. They're also useful as camp pillows, support for your legs, or insulation under your feet while paddling, and they make a great air

splint for field treatment of some injuries. All in all, they're handy little buggers.

There are also paddle floats that do not need any inflating. These are typically large foam blocks that have a cover with a sleeve to hold a paddle blade. These foam paddle floats have some advantages: they can be rigged quickly since no inflation is needed, and they have few parts that can fail. They also do not depend on the paddler to do much other than slip the paddle blade into the sleeve and clip a buckle or two. And many paddlers argue that in very cold water it would be difficult to inflate a bladder-style float, and in extremely cold areas the valves may actually freeze. However, few paddlers like the bulk and rigidity of the foam paddle floats since they are difficult to store on deck or fit into the cockpit for quick accessibility.

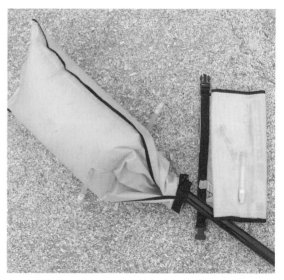

A paddle float is an essential piece of safety gear. Be sure it provides adequate buoyancy and has noncorrosive hardware. Inflation tubes should be long enough to use easily even with cold hands.

Inflatable sponsons such as Sea Wings attach to either side of your kayak to stabilize it. These clip into hardware mounted on either side of the cockpit and can then be inflated. They generally offer more flotation and stability than a paddle float but take longer to employ. They can also be used as "training wheels" if needed or kept in place for swimming or snorkeling to make repeated reentry easier.

The rescue sling is a piece of $\frac{5}{16}$- to $\frac{3}{8}$-inch-diameter (8–9 mm) floating line about 13 feet (4 m) long that's made into a loop with a couple of double fisherman's knots (see page 271). This loop is handy for giving a boost to kayakers as they climb back into the cockpit from the water with or without help (see pages 137–38). Even if you rarely use a rescue sling for reentering, a piece of floating line stored under your deck rigging is a useful thing. Aside from using it for a reentry aid, I've used mine for hanging food from pesky raccoons, securing a tarp as a windbreak, and even lassoing wayward gear that slipped out of the boat during a landing. Some paddlers prefer to use nylon webbing for their slings, but I find nylon harder to work with when my hands are cold and clumsy.

Spare Paddles and Paddle Leashes

Since you probably had trouble making up your mind about which paddle to purchase, you can use the excuse of needing a spare paddle to justify buying another one! It's sensible to carry a spare paddle. A ferrule could jam or a shaft could break on your primary paddle. I even know of one instance in which a paddle floated off with the tide one night

after being left out by a careless paddler. Having a spare also means you can carry two distinctly different paddle designs for use in different conditions. This is a luxury not to be overlooked.

A paddle leash tethers the paddle to you or your boat. Some leashes loop around the paddle shaft and then loop your wrist to keep wayward paddles very close at hand. Others tether to the deck rigging or an eyelet on the forward deck. Paddle leashes attached to boats are handy if you capsize; they allow you to hang on to both your boat and your paddle at the same time. If you lose your grip on both, your paddle will serve as something of a sea anchor on your boat until you can catch up to it.

Paddle leashes are handy for keeping your paddle secure if you're diving or swimming off your boat. If you ever need to toss your paddle out of the way to change clothing or the film in your camera, you don't have to worry about it floating off. But you'll have to

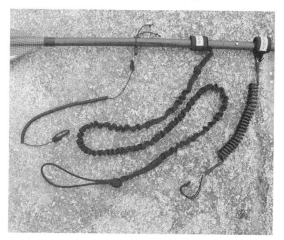

Paddle leashes allow you to tether your paddle to the boat or to your wrist.

put up with a piece of line flopping around as you paddle and always wonder if you'll get tangled up in it should you capsize.

Signaling Devices

You'll need signaling equipment in case you ever need to get someone's attention while on the water. Otherwise, you'll despair as all those friendly people wave at you as you sit yelling and waving your hands or paddle in mounting frustration. You'll need both sound and visual signaling devices for both day and night uses. The bigger and more varied your arsenal, the better off you'll be.

Signaling devices, with the exception of a whistle and flashlight, are for emergency purposes only. Sending up a flare or setting off a smoke canister is an irreversible call for immediate help. To use them otherwise is unwise and illegal.

Flares

Flares are your real visual firepower. Even though the small pencil flares that can fit in your pocket soar over 300 feet (90 m) into the air, the overall effect is pretty puny. The larger and more expensive parachute flares not only go much higher but also majestically float back to earth while putting on an aerial show of bright orange or red. Also consider carrying handheld flares that can be staked on an island shore or held aloft to mark your position. In the case of aerial flares, carry at least three at a time. Radio, visual, or sound emergency signals are normally given in threes. Besides, the first flare you send up will probably be ignored, the second one will get people's attention, but they may remain unconvinced ("it's probably

just kids shooting off fireworks"), and the third should convince them that something's amiss. Flares are useful as day and night signaling devices. Each flare is marked with an expiration date. Always have fresh flares on board, and inspect them regularly.

Strobes

Strobes are great for signaling at night. An emergency strobe can be worn high on the back of your life vest or even attached to your boat. These devices are quite noticeable after dark and are a fairly inexpensive piece of equipment for marking your position. Keep the contacts clean and the batteries fresh and put silicon grease around the O-ring seal on a regular basis. Always keep your strobe in working order.

Dye, Smoke, and Mirrors

Small smoke canisters can be carried easily and set off to produce a billowing cloud of orange smoke. This is a daytime signal only and on a windy day will dissipate quickly. Like smoke, dye markers are useful for marking your position if someone is already looking in the general vicinity (like a search helicopter). Dye markers secrete a fluorescent green or orange dye that is quite noticeable from the air or from a high vantage point on land. Although these pieces of equipment might fit into a pocket, be careful when carrying them to ensure you don't accidentally trigger them. The chemical residue from a smoke canister is especially difficult to remove from clothing and equipment. Store both smoke canisters and dye markers in a dry container when not paddling.

A signaling mirror can be useful on sunny or partly sunny days. You're simply reflect-

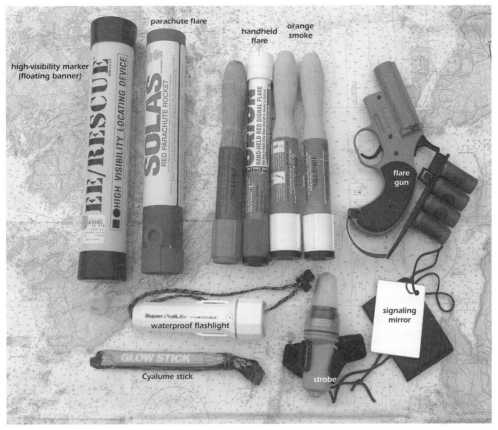

The greater the variety and firepower of your visual signal arsenal, the better your chance of being noticed. Be sure to keep these up to date. (See also the illustration on page 231.)

ing sunlight off the mirror's surface to gain someone's attention. Mirrors put out a pretty impressive flash, but they're too often ignored as an initial signal of distress. But they're useful if someone is already looking for you or you simply want to get someone's attention within your paddling group.

Flashlight

A waterproof flashlight is essential for any trip that might include a late day or an overnight. A flashlight can be used to signal your position, but it's not viewed as an emergency distress signal unless you're signaling an SOS in Morse code and lucky enough to find someone on the other end who understands you. But the U.S. Coast Guard requires that after sunset you use a white light to signify your presence on the water and to designate you as a human-powered vessel. The light must be readily available to help prevent a collision. You can easily mount a flashlight under your deck rigging for a quick running light, though beware, the light will attract insects and the creatures that feed on them!

A headlamp can be used instead of a flashlight, though it may interrupt the night vision of your paddling partners when you look in their direction. It may also attract insects, but a headlamp has the advantage of freeing your hands for paddling. Sometimes it's useful to continue paddling while directing or sweeping light over an area.

Sound Signals

Your voice won't carry very far or last very long in a real emergency. A rescue whistle is shrill and works well for communications within the group. A whistle is louder than your voice, but it still doesn't carry very far on a windy day. Air horns are much louder for signaling your position in the fog or in an emergency. There are some models that you blow, whereas others operate off compressed air. Manual foghorns are superior to the canister style because you don't have to worry about the amount of charge remaining.

VHF Radios and Cell Phones

Electronics are a wonderful thing, and the convenience of carrying a VHF radio and cell phone offers you an easy fallback method of communicating. VHF radios broadcast weather channels, emergency channels that are constantly monitored by the coast guard, ship-to-ship communication channels, marine operator–monitored channels for communications to land phones, and general channels that allow you to chat with other vessels on the water or nearby marinas. A VHF radio gives you the ability to put out a distress call to the people who can help you the quickest: the coast guard and other boats in the area.

VHF radios are powered by nickel-cadmium batteries that must stay dry and

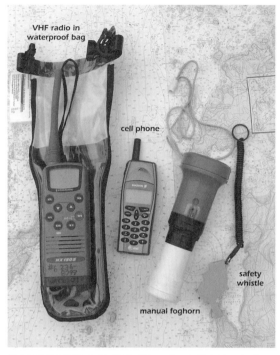

Sound signaling devices range from the low-tech, pealess whistle to VHF radio.

charged. Carry a spare battery pack for trips longer than a day or two, and consider using a weather radio for monitoring weather reports to conserve your VHF batteries. Carry your radio in a waterproof casing that allows you to use it while it's in the case. Trying to remove the radio and screw in an antenna to make a call is too slow and cumbersome if time is of the essence (like a ferry bearing down on you in low visibility).

Cell phones have become a common item among sea kayakers' gear. It makes sense to have a simple and easy way to contact someone on shore for any updates on your landing time or location, but it certainly rankles when you hear one ring with some news tidbit from home. It's a personal matter as to how and when you use a cellular phone while on a pad-

VHF RADIO PROCEDURE

You must learn the operating rules for VHF radio transmissions. These have been established to keep certain channels open for distress calls only and reduce the channel overcrowding that can occur in busy boating areas. Unless you're using another channel for communication, your radio should be set on channel 16, the distress and safety frequency. Never use channel 16 for any transmissions except distress calls and initial contacts with other vessels before moving to another channel. This channel must be kept open so that any distress signals can be heard at all times. There are three levels of denoting priority messages that have the "right-of-way" on the radio channel. These will be broadcast as *Mayday*, which is a universal distress signal (in danger of death); *Pan-Pan* (pronounced *pahn-pahn*), which is an urgent message priority (for example, a guide sending an alert about a lost paddler); *Sécurité* (pronounced *say-cure-e-tay*), which is a safety announcement (for example, you're alerting boats to your presence in foggy conditions). These messages should be announced by repeating your message priority three times (Pan-Pan, Pan-Pan, Pan-Pan), establishing your call sign (like "Acme Kayak, WGB six-zero-two"), your position (if applicable), and then making your announcement.

Channel 9 is now the most common VHF radio channel for hailing other vessels before moving to another channel for conversation. Channels 68, 69, 71, 72, 78, and others are for ship-to-ship communications, with regional preferences. Channel 22 is normally used if you're communicating with a coast guard vessel. Marine operators will typically use one or two channels that are a regional preference and can be found by checking local cruising guides or at a nearby marina (sadly, many paddlesports shops are unable to give you this information). If you're expecting a call from a marine operator, monitor this channel.

VHF radios transmit over an area slightly greater than line of sight. When using a VHF radio, find an open piece of water or high spot on an island to improve reception and transmission.

When you purchase a VHF radio, you'll receive instructions and an application for registering your call sign, or call name. Registering is a simple procedure and establishes your identity for making or receiving calls. When you use the VHF radio, state your call name at the beginning of your message and at the end. It's also helpful to say "over" when you finish each snippet of conversation so the person on the other end knows he or she can speak without missing any of your communication. It's important to become familiar and comfortable with your VHF radio, not only from a safety standpoint, but also because it broadcasts to other boaters that sea kayakers understand proper operating procedures.

dling trip. It might be wise to talk this over with your paddling partners since some folks, myself included, feel that cell phone use on a paddling trip should be restricted to emergencies only (or for calls for takeout pizza).

Other Safety Essentials

First-Aid Kit

I keep two first-aid kits packed and ready to go. One includes the basics for a day's paddle and is always kept close at hand; the second kit is stored in the bow hatch and includes items that might be necessary for longer trips when help is more than a quick sprint away. Even the second kit would have to be beefed up for long expeditions when help might be a day or more away. There are several companies that market ready-made wilderness first-aid kits, and some even have specialty kits for paddlesports. Store your kit in a waterproof container or dry bag where the contents are easily accessible. Everyone in your group should be aware of where the first-aid kit is stored (you might be the one injured) and how to call for emergency help.

Consider enrolling in a wilderness first-aid course where you can learn techniques suitable for field use when immediate help isn't available. If you're interested in longer expeditions, consider pursuing a Wilderness First Responder or Wilderness EMT certification, as well.

Repair Kit

Your repair kit should include spares and repairs for all the little bits and pieces that are prone to breaking, vibrating off your boat, jamming, tearing, unraveling . . . well, you get the point. A repair kit has all the goodies that will get you up and running quickly and make you a hero to your paddling buddies. Throw all these goodies in a large-mouth Nalgene bottle and toss it into a hatch whenever you go paddling. That little machine screw that holds the rudder cable in place is just waiting for you to forget so it can fall out in deep water. Don't say I didn't warn you.

Suggestions for gear inspections are in chapter 13; the contents of your repair kit are listed on page 301.

Towlines

A towline should be a standard item for most any paddling trip. Sea kayak towlines are usually 20 to 50 feet (6–15 m) long and include a length of bungee to absorb the lurches and

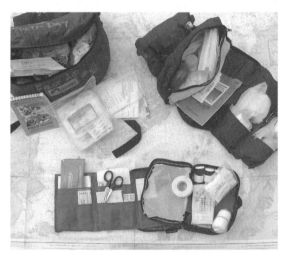

What you carry in your first-aid kit will vary with the nature of your trip. The pack at bottom is useful for shorter trips or ones close to mainland services. Longer trips or explorations in remote areas require more extensive supplies and knowledge.

jerks of paddling in seas. The long length is needed to avoid having the towed kayak surf down a wave and plow into the towing kayak, a common scenario with short towlines.

Most towlines are worn around the waist (never loop them over your shoulder) and should include a quick-release feature, similar to a scuba diver's weight belt. Some towlines mount directly on the boat, either on the deck or around the cockpit coaming. They also include a quick release for safety. Towlines are usually clipped to the bow of the towed boat by carabiner, which should be checked regularly for corrosion.

Shorter towlines may be used for close-contact tows and are often carried on the life vest. These *pigtails* or *cow tails* may be only 3 to 10 feet (0.9–3 m) in length. They are handy for corralling an empty boat during an assisted reentry, for towing over short sprints to shore, or for stabilizing a towed paddler. For a discussion of towing techniques, see pages 254–56.

CLOTHING AS SAFETY GEAR

Anytime you combine the elements of wind, water, and sun, you create a need for pro-

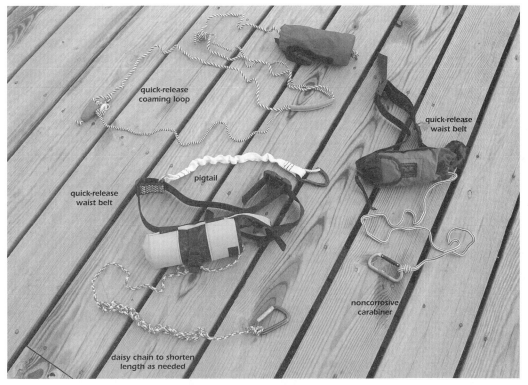

Towlines are worn around the waist or attached to the kayak. They should include a quick release for the tower.

tective clothing. Clothing for sea kayakers is more about safety than fashion. It's about keeping core temperatures protected and skin hidden from the effects of ultraviolet rays. The majority of sea kayaking deaths have involved cold water, often aggravated by wind. Most victims were not prepared for immersion. Many were reasonably dressed for the air temperatures but unprepared for the stunningly cold water temperatures.

Cold-Water Clothing

Hypothermia occurs when the body cools below its normal core temperature. Blood is pulled from the skin surface and extremities to maintain a core temperature and protect vital organs. Shivering tries to create body heat as muscles fire with abandon. The early stages of hypothermia can produce clumsiness as manual dexterity is lost. Often, mildly hypothermic paddlers will become detached and even lethargic, being slow to respond to commands or questions. These symptoms can be disastrous for paddlers and can happen quickly when the person is immersed in cold water. We need our manual dexterity and mental acuity on the water. If we turn passive and clumsy, we're asking for big trouble.

Hypothermia cannot be taken lightly by any sea kayaker paddling in areas with water temperatures below the 70s (below about 21°C). The top table on page 82 shows that even moderate water temperatures are of concern if there is a prolonged immersion. Ignoring the potential for immersion and the disastrous effects of hypothermia is a game of chicken with mighty big stakes. Proper clothing is our best defense against hypothermia.

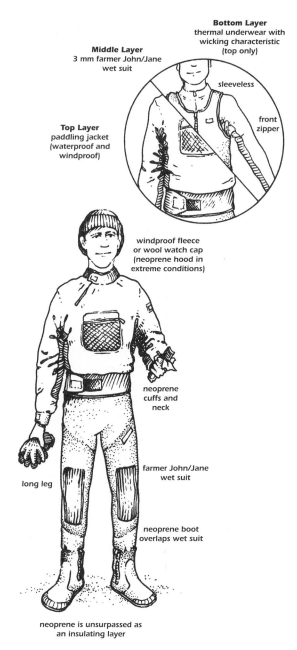

Bottom Layer thermal underwear with wicking characteristic (top only)

Middle Layer 3 mm farmer John/Jane wet suit

sleeveless

front zipper

Top Layer paddling jacket (waterproof and windproof)

windproof fleece or wool watch cap (neoprene hood in extreme conditions)

neoprene cuffs and neck

farmer John/Jane wet suit

long leg

neoprene boot overlaps wet suit

neoprene is unsurpassed as an insulating layer

Basic clothing for staying warm and dry should include synthetic layers next to the skin, an intermediate layer of neoprene for insulation, and a top layer that is water- and windproof.

For more information on hypothermia, see pages 262–63.

Both wet suits and dry suits will protect the body when immersed in cold water. Wet suits, which are made of closed-cell material, trap a thin layer of water against the body, which is rapidly heated and insulated by the material. The body remains warm until this layer of insulation is overwhelmed. Wet suits come in a wide range of thicknesses, from 0.5 to 6 mm. The workhorse of paddling wet suits is usually a 3 mm farmer John or Jane. These are sleeveless wet suits with full legs that are common throughout the watersports industry. Thicker wet suits, common among scuba divers, are less comfortable for paddling. Thinner versions are more comfortable but offer less protection and insulation. If you will paddle regularly in water temperatures below 60°F (15°C), you should stay with a 3 mm model (or thicker under challenging conditions and water temperatures under 50°F/10°C). In warmer waters, you might consider thinner versions or the "shortys," which reach to only about midthigh.

You still need to wear a thermal underwear top under your wet suit and a windproof layer, like a paddling jacket, on top. The thermal top will wick moisture away from your skin and continue to warm you even when wet. The outer windproof layer will prevent evaporative cooling across the surface of the wet suit and your skin. Typically, paddlers prefer light- to midweight thermal pieces, which also serve as rash guards in sensitive areas like under the arms.

Of course, the best way to stay warm is to remain dry, and the more area of your body that remains the dry, the better. Dry suits enclose the body in a waterproof material that is most often sealed at the neck, ankles, and wrists with latex gaskets. Dry suits have a durable and bulky zipper either across the chest or the top of the back for entry and final lockdown. You may also add waterproof socks (feet always get the coldest, so seriously consider this option) and hoods to dry suits for maximum protection.

Dry suits are waterproof, but it's their use of breathable membranes such as Gore-Tex that makes them so comfortable to wear. The nonbreathable versions can create an internal steam bath that will leave you soaked. Regardless of the actual dry-suit material, wear thermal layers underneath your dry suit since you can feel the cold water through the material even as you remain dry. These layers will also help transport your moisture to the surface, where it can be expelled through the membrane. Dry suits are windproof, so you'll be protected from convective cooling when you emerge from the water, and the insulating layers inside the dry suit will keep you toasty.

Dry suits with breathable membranes are typically five to six times as expensive as the average wet suit. They'll cost less than your boat, but more than your paddle! They require some basic maintenance to protect the latex gaskets and keep the layered membrane unclogged (see page 289).

Dry suits can be a challenge when it's time to relieve yourself. They are not easy to slip on and off, and the one-piece versions leave your entire upper body exposed to chilly winds when you need to drop them to below waist levels. Many models have a drop seat or zip-

The Effect of Water Temperature on the Body

Water Temperature	Useful Work	Unconscious
32.5°F (0.3°C)	less than 5 min.	less than 15 min.
40°F (4.5°C)	7.5 min.	30 min.
50°F (10°C)	15 min.	60 min.
60°F (15°C)	30 min.	2 h
70°F (20°C)	45 min.	3 h

Adapted from the findings of A. F. Davidson, *American Whitewater*, 1966.

Water Temperature Table

Location	Jan.	March	May	July	Aug.	Sept.	Nov.
Myrtle Beach SC	48°F (8.9°C)	55°F (12.8°C)	72.5°F (22.5°C)	82°F (27.8°C)	83°F (28°C)	80°F (6.7°C)	61°F (16.1°C)
Key West FL	69°F (20.5°C)	75°F (23.8°C)	82.5°F (28°C)	87°F (30.5°C)	87°F (30.5°C)	86°F (30°C)	76°F (24.4°C)
Grand Isle LA	61°F (16°C)	64°F (17.8°C)	77°F (25°C)	85°F (29.4°C)	85°F (29.4°C)	83°F (28.3°C)	70°F (21.1°C)
Bar Harbor ME	38°F (3.3°C)	38°F (3.3°C)	48°F (9.4°C)	58°F (15°C)	60°F (15.6°C)	57°F (14.4°C)	52°F (11.1°C)
Port Townsend WA	44°F (6.7°C)	46°F (7.8°C)	49.5°F (9.7°C)	52°F (11.1°C)	54°F (12.2°C)	54°F (12.2°C)	50°F (10°C)
Santa Barbara CA	56°F (13.3°C)	57°F (13.8°C)	59.5°F (15.2°C)	63°F (17.2°C)	64.5°F (18°C)	64°F (17.8°C)	60°F (15.5°C)
Oceanside CA	57°F (13.8°C)	58°F (14.4°C)	61.5°F (16.4°C)	66.5°F (19.2°C)	69°F (20.6°C)	66.5°F (19.2°C)	61°F (16.1°C)
Anchorage AK	31°F (−0.5°C)	32°F (0°C)	44°F (6.7°C)	58°F (14.4°C)	57°F (13.9°C)	53°F (11.7°C)	34°F (1.1°C)
Honolulu HI	76°F (24.4°C)	76°F (24.4°C)	72°F (22.2°C)	74°F (23.3°C)	75°F (23.8°C)	75°F (23.8°C)	74°F (23.3°C)
Lake Superior	37.4°F (3°C)	33.8°F (1°C)	35.6°F (2°C)	55.4°F (13°C)	60.8°F (16°C)	62.6°F (17°C)	46.4°F (8°C)
Lake Michigan	39.2°F (4°C)	33.8°F (1°C)	37.4°F (3°C)	60.8°F (16°C)	71.6°F (22°C)	66.2°F (19°C)	50°F (10°C)

Coastal data is adapted from the National Oceanographic Data Center's *Coastal Water Temperature Guide 2010*. Data on the Great Lakes is adapted from water temperature graphs plotted by the Great Lakes Environmental Research Laboratory.

pered fly, which are features useful for both men and women (women can use the Freshette, a urine funnel, with the zippered fly). Adding these features will increase the cost of the dry suit and add some bulk from the extra zippers but their convenience may be well worth it.

GASP! COLD WATER!

We've all been unexpectedly doused with very cold water: your first reaction was probably to gasp. Now imagine suddenly immersing your head in cold water and what might happen if you were to gasp. Even if you're just bobbing in cold water, the shock of it may initially quicken your breathing and leave you feeling as if you can't get a good deep breath. (Watch those daredevil kids who are the first to jump in the swimming pool or lake each spring.)

This phenomenon has often been called *cold shock*. It has been suspected for years that many of the drownings due to hypothermia may have actually occurred as the result of this gasp reflex, or cold shock. While everyone seems to agree that sudden immersion in very cold water can make a person gasp, many are uncomfortable with using the term *shock* to describe anything outside of the confines of its exact medical definition. So, over the past ten years, the term *cold shock* has been less frequently used. No matter what we call it, we still instinctively gasp when plunged into cold water.

The only way to protect against a gasp reflex (other than not paddling in cold water) is to insulate the body and especially the head from sudden exposure. Neoprene beanies or full hoods will help insulate you from the sudden shock of immersing your head in cold water—even a knitted, close-fitting wool cap will help. If you plan to paddle in cold water temperatures, especially in rough water, you need to protect your head as well as the rest of your body. If you don't, you could be left gasping.

Head coverings provide insulation, shade, or warmth. For information on helmets, see pages 89–90.

Once water temperatures reach well into the 60s (about 18–20°C), you have more choices in paddling clothing. Stay with quick-drying materials like Supplex nylon, or lighter-weight versions of Gore-Tex or Sympatex. Always avoid cotton clothing for on-water activities. Cotton will cool you down and becomes heavy when wet. Use wicking fabrics against your skin and waterproof-windproof layers on the outside. If you're chilly, use fleece or pile as a midlayer for warmth. These synthetic materials are lightweight and dry quickly. Wool continues to insulate when wet but can absorb water and grow heavy. Don't forget to wear a hat to help stay warm.

To protect your hands when paddling in cold water conditions, consider neoprene gloves, mittens, or pogies. Pogies attach to your paddle shaft and allow you to slip your hand inside for a good paddling grip. Pogies can be made from nylon and have a fleece lining around the hand for warmth, or they can be made of neoprene.

Most paddlers find the neoprene gloves used by scuba divers to be too thick for comfort and a good paddling grip. You want to avoid having to compress a thick material to have a good grip on the paddle shaft. Otherwise, you'll get forearm or hand cramps. Popular neoprene paddling gloves fall within the 0.5 to 3.0 mm thickness range. If your hands tend to get cold quickly, consider packing along a few small heat packs that you can store in a life vest or sprayskirt pocket. Acti-

Dry suits provide complete protection from the water with latex gaskets at the wrists, neck, and ankles. The best dry suits are constructed of multi-layered waterproof but breathable membranes that allow body moisture to escape while keeping the elements out.

A TOUGH DECISION

Deciding when to leave your wet suit or dry suit at home is critical. Even if the water temperatures are in the 60s (15–20°C), you can quickly become hypothermic if immersed. You need to factor many variables into your decision. How likely is immersion? (With surfing it's a sure bet.) Are you prone to getting cold quickly and having trouble rewarming? How solid are your boating skills (especially rolling and solo reentry) and your balance and comfort level in your boat? Are there aggravating factors such as wind? How accessible is the shore, and what does it offer if you need to warm up? Who are your paddling partners, how prepared are they, and how strong are your skills in relation to theirs? (Are they expecting you to take care of them?)

You can never go wrong by erring on the conservative side when deciding whether to wear a wet suit or dry suit. The worst that can happen is that you get overheated, which can be quickly remedied when you're surrounded by cold water.

One popular option for dry suits is an integral waterproof but breathable sock. Since feet often get cold (and don't have a chance to move much in a kayak), consider this option. It also eliminates a set of latex gaskets that would need to be maintained and often replaced.

Pogies (far left and far right) attach to the paddle shaft and provide protection from cold wind and water. The comfort and grip of neoprene gloves (center) vary depending on their thickness and the use of additional materials.

HOW YOU GET COLD

There are four ways your body can be robbed of heat, and all can occur on a given kayak trip under the right conditions.

Radiation: Heat flows from warmer objects to cooler objects. Since your body is often warmer than the air, it will readily lose its heat if exposed to a cooling breeze. Heat loss through radiation can be minimized by covering skin and wearing a hat to minimize your exposure.

Evaporation: When you sweat, moisture leaves your body and takes some of your body heat with it. This helps cool you on a hot day but will also result in heat loss on cooler days. Use wicking fabrics as your bottom layer since they transport moisture away from the surface of your skin and minimize evaporative cooling. Cotton will absorb moisture and hold it against your skin, which will enhance evaporative cooling.

Conduction: Heat is lost through conduction when a warm object is in direct contact with a cooler object. When your body is in direct contact with cold water, you'll rapidly lose heat through conduction. In fact you lose heat up to thirty-two times faster in water of a given temperature than you do in air of the same temperature. To avoid conductive heat loss, you'll need to insulate your body from direct contact. Neoprene is unsurpassed as an insulating material.

Convection: Convective heat loss occurs by movement of air. On a cold, windy day, your body will rapidly lose heat unless it's protected with windproof materials.

You can see that your own heat loss can be prevented or minimized by addressing the ways you lose heat to the surrounding environment. Layering performance fabrics and making sure you're properly insulated or kept completely dry will not only be more comfortable but also may well save your life.

vating one of these for a quick hit of warmth while under way is a godsend.

Warm-Weather Clothing

Paddling in warm climates is mostly about comfort and protection from the sun. You should look to quick-drying fabrics that do not have any seams that will chafe during the repetitive motions of paddling or while in a seated position for hours at a time. Avoid metal zippers, and consider Velcro closures and light colors that will keep you cool. Many fabrics will provide additional sun protection with special weaves and treatments, usually in the SPF 30 range. Don't forget to include

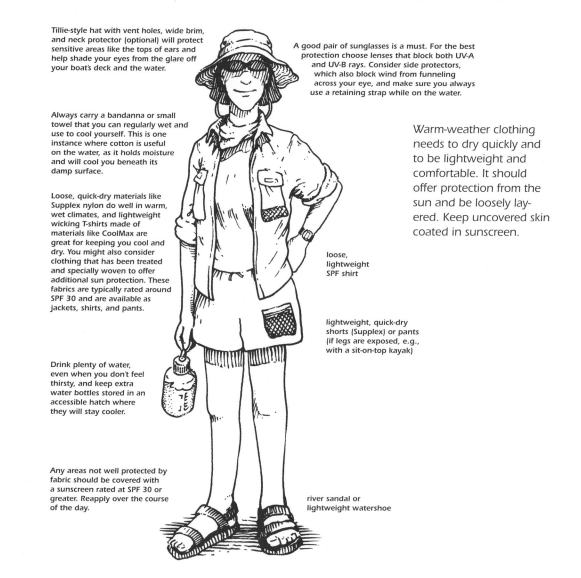

Tillie-style hat with vent holes, wide brim, and neck protector (optional) will protect sensitive areas like the tops of ears and help shade your eyes from the glare off your boat's deck and the water.

A good pair of sunglasses is a must. For the best protection choose lenses that block both UV-A and UV-B rays. Consider side protectors, which also block wind from funneling across your eye, and make sure you always use a retaining strap while on the water.

Always carry a bandanna or small towel that you can regularly wet and use to cool yourself. This is one instance where cotton is useful on the water, as it holds moisture and will cool you beneath its damp surface.

Loose, quick-dry materials like Supplex nylon do well in warm, wet climates, and lightweight wicking T-shirts made of materials like CoolMax are great for keeping you cool and dry. You might also consider clothing that has been treated and specially woven to offer additional sun protection. These fabrics are typically rated around SPF 30 and are available as jackets, shirts, and pants.

Drink plenty of water, even when you don't feel thirsty, and keep extra water bottles stored in an accessible hatch where they will stay cooler.

Any areas not well protected by fabric should be covered with a sunscreen rated at SPF 30 or greater. Reapply over the course of the day.

Warm-weather clothing needs to dry quickly and to be lightweight and comfortable. It should offer protection from the sun and be loosely layered. Keep uncovered skin coated in sunscreen.

loose, lightweight SPF shirt

lightweight, quick-dry shorts (Supplex) or pants (if legs are exposed, e.g., with a sit-on-top kayak)

river sandal or lightweight watershoe

a hat for shade and a bandanna that can be soaked to cool you down.

Footwear

You need some pretty rugged footwear for paddling since it's likely you'll be scrambling around on barnacles and shells once you go ashore. Neoprene boots, 4 to 6 mm thick, provide warmth and plenty of protection once you're out of the boat. You can also get lighter neoprene versions in the 2.5 to 4 mm range and may opt for a lower cut if your paddling is primarily in warmer seasons. The foot beds on the boots must be tough enough to stand up to your intended use. If you're primarily landing and launching from beaches full of rocks or crushed shell, use a foot bed that is at least 7 mm thick, and consider models with additional stiffening and protection built into the sole. If you're paddling primarily in areas with sand beaches,

the thin soles found on common watershoes may be just fine.

The ubiquitous river sandal is a popular footwear choice for many paddlers. The comfortable soles are usually rugged enough for scrambling around on rocks (though they wear out quickly under these conditions). Add neoprene socks for warmth and to help keep pebbles from torturing the soles of your feet. There have been incidents in which river sandal straps caught on foot braces and produced some harrowing moments for paddlers trying to wet-exit their boats. So, keep the straps properly tightened and loose ends tucked in or trimmed. There are numerous watershoes that range from the high tech to the basic, with prices from $15 to $150. Be sure that whatever you choose for footwear is comfortable when you're in the paddling position. Often, an edge or a seam that isn't noticeable during a test walk around the store will haunt you as it rubs uncomfortably during paddling.

Your paddling conditions and landing sites will determine your choice among the many footwear options. Your footwear should not make it difficult for you to exit your kayak, nor should it chafe uncomfortably when you're in the paddling position.

NAVIGATIONAL GEAR

Unless you plan on paddling next to a shore-line whenever you set out, you're going to need a compass, preferably one you can mount on the deck of your kayak. There are several styles of deck-mounted compasses—some are removable, others are firmly mounted to a deck plate that is then attached to the boat and sealed. Polyethylene boats almost always use removable deck compasses since there is too much flex in their decks to mount and seal a compass properly.

A deck compass is normally mounted on the forward edge of the deck rigging, though some paddlers place theirs as far away as the forward hatch cover (it should be easy to read without leaning forward and squinting). Center the compass on the centerline of your kayak for the best accuracy. If your compass is removable, don't let it slip to the side, and check that the lubber line, the line through the center of the compass circle, is always set on the centerline of the kayak. Make sure you can read your compass from your cockpit,

Compasses can either be mounted permanently to the deck or be removable. A handheld compass is useful as backup and to check for deviation.

A GPS unit can store a surprising amount of data for retrieval while under way. You still need a chart and compass as backup in case of electronic meltdown.

even under low-light conditions, before you permanently attach it. Lighted compasses are available for night paddling.

A great backup to your deck compass, a handheld compass allows you to check for deviation in your primary compass. Deviation occurs when iron, steel, or other ferrous materials are close enough to a compass to disturb its readings. If you stand well away from the boat but perfectly aligned with the deck compass, you should get the same reading. Otherwise, something is causing the compass to deviate from magnetic north. Be sure you didn't pack your flashlight or cast-iron skillet too close.

A handheld compass also makes it easy to take a bearing on landmarks that are perpendicular to your boat. Rather than turning your boat around to point at the landmark, you can sight your handheld compass along that line for your bearing.

A GPS (global positioning system) unit makes use of satellite positions to pinpoint your exact location or help you paddle a course to another location programmed into your unit. This system comes from military technology and is able to pinpoint your location with impressive accuracy. In the past few years, GPS units have come down in price (less than $100) so that they are quite affordable. They require batteries, so pack a spare set, and double-check things by using your chart and compass rose (see page 207). A GPS also makes it a cinch to determine your paddling speed, total distance traveled, and distances between points.

A GPS doesn't provide you with any information that you can't get by using your chart, compass, and brain. So don't get so enamored with this technology that you forget how to use any or all three of these tools.

There are several basic navigational tools that you'll depend on for reading charts, plotting courses, and determining distances. Get a good chartcase that will fit on your deck and keep your chart reasonably dry (condensation is always a problem). For trip planning, you'll want a set of parallel rulers and dividers. A course plotter, or courser, usually an acetate sheet overlay with parallel lines etched on the surface, can do almost everything parallel rulers can do and is easier to use when under way. For more discussion of these tools and how to use them, see chapter 8.

OTHER USEFUL STUFF

Safety Helmets

Helmets are a given in the world of whitewater kayaking but may be optional for most sea kayakers. If you're paddling in rock gardens or surfing, they are a must! It's too easy to get bopped on the head by another boat or piece of ledge even when playing in gentle surf. Kayaking helmets are padded to absorb shocks and may be individually sized or adjustable for a proper fit. There will be water drain holes across the top of the helmet and an adjustable chin strap. There are beefed-up versions for extreme kayakers with full face masks or chin guards.

If you're paddling in cold-water conditions, consider sizing your helmet to allow a neoprene beanie or hood to fit underneath. A beanie or hood with a bill will not only

A safety helmet is essential in rock gardens and surf. These "brain buckets" should protect the entire head and allow water to drain quickly. You can add an insulating layer underneath and/or a bill to help water drain away from your face.

insulate your head but also keep water from draining directly into your eyes after a roll or wave hit.

When exploring areas that may include rocky shorelines with surf or rock gardens, pack a helmet and don it as you near these areas even if you don't want to wear it for the entire trip. The main thing is to protect that noggin of yours!

Dry Bags

You can't have too many dry bags. These vinyl or urethane-coated nylon bags have radio-frequency-welded seams that make them completely waterproof when they're correctly closed. The most common closure has a roll top that clips together in the front and creates a handy carrying grip. Dry bags come in a wide range of sizes and shapes with and without clear windows, so you can figure out what you put in each one or hide their contents if you choose.

Some bags are tapered so they can fit nicely in the bow or stern of a touring boat, and some even have purge valves that let you compress the contents and squeeze out every last square inch of space available. Urethane-coated nylon bags are easier to slide into tight spaces and are more abrasion resistant than their vinyl cousins, though they cost a bit more. The most common dry bag is the round-bottom bag made of 13- to 20-ounce (369–567 g) vinyl fabric. With any dry bag, look for solidly made seams that do not pucker or have loose threads, and check the quality of the material and its weight (thicker fabric is more durable).

Many companies are looking for other materials to replace the PVC versions in order to lessen the environmental impact of this material. Urethane-coated nylon bags and other PVC-free materials are available in a wide variety of shapes and styles. These PVC-free dry bags are usually more expensive, but as the market demand grows and more research is given to new waterproof fabrics and coatings, PVC bags may become a thing of the past. Many outdoor-gear stores have decided to ban them from their shelves,

Dry bags come in all sizes, shapes, and materials. You'll appreciate having an assortment at hand when it comes time to pack for longer trips. Label or color code your dry bags to avoid confusion.

which may hasten the demise of PVC in the outdoor sports market.

Sea Anchors or Drogues

Sea anchors and drogues are set to hold a kayak at a favorable angle to the wind. These are not anchors that are set on the bottom, but rather devices that float just below the water's surface to create sufficient drag to help keep the kayak from broaching in heavy seas or slow its downwind motion. Sea anchors are normally set from the bow so that the paddler can be pointing into the wind and seas when paddling has ceased. Sea anchors are useful for taking a break during long, windy crossings or for minimizing downwind loss of position during emergencies.

The term *drogue* is commonly used to denote a sea anchor that may be set from the stern and merely slows progress and keeps the boat from broaching or helps settle it in rough seas. A kayaker would continue to paddle after setting a drogue.

Sea anchors and drogues are usually nylon (though traditionalists may use canvas) cones or parachutes that can spill water from their openings when being retrieved. There are several ingenious designs on the kayak market. Anchors and drogues shouldn't necessarily be viewed as extreme safety devices; many paddlers regularly use them if their paddling area includes long, open crossings or if they want to swim or dive in deep water. In an emergency, a piece of wood, spare paddle, or open dry bag can be used as a sea anchor.

EPIRBs

Emergency position-indicating radio beacons (EPIRBs) are electronic devices that transmit a signal pinpointing their location for emergency searches. They are used by pilots, seagoing vessels, alpinists, and kayakers who paddle in remote locations. Once activated, an EPIRB signal may be picked up by satellite and relayed to emergency stations, or it is broadcast over channels regularly monitored by aircraft or the military.

The several classes of EPIRBs differ in range, ruggedness, and cost. Some are automatically triggered by jarring impact or submersion, others must be manually triggered. Once activated, they set in motion an emergency response, so any accidental triggering must be reported immediately. Batteries and operational readiness must be checked

Sea anchors deploy from the bow and can help hold your position in headwinds or strong currents.

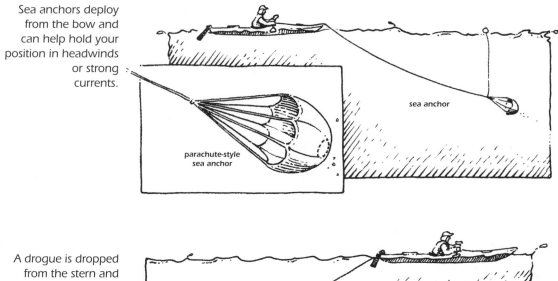

parachute-style sea anchor

sea anchor

A drogue is dropped from the stern and can help keep your kayak from broaching in following seas.

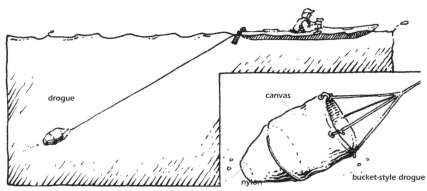

drogue

canvas

nylon

bucket-style drogue

EPIRBs are for emergency use only and are normally carried only by kayakers undertaking extremely challenging or remote explorations.

regularly, and any EPIRB used for kayaking should have a flotation collar. EPIRBs must be registered in a manner similar to VHF radio registration.

Handheld Barometers and Anemometers

Kayakers now have the option of carrying small barometers that measure the changes in atmospheric pressure, and anemometers that measure wind speeds. These handheld versions are not as rugged or accurate as the large versions that weather stations and airports use, but they are fun to use and educational.

They're a handy way of providing information to help you determine weather and weather trends and conditions at your exact location. If you paddle in remote areas or out of range of weather broadcasts, these can be especially useful.

4

Getting to Know Your Kayak

If you're new to this sport, you may still view your kayak with a little bit of distrust. You need more time locking down hatch covers, lifting rudders, scrambling around in the depths of the cockpit, and securing the boat to the roof of your car. You need to find out all its idiosyncrasies and adjust to its temperament. It's time to build a partnership.

SEATING AND FOOT BRACE ADJUSTMENT

There is no reason to be uncomfortable in your boat. Sure, you might be stiff after being confined in the cockpit for several hours straight, but your seatback should provide adequate back support and your feet should

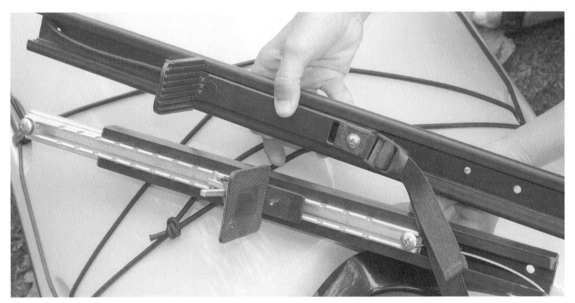

Adjust foot braces for leg length and lock into place. The foot brace track may also slide along a second track to allow use of a rudder system.

be resting comfortably on foot braces. There are many different seat and backrest designs available in today's market. Your kayak probably has some way to adjust the pitch of the backrest, either with a jam cleat and line or a nylon strap and D-ring. Even if you're a born sloucher, you'll appreciate some back support, so snug things up before setting out.

It's rare for kayaks to have a sliding seat-base adjustment. Instead, adjustments for leg length are made with sliding foot brace pedals that lock into position. Most manufacturers use a notched track (see photo on page 94) that allows for plenty of adjustment. In kayaks with rudders, these notched tracks slide along a second track that allows you to have foot control of your rudder system. Sometimes, adjusting your foot braces is frustrating because the track is sliding as you're trying to make the adjustment. Keep it from sliding while you make the adjustments and be sure that each side is set for the same leg length. Unless you're sharing your

kayak with someone else, you shouldn't have to make this adjustment again.

The proper position for paddling forms a diamond shape with your lower body. Sit erect and rest your feet on the foot brace pedals with your heels pointed in toward the centerline of the boat. Your upper leg should be out under the thigh braces with your knees toward the shoulders of the boat. You shouldn't feel jammed into this position, but you should feel as if you have control of your boat with your lower body. Rock the boat back and forth using your lower body only. You may have to make a minor position adjustment after paddling for an hour or so. The big adjustments are done more easily on land, but it's easy to make a quick one while on the water (get someone to stabilize your boat while you do this). For problems with numb feet, see pages 261–62.

When you operate the kayak's rudder, you'll feel the tracks sliding with foot pressure on either side. Get used to balancing

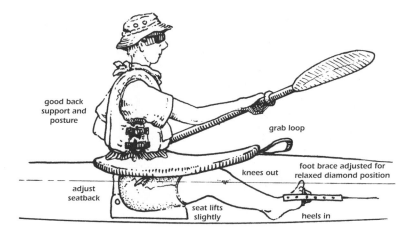

good back support and posture

grab loop

knees out

foot brace adjusted for relaxed diamond position

adjust seatback

seat lifts slightly

heels in

With your feet on the foot braces, your lower body should form a relaxed diamond with your heels in toward the center of the boat and your knees out underneath the shoulders of the boat. This position increases your boat control and paddling efficiency. Use good posture and be sure your back and upper legs are adequately supported by your seat.

your foot pressure so the angle of your rudder remains where you need it.

CUSTOMIZING YOUR KAYAK

Most paddlers find that a bit of padding added here and there in the cockpit helps to customize the fit of their boat. You can pad the area where your knees touch the inside of the boat, make the thigh braces more snug and supportive, add hip padding on the seat sides, or beef up your back support. You'll be working with 1- and 3-inch-thick (25–75 mm) closed-cell foam (often known by the name brand Minicel) that you can use to block out a more comfortable fit. Then you can shape these foam pieces until they fit the contours of both your body and the cockpit.

If you're just starting out, paddle your boat for a while before thinking about customizing the fit. Or, attach pieces of foam in place with duct tape for some test trials before gluing them in place.

To customize the fit of your boat, you'll need the following.

- closed-cell foam (½, 1, and 3 in./12, 25, and 50 mm thick)
- X-Acto knife
- utility (razor) knife or sharp kitchen knife
- waterproof contact cement
- duct tape
- mesh sandpaper (such as Dragon Skin)
- Sureform rasp
- 100-grit sandpaper (for roughing the boat surface to be glued)
- clean sponge and dry rag

- pencil
- small brush for applying cement
- rubber or latex gloves
- acetone (for prepping surfaces on composite boats; keep away from high heat or flames)

First, sit in your boat and decide exactly what you need. With a pencil, outline the areas in your cockpit where you want to add foam. This will give you the general shape and size of the foam pieces. Cut a layer of foam to match these marks. Don't worry about the exact thickness yet. Using duct tape, position these pieces in place.

Customizing your boat is naturally a trial-and-error procedure, so you want to be reasonably sure about the placement of the foam before you glue it into place. Removing foam and glue residues from the boat surface is possible, though not easy.

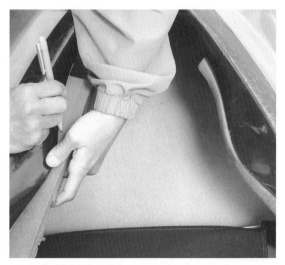

Customize the fit of your boat by placing foam padding on the underside of the thigh braces and around the seat. Mark pieces and then carve to fit.

Attach carved foam to the boat with waterproof contact cement. These pieces can be formed with a small Sureform rasp and then smoothed with mesh sandpaper.

Next, determine the thickness you need by wedging additional pieces of foam into place. Cut away areas where foam is too thick and do some rough carving to get the pieces contoured to your body.

Once you're satisfied with the rough shape and placement of the foam, ready the boat surfaces for gluing. On composite boats, prep the working surface with acetone; on polyethylene boats, use sandpaper to rough up the surface. Thinly coat the surface of both the boat and the foam with glue and wait until both of these surfaces are ready to join (follow product directions). Place the foam in position—you'll only get one chance!—and press firmly over the entire surface. Climb back into the cockpit and use a pencil to mark the areas to be smoothed and contoured to finalize the fit. Use the rasp to form the pieces and the mesh sandpaper to smooth their finish.

GETTING YOUR KAYAK TO AND FROM THE WATER

One of the easiest boat carries is with a person at either end. Most boats are equipped with carrying handles, or toggles. If the boat is loaded, also cup your hand underneath and balance it against your hip. Toggles can break under heavy loads, and a firm backup grip on your part can't hurt.

My favorite way to get a boat to the water is with a small kayak trolley or cart. You can

A kayak cart allows you to easily get your boat to and from the water. Most models fold up or disassemble for storage in a hatch. Carts can be positioned near the center of the boat (top) or at the stern (bottom).

attach a kayak cart over the stern or in the middle of the boat and roll the boat wherever needed. You can throw your gear in for one trip and keep it simple. If the terrain is rough, take care that the cart stays firmly attached to the boat. Most kayak carts fold up or disassemble for storing inside your boat if you need the cart along for the trip or don't want to return it to your car (you would just have to retrieve it, anyway).

You may choose to carry your boat on your shoulder for a solo trip to the launch site (see photos on page 99). There are good ways and not-so-good ways to accomplish this. You'll know which is which by the feel of your lower back the next morning.

To carry your boat solo, get the boat's weight resting on your thigh and then turn the cockpit to rest on your shoulder. Let your legs do most of the work, and keep your back straight.

1. Bend your knees slightly and slide the boat (deck out) up your leg by grabbing it with both hands inside the cockpit rim.
2. Rest the boat on your thigh, then roll the cockpit up and toward you until you can begin to get your shoulder inside it.
3. Shift the weight of the boat from your thigh to your shoulder. Use your arms to steady the boat as you straighten your legs.
4. As the boat rests on your shoulder, find its balance point to make the carry easier. If the coaming digs into your shoulder, use a life vest for padding.

Some boat models are difficult to balance, and longer boats may be unwieldy on a windy day.

CARTOPPING YOUR KAYAK

Getting boats on and off your car is often the most difficult part of going paddling. You'll probably try several methods before working out the best series of moves and methods of securing your boat. Cartop racks and accessories are available for even problematic vehicles like campers and convertibles. Some systems are as simple as foam blocks and a couple of tie-down straps; some are engineering marvels created for a specific vehicle model and year.

Consider the following when choosing a cartop carrier.

- Properly protect your vehicle. There's no reason for a roof or hatchback to be scratched or abraded in any way. Clean grit off the bottom of foam blocks, use a bath mat or thick towel to protect the back edge of the roof, and remember to hose off salt water that may remain on the roof of your vehicle.
- Support your kayak adequately. Ideally, you should support the kayak at the bulkheads, a particularly strong area. Generally, it's better to carry a kayak on its shoulders, or side, or on its hull since these areas are stronger and less prone to flexing (gently push down on the deck, shoulders, and hull of your boat to feel the differences in strength and flexibility). Remember to brush off grit from all areas that are being placed in cradles or foam blocks so the kayak won't be abraded.
- Secure your kayak to your cartop equipment, and secure the cartop equipment to your vehicle. For example: if you're using foam blocks for carrying your kayak (and no roof rack), secure your kayak to the foam blocks, then place your boat and blocks on your rooftop (solo loading may require changes in this step), and secure all this in place. By following this procedure, the blocks won't dislodge when under way. A roof rack system such as those made by Thule or Yakima is attached to your vehicle, and then your kayak is attached to this system. (Be sure you're aware of the load limits of your roof rack system.)

- Tie lines (¼–⅜ in./6–9 mm diameter nonstretch line) from the bow and the stern of your boat to the vehicle (most modern bumpers make this something of a challenge). Anchoring each line at two points to form an A is best. These lines help stabilize the boat in high winds and may buy you some time if one of your tie-down straps fails (a rarity).
- If you're traveling long distances or expect strong winds (especially crosswinds), consider using a backup line (often called a *belly*, or *perimeter*, *line*) in addition to the tie-down straps for added insurance. This redundant line may buy you enough time to pull off the road (without losing your kayak) if any part of your cartop system fails.

Attach bow lines to the top of the kayak and then to two points on the car's bumpers; do the same at the stern. These bow and stern lines help hold the boat steady in strong winds and should always be used if the kayak extends well beyond the roof area.

Top: When loading from the side, place the bow in the cradle (or foam block). On hard surfaces, protect the stern by placing your life vest beneath. Add attachments to the roof rack system (e.g., Thule Outrigger, Yakima Boat Loader) to extend its length.
Bottom: Now load the stern of the boat. A small stepladder or milk crate can be used for an easy step-up if you need more height to reach. On windy days, strap the bow loosely in place while you lift the stern. Once the boat is settled in both cradles, secure all lines.

- Anytime you travel with boats on top of your car, you should stop and check all lines after a short period of driving. If anything is amiss, fix it. Then as you continue to drive, pay attention to any troubling sounds issuing from the top of your car. Often this will be the first warning you get that something is loose or broken or has slipped.

LOADING A BOAT ONTO A VEHICLE

We've talked about ways to carry your kayak on your vehicle, but what about getting the boat up there in the first place? Here's where you might have to be creative, especially if you fall into the short person, tall vehicle category. What might take a 6-foot 4-inch (193 cm) person one move may require four moves from a 5-foot 4-inch (162 cm) person. But the result is the same: you've loaded your boat and you're ready to go paddling.

If you need to load your boat onto your vehicle by yourself, simply work with one end of the boat at a time. This may sound obvious, but I've seen folks struggle to lift the entire boat, often with disastrous results. There's no need for this if you accept that you will need to take multiple steps to get the boat on top of your car. Useful things to have close at hand include a small stepladder or milk crate for an easy step-up, a towel or bath mat to protect the vehicle, some short pieces of line to temporarily secure things, and a life vest or pad to protect the kayak from grinding against the ground, driveway, or parking lot.

Loading from the Rear of the Vehicle

If you are loading from the rear of the vehicle, place a thick towel or bath mat over the roof edge or hatchback to protect your car. A bath mat with rubber backing works well since it doesn't slide around as you push the kayak over its surface. The towel or mat not only protects your vehicle but makes sliding the kayak up and onto the roof of your car much easier (and removes grit from the hull as you do so).

Pick up the bow of your boat and place it on the covered roof or hatchback. If your vehicle is tall and squared off in the back (many SUVs have this configuration), you may be better served to load from the side (next section). Make sure you have protected the stern of your boat from grinding on the ground or asphalt as you lift the bow (position your life vest or other padding under it). You will also have to be aware of the balance of the bow on the vehicle before you move to the stern. If you are concerned about the bow rolling off, position another towel or a

Placing a towel or bath mat over the rear of the vehicle not only protects the vehicle but makes sliding the kayak up and onto the roof much easier.

You can line kayak cradles with nylon hose or carpet, or purchase roller cradles to make it easy to slide the kayak into place when loading from the rear of a vehicle.

soft piece of gear against it to help hold it in place.

As you lift the stern, you can carefully slide the bow up onto a roof rack or into a set of kayak cradles. If you are using foam blocks directly on your cartop, you may find you need to repeatedly lift and push the boat since foam blocks do not slide easily. If you are using foam blocks on a roof rack, you may find it easier to place the blocks under your boat after you have it positioned on the roof rack. If the kayak cradles on your roof rack don't allow your kayak to slide, consider covering them with old pantyhose or carpet pieces to make sliding easier. Some rack systems offer a roller bar at the rear or rollers built into the cradles; both are helpful when loading from the rear of the vehicle.

As you slide the kayak up and onto the roof of your vehicle, you may reach a point where

your bow is pointing skyward and you are not tall enough to ease the boat into place. This is where a small stepladder or milk crate placed at the rear of your vehicle for an easy step-up is useful. With this increased height you can then gently lower the boat into place. Secure the boat to the cradles (foam or rack) and then continue to secure the boat as discussed on page 99–101.

Loading from the Side of the Vehicle

If you are loading from the side of the vehicle, you may want to use cradles that open to the side ("J"-cradles) or use an attachment such as the Thule Outrigger or Yakima Boat Loader, both of which provide a temporary place to park your boat on the edge of the rack system. These attachments extend the

Loading from the side with a small car is quite simple with "J"-style cradles. If you are concerned about the bow slipping out as you load, use a piece of line to temporarily close the "J" for extra security.

Using a rack extension bar as a temporary place to park the bow is handy. Position a life vest under the stern of the kayak to protect it, and have something close at hand for an easy step-up (here, a milk crate).

A rack extension bar (available from both Yakima and Thule) is particularly useful with tall vehicles or for use with "J"-style cradles.

Once the stern is set in place, the bow can be moved into its cradle and the kayak readied for tie-down.

Ideally, straps should be set outside of the cockpit area (this is most important for composite boats). Snug down all straps and check over all rack and cradle hardware. Tighten as needed before driving off.

rack bars out from the vehicle for easier loading, especially on taller vehicles (depending on your vehicle, you may need to use side cradles and a rack bar extension device). Whatever method you choose, be sure the boat is secure during the intermediate steps. You can use a short piece of line for temporarily securing the boat in place—see knots on pages 106–7 for some tips.

Loading from the side uses methods similar to those for loading from the rear of the vehicle. You should place the bow into the forward cradle (side open or regular cupped version) or temporarily park it alongside the cradle. The stern of the boat is out and away from the vehicle at an angle that makes this possible. Be sure to secure the bow with a quick loop of line before moving to the stern. Now lift the stern, move toward the vehicle, and set the boat into the rear cradle. If you temporarily parked the bow on a rack extender, then lift the bow and set it into place in the forward cradle. Secure the boat to the cradles with your tie-down straps and continue to secure the boat as previously discussed.

Carrying Gear Inside Your Boat

You'll be tempted to store gear inside your boat while it is traveling on top of your car. That's fine, but you will need to take special care to prevent it from blowing out as you travel. I've seen many pieces of gear (sponges, sprayskirts, half of a paddle, even a wet suit!) alongside roads; I'm sure these articles simply blew out of the cockpit. Use a cockpit cover that is either tied off or clipped to the deck rigging, and regularly check that the cover has not popped free of the coaming.

Useful Knots for Kayakers

Knowing how to tie a knot is becoming a lost art. Several knots are simple to learn and useful to kayakers (I urge you to learn more than just these few). I always carry a bag with tie-down straps and several pieces of line (4–20 feet in length) that have a bowline tied on one end. The bowline on one end allows you to quickly anchor the line around a rack bar, car bumper, or piece of gear by running the free end through the bowline loop. With this anchored line in place, you can proceed to secure all manner of things. This quick tie-off is easily undone and fast enough to put in place even during stressful moments (such as an unsecured boat trying to blow off a rack). Additional knots are covered in chapter 11.

A **half hitch** is useful for finishing off a trucker's hitch or taut-line hitch. Half hitches are great for using up one end of a line, and they add supportive bites to finish many other knots.

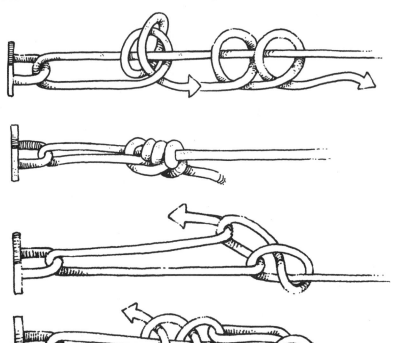

The **taut-line (rolling) hitch** is useful for anchoring the bow and stern lines. This knot slides freely but will jam when under a load. The ends should be made off using a series of half hitches.

The **trucker's hitch** is stronger than a taut-line hitch and gives you good leverage when tightening. It requires more line length and is harder to tie on thick or stiff line than the taut-line version.

The **bowline** creates a bombproof loop at the end of a piece of line that is still easy to remove when needed. A bowline may be used when attaching the bow or stern lines to the boat.

TRAILERS

In addition to cartop systems for carrying kayaks, small trailers are available for recreational use (you don't need the heavier versions designed for commercial use). Towed behind your vehicle, the trailers can carry from one to six boats at a time. They require that your vehicle be equipped with a trailer hitch, and they must be hooked up to your vehicle's electrical system to power the lights on the back of the trailer. Most states require you to register these trailers, but the cost is generally reasonable. Learning to tow a trailer like a pro is a bit of a challenge. Practice turning, braking, and reversing in a large parking lot before going prime time!

When using a trailer, you will also need to regularly check and maintain wheel bearings, tire treads, and electrical connections (the most common maintenance problem).

GETTING INTO AND OUT OF THE KAYAK

Novice kayakers are often left at the water's edge nervously eyeing their boat and trying to visualize just how to get into the darned thing. Or worse, they're unceremoniously dumped into the water when they first attempt to enter the boat. It just isn't obvious how to make this move successfully for the first time.

At the launch site, first envision a way to stabilize your boat by anchoring it to something solid like a low dock, river bank, or shallow bottom. You can do this by using your paddle as a bridge. Place the paddle behind the rear cockpit coaming and perpendicular to the boat, allowing the blade farthest away to settle on the bottom or on the dock or bank. This creates a system of support that allows you to hop in and out while the kayak remains stationary.

Enter or exit your boat only from the supported side and remember to hold the paddle firmly in place by clamping one end of the shaft against the rear cockpit coaming so it remains perpendicular to the boat throughout the process. You may park yourself temporarily on the edge of the boat and then lean on the paddle for support while you put first one leg and then the other into the cockpit before lowering yourself into the seat (see photos on page 108). As long as the paddle remains perpendicular and anchored to something solid, you'll have no problem.

This method of getting into and out of your boat will serve you well under most circumstances. But what about a high dock or pier ladder? The same principles apply as you transfer your weight to and from the boat while it remains anchored to something solid. A high dock prevents you from using your paddle as the bridge; instead, use your hands and then arms to anchor your boat to the dock as you transfer your weight to and from the

Getting into and out of the boat. **Left:** Make sure the back of the paddle blade is grounded on the bottom or a piece of shore and held firmly in place perpendicular to the boat. **Right:** Lean on the grounded paddle for support while you tuck your feet into the cockpit. Your paddle holds the boat in place. Reverse these steps to exit the boat.

dock. You might tether your kayak to the dock so it doesn't float away while you make these moves, but you might need help to cast off.

A pier ladder can be challenging, but the moves are still the same. You may even use your paddle through the ladder rungs to help hold the boat in place if the conditions are calm. Transfer your weight to and from the ladder much as you did for the high dock, but you'll have less surface to accomplish this on the ladder. The main things to keep in mind are to take each step slowly and to support yourself firmly. If the boat starts to move out from underneath you, reposition yourself as the bridge that anchors your boat to the ladder or dock before proceeding.

Getting into and out of the boat at a dock. **Left:** Using both hands, transfer your weight from your cockpit to the dock (or dock to cockpit). **Right:** Keep your feet in the cockpit until you are seated on the dock and can secure your boat. (If you're entering the boat, swing your legs directly into the cockpit and place your feet on either side of the boat's centerline as you transfer your weight from the dock into the cockpit.)

5

Controlling Your Kayak

Once you're in your boat and on the water, the real learning process begins. You may feel unsteady or may not feel that you can make your kayak go exactly where you want it to. Remember, you're the student; your kayak is designed to handle wind and waves, but you must learn your kayak's nuances and temperament.

BALANCE AND THE ART OF STAYING UPRIGHT

First, sit in the kayak in calm water with your paddle out of the water and gently lift one thigh and then the other from the seat. Does the boat twitch or sit quietly underneath you? Now rock the boat back and forth using your thighs and knees to lift one shoulder of the boat and then the other. Keep your upper body still and over the center point of the cockpit while only your lower body rocks the boat. Think of your upper and lower body being connected by a swivel joint that allows you to rotate and swing freely at the hips. Now, when the boat begins to tip in a direction you want to avoid, simply swing your hip on the downward side back up to bring the boat level again. You'll probably be surprised at the amount of control you have using just your lower body.

Now get someone to spot you in shallow water and bring the boat up on its edge while keeping your upper body over the center of your boat's buoyancy (now the shoulder of the kayak). Your body will form a J when you do this. Your spotter can take some of your weight as you get comfortable with this move

Practicing J-leans is useful for determining your boat's balance points and getting comfortable with your balance and flexibility in your boat. At first, use a spotter or a dock edge for support.

and lean the boat farther on its edge and hold it there, even to the point of water entering the cockpit. Be sure to do this J-lean (also called a *knee hang*) on both sides of the boat and try to balance it on edge with little or no weight supported by your spotter. You're now finding the balance points of your kayak. If you lean away from the boat's center of buoyancy, you'll capsize without the support of your paddle and a quick corrective stroke called a *brace* (see pages 119–21).

Being able to lean your kayak will come in handy. It'll allow you to stabilize your boat as waves pass under its hull, change the boat's configuration by leaning it on edge to make a turning stroke, and make subtle course corrections while you're under way. Practicing J-leans will also help you relax in your boat. Your kayak can handle sizable seas and rough water, but only if you remain relaxed, let-

ting your hips swing fluidly with the boat's motion. Let your lower body absorb the little twitches and shakes that your boat makes as it sits in and moves through the water. If your hips are stiff and locked in place, these little twitches will travel up your torso and be magnified, making you feel unstable. Don't be a "twitch magnifier"; relax and enjoy making the subtle adjustments to the water conditions and your kayak's temperament. Remember the saying of the wise kayaker, "loose hips save ships."

YOUR PADDLE GRIP

Before practicing any paddle strokes, it's important to learn the proper way to hold the paddle. Hold your paddle shaft up to your shoulders with the shaft centered on your

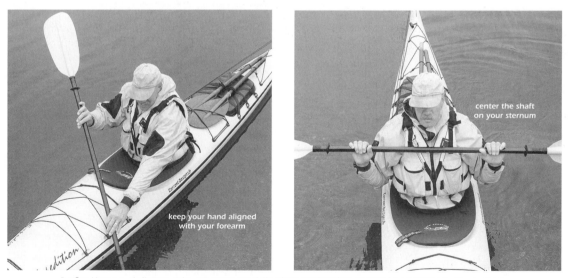

Left: Keep a delicate grip on your paddle that maintains control but allows your upper hand and forearm to relax. **Right:** Your paddle grip should position your hands outside your shoulders and equidistant from the center of the paddle shaft.

TO FEATHER OR NOT TO FEATHER

Whether you choose to orient your paddle blades in an unfeathered (same plane) position or a feathered (offset planes) position is strictly a personal matter (see Feathering and Other Weighty Matters, page 66). An unfeathered paddle has to push a blade face through headwinds and waves when moving forward; a feathered blade exposes the blade face to a crosswind where it can be more easily snatched from your hand. I know paddlers who move from one setting to another depending on the paddling conditions. If you do this, make sure you're still quick to determine your paddle blade's orientation as you move from one style to the other (personally, I can't).

If you want a feathered paddle, you'll have to decide on the feather angle. This typically ranges from 45 to 90 degrees. There are strong feelings associated with various feather angles. As you edge toward 90 degrees, the potential stress on the wrist is noticeable and should be of some concern. But in the 45- to 75-degree range, personal preferences begin to prevail. Everybody has his or her favorite angle and will argue convincingly about its merits. If at all possible, try paddles with different feather angles, or better still, try the same paddle with different feather angles. Some models even allow you to set the angle yourself.

Over the past several years, feather angles have gradually decreased as more people began noticing the effects of years of repetitive motion on their wrists. Whatever feather angle you choose, make an effort to keep your wrist and the back of your hand aligned with your forearm throughout your forward stroke. This protects your wrist and avoids placing undue torque on the joint and causing injury.

You may choose a feather angle (or an unfeathered version) that is comfortable for your style of paddling. The blades shown here range from a 90-degree feather (far left) to an unfeathered (far right). Be sure that your choice does not place undue torque on your wrist during your forward stroke.

chest. Position your hands slightly outside of your shoulder width (see the right-side photo on page 110). Most paddles have indexed, or oval, areas, on the paddle shaft for your grip; some even have rubberized grips for precise hand placement. Keep your hands at a comfortable spot that is equidistant from the center of the shaft. Allowing your hands to travel along the shaft during your forward stroke will result in an imbalance that may put you off course or adversely affect the power of your stroke.

When you hold your paddle, keep your grip relaxed and be sure that the wrist and back of the hand are aligned with your forearm. A relaxed and properly aligned grip will prevent the repetitive motion injuries that plague some kayakers. Different strokes may use the power face or the back face of the blade, but your hand placement doesn't change. This allows you to gain a reflexive knowledge of your paddle's position and orientation at all times.

FORWARD STROKE

The forward stroke is the workhorse of your repertoire. Because you'll be dependent on its repeated motion to click off mile after mile as you explore the seascape around you, this is not a stroke to take lightly or grow complacent about. Your forward stroke will mark you as a veteran kayaker or an unsure novice. More important, the quality of your forward stroke will mean the difference between an efficient cruise or a long slog to your destination. So, take the time to develop a smooth and effective forward stroke: it's well worth the effort. Don't worry about speed at first. Your speed will pick up as your forward stroke becomes more smooth and efficient.

The forward stroke is driven by your torso as it rotates from side to side. Many paddlers use only their arms to drive the stroke, much like a cyclist's leg motion. This is a weaker and more wasteful way to paddle since it uses only the smaller muscles of the arm rather than the more powerful muscles of the torso and abdomen. The arms should be kept fairly straight with only a slight bend at the elbow throughout the stroke. This keeps the paddle shaft well away and parallel to your torso and shoulders. Think of your arms as mere connective shafts between the paddle and your torso—the engine that drives the paddle.

The forward stroke starts as you place the paddle blade into the water at about your ankle. Let your torso unwind to drive your upper hand forward, bringing the blade through the water where it exits alongside your hip. This motion automatically sets up the stroke on the opposite side so that the motion is continuous and fluid as your torso rotates throughout the stroke. As each stroke is made, the ball of your foot should press gently on the foot brace on the side of your stroke. This brings your legs into service and solidifies your lower-body control of the boat. Don't let the boat rock or plunge with each stroke, which wastes forward momentum.

At first your forward stroke may feel awkward. Stick with it and allow your body to establish the muscle memory required to make this stroke natural and graceful. Sit upright, remember to relax, and find a fluid motion that you can use for mile after mile. Try to develop a cadence that is comfortable and can be maintained for at least twenty minutes without pause. As you practice your forward stroke, monitor the following.

- *Wrist:* Your wrist should not move side to side or bend back and forth with each stroke. Keep your wrist straight and your hand relaxed. The back of your hand should be in line with your forearm.

1. The catch of the forward stroke should be placed alongside your shin. Note that there is little bend in the elbow. **2.** Keep the top hand relaxed as it pushes through the stroke. **3.** The forward stroke moves alongside the boat and exits at the hip or just aft of it. Keep the shaft squared and away from the torso. **4.** The boat should remain flat in the water as you move the stroke from side to side. During all phases of the stroke, the back of your hand and forearm should remain aligned. The wrist should not move from side to side.

- *Upper hand:* Your upper hand should not cross the centerline of your boat during the forward stroke. For a relaxed touring stroke, it should remain at about chin level or lower. If you lose sight of it, it's too high. Your upper hand should remain relaxed and even partially open as it pushes through the forward stroke.

- *Elbows:* Your elbows should be bent only slightly throughout the forward stroke, which keeps the paddle shaft out in front and squared with your torso. Don't pump your arms in a bicycling motion. Imagine something really smelly on the paddle shaft that you'd rather keep well away from you.

THE TORSO TOOL

Teaching the forward stroke is not easy. Students often insist they are rotating their torsos when in fact they're only swinging their shoulders. It's difficult to monitor the side-to-side motion of your torso, and with no muscle memory to fall back on, you don't know how it should feel.

One day, inspiration hit two fellow instructors, Matthew Levin and Vaughn Smith, and they invented the (drum roll, please) Torso Tool. Luckily, they had a large pool of willing (and gullible) novice kayakers for guinea pigs, and by the end of one paddling season the final design was in place.

The Torso Tool has become the truth serum of forward stroke practice. It uses a rod to extend the plane of the torso to a length slightly longer than a typical paddle shaft. If the student doesn't rotate the torso and keep it parallel to the paddle shaft throughout the stroke, the paddle blade clunks against the end of the rod. The student receives immediate feedback and learns not only to rotate the torso but also to keep the shaft away from the upper body so it can result in a more powerful and efficient stroke.

I began to use it in classes and was amazed that students were willing to wear it and even more amazed at how quickly they picked up the idea of torso rotation from it. Some instructors even joked about attaching shock electrodes to speed the learning process and dubbing it the "Torture Tool." All this silliness aside, it takes time and an awareness of your own movements to learn proper torso rotation.

The Torso Tool extends the plane of your shoulders and helps teach the torso rotation needed for an efficient forward stroke. Students practice keeping the paddle shaft parallel to the Torso Tool until this motion feels more natural.

- *Posture:* You should be sitting upright with your lower body in a diamond shape and your feet resting on the foot brace pedals. Don't lean forward or slouch during the forward stroke. This will limit your torso rotation. You should be looking forward of the boat (don't fixate on the bow).
- *Torso:* Imagine having a bell attached to your belly button. It would ring

with each stroke as your torso rotates from side to side. Keep the torso squared with the paddle shaft so that a box is formed by your chest, two arms, and the paddle shaft.

Power Forward (Sprint) Stroke

Occasionally, you need to step up the pace and really drive your forward stroke for a quick sprint. To do this, simply increase your cadence and the angle of your stroke. Your upper hand will be higher, at about forehead height, and the paddle blade will be angled more vertically in the water. You must use your torso to drive a power forward stroke since you're calling on all your resources for a quick sprint.

Back Stroke

The back stroke seems obvious, yet it's the stroke most often performed incorrectly. The back stroke uses the back face of the blade, so don't be tempted to turn the paddle over or change your hands from the forward stroke position. Your torso plays an important role in the back stroke, as well. Rotating it not only drives the stroke but allows you to look behind you as you plant the blade for each stroke. Consider flattening the blade face a bit as you make a back stroke. This gives you more support during the stroke since you use more blade area against the surface of the water. Be sure you look at the paddle blade as you plant it in the water for each stroke. You don't want to catch the blade under the edge of the boat and capsize.

A power forward stroke (shown) uses a higher angle and more aggressive setup than a typical touring stroke.

1. The back stroke uses the back face of the paddle blade, which may be flattened toward the water for additional support if needed. Look at the blade placement and keep your torso parallel to the paddle shaft. **2.** The back stroke moves alongside the boat and exits the water at your foot.

Back strokes are also used to stop the boat. If you're charging toward something and need to slam on the brakes, a series of very quick back strokes will do the trick. Back strokes used for stopping are shorter and made at a faster cadence than those used to travel backward.

TURNING (SWEEP) STROKES

Touring kayaks are designed for efficient travel, where maintaining a straight line course is more important than the ability to turn quickly. But you still need to turn your boat, and an understanding of boat dynamics will make this easier. The longer waterline lengths on touring kayaks prevent making a snappy turn. Decreasing this waterline length by leaning the boat on edge allows you to turn the boat more readily. So, leaning your kayak is part of making a turning, or sweep, stroke.

If you make a forward stroke on one side of your boat, it turns away from the side the stroke was made on. If you reach out away from the boat and execute a stroke that sweeps in a wide arc on one side, the boat will turn even more readily away from the side of the stroke. If you now combine this sweeping stroke with a boat lean toward the stroke, you'll have the makings of a fine forward sweep stroke. But there are several refinements you should heed before practicing this stroke.

- When you lean your boat, keep your upper body centered over the shoul-

der of the boat (J-lean) as we discussed earlier in this chapter. Lean into the stroke since you'll gain support from your paddle blade as it moves through the water. The deeper you lean, the more you shorten the waterline length of your boat and aid the turning stroke.

1. The sweep stroke begins at your foot and travels in a wide arc. **2.** A boat lean toward the stroke makes the sweep stroke more effective. **3.** Continue to watch the paddle blade as it travels toward the stern of the boat.

- Use the power face of your paddle blade during the forward sweep stroke. Consider flattening it a bit toward the water to gain even more support. Plant the blade up by your foot and sweep it out away from the boat and back to the stern during the sweep stroke.

- Remember to rotate your torso and use your upper hand to drive the stroke, keeping the shaft low and parallel to your belly. Keep your upper hand low and close to the cockpit coaming and your elbow close to your body. This gives you a longer reach for a wider arc and more powerful turn.

- Watch the paddle blade throughout the stroke and ensure that it exits the water before reaching the edge of your boat. Follow the blade with your torso and your eyes.

- As you recover from a sweep stroke and set up for the next one, tilt the back face of the blade so it's parallel to the water (not in the water). This is done by rolling the wrists slightly forward, turning the knuckles down. Being ready to slap the water with the back face of the blade for support will give you confidence to maintain your boat lean while you're setting up for your next sweep stroke.

- Use the entire range of the stroke from bow to stern. The latter half of the stroke is more powerful since the stern is freer to swing in response to the stroke. But don't attempt to go beyond a point where you cannot rotate your torso to keep a close eye on the paddle blade.

Don't let all the refinements to the sweep stroke intimidate you. All you're doing is paddling on one side of your boat to make it turn the other way. You reach out farther and lean the boat to make it snappier and more responsive. You monitor the subtleties of your blade angles so you have support through all phases of the stroke.

When you first practice sweep strokes, keep your boat flat in the water. Smooth out the motion of the paddle and your torso rotation before adding your boat lean. Then add your boat lean and adjust the blade angle for additional support. You'll find the sweep stroke to be graceful and a real confidence booster once you've smoothed things out.

Reverse Sweep Stroke

A reverse sweep is simply a turning stroke that starts from the stern of the boat and sweeps toward the bow. A reverse sweep stroke makes the bow swing toward the side of the stroke. The reverse sweep uses the back face of the paddle blade and can be enhanced by the same refinements that came into play with the forward sweep stroke: torso rotation, boat lean, and adjustment of the blade angle for support.

A reverse sweep slows and will eventually stop your forward momentum and is a decided change of course. Coupling a reverse sweep on one side with a forward sweep on the other side allows you to turn your boat in a tight spot like a boat slip or launch area. Reverse sweeps are also handy when you want to stop your forward momentum to turn and look behind you. (See also low brace turns on page 121.)

Using the back face of the blade, the reverse sweep stroke begins at the stern and then travels in a wide arc toward the bow. Leaning the boat toward the stroke makes it more effective; flattening the blade toward the water provides more support.

SUPPORT STROKES (BRACES)

Two powerful tools for staying upright in your boat are your balance and the support of your paddle. If you've ever done a belly flop from a diving board, you can appreciate that water has a surprising resistance to being slapped with a flat object (like your unfortunate belly!). You can use your paddle blade the same way by slapping the water to gain a quick bit of support. These support strokes are called *braces* and come in variety of fashions: slap (low and high) and sculling (low and high).

Naming a brace low or high is based on whether you're using the power face or the back face of the blade for support. If you use the power face, you're doing a high brace. Your knuckles will roll up to bring the power face parallel to the water. If you use the back face, you're doing a low brace. Your knuckles

will roll down to bring the back face parallel to the water. You may use a high or low brace on either side of the boat.

If your boat begins to tip to one side, use both your paddle and your lower body to regain your balance. Your paddle blade will slap the water while your lower body swings the boat back up under you (and gets your upper body back over the center of the boat's buoyancy where it belongs).

A slap brace is a short-lived move. It buys you just enough time to snap the boat back to a more stable position underneath you. You must snatch the paddle blade from the water before it dives and takes you with it. A quick roll of the wrists will make it easy for the blade to be lifted from the water. If the blade has begun to dive, this roll of the wrists will put the paddle blade on its edge so you're not lifting water as well as your paddle blade—a surefire recipe for a capsize.

If you need more than momentary support from your paddle, use a sculling brace. This is a leisurely way of regaining balance and supporting yourself on the surface of the water (it's also a great way to learn more about you and your boat's balance points). A sculling brace requires paddle movement. It's this constant movement of the paddle blade with the leading edge lifted that buys you support.

The movement of the paddle blade during a sculling brace follows an elongated figure-eight pattern (think of spreading peanut butter on the surface of the water). This movement is slow and controlled, and you must take great care to keep the leading edge of the paddle blade lifted throughout the stroke. As long as you continue to move

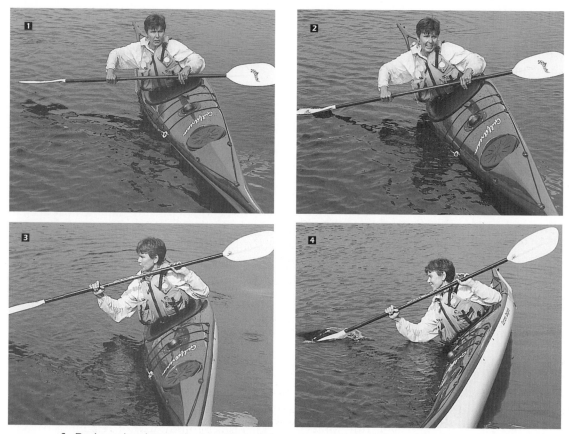

1. During a low brace, the knuckles roll down to use the back face of the blade. **2.** The back face is slapped against the water for support. **3.** The high brace requires you to roll your knuckles up to position the power face parallel to the water. **4.** The power face is slapped against the water for support while the boat is brought underneath you.

the paddle and keep it correctly oriented, you have support. The leading edge of your paddle will shift from one edge of the blade to the other as you move the blade back and forth in the water. You can continue the sculling brace indefinitely until you regain your balance and bring the boat underneath you and are sitting upright.

Don't flail your paddle on the surface of the water, creating a lot of foam and splashing. Water is denser and more supportive than froth at the surface. Try to make your sculling motion just underneath the surface of the water and cover three or more feet from one end of your blade's path to the other. The density of the water may make it more difficult for you to move your paddle, but be aware that this density also brings support.

Remember that a sculling brace can use the power face (high sculling brace) or the back face (low sculling brace) and be made on either side of the boat. You may find it easier

A sculling brace relies on the movement of the paddle blade through the water for support. Sculling braces can be low (using back face) or high (using power face). Here, a high sculling brace moves the power face in elongated sweeps beside the boat. Notice that the leading edge of the blade is lifted.

to scull on one side or the other or with either the power face or the back face. Take the time to practice these sculling braces in a variety of ways to broaden your stroke repertoire and gain more confidence in your ability to maintain or regain your balance.

Low Brace Turns

This stroke combines the support of a low brace and the blade path of a reverse sweep stroke. It's a graceful way to execute a reverse sweep and stop forward momentum. Imagine paddling toward a dock that is perpendicular to your boat's path. Now just before reaching the dock (you don't want to impale it with your bow), lean into a reverse sweep that uses the flattened back face of the blade for the full support of a brace. Your boat will make a snappy swing to bring you alongside and parallel to the dock. This dynamic brace is useful and will wow the crowds at the dock.

A low brace turn is a dynamic brace stroke made when the boat has forward momentum. It is a snappy way to bring the boat around sharply while stopping forward momentum. The back face of the blade is swept from the stern to the bow as the boat pivots around it. Here, the boat is swinging to the paddler's right as she makes a low brace turn on the right.

DRAW STROKES

Every time I try to parallel park my car, I find myself wishing I could use a draw stroke. I would plant that imaginary paddle blade alongside the curb and pull my car sideways right into the slot. Instead, I go back and forth, never getting the midpoint of the car any closer to the curb until I finally give up and find another parking spot. A draw stroke is way easier to learn than a parallel parking maneuver.

A draw stroke moves the boat sideways, which allows you to pull alongside a dock or another boat or pick up some flotsam in the water. It's a handy stroke and can even be used with some forward momentum to make a side-slipping maneuver. There are several ways to execute a draw stroke, depending on what you need from the stroke and your own sense of style.

The draw stroke requires some flexibility at the waist. You need to rotate your torso

1. The draw stroke is planted alongside the boat (about even with your hip), and the boat is pulled toward the power face. Twist your torso to face the paddle shaft and get both hands outside of the boat to help power the stroke.

2. The blade can be sliced through the water to set up for the next draw stroke. Called an *in-water recovery*, this is quieter and more graceful than pulling the paddle out of the water with each stroke.

toward the side of your boat with the paddle shaft perpendicular to the water and the blade parallel to the boat. Now reach out from the side of the boat and plant the lower paddle blade in the water, with the power face toward you, and pull your boat to the blade. Your top hand should be at forehead height, with your lower hand reaching out from your hip to plant the blade and pull in toward the boat.

You should try to keep the shaft vertical and both hands outside the edge of your boat, but this isn't easily done. Often, the boat is too wide or your arms too short. Always strive to square your shoulders and torso with the vertical shaft and watch the paddle blade placement and movement throughout the stroke. To set up for the next draw stroke, simply lift the paddle blade out of the water and replant it for the next stroke. If you want to earn style points and keep things quiet, use an in-water recovery for your draw stroke. To do this, roll your wrists so the edge of the blade is perpendicular to the boat. Slice this edge through the water away from the boat, and then set the blade parallel to the boat for the next stroke. This makes for a more graceful but somewhat slower draw stroke. If you need a quick and powerful draw stroke, remove the blade from the water with each stroke and pump your arms like pistons as you pull the boat sideward. This won't earn you any style points, but it gets the job done quickly and with power.

As your boat moves sideways during a draw stroke, water will pile up alongside the boat. Try leaning slightly away from the stroke so you don't bulldoze water but instead allow it to slip beneath the hull. If you're having trouble reaching to the side of your boat during your draw stroke, leaning the boat away from the stroke will only make this more difficult. The best you can hope for may be to keep your boat flat in the water.

If you'd like to gain some support during the draw stroke, simply turn it into a sculling draw stroke. Move the paddle blade through the water alongside your boat in figure eights as you pull toward the boat (think of spreading peanut butter along the side of

The sculling draw stroke uses the power face in a sculling motion parallel to the boat's edge. You can fine-tune the boat's sideward motion using a sculling draw stroke. The leading edge of the power face is turned slightly outward throughout the stroke.

your cockpit). Keep your lower elbow close to your side and the top hand at forehead height. Remember to avoid leaning into this stroke since that slows the sideward movement of the boat. The advantage of using this sculling motion is that a quick drop of the upper elbow can turn this stroke into a sculling brace when needed, the paddle shaft moving from perpendicular to parallel with the water. Throughout the sculling draw stroke, use your torso rotation to power the stroke. The sculling motion is much more powerful and precise when your torso drives the paddle shaft rather than your arms. Your paddle will mirror the movements of your torso while your arms connect the two.

A sculling draw stroke also allows you to fine-tune your sideward motion. If the bow is swinging too much, move your sculling motion slightly behind the cockpit. If the stern is swinging too much, move the sculling motion slightly forward. Being able to make these minor adjustments will make you a parallel parking ace.

Sometimes it's helpful to move the boat sideways while under way. If you need to pull into a dock, you can paddle alongside, stop, and then use a draw stroke to get there. Or, you can paddle forward and set an angled blade in the water that draws your boat alongside the dock by using the forward momentum of your boat. Called a *sideslip maneuver*, this garners lots of style points (another way to wow the crowds at the dock!).

If you plant a draw stroke parallel to your boat while moving forward, the blade would simply slice through the water. If you plant that blade at an angle from the side of the boat, your forward momentum will pull your boat sideways. This is a static draw stroke,

A sideslip maneuver sets a static draw stroke alongside the boat to pull it sideways while moving forward. This is useful for pulling alongside docks or another boat.

A static bow stroke can be set at the bow to bring the bow around sharply. This stroke uses the power face and is aided by a boat lean away from the stroke.

which means the blade is not moving but simply planted alongside the boat. It's your forward momentum that does the work.

A static draw stroke may also be moved forward to guide the bow sideways while under way. Plant the paddle blade at an angle up by your foot, and the bow swings dramatically toward the blade. This is handy when winding in and out of kayak traffic and can be accentuated by leaning away from the stroke to allow water to pass easily under the bow. After a quick correction with this static bow draw, you can move directly into a forward stroke to continue on your way. These stroke combinations are not only stylish but also efficient. Moving through a repertoire of strokes as needed while under way is an impressive show of skill and confidence in your boat handling.

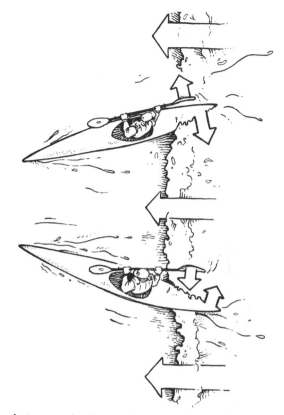

A stern pry (top) uses the back face to force the boat away from the paddle blade. During ruddering strokes, keep the paddle shaft low and alongside the boat and your elbows low and close to your torso. The stern draw (bottom) uses the power face to pull the stern toward the paddle blade and swing the bow in the opposite direction.

STERN (RUDDERING) STROKES

As your kayak moves forward through the water, the water parts and flows down the sides of the boat. The different lateral pressures at play along the side of the boat shift forward as the boat moves in that direction. At the stern, which is behind the widest part of the kayak, there is an area of lower lateral pressure, which allows the stern to swing more freely from side to side than the bow. So it stands to reason that making a stroke at the stern will produce a snappy response from the back half of the boat.

Strokes at the stern are often called *ruddering strokes* but are more accurately called a *stern draw* or a *stern pry*. A stern draw pulls the stern to the paddle blade; a stern pry

Stern rudder strokes are most often used during surfing to keep the boat aligned on a wave.

STROKES FOR A DOUBLE KAYAK

Maneuvering a double kayak may require the two paddlers to make different strokes depending on their position in the boat. Taking a cue from canoeing, the bow paddler may make the most useful stroke to control the bow while the stern paddler will coordinate her stroke to move the stern in concert. Tandem kayakers can also make good use of a rudder system for boat control.

To turn a tandem kayak while under way, have the bow paddler use a static bow draw on the side the boat is turning toward while the stern paddler uses a sweep stroke on the opposite side. This will continue forward momentum while the bow is being set over and the stern swings into the turn as well. If you need to turn without forward momentum, the bow paddler should make a sweep stroke on the side away from the turn while the stern paddler uses a reverse sweep on the opposite side.

Remember that the stern of a tandem can be moved side to side far more easily than the bow (as long as the rudder isn't dropped). So using the bow as the pivot around which the stern moves is often the easiest way to maneuver, unless you prefer the turn to be wide and gradual. In that case, sweep strokes on the same side will continue your forward momentum and gradually turn the boat in a wide arc.

Top: A forward stroke in a double kayak should be in synchrony. The bow paddler sets the pace, and the stern paddler follows the lead. **Bottom:** To turn a double kayak in place, use a forward sweep at the bow on one side and a reverse sweep at the stern on the other side.

pushes the boat away from the paddle blade. As you move the stern of your boat from side to side, the bow will swing from side to side in the opposite direction.

A stern draw pulls the power face of the blade in toward the stern (similar to the tail end of a sweep stroke) and swings the stern toward the blade. In other words, a stern draw on the right side swings the stern to the right and the bow moves to the left. A stern pry is set alongside the boat well behind the cockpit, and it pushes the back face of the paddle blade out from the boat. A stern pry on the right moves the stern to the left as the bow moves to the right.

Stern strokes are very effective when you're surfing or paddling in following seas (seas from behind), where you must keep your boat on a line to avoid broaching (getting caught parallel to a wave). Slowing your forward momentum in this situation is not a problem, and the quick response you gain from a stroke at the stern is helpful. You may even need to keep your paddle blade in the water at the stern, employing a pry or draw to keep your boat straight as you accelerate down the face of a wave.

PUTTING IT ALL TOGETHER

As you get more comfortable in your boat, you'll begin to combine strokes in a fluid manner for more effective boat handling. Practicing combinations of paddling strokes and playing around with boat leans and blade placements is fun. You may only travel 50 feet (15 m) in any one direction as you move through your repertoire of paddling strokes, savoring this graceful ballet. Try paddling among obstacles without losing your forward momentum. Use your static bow draw and then slip flawlessly into a forward stroke to continue on your way. You'll probably find it very satisfying to move quietly and gracefully through the water.

Freestyle kayaking takes this to another level as paddlers move through choreographed strokes set to music. Boat leans are dramatic, and the confidence these freestyle paddlers have in their balance and boat control is very impressive. Whether or not you choose to pursue freestyle kayaking as a discipline, practicing your paddling repertoire makes sense and is a great confidence builder.

ADAPTIVE PADDLING

Learning a new skill like kayaking requires ability and a willingness to try something new. Having a disability does not keep a

Freestyle champion Karen Knight demonstrates a freestyle paddling maneuver. Practicing a sequence of choreographed paddling moves is a great way to build confidence in your boat control and balance.

Often, a disability on land disappears on the water.

person from doing this but may require adaptations to pieces of equipment. Many disabilities that make a body uncooperative on land will disappear on the water.

This book cannot possibly cover the growing number of equipment adaptations for the entire range of disabilities, both physical and mental. But I would like to throw out a few suggestions for how best to proceed for general categories of disabilities and point out adaptations that have been successful. Many times a strategically placed piece of support or the simple act of assisting someone as he or she prepares to launch will allow access to this sport.

If adaptations are made to the equipment, be sure they do not hinder your ability to exit the boat during a capsize. It's important to test adaptations in a controlled setting with a paddling partner before setting

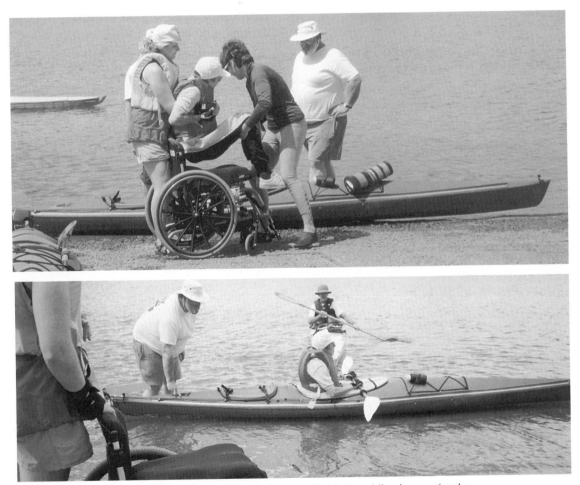

A disability on land does not mean a disabled paddler. It may simply require adaptation to equipment.

out on open water. If you have a disability that makes you susceptible to bruising and abrasions, add padding inside the cockpit for protection. Some medications may increase your sensitivity to sunlight and dehydration, so take care to stay hydrated and protected from the sun. Prostheses must be waterproof or well protected from any water or salt air damage.

Adaptations for Lower-Body Disabilities

A lower-body disability may make it more difficult to enter and exit a kayak. Adding grab handles to the sides of the boat may help you with weight transfers, and setting up an intermediate platform like a cooler can help prepare you to enter the boat. Often, sit-on-top models are easier for paddlers with lower-body disabilities to get into and out of.

Once in the boat, be sure that your legs are properly placed so that your balance will not be affected. In the case of a lower-limb amputation, you may need to add some weight to the lighter side of the boat for proper trim. Hemiplegia and paraplegia may require padding for the legs so that they don't shift unexpectedly and affect your balance in the boat. If you're having difficulty maintaining a seated position, additional adaptations may be needed, such as adding foam to lift the front seat edge.

Adaptations for Upper-Body Disabilities

If you're having difficulty holding or controlling your paddle, you may be able to adapt

Sit-on-top kayaks are often useful for adapting to a lower-body disability. Padding can be used for comfort and to keep legs blocked into place.

This equipment adaptation allows the paddle weight to rest on a small platform in the boat.

the grip or simply hold the paddle in a lower position and use a slower cadence during your forward stroke. Numerous grip adaptations for paddles can hold hands in place on the paddle shaft. Some are as simple as a rubber strap held in place with two wire ties; others are complex hand wraps and braces. For an upper-limb amputation, there are attachments available for a prosthesis that will grip a kayak paddle. If your amputation is high on the arm, be sure your life vest will stay on when you're floating in the water. If not, you may need to add a crotch strap, available from most life vest manufacturers.

Neck and trunk disabilities may require adaptations for back support and significant seat adaptations. You may need to make cockpit adaptations with Minicel foam that will allow you to paddle in a stable seated position. Be careful about raising your center of gravity, since it will affect your stability in the boat. If your trunk balance is seriously impaired, consider using a double kayak with another paddler. This offers a more stable platform, and your paddling partner can help counterbalance you in the kayak.

Hearing and Visual Impairments

Hearing and visual impairments require adaptations in group communication and signaling devices. If you have a hearing impairment, everyone in your group should have a visual means of communicating. You can rely on hand signals (see page 251) and the use of small, bright flags to facilitate communication on the water.

A paddler with a visual impairment may need to be paired with a paddler without a visual impairment so that verbal directions and descriptions may be given for both safety and fun. You can pair up by using a double kayak or two single models paddling close to each other. Group communication can be accomplished through sound signals using whistles or small bells. If you're having difficulty maintaining paddle orientation, tape a toothpick or other small marker along the paddle shaft so the marker aligns with the top edge of the paddle blade. This will help the paddler keep the power face facing him or her.

Mental Impairments

If you're paddling with someone who has a mental impairment, demonstrate important kayaking skills and allow time for practice and encouragement. You may need to do this in each new setting if skills do not transfer because of a change in location.

You may also need to be particularly sensitive to your paddling partner and any discomfort, thirst, or fatigue on his or her part. Paddlers with mental impairments may not communicate these needs, so you'll need to ascertain them as you spend time together on the water.

6

Getting into and out of the Water

"Hey, that's why they call it a watersport," I yelled to the first-time kayaker who had capsized a few feet after his first paddle stroke. Many novice sea kayakers are appalled by the idea of actually ending up in the water. You really do need to accept the inevitability of getting wet. Instead of fretting about this, learn the skills to control when and how you get wet. Then relax and enjoy your paddling!

Anytime you paddle away from shore, you're leaving behind the comfortable safety nets of harbormasters, mooring floats, and other boaters. It means taking care of yourself and others with the tools at hand: your boat, paddle, life vest, safety equipment, and—most important—your brain. One of the biggest challenges you may face is an unexpected capsize by you or someone in your group. Having the skills and equipment to deal with this quickly and effectively will make you more confident as a paddler and broaden your range of paddling choices.

Before learning how to get back into your boat from the water, let's be sure you understand how to get out of, or wet exit, your boat.

THE WET EXIT

The term *wet exit* is just a bit of kayaking jargon for getting out of your boat after you flip upside down. There are myriad ways you'll find yourself in this position, ranging from well planned to comical. Before you practice your first wet exit, consider swimming your boat just off a nearby shore (be sure to wear your life vest). Now, try crawling around on the deck or turning the boat over and sticking your head up inside. See if you can enter the overturned boat and hang upside down. After all, it's a watersport, and your kayak is just another water toy!

You may have concerns about getting stuck inside the boat or have qualms about the sprayskirt trapping you in place. The best way to deal with these concerns is to practice wet exits until you can remain relaxed and convinced that you can exit the boat even when the capsize is unexpected.

First practice a few dry exits on land to make sure your sprayskirt is properly sized and easy to pull from the cockpit coaming.

Sit in your boat and attach your sprayskirt, making sure the grab loop is not tucked in or caught on anything on the deck of your boat. Now put your feet on the foot brace pedals with your lower body in the diamond position for paddling. The first thing to do in a wet exit is lean forward. This frees your hips from the seat and allows your legs to swing out of the cockpit. This position also brings you close to the grab loop of your sprayskirt at the forward part of the coaming. It also makes it easy to reach up and slap the hull several times to get the attention of someone in your group.

Get in the habit of wet-exiting your boat in a consistent manner. **1.** Lean forward and hold onto your paddle when you find yourself upside down. **2.** Pull the grab loop and clear the sprayskirt from the coaming. **3.** Continue to lean forward and push your hips free of the cockpit. Your legs will follow as you forward roll to the surface. **4.** Grab the boat immediately and continue to hold your paddle.

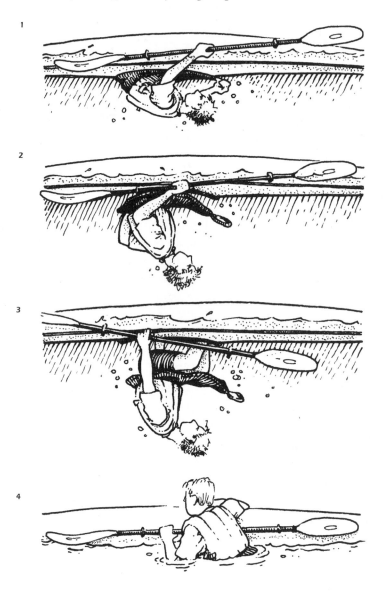

As you lean forward, reach for the grab loop and pull it away from you and then back toward your chest. Pulling the grab loop away from you first ensures it's completely free of the coaming (some boats have deeper cockpit rims than others). Now, while you're leaning forward, tuck your thumbs inside the coaming and sweep them all around. This is a redundant measure to be sure the sprayskirt is free of the coaming and you aren't holding it in place alongside your hips. Continue to lean forward and shrug off the boat like a pair of tight jeans. Now do these steps with your eyes closed. You're ready for the water. (If you're still not convinced, try these steps while you hold your breath. You'll find you have plenty of time before you run out of air.)

If you prefer, practice your first few wet exits without attaching your sprayskirt or with someone spotting you in shallow water (not so shallow that you'd hit your head on the bottom). Most people come out of their boats so quickly during wet-exit practice that the tops of their heads don't even get wet! When you bob to the water alongside your boat, be sure to maintain a firm hold on your paddle and your boat. You don't want to chase either of these while you're in the water. An overturned boat can blow away from you faster than you can swim to retrieve it, leaving you without this precious piece of equipment.

When you're ready, try to hang upside down in your boat for a few seconds (try reciting the alphabet before exiting) to become comfortable being underwater in your boat. This will come in handy when you begin practicing kayak rolls (see pages 151–59). After your first few wet exits, you'll probably wonder what all the fuss was about!

Try this fun practice drill: have a friend stand in shallow water and rock your boat and make big splashes in the water as you turn your boat over and exit it. It gets surprisingly noisy underwater, and this is a good simulation of rough water.

THE SOLO REENTRY

Getting back into your boat from the water is a matter of balance and making good use of the safety equipment at hand: paddle, paddle float, bilge pump, and rescue sling. All pieces of safety equipment should be accessible from both your cockpit and from the water.

Since it's imperative to hold onto your boat at all times, look for rudder or perimeter lines so you can loop an arm through and still have use of both hands. You may find it easier to maintain a hold on your boat while it's upside down than after you have righted it. With the boat upside down, you can slip a foot into the cockpit to keep it corralled. Also, you may find that an empty boat that is upright in the water is more likely to be affected by strong winds. If seas are rough, you may also want to minimize exposing an open cockpit to any breaking waves.

When it's time to flip the boat over, do so quickly and decisively. You want to minimize the amount of water you scoop up. Try placing your hands on either side of the cockpit coaming and then use a scissors kick to push the boat up while you flip it over. Never lose contact with the boat. Smaller paddlers in wider boats may not be able to place their hands on either side of the cockpit. In this case, you'll only be able to push up quickly

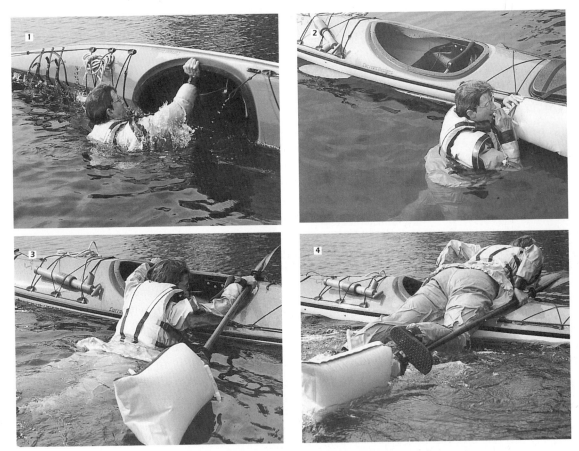

1. A quick flip of your boat will scoop less water into the cockpit. **2.** Never lose contact with your boat. Here, my arm is looped through a rudder line as the paddle float is inflated. **3.** Position the paddle float perpendicular to and away from the side of the boat. Bring your feet to the surface behind you and flutter kick as you pull yourself onto the boat. **4.** You can hook an ankle on the paddle shaft once you're out of the water to help stabilize your position.

and strongly on the side nearest to you to flip the boat over.

Retrieve your paddle float and place it over one of the paddle blades. Snap or buckle any retaining straps before you begin inflating the paddle float. Fully inflate the paddle float using both valves (most paddle floats have two chambers with separate valves). If you haven't returned the boat to an upright position, do this now.

Lay the paddle across the back of the cockpit coaming as when entering the boat from a launch site (see pages 107–8). The end with the paddle float should be in the water perpendicular to the boat as far from the boat as possible. This will serve as a buoyant outrig-

TIPS FOR PADDLE-FLOAT REENTRY

Although you may be paddling with others, you should always be ready to take care of yourself. This means always carrying a paddle float and bilge pump and knowing how to use them quickly and effectively.

- Never lose contact with your boat or your paddle. A paddle leash is handy in these situations since it not only keeps your paddle close by but also might serve to retrieve your boat as well.
- If you have deck rigging behind your cockpit, you may use this to help hold the paddle in place during your reentry. Slide the bare paddle blade under this rigging with the power face down for the best fit. You should practice a reentry without relying on this deck rigging since it may fail or be blocked with other gear.
- Do not try to "chin up" onto the boat. Instead, think of swimming up onto the boat as you would the edge of a pool. Take the time to bring your feet to the surface behind you before making this move.
- You may swim onto the boat from either side of the paddle shaft as long as you're holding it firmly in place. Try a reentry on both sides and see which works best for you. Some paddlers prefer having the cockpit coaming as a handhold; others prefer the flatter surface of the rear deck for a reentry.
- Unless you're forced to exit the area immediately, take the time to remove the water from your cockpit. A boat with water sloshing in the cockpit is more likely to capsize again.
- If there are strong winds, try to position the overturned boat with the bow pointing into the wind. This will present less of the boat's surface to the wind during the reentry and may help keep the boat pointed into any seas.
- Before reentering the boat, check any rudder cables. These often get crossed during a capsize, and you can't reach to fix them from the cockpit.

ger to support you as you reenter the cockpit. Face the cockpit and reach across it to grab the cockpit coaming with your hand closest to the bow while you continue to keep the paddle shaft clamped firmly to the coaming with your other hand. Kick your feet a few times behind you to bring them to the surface and then swim up and onto your boat over the cockpit. You may choose to hook an ankle over the paddle shaft to stabilize things before swinging one leg up and over the cockpit.

Be sure to favor the supported side (the one with the paddle float) of the boat with most of your weight. If too much of your weight falls on the unsupported side, you'll capsize again (sending the paddle float on a trajectory that instructors call the "yellow rainbow"). Once your belly is over the cockpit, turn toward the stern of the boat and inch in that direc-

1. Stay low and keep your eyes on the paddle float as you work your way toward the stern. The paddle float must remain perpendicular to the boat and in the water for the best support. **2.** Once your belly is over the seat, make the final turn to a seated position toward the side supported by the paddle float. Watch the float throughout this process. **3.** Continue to favor the supported side of the boat as you reseat yourself in the cockpit. **4.** Bring your paddle in front of you and continue to use the paddle float for support while you pump the boat dry.

tion, and be sure to stay low and favor the supported side of the boat. Throughout this phase, look directly at the paddle float. Slide your hand down the shaft so you naturally lean in this direction for support. Once you've inched to the stern enough to bring your feet into the cockpit, begin inching backward until your legs are in and your belly is now over the seat. Make a slow and controlled turn to sit in the seat while you continue to watch the paddle float and favor that side with your weight.

Once you're seated in the boat, quickly bring the paddle shaft over your head and place it across the coaming directly in front of you. Keep the blade with the paddle float extended out into the water so you can continue to use it for support. If your boat still has enough water in it to make it unsteady, your paddle float will help stabilize things while you pump the water out. You can help hold the paddle shaft in place by pushing down on it with your forearms. This will free your hands so you can use your bilge pump to remove any water from the boat. If you're taking water over the coaming from rough seas, before operating the bilge pump you should reattach your sprayskirt, keeping just enough of an opening to use the bilge pump. During the pumping process, remember to lean toward the paddle float for additional support.

Once you're pumped out, begin assessing the situation. You may do well to add a layer of clothing or a hat, have a quick snack of high energy food, or take in some fluids. Obviously, you must respond to the paddling conditions, some of which may have caused your capsize. Before you continue paddling, attach your sprayskirt fully, and stow your deflated paddle float and bilge pump.

The paddle-float reentry is a balancing act. As with any finely balanced maneuver, haste is your biggest enemy. Try to make your movements controlled, keep your center of gravity low and close to the boat, and always remember to look at your paddle float. The conditions that caused you to capsize in the first place are probably still a factor, so your balance and control are critical.

The paddle-float reentry is a tricky technique to perform even under ideal conditions. Paddling conditions that might have caused a capsize make this technique even more challenging. But it makes sense to practice and groove your paddle-float reentry because

other methods like kayak rolls are not bomb-proof. And, even though you may travel with skilled paddlers, you need to be able to take care of yourself and not rely on the skills or equipment of other paddlers.

Adding a Rescue Sling

A rescue sling adds another piece of equipment and a few more moves to your paddle-float reentry, but it also adds some advantages. You'll get a boost up onto the boat and be able to use your leg muscles rather than depend on just your arms. The sling also helps hold

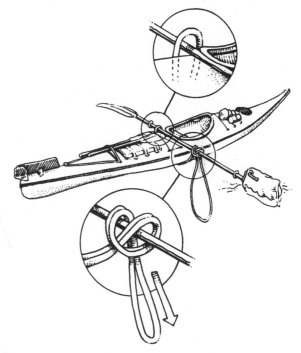

For a solo reentry, rig a foot stirrup. Loop one end on the paddle shaft close to the bare paddle blade (not the blade with the float). Bring the loose loop end under the boat and wrap it around the paddle shaft next to the side of the boat, with the paddle float supporting the paddle.

the paddle shaft perpendicular and firmly to the boat.

The rescue sling is a 13- to 15-foot (4–4.6 m) piece of floating line with the ends tied to form a loop (use a double fisherman's

A foot stirrup helps hold the paddle in place and provides an easy boost up onto the boat.

knot, see page 271). Once the paddle float is inflated and you're ready to reenter your boat, loop the sling over the bare blade and allow it to trail in the water on the far side of the boat. Reach under the boat to pull the sling toward you. If you can't reach the sling, push and swim your boat a few feet until you can reach under the boat and grab it.

Take this loose loop of the sling and wrap it over the paddle shaft a couple of turns. Taking one turn over the other will help hold the sling in position. You should now have a small loop extending from the paddle shaft at your side. This small loop may be used as a foot stirrup for you to lift yourself onto the boat. Put only your toes into the stirrup so it will be easier to slip your foot out when needed. You still need to favor the supported side of the boat and continue to look at your paddle float. Once you're seated in the cockpit, you can still quickly bring the paddle shaft in front of you. The sling won't impede this but will pull free as you lift the paddle. Most paddlers find the rescue sling a welcome aid to their reentry.

Another way to use the sling is to simply loop it around the cockpit coaming and allow it to trail in the water. You can step onto this with one or both feet for a boost onto the boat. If this step up is too deep, take a couple of quick hitches in the sling to shorten it. Although using the sling in this fashion is faster than using the sling and the paddle, it doesn't help lock your paddle in place. You may also find that you're more likely to scoop water into the cockpit as you reenter the boat. Practice both methods until you're comfortable performing them, then decide the pros and cons of each.

SIT-ON-TOP KAYAK REENTRY

A reentry technique for a sit-on-top kayak is quite simple, given the boat's design. You'll need to flip the boat back over (if it indeed turned over) and maintain contact with it at all times. You can use the gear straps or any perimeter lines to help flip the boat upright.

Once the boat is upright, swim up and onto the deck of the sit-on-top kayak belly first. Roll yourself over and into the seat and then swing your legs up onto the boat. Very simple! Since sit-on-top kayaks are self-bailing, there won't be any water to remove from the boat.

It's rare that you need to use a paddle float during a sit-on-top kayak reentry, but it's employed the same way as in decked boats. You might have a bit more trouble keeping the paddle shaft from slipping off the boat as you begin to reenter. In this case, look for ways to hold the paddle shaft against a seatback or gear strap edge to keep it firmly in position. Most sit-on-top designs are extremely stable and allow easy reentry over the side. If you need a boost onto the boat, use a rescue sling in the same fashion as you do for decked kayaks.

1. Reenter a sit-on-top by swimming up to the side of the boat alongside the seat. **2.** Swim over the edge and pull yourself up much as you would at the edge of a swimming pool, then roll your body into the seat.

Reentering a Double Kayak

Most of the techniques for reentering a double kayak are the same ones we use for the solo reentry, but there are a few subtleties.

You and your paddling partner will need to communicate throughout the process and assess the situation and each other's condition. Turning a double kayak upright requires a simultaneous effort and may be quite difficult if the boat is heavily loaded. Use the same method to flip a double that you used to flip a single kayak, but coordinate your efforts. If you're unable to flip the double kayak over in this way, both paddlers may need to drape themselves over the hull and pull the cockpit coaming toward them by using their own body weight as they roll backward into the water. However, this will scoop more water into the cockpits.

You have a decided advantage when reentering a double. One paddler can help stabilize the boat while the other crawls in. During the first paddler's reentry, the second paddler may stabilize the boat by acting as a counterbalance to the first paddler's weight. The second paddler may remain in the water and hold the cockpit coaming from the opposite side of the boat until the first paddler is settled in place. Now the boat can be

1. Flipping a double kayak upright requires the coordinated effort of two paddlers. **2.** One paddler should stabilize the boat while the other crawls aboard. **3.** The second paddler enters while the first uses a sculling brace (here, a low one) for support. Paddle floats may also be used for additional support if needed.

stabilized by the first paddler as the second paddler reenters the boat. This may be done by using a sculling brace for support or even using an extended paddle with a paddle float until the second paddler is settled in place.

A double kayak can take on a great deal of water, so both paddlers need bilge pumps. You may choose to use a paddle float and rescue sling for a boost up onto the boat at any point.

When reentering a double kayak, you need to agree upon who goes first. Rather than make some rule about which paddler reenters first, consider the following.

- One paddler may be clearly weaker or less prepared for cold-water immersion. In this case, it might be wise to get that person out of the water and back into the boat first. The stronger paddler may even need to assist with this if her partner is weak or cold (a rescue sling may also be used).
- Both paddlers are prepared for immersion but one paddler is more skilled. Here, the skilled paddler should consider entering the boat first. That way, she may use her bracing skills to help stabilize the boat while the second paddler reenters. The exception may occur when there is a significant weight difference between the paddlers. The weight of the more skilled paddler who reenters at the stern may make the bow too high for the second paddler to reenter.
- Both paddlers are equally skilled and prepared for immersion. In this case, it might be best to let the stern pad-

dler enter first. From the stern position, she can see and better assist the second paddler's reentry if needed. But in this scenario, you may again encounter the problem of having a significant weight disparity between the two paddlers.

THE ASSISTED REENTRY

Enlisting the aid of another paddler after a capsize is a definite advantage. This person is out of the water and able to counterbalance your reentry and help corral any wayward pieces of gear. But you should never count on assistance, since your paddling partners may have their hands full with their own troubles in challenging conditions.

Anytime a paddler has to exit the boat, you're faced with two things: getting him back into the boat and getting any water out of the boat. Conditions will dictate in which order and how you accomplish these two feats. Surf or extremely cold conditions may force you to get the swimmer back into the boat immediately. If conditions are less extreme, you may delay reentry and empty the boat first.

There are many assisted rescues, each with its own advantages and disadvantages. You should practice several techniques and decide which would work best for you under various conditions. To put your faith in one method is shortsighted. Getting comfortable with a variety of techniques gives you even more tools for dealing with a host of challenges.

Before we get into the nitty-gritty of assisted techniques, review these tips that apply to all methods. Throughout our discussion of the rescue process, I'll refer to the capsized paddler as the swimmer.

During an assisted rescue, remember the following.

- Before approaching closely, determine if the swimmer is uninjured and coherent. You don't need to be capsized by a panic-stricken swimmer. You also need to determine if an injury or some other factor will affect your choice of rescue technique. Talk to the swimmer and get answers to simple questions: Are you OK? Are you getting cold? Do you have your paddle? A nod of the head is not a sufficient answer. You need to hear from the swimmer since this will also give you feedback about her condition.

- Speak to the swimmer in a calm, confident voice. Take charge of the situation and keep instructions simple. Be sure the swimmer acknowledges any instructions.

- Be sure the swimmer holds on to the boat at all times. If the swimmer becomes separated from her boat, the situation will be much more difficult. Now you have to retrieve a boat and a swimmer. Have the swimmer hold on to the paddle until you're ready to take it.

- A swimmer who is injured or has a medical problem must be handled according to emergency medicine protocol. This may preempt any assisted reentry technique.

- A swimmer who is cold and not prepared for cold-water immersion must be dealt with immediately. Get the swimmer out of the water. If you can't get her back into the boat immediately, have her lie across the stern deck of your boat. Communicate constantly to monitor her condition.

- Get to the capsized boat at any angle you can and grab it. Don't waste time trying to paddle into the perfect position. It's much easier and faster to grab the capsized boat, lean into it, and use your hands to maneuver around to the correct position. Don't try to push the capsized boat around; instead, swing your boat around the capsized boat.

- Consider what tools you have at your disposal. You have your boat, paddle, paddle float, rescue sling, bilge pump, and possibly another paddler in your group. You may choose to use some or all of these invaluable tools depending on the conditions.

- Remember that the swimmer's boat offers stability and flotation. You can lean across or on the swimmer's boat and be completely stable as you help with the reentry.

- Once the swimmer is back in the boat, be sure she is ready to resume paddling. A recapsize is most likely immediately following a reentry. Unless you have to get out of an area quickly, take the time to see if all her gear is back in place and the sprayskirt properly attached. Check rudder lines and hatch covers, and see if another layer of clothing, liquids, or a quick snack might be in order.

ESCALATING COMPLICATIONS

During a surf clinic, students frequently capsize. That is why we make sure everyone is comfortable with both solo and assisted reentry techniques before we begin. Students will often help one another reenter, and a buddy system is used to manage the group in these conditions.

During one surf clinic, which had been going pretty much as planned, one student capsized and did not hang on to his boat (he later said he was planning on body surfing to the beach and retrieving it later). The boat began drifting away from him, and one instructor (me) paddled after it. The second instructor got the swimmer onto his back deck until he could reenter his boat, and his buddy helped retrieve other gear that had floated free. During this time, two other students capsized, excited by all the commotion. With both instructors tied up with the original swimmer and corralling the wayward boat, the scene began to look like a comedy of errors.

Everything worked out fine because of the buddy system, and the students had the skills to assist one another during a reentry. But it points out that the simple mistake of not holding on to the boat after a capsize led to an escalation of complications and made things far more difficult than they needed to be.

Remember the tips already outlined. During the following descriptions of assisted reentry techniques, assume they have been followed.

T-Rescues

All styles of T-rescues allow you to drain the water from the capsized boat before the swimmer reenters it. This does not take much time or strength unless the overturned boat is heavily loaded. When you reach the overturned boat, you should bring the swimmer's bow perpendicular to your cockpit, forming a T. I find this to be far more stable than having it alongside, or worse yet, slightly behind you as you begin to lift the boat. The swimmer should move to the stern of their own boat, maintaining contact with the boat at all times. You can then direct the swimmer to push down on the stern as you lift the bow onto your cockpit. While you may be able to lift the bow without the swimmer's aid, pushing down at the stern helps break the vacuum as the swimmer's cockpit clears the water.

Now that the bow of the overturned boat is across your cockpit, it can be lifted until the water drains from its cockpit. If you cannot lift the bow of the swimmer's boat, pull it farther across your cockpit until it's able to drain. You should then roll the boat upright (communicating this action to the swimmer), being careful not to refill the boat with water, and align the two boats in opposite directions.

Aligning the two boats in opposite directions (bow to stern) is best because it gives you access to easy handholds on the front of the coaming and allows you to watch the swimmer throughout the reentry. This position also keeps you from getting in the way of the swimmer and keeps fingers from getting mashed or pinched during the process.

1. The rescuer leans into the overturned boat and "walks" around the boat toward a position at the bow. This is much quicker than paddling into this position. **2.** The rescuer lifts the bow while the swimmer helps by pushing down at the stern. The cockpit needs to be free of the water to drain during a T-shakeout rescue.

Use both hands to firmly hold the front of the cockpit coaming on the swimmer's boat and lean across the foredeck, keeping your elbows low. This will allow you to keep the swimmer's boat stable and to counterbalance movements to either side.

Before the swimmer reenters, you'll need to take his paddle. You can store this paddle with your own under the deck rigging. You may opt to tuck them under your arms as you lean across the swimmer's deck or use a paddle leash. If the decks are highly crowned or of significantly different heights, storing the paddles under your arms may be too awkward.

Have the swimmer come across his boat in the same manner as a paddle-float reentry. This will be even easier with you stabilizing the boat. The swimmer should still remain low and on his belly, pointed toward the stern of his boat. Once the swimmer has tucked his feet into the cockpit and positioned himself over the seat, he may turn toward you to sit down.

1. The rescuer leans toward the swimmer's boat and uses both hands to grasp the boat inside the cockpit (the thigh braces make good handholds) as the swimmer climbs aboard. **2.** Once the swimmer's legs are in the cockpit, he can turn toward the rescuer and slide into a seated position while the rescuer continues to stabilize the boat. **3.** The rescuer makes sure the swimmer is OK and ready to continue paddling before she lets go of his boat. Gear needs to be stowed and the sprayskirt in place before the swimmer is handed his paddle and released.

This T-shakeout method can be used only on boats that have a rear bulkhead. As the bow is lifted, the water rushes toward the stern where it hits the rear bulkhead and spills from the boat.

If the swimmer's boat does not have a rear bulkhead, you'll need to drag the swimmer's overturned boat across your cockpit until the two boats form an "X." By rocking the overturned boat in a seesaw motion, you can drain water from both ends of the boat before it's turned upright and put back into the water alongside the rescuer's boat. Obviously, your sprayskirt will keep the draining water from being dumped into your cockpit. This rescue is awkward and may be impossible with a heavily loaded boat, but it offers you an option for getting water out of a boat without bulkheads besides pumping. This method can be tough on composite boats since dragging them across another boat can scratch or gouge the gelcoat, and if the capsized boat is swamped, it could even collapse the deck of a composite boat.

Reenter and Pump

This method is the quickest way to get a swimmer back into the boat but doesn't empty water from the capsized boat before the swimmer reenters. You should pull alongside the capsized boat and reach across the hull to pull it upright. You may need the help of the swimmer to roll the boat over. Another paddler in the group may also be enlisted to serve as a counterbalance to your boat if needed.

The rescued swimmer is now seated in a boat full of water and must not lose the stability that you provide. You'll need to get the water out of the boat using a bilge pump or bailer. If possible, let the swimmer pump, since this may serve to warm him up and allows you to keep a firm hold on the boat for stability. You may choose to pump the boat, but be sure the swimmer is holding on to your boat with both hands (using a paddle to

During a reenter-and-pump rescue, the rescuer comes alongside the swimmer's boat and quickly flips it right side up. Water is pumped from the boat after the swimmer is aboard.

bridge and help stabilize the two boats may be useful). Using both pumps is the quickest way to remove the water, as long as the swimmer is stable.

The reenter-and-pump method may be used on any style boat, single or double. It offers a quick reentry for the swimmer and may be the only method possible if the swimmer's boat is heavily loaded. The disadvantage of this method is that the boat will have a lot of water in it during reentry, and it takes some prolonged effort to pump the cockpit dry.

Other Variations

Another variation on the assisted rescue theme brings the swimmer aboard from a position between the two boats. This can be used with any T-rescue or reenter-and-pump scenario. For this method, bring the

1. A swimmer can reenter her boat from a position between the two boats. **2.** The swimmer drapes her arms over the two boats and then leans back and swings her legs into the cockpit. The rescuer stabilizes the boat with both hands. **3.** The swimmer slides into the cockpit and seats herself. The rescuer continues to stabilize the boat until the swimmer is ready to resume paddling.

WHAT NOW?

When Vaughan Smith and I filmed a sea kayak rescue technique video, *What Now?*, we decided to demonstrate assisted techniques with me as the rescuer and Vaughan as the swimmer. Vaughan is 6 feet, 4 inches (193 cm) tall and weighs 220 pounds (99 kg). I am 5 feet, 4 inches (162 cm) tall and weigh 125 pounds (56 kg). When teaching rescues, we found that students were concerned about the size and strength differences between the rescuer and the swimmer. Couples often entered a class unconvinced that the wife could rescue the husband. Of course, they were often unconcerned about this since they erroneously assumed that the wife would be the one who would need to be rescued in the first place!

By showing that size disparity was not an issue, we convinced students that they could rescue someone nearly twice their size. This was a real confidence boost for everyone.

two boats alongside each other in the usual fashion (bow to stern). The swimmer comes between the two with one arm over his stern deck and the other over your forward deck. When the swimmer nears the cockpit area, he then leans back and swings his legs up into the cockpit and then scoots in. You should continue to stabilize the boat by grasping the forward portion of the cockpit coaming throughout the procedure.

If your boat has a high crown to the forward deck, it may be better to position the boats pointing in the same direction. This offers a flatter surface to the swimmer and may facilitate the reentry. It does have the disadvantage of pointing you away from the reentry.

Some people find that this method of bringing the swimmer between the boats works very well. Others are unable to get themselves into the boat in this manner, and it's been known to put undue stress on the swimmer's shoulders. But this gives you yet another option for getting a swimmer back into the boat. Again, the more you practice a variety of techniques, the better prepared you'll be for whatever is thrown your way.

The Scoop Rescue

This reentry technique is useful for getting someone who is injured, unconscious, or disabled back into the boat. You must first use emergency medical protocol and assess the situation if you have an injured or unconscious paddler. If it's appropriate to get this person into the boat, the best way may be the scoop rescue.

The scoop rescue positions your boat alongside the swimmer's boat. You'll need to get the swimmer's boat on its side and partially submerged to make the cockpit accessible. This allows the swimmer to be helped into the cockpit and positioned over the seat. Once the swimmer is in the boat, the rescuer must pull the boat upright. This will require you to reach across the cockpit and roll back with the swimmer's boat until it's upright.

The scoop rescue submerges the swimmer's cockpit and scoops her into it. Then the rescuer leans back to pull the swimmer and her boat upright. This may require the help of another paddler positioned outside the rescuer's boat.

The swimmer may help you by shifting her weight in your direction or even pulling her weight up with her hands. It's helpful to have another paddler positioned on the other side of the rescuer's boat to help stabilize and provide a stronger counterweight during the scoop itself.

Obviously, you need to remove the water in the cockpit before continuing. If the swimmer is unable to paddle, make sure she's stabilized before setting up a tow to safety (see towing techniques, pages 254–56). The scoop rescue is not easily done, but there are few options if you have a paddler with a lower-body disability or injury or an unconscious victim.

Assisted Reentry Techniques for Double Kayaks

The same principles and many of the same procedures used for single kayaks can be used for double kayaks. The main differences are that you now have two paddlers to get back into the boat, and you'll probably not be able to lift a double and empty it before reentering it. You'll need to pull alongside and roll the kayak upright with the aid of the two swimmers.

After reentry, both paddlers should immediately begin pumping out the double, since there will be a great deal of water to remove. Continue to stabilize the boat until everyone is ready to resume paddling, and even switch off roles until the pumping is completed.

Close-By Rescues

Some assisted rescues developed by white-water kayakers are useful in situations where paddlers are close together or paddle together regularly and thus have the presence of mind to hang out underwater until their

The overturned paddler bangs on the bottom of the boat to get the rescuer's attention and then sweeps his hands parallel to the sides of the boat.

Once the overturned paddler contacts the rescuer's boat, he can hold the bow
and hip snap into an upright position.

In a variation of this rescue, the rescuer may come alongside and guide the overturned paddler's hands onto his paddle shaft. Using the paddle shaft across the boats for support, the
overturned paddler can hip snap into an upright position.

buddy comes to the rescue. All these should start with the capsized paddler banging on the bottom of the overturned boat to get the attention of someone in the group. Then, the upside-down paddler must continue to sweep his hands back and forth along both sides of the boat until he contacts the bow, paddle shaft, or hands of his rescuer.

The most popular of these rescues brings the bow of the rescuer's boat perpendicular to the overturned kayak and within reach of the sweeping hands of the upside-down paddler. The bow can then be grasped and the overturned paddler can use a hip snap to bring his own boat back under him. This rescue works well if executed quickly and in conditions that would not impale the overturned boat with the rescuer's bow.

The rescuer may choose to pull alongside and place her paddle shaft across the overturned boat hull and help guide the overturned paddler's hands onto the shaft. From this position, the overturned paddler can take a breath of air before executing a hip snap into an upright position.

A FINAL WORD ON RESCUES

Often, reentry techniques are simply a useful means to get back into your boat after swimming or practicing rolls (which weren't all successful). At these times using the term *rescue* seems far too melodramatic. Some paddlers complain that too much emphasis is given to these techniques, which may never be required of the majority of kayakers. The problem is, even well-planned outings can go awry, and it's comforting to know you have

some strong tools at your disposal to deal with those situations.

Many of the techniques we've discussed seem awkward or clumsy at best. Rough seas only make them more challenging, so practicing these techniques once in calm waters is not sufficient. Start out in calm conditions in shallow water, but once you get comfortable with the moves in these conditions, up the ante. Try solo and assisted reentries on a windy day with some choppy waves. Choose a site with a soft landing and a day with an onshore breeze. Have your partner on standby just in case you need help. Real conditions will help you develop real responses and skills.

Another good way to really groove reentry techniques is to teach them to someone else (or at least pretend to). Describe each step and where things could go wrong. Have a friend call out a scenario and then reenact it. Review and defend your choices of methods and equipment. This forces you to think through things by doing them rather than just accept the word of an instructor or this book.

ROLLING

Rolling is an inherent part of kayaking, with traditions dating back hundreds of years. Rolling is one of the most rewarding skills you can learn as a kayaker, and yet to tag your success as a fledgling kayaker to this one maneuver is chancy. Rolling your kayak means being able to stay in your boat in challenging conditions, which is a huge plus. As important, rolling builds a certain self-

Top: Greenland national champion Maligiaq demonstrates paddling while upside down. Being comfortable underwater is key to successful rolling. **Bottom:** Some rolls require excellent balance and flexibility. Here Maligiaq hand-rolls his boat upright. For more on hand rolls, see pages 157–59.

confidence that allows you to relax and even relish playing in conditions that might stress a paddler whose main concern is to remain upright at all times.

Some kayak historians have documented an incredible array of rolling styles, each suited to specific conditions or local traditions. To eschew rolling is to miss out on this fun pursuit of learning new skills and practicing moves connected to a distant past. And yet, I've seen kayakers miserable over not "getting their roll" or losing the skill after

ONSIDE OR OFFSIDE?

Some instructors refer to rolls as "onside" or "offside," forever lending strength to one side and tagging the other with a certain weakness of spirit. This manner of describing rolls was used to note whether a roll was made on the side of your major, or control, hand (the control hand is the one that maintains its grip position on a feathered paddle shaft). It was also useful to distinguish one side of the boat from the other. Of course, any distinction was specific to the individual paddler since some people used their left hand as their control hand (and thus, their onside was to the left). As feather angles have become less severe and unfeathered paddles have become common, the need to note adjustments to the precise hand-blade angle became less important or nonexistent. So, the use of terms like *onside* and *offside* has begun to fade.

If you're like most paddlers, your strokes and rolls are stronger on one side than the other. You probably throw a baseball better with one hand than the other, also. Years ago, I had a rolling instructor who refused to acknowledge that one side was different from the other and made students practice on both sides equally. As he said, "My students don't have offsides!" It worked: almost all of us developed a roll on both sides, which was especially handy on rivers when a rock prevented a roll setup on one side or the other.

Sea kayakers are not prone to refer to rolls as onside or offside, especially Greenland technique aficionados, with their unfeathered paddles. Maybe we should adopt a nautical bent and use the terms *port* (left side when facing forward) and *starboard* (right side when facing forward).

years of paddling. These same paddlers were often safe and thoughtful kayakers. They just couldn't seem to learn the roll or count on performing this maneuver in any consistent manner, especially under challenging conditions.

So I would urge everyone to try to learn to roll. It's fun, and you'll be a more relaxed and safe paddler if you have this tool in your back pocket. But if you just can't seem to learn this skill with any consistency, don't let it get you down. You'll just need to be more cautious and conservative in your trip planning, and be sure your reentry skills are solid. Frankly, I'd be willing to bet that only a small percentage of sea kayakers have a consistent

combat roll that will bail them out in real conditions.

Rolling requires flexibility at your waist and hips and a certain sangfroid about hanging out underwater. The elements of a roll are the *setup* (getting into position to begin the roll), the *support phase* (using your paddle, hands, or a float for support on the water), and the *hip snap* (bringing the boat underneath you to sit upright). In some rolls, certain elements may be simultaneous, while other rolls may have you languishing in the support phase before deciding when you wish to move into your hip snap. As you learn a wide variety of rolling maneuvers, try to break each style of roll down into these components and master each one. If your roll fails, this will help you pinpoint where things went wrong and correct your technique.

The Sweep Roll

This is one of the most common rolls for kayakers. Its support phase is solid and forgiving, and it's relatively easy to learn because it mimics a sweep stroke. Like many other rolls, the sweep stroke begins with a setup alongside the boat. It's important to get your paddle blades out of the water and correctly oriented parallel to the boat. Twist your torso to bring your chest parallel to your paddle shaft and the boat. You should also look at your forward paddle blade (even if you close your eyes, orient your head in this direction).

Your forward paddle blade will sweep along the surface of the water with a rising blade angle just like your forward sweep stroke. This climbing angle and the sweeping movement will give you ample support to snap the boat back underneath you into an upright position. As with any roll, it's key that your head be the last thing out of the water. Watching the paddle blade through its sweep as the boat rolls underneath you will help accomplish this. Your hip snap begins shortly after your paddle sweep begins. Continue your sweeping motion throughout its full range until the boat is underneath you and you're sitting upright (see illustration opposite).

The C-to-C Roll

This is an elegant roll that uses the slap of a high brace for support at the same time that a strong hip snap brings the boat upright. The setup is the same one used for the sweep

stroke. But instead of beginning a sweep stroke for support, the paddle is brought perpendicular to the boat and then a high brace is slapped against the surface of the water at the same time the hips are snapped. Again, the head should be the last thing out of the water, so watch the blade until you're upright.

One advantage of the C-to-C roll is that it leaves you in a position ready to brace or paddle forward. The C-to-C roll was developed by whitewater paddlers and quickly caught on in the whitewater instructional community. For teaching purposes, it can be broken down into discrete elements and is a quick roll that can be critical in whitewater conditions. The body forms the initial C during the setup phase, and the second C occurs as the hip snap brings the boat underneath while the paddler is in the bracing position (see illustration on page 156).

Extended Paddle Rolls

Sea kayakers often have an advantage when it comes to rolling. We don't necessarily need a fast roll, just an effective one. For this reason, we can use extended paddles or prolonged support phases in our rolls. The disadvantage of an extended paddle roll is that you're changing your hand placement from its normal position on the paddle shaft. Rearranging your paddle grip takes time and may confuse your normally quick grasp of your paddle blades' orientation (see photos on page 157).

One of the easiest rolls to learn is the Pawlata roll, which is a sweep roll using an extended paddle. When you use an extended paddle blade, you're grasping the aft paddle blade edge with one hand. This extends the other paddle blade farther out from the boat

1

2

3

4

1. To set up for a sweep roll, punch the paddle skyward and alongside your boat. **2.** Begin the blade's sweeping motion with a climbing angle to the leading edge of the paddle blade for lift and support. **3.** As you move through the sweep, orient your face and torso toward the blade (you can look right at it) and snap your hips to bring the boat underneath you. **4.** As you complete the sweep roll, make sure your paddle blade is out of the water at the stern. At the finish of a sweep roll, you'll be leaning slightly back and turned toward the working side.

1. Set up for your C-to-C roll by punching the paddle skyward and alongside your boat. You should feel air on your wrists.
2. Position the paddle in a high brace position with the working blade face above or as close to the surface as possible. **3.** Snap your hip and lift your knee to bring the boat underneath you as you gain support from the downward slap of your paddle blade.
4. Lift your head only when you are fully upright; it should be last to leave the water. Finish facing forward in a high brace position.

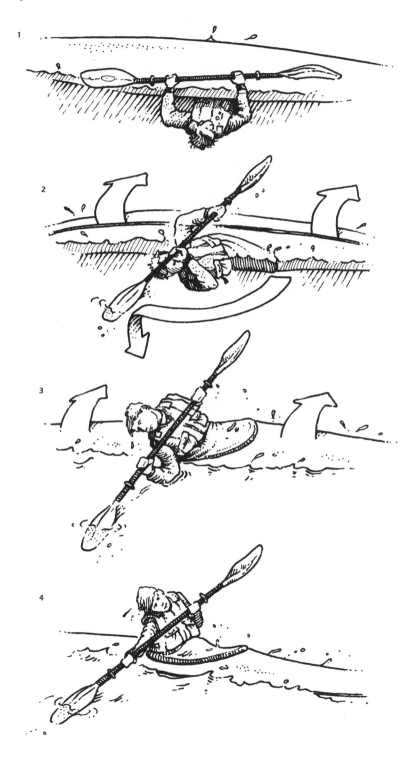

1. Set up for the Pawlata roll by gripping the rear blade of the paddle along its farthest edge. Slide your other hand down the paddle shaft to a comfortable position a bit more than shoulder-width apart. Punch the paddle skyward, with the working blade oriented with its power face parallel to the water. **2.** The extended sweep of the Pawlata roll is extremely supportive. The leading edge of the blade is slightly lifted.

during the sweeping motion, buying you extra support when you need it.

The setup phase in the Pawlata roll may be somewhat slow until you get comfortable with the hand position even with your eyes closed. The support phase can be luxuriantly slow. In fact, many paddlers find that moving an extended paddle through a sweeping arc cannot be done quickly. Although you should attempt to keep the sweeping blade on the surface of the water, there's enough support from the extended paddle to perform this roll successfully with the blade underwater as long as its leading edge is raised.

You can also use an extended paddle for a C-to-C roll to gain extra support and for a variety of other rolls like the Steyr roll (see illustration page 158). There is an incredible variety of rolls, and entire books are devoted to this subdiscipline of kayaking. Practicing these skills is fun and a great confidence builder. Many paddlers will use a traditional Greenland paddle or a hand paddle to practice rolls. The buoyancy and design of these wood paddles may facilitate learning and performing these rolls.

Hand Rolls

Hand-rolling a kayak demands excellent technique. The support phase is brief and minimal (I have seen a "no-hands" roll, the ultimate in

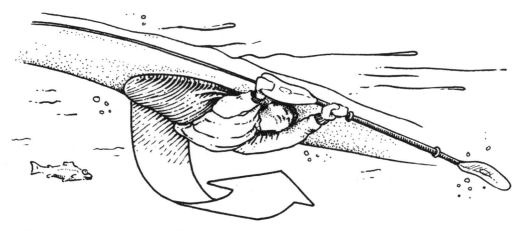

The Steyr roll uses an extended paddle for support but sets up with the paddler lying on the back deck with the paddle held parallel to the stern deck of the boat. The setup for this roll is awkward and requires flexibility. The actual execution of the roll uses a supportive reverse sweep motion with the paddle blade.

LEARNING TO ROLL

Several things will help you learn a roll faster and more comfortably:

- warm, clear water
- a dive mask, or swim goggles and nose clips
- use of a whitewater kayak that fits snugly
- a good instructor

Once you get the moves down and smooth out the rough spots, you can move to your sea kayak and more realistic conditions. Most whitewater kayaks are considerably easier to roll than their longer seagoing cousins. But once you groove your rolling skills, you shouldn't have any problem rolling your sea kayak (if the kayak is heavily loaded, be sure everything is well secured).

One method for learning a roll is to place a paddle float on one blade for additional support until you learn the positions and movements of the roll. If you use a dual chamber paddle float, inflate only one chamber on the back face of the blade. This way, you can still get a good climbing angle if you're practicing a sweep roll. As you get more comfortable, let more and more air out of the float until you're no longer dependent on it. You may also choose to start with extended paddle rolls, which give you better leverage, and then move into rolls that use your regular hand position on the paddle shaft.

minimalism!). The two most popular hand rolls are the C-to-C roll and the sweep roll (often with a slashing motion at the end). Many paddlers wear webbed neoprene gloves to practice hand rolls to get more support.

One way to work toward a hand roll is to use a paddle float or a traditional hand paddle (see photo). These will give you some support but less than a paddle blade would. In the case of the paddle float, you can gradually lessen the support by deflating the float over time. Once you're comfortable with several different rolls using your paddle, try some of these techniques. Even if you never nail a hand roll, it will help you refine your rolling technique. Any time you roll, try to use as little support on the water as possible.

Webbed neoprene gloves and a small hand paddle will help you learn a hand roll.

A paddle float can be used as an aid for learning and practicing rolls. Only the float chamber on the back face of the blade should be inflated. The buoyancy of the float can be reduced until it is no longer needed.

7

Real-Life Paddling

We've theorized about design, gotten up to speed on how to put your boat through its paces on the water, and given you the tools and techniques to deal with capsizes. But what about all those real-life factors like wind, tidal current, waves, and weather? How do you prepare or practice for these things? The answer is, you strive to understand them.

Once you understand the underlying principles of wind and waves, or approaching weather fronts, then you can develop a strategy to deal with them. You can plan a trip that minimizes the negative impact of these things. That's not to say that you'll never experience a hard slog against a headwind or stiff current or get soaked on a raw, cold day. But you can learn to manage these factors once you understand how to predict their presence and effects on you and your kayak.

STAYING ON COURSE

Sometimes staying on course is as simple as pointing your bow at a destination and paddling toward it. Quite often, though, conditions conspire to set you off course. When you're kayaking, you want to paddle a given course and waste as little energy as possible. The quickest way to waste energy is to lose your forward momentum. Novice paddlers often do this—they get too far off course and then have to stop and bring the boat back on line. You can avoid this "snake-wake" style of paddling if you learn to monitor your boat's course and make corrections early and often.

Think about how you walk up a set of stairs. You aren't aware that you're monitoring your progress and judging where to place each foot as you climb. You must learn this same sensitivity to your boat as it moves through the water. Each little lurch off course should bring an automatic response from you in correction.

Get used to looking ahead as you paddle. Pick out an object or series of objects that you can use to gauge your kayak's position (see Ranges, pages 212–14). When your boat begins to stray off course, you can react quickly and accordingly. Bringing your boat back on course requires little more than a shifting of your weight in the cockpit.

To make this course adjustment maneuver, slightly lift your hip and knee on one side of the boat, which leaves your weight unevenly distributed in the seat. This subtly changes

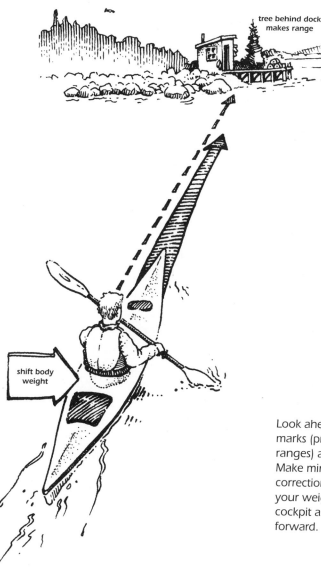

tree behind dock makes range

shift body weight

Look ahead to land-marks (preferably ranges) as you paddle. Make minor course corrections by shifting your weight in the cockpit as you paddle forward.

the hull's balance, causing one side to ride a bit lower in the water. If you continue to paddle forward, you'll find that the boat gradually moves away from the weighted side. For example, if your boat was beginning to stray off course to the left, you would want to weight the left side of the boat with a slight lift of the hip and knee on the right side. You continue to paddle forward until the boat is back on course, shifting back to a normal position in your seat. This subtle course correction doesn't lose any forward momentum.

These course corrections are not as decisive as turning strokes and should be made within the rhythm of your forward stroke cadence. Your strokes should be continuous and smooth, and your weight shift should become second nature as you respond to your boat's movement through the water.

WIND: DON'T LET IT PUSH YOU AROUND

I find paddling in strong winds to be one of the most difficult things about sea kayaking. Wind has always been my nemesis, dogging my every stroke with discouragement. I've wasted as much energy disliking wind as I've used dealing with it! Finally, I realized that I was missing way too many opportunities to go paddling while I waited for perfect conditions (a 5–10 knot breeze in my case) that are less reliable than a dime store wristwatch. So I outgrew my aversion to windy days, or at least accepted their inevitability, because I learned how to deal with them.

Different wind directions affect your boat in different ways. Above-water and below-water forces act on your boat as it sits in or moves through the water. Imagine a kayak sitting still in the water. A tailwind or headwind would have a minimal effect since the wind would be blowing along the length of the boat with very little to impede its flow. Now imagine a crosswind. The boat would be caught broadside by the wind and be pushed sideways through the water. But we care more about what our kayak does as it

moves through the water on a windy day. So we must consider below-water forces, as well.

Paddling in Crosswinds

Paddling in a crosswind requires some adjustments to your paddling to stay on course. There are above-water forces that blow the boat sideways—the same ones that are in effect while sitting still. The below-water forces are a bit more complicated than they are for the stationary boat.

As the boat moves forward through the water, the bow parts the water, which flows down the sides of the boat. The stern, which is behind the widest part of the boat, has less lateral pressure acting on it. With less water pressure on either side of the stern, it may swing more freely than the bow. In addition, lateral pressure begins to "stack up" at the bow as it moves forward and is greatest on the downwind side because of the sideways component created by a crosswind. The bow wants to swing upwind away from this higher pressure, as the stern is free to swing downwind. The result is that the boat has a tendency to weathercock, or swing up into the wind as it moves through the water. Some kayak designs are quick to do this; others are more resistant. If you paddle in a crosswind, you'll need to deal with your boat's tendency to weathercock if you hope to keep your boat on course.

If your boat has only a minor tendency to weathercock, the subtle adjustments we talked about for staying on course will be sufficient. If the crossing is long or the winds strong, you might have to make more decisive adjustments. You may do this by using a skeg or rudder or by leaning the boat into the wind. Dropping a skeg or rudder blade into the water creates more lateral pressure

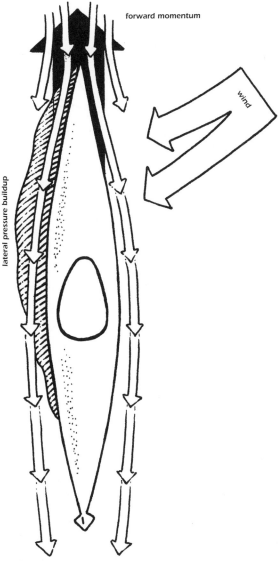

forward momentum

wind

lateral pressure buildup

Paddling in a crosswind creates different lateral pressures along the boat. As the lateral pressure stacks up at the downwind bow, the boat begins to weathercock (swing its bow into the wind).

at the stern, which helps hold the stern in place and enhances tracking. This is often the easiest way to counteract the effects of weathercocking if the crossing is long or the boat heavily loaded. (Also check the trim of your boat; a too-heavy bow accentuates weathercocking.)

Leaning the boat into the wind and paddling forward will help the boat hold its course. This may need to be a decisive lean, as opposed to the unequal weighting created by a slight lift of the hip and knee described on pages 160–62. Leaning the boat into the wind may also help stabilize your boat in beam seas (waves striking the side of the boat) created by crosswinds. If you continue to have difficulty staying on course in a crosswind, consider adjusting your stroke so that the upwind (or weather side) stroke is stronger, or reach out to make more of a sweep stroke on that side of the boat. Any of these adjustments will work to keep your kayak on a straight course while paddling in a crosswind.

Strong crosswinds and beam seas will also require good timing on your paddle strokes. You don't want to plant a forward stroke on the downwind side just as a wave passes beneath the hull. The boat might trip over the paddle blade and capsize. Instead, make your downwind strokes after the wave has passed beneath your hull and your upwind strokes on the crest of the wave, or just after it passes. Strong crosswinds may also try to snatch your paddle from your hand, especially feathered paddles. If the wind catches a blade, let the upwind side go, hang on with your downwind hand, and retrieve it. You may find that hunching down slightly in the cockpit and keeping the upwind stroke as low

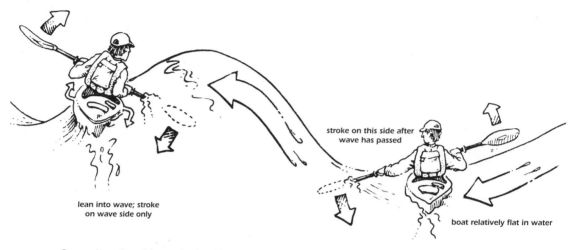

lean into wave; stroke
on wave side only

stroke on this side after
wave has passed

boat relatively flat in water

Stay relaxed and loose in the hips while paddling in beam seas. Make your stroke on the upwind side and lean into the wave as it lifts you. Make your stroke on the downwind side after the wave passes.

as possible will help. In general, the less profile you present to the wind, the better.

Not to put too fine a point on it, but we should also discuss wind angles that fall between a true crosswind and either a tailwind or headwind. These winds are said to be *quartering* and are either off the stern quarter or off the bow quarter. As you might expect, dealing with a quartering wind is much like dealing with a combination of a crosswind and either a headwind or tailwind. Staying on course may require you to lean your boat and make adjustments to your forward stroke similar to those used in crosswinds.

You'll also need to deal with any seas these quartering winds have created. Waves off the bow quarter are pretty straightforward; you can see them coming and adjust accordingly. Waves off the stern quarter are more disconcerting. They are often more difficult to anticipate since they come from over your shoulder, and they may help swing the stern downwind as they pass. This can make for tough going since you'll need to correct for this swing and be ready to brace if you broach (get caught sideways to the wave). Seas off the stern quarter can often be very frustrating since you're dealing with the worst components of both crosswinds and following seas at the same time! Try to discern the timing between waves and make your stroke adjustments as the wave lifts the boat. You'll need to fine-tune your balance and be ready with a quick brace if you broach.

Paddling into the Wind

Kayaking in a headwind won't require you to make a lot of adjustments to your paddling, but it may require an attitude adjustment. It's very easy to get discouraged when you're bucking a headwind. You feel like you can't pause or let up without losing ground. It's even hard to talk to your paddling partner since every time you turn your head, wind is whistling in (not through!) your ears.

Pay close attention to the wind and try to listen for any rhythm in its blowing. Wind is rarely steady but will lurch and pause like a poorly trained dog on a leash. Paddle a bit harder during those brief letups and keep a steady pace during the gusts. Increase the cadence of your stroke, and keep your paddle angle low so there is less exposure to the wind. Try to shorten your stroke, as well. It may not look as smooth and graceful, but a shortened stroke will keep a blade in the water and maintain your forward momentum.

It's important to relax and power your stroke with plenty of torso rotation. You'll need everything working efficiently if you're faced with a long paddle in strong headwinds. At some point, you may be convinced that you're not moving forward. Observe a piece of nearby shoreline or object to the side. You'll see that you're indeed moving even if you feel like you're standing still. I always envision throwing a ball well in front of my boat and then paddling to that spot. Once there, I throw it again. By breaking the distance into short segments that I can visualize, I get a series of small rewards instead of looking across a long crossing and getting discouraged.

Look for any windbreaks you can find. Even a small ledge might offer a place to duck behind for a quick breather. When you leave the windbreak's protection, you need to have plenty of momentum as you reset your course. If you must take a break during a long piece of exposed paddling, set a sea anchor to help maintain your position. If you're pad-

dling into the wind, you probably won't need to make many corrections to stay on course, but you may need to make corrections to your travel time. (See chapter 8 for more on this topic.)

Paddling with the Wind

It doesn't get any better than paddling with a nice tailwind. With the wind at your back, you're largely unaware of its presence as you get a helpful boost to your paddling. But if the winds are strong and seas have begun to form, that handy tailwind might be more trouble than it's worth.

Paddling in following seas can be unsettling because the stern may be suddenly lifted and make your boat feel unstable. Rather than feel at the mercy of these conditions, work within their rhythm. Time the interval between waves as they pass beneath your hull. Now when your stern is lifted, keep the boat pointed down the face of the wave for a free ride. Continue to paddle with an easy cadence and keep it steady when you hit the trough of the wave. Don't paddle hard up the back face of the wave as it passes underneath you, but continue to paddle forward until the next wave lifts your stern.

The key to paddling in following seas is to maintain momentum. Don't waste valuable energy wallowing in the trough or pulling hard to paddle uphill on the back face of a wave. Keep the boat pointed forward and moving with the rhythm of the seas that pass beneath the hull: fast on the downhill and slowing, but still moving, on the uphill.

If the waves are steep, you'll need to be sure that your bow does not pearl, or bury

LEE VERSUS WEATHER

Sailors and other small boat operators will often use the terms *lee* and *weather* to denote a wind direction in relation to their boat or to describe a shore in relation to the wind. *Lee* refers to the direction toward which the wind blows. *Weather* refers to the direction from which the wind is coming. Thus, the weather side of a boat is the side upon which the wind is blowing, or striking. So, when the bow of a boat swings upwind (windward), or to weather, the boat is said to *weathercock*. When the bow falls off the wind, or swings to lee, the boat is said to *leecock* (some say *weathervane*, but this is confusing).

Most sailboats are designed with a slight weather helm. That is, they're designed to turn slightly to windward, which requires little helm to keep the boat on course. A leeward helm, on the other hand, is more difficult to keep on course and can be unsafe. The same is true of a kayak. It's easier to control a boat that weathercocks than one that leecocks, because it's difficult to turn back into a strong wind. Usually, if a kayak is falling off the wind, or leecocking, it's because of improper loading and poor trim, not because of the boat's design.

You may also use the terms *lee* and *weather* to refer to a shore, either mainland or island. The shore from which the wind is blowing is the weather (windward) shore; the shore toward which the wind is blowing is the lee shore. In strong winds, you'd do well to avoid lee shores since they feel the full force of the wind, which may make landing or launching difficult. Do not confuse *lee shore* with *in the lee*, a phrase that refers to an object that is sheltered from the wind. Thus, you may pull into the lee of an island to catch a breather from the wind, but on the lee shore you would take a beating from that wind.

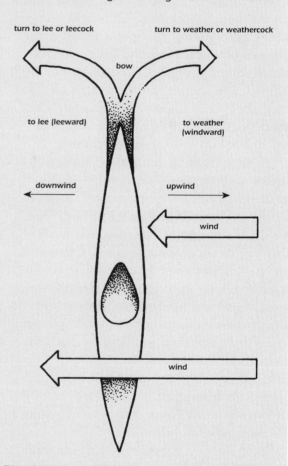

Directions in relation to the wind may be given as windward (to weather—on the side the wind is coming from), or leeward (the side toward which the wind is blowing). If a boat turns into the wind, or to weather, the boat is said to *weathercock*. If it turns away from the wind, or to lee, it is said to *leecock*.

Many nautical terms and their common pronunciations can be confusing at first. Being comfortable with these terms is useful since they are precise references to wind direction in relation to the boat or a piece of shore, and they will allow you to glean useful information from the many books on seamanship and small-boat handling.

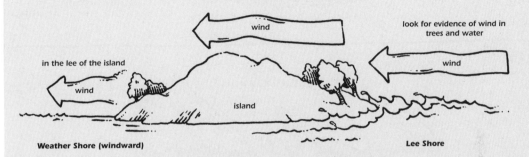

When discussing a piece of shore (mainland or island), the shore onto which the wind is blowing is the lee shore. The windward, or weather, shore is the one from which the wind is blowing. You may use the protection of land (or an object), paddling in its lee.

TIPS FOR PADDLING IN WIND

Here's a quick review of how to paddle in winds and wind-created waves.

- Keep moving. A stationary boat is more difficult to control and bring back on course. Present a low profile to the wind. If needed, hunch in the cockpit, and keep the paddle angle low.
- Try to discern a rhythm to the wind and wave conditions. Paddle hardest when there's a letup. Maintain a steady cadence when the going is toughest.
- Look for any windbreaks, however fleeting. Stronger paddlers may even serve as a temporary windbreak (be sure there's enough spacing to prevent a collision).
- Often, wind will build over the course of the day during the summer months, with lighter conditions in the early morning and around sunset. Plan the exposed portions of your paddling trip for these times.
- Remember that wind is just air with an attitude: it isn't out to get you. If the conditions are beyond your abilities, declare a windbound holiday.

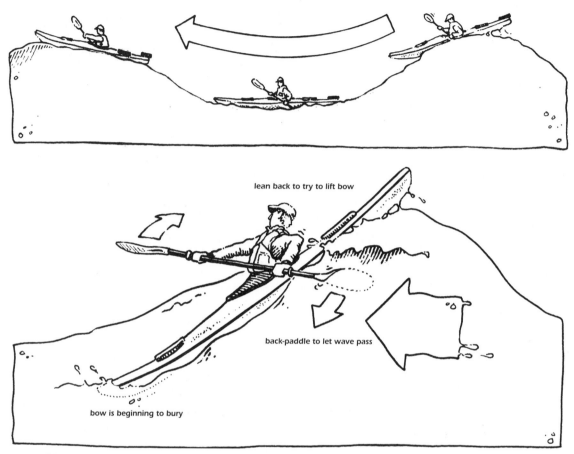

lean back to try to lift bow

back-paddle to let wave pass

bow is beginning to bury

Top: When paddling in following seas, develop a pattern that takes advantage of the wave's movement and try to keep your boat perpendicular to the waves. The best time to make corrections is at the crest of a wave when more of your boat is out of the water. **Bottom:** To avoid pearling, lean back to try and lift the bow. You may even need to back-paddle if the bow begins to bury itself. If the bow is held underwater as a steep wave passes, you'll be pitched forward (pitchpoled) as the wave breaks.

itself as the stern is lifted. Pearling can lead to broaching, or even pitchpoling, which is kind of what it sounds like: your boat, standing on its bow, is thrown over by the wave. It's not something to look forward to, especially in a loaded boat. To avoid pearling, lean back as you slide down the face of the wave. This will keep the bow up on top of the water until the wave passes. If you must, you can slow the boat with a few quick back strokes if the bow is beginning to dive.

Take care to stay pointed down the face of the wave and avoid broaching. Ideally, you don't want to slow your free ride, so lean the boat and make a quick sweep stroke if you need to straighten things out. This is easiest to do as the boat is lifted by the wave and some of its length is out of the water.

If you have a lot of momentum down the wave face, you may need to plant a stern rudder stroke to straighten the boat out and slow your speed. If you begin to broach, be ready to brace and lean into the wave. Be careful to plant the brace on top of the wave and lift your downhill hip and knee. Remain loose in the hips so you can react quickly when the boat swings back around or falls off the wave.

WIND AND TOPOGRAPHY

The flow of the wind is rarely unimpeded. It swirls around small islands, roars down canyons, and lurks behind points of land. Sea kayakers need to be aware of how topography affects wind—it can be friend or foe. We've talked about looking for windbreaks when you need a breather, a rather obvious use of topography. And we discuss later how the heating and cooling of the coastline actually generates local, predictable winds (see page 171). Now, let's look at how we might predict a wind's behavior in our paddling area by the topography it encounters.

Weather reports will give the wind speed and direction. The wind speed is generally given in knots, or nautical miles per hour (see chapter 8 for more on wind), and the wind direction given as a compass point (for example, northwest or southeast) from which the wind is blowing. For example, a southwest wind is blowing from the southwest. Knowing this information is invaluable for trip planning, but it's still incomplete. You need to relate the wind to where you're paddling.

The Beaufort scale (see table page 170) was created in 1808 to indicate the effect wind would have on a full-rigged frigate under sail. Today, the Beaufort scale includes descriptions of the effect of wind on land features such as trees or a flag. The wind is now defined by actual wind speed in knots in addition to the original Beaufort scale of "forces." These levels of wind run from force 1 to force 12. It is interesting to note that the force of the wind increases as the square of its speed. That is to say, as the wind speed doubles, its force on your kayak (and you) quadruples. This is why you feel such a big difference in the force of the wind when moving from one Beaufort wind scale level to the next.

The Beaufort scale can predict conditions you might see at a given wind velocity, or conversely, what velocity wind you're experiencing based on your observations. It does not take into consideration fetch, swell, heavy rain, tidal current, and other factors that could affect these conditions. Using the scale as a reference lets you then consider other factors that might enhance or diminish the conditions.

Sea kayakers, armed with nautical charts and topographical maps, should be able to predict a good deal about a given wind's behavior. You may be able to plan a day of paddling that leaves you protected from wind by hugging a piece of shoreline. Or you might configure your trip so that you'll face a headwind in the morning but have the wind at your back for the return leg home.

Beware of long, narrow stretches of water that will funnel any winds that blow along their axis. Look for headlands that might keep the wind at bay while you enjoy placid

Beaufort Wind Scale

Beaufort Number	Wind Speed (knots)	Wind Description	Water Description	Land Description
no force	less than 1 knot	calm	flat calm	nothing stirring
1	1–3	light air	ripples	smoke drifts gently according to wind direction
2	4–6	light breeze	small wavelets	air movement can be felt on your face
3	7–10	gentle breeze	scattered white-caps and large wavelets	leaves and twigs in motion
4	11–16	moderate breeze	lots of whitecaps; small waves lengthen	loose paper blows around; small branches move
5	17–21	fresh breeze	mostly whitecaps with spray; moderate waves	flags ripple; small trees begin to sway
6	22–27	strong breeze	whitecaps everywhere; more spray	larger trees and branches move; whistling heard in sailboat rigging
7	28–33	near gale	foam from waves begins blowing in streaks; sea heaps up	whole tree sways; your skirt gets blown up around your face
8	34–40	gale	foam is blown in well-defined streaks; crests begin breaking	branches and twigs torn from trees; you have trouble making headway on foot
9	41–47	strong gale	dense streaking; spray reduces visibility	roof shingles peeled from houses
10	48–55	whole gale	sea begins to roll and look white; visibility poor	trees uprooted; structural damage to buildings
11	56–63	violent storm	sea covered with white foam patches; large waves	widespread damage
12	64+	hurricane	air filled with foam and spray; almost no visibility	major, widespread damage

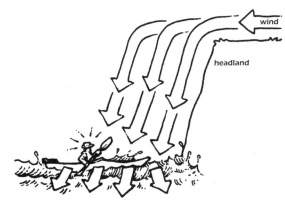

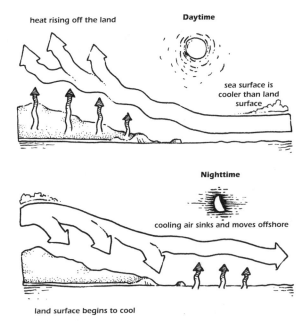

Williwaws, or wind spills, may splash on the water and an unsuspecting paddler, at forces greater than the wind that created them. They can create turbulence and confused water conditions.

On a sunny summer day, hot air rises from the warmed land. The cooler air over the water is drawn into these areas and creates the common sea breeze. The process reverses in the evening but is weaker and creates only a mild land breeze.

conditions in their lee. But know that once you round the headland, you'll be blasted with the full force of the wind.

If you're paddling along a steep piece of shoreline, you'll need to be aware of the potential for wind spilling over the edge. These sudden downdrafts, also called *williwaws*, may strike the water with a force greater than the wind that created them and can capsize an unsuspecting kayaker. I once paddled on the Great Salt Lake at sunset when there was barely a ripple on the water. But as we paddled along a high point of land that rolled off into the distance, paddlers started toppling like bowling pins. We were experiencing williwaws that made it difficult to stay upright without good bracing skills. It was an amazing feeling to look across the glassy water and then feel this fierce blast of wind from above.

Some of the easiest winds to predict are the sea breezes that build on a sunny, warm day along coastal waters. As the land is warmed by the sun, hot air rises to create an area of low pressure along the shoreline. Cooler air above the water is pulled into these areas and sets up an onshore breeze. This sea breeze begins around late morning in most coastal areas and will generally build through the afternoon hours. These predictable winds can reach a steady 15 knots or so before dissipating as the sun loses its strength in the late afternoon. A land breeze may occur as these conditions reverse during the evening hours but will be considerably weaker as it blows offshore.

DEFINING A WAVE

The following terms are used to describe a wave.

- **crest:** the high point of a wave
- **trough:** the low point of a wave
- **length:** the horizontal distance from one wave crest to the next
- **height:** the vertical distance from the trough to the crest
- **period:** the time for a wave crest to travel the distance equal to one wave length

Imagine timing wave crests as they pass a piling or the spindle of a day beacon. The period is the time it takes for one wave length, or two successive crests, to pass this mark. A wave period is usually measured in seconds. Ripples have wave periods of only fractions of a second, fully developed seas range from 5 to 12 seconds, the swell from 6 to 22 seconds.

There is an interesting relationship between a wave's length and height: a wave's height may not be greater than $\frac{1}{7}$ of its length (or its angle at the crest less than 120 degrees). If this maximum wave steepness is exceeded, the wave breaks.

WAVES: WHAT TO EXPECT AND WHY

The waves that are most important to sea kayakers are those raised by the wind. Although events like landslides, earthquakes, and the passage of a large ship can create waves, it's the wind that creates the ripples, whitecaps, and swell that affect our days of paddling. We are primarily concerned with the size of waves

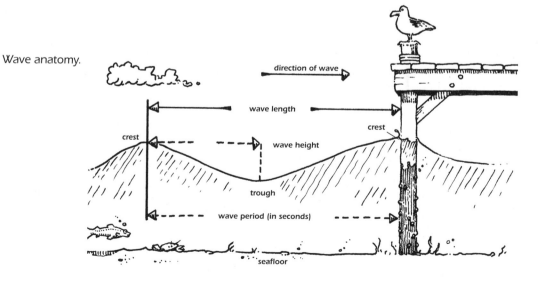

Wave anatomy.

and their potential to do us harm or provide play time. Three factors affect wave size:

- the wind's velocity
- the duration of the time the wind blows
- the extent of open water over which it blows (the fetch)

Not all big waves are bad waves; it usually takes the topography of the land underneath the water to release their power. The illustration on page 172 shows the parts of a wave. It's useful to know these terms since marine forecasts often include data from offshore buoys that include terms like *wave period* and *wave height*.

The Development of a Wave

Knowing the three factors that affect the size of a wave can help us predict what we'll see when paddling. From our charts, we can ascertain the fetch. From our weather radio and Internet sites, we can find out the wind's velocity and for how long it has maintained that velocity from that direction. While the formula for precisely calculating wave size isn't something the average sea kayaker commits to memory, simply knowing these three factors play a role is useful. Thus, paddling among islands along the coast of Maine, with its small fetch, will hardly give me the elevator rides I can expect along much of the California coast, where wind may have blown across hundreds of miles of open ocean. That's one reason surfers congregate on the beaches of California and shun Maine.

Waves finally reach a point where they have absorbed all the energy they can from wind of a given velocity. These fully developed seas will not continue to grow even if more time and fetch are added to the equation. The table on the next page shows con-

A long fetch with sustained winds can create mature waves that roll toward shore in a predictable fashion. These are fairly common along much of the Pacific coast.

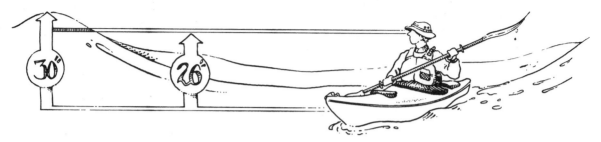

It's easy to misjudge wave heights when your eyes are only
26 to 30 inches (66–76 cm) above the water.

ditions in fully developed seas. If you look at the figures in this table, you'll see that it takes a pretty potent combination of time, velocity, and fetch to create a fully developed sea. When you're estimating wave height from the cockpit of your kayak, keep this table in mind. It's very easy to overestimate the size of a wave when your eye level is only 26 to 30 inches (66–76 cm) above the water. That towering wall of water descending on you may pack embarrassingly small statistics. So, before you tell your epic tales of adventure paddling, check the feasibility of your wave height estimates!

It's also handy to understand the concept of *swell*. Waves may develop out at sea from a storm that occurs over these deep waters.

As these waves move out from the winds that generated them, they gradually change and begin to move in groups of similar wave period and height. These groups of similar waves become more rounded and symmetrical. They are predictable enough that the time of their arrival on some far shore can be determined fairly accurately (remember that congregation of surfers in California). These wave trains move across deep water with little loss of energy until they finally spend themselves against some shoreline.

The Death of a Wave

I like to think that waves never really die, they just reform and gather their energy for

Conditions in Fully Developed Seas

Wind (velocity in knots)	Fetch (nautical miles)	Time (hours)	Average Wave Height (feet)	Average Height of the Highest 10%
10	10	2.4	0.9	1.8
15	34	6	2.5	5
20	75	10	5	10
25	160	16	9	18
30	280	23	14	28
50	1420	69	48	99

Adapted from Willard Bascom, *Waves and Beaches.*

another day. Most waves never make it to shore. Instead, they are overlaid with a multitude of other waves, both small and large—sort of "old seas meet new seas." Waves that do make it to shore will break in a predictable fashion. As a wave nears the shore, it begins to steepen as the shallow bottom creates drag. The crest begins to move more rapidly than the water below and finally falls forward, or breaks. A gradually sloping bottom allows the wave to gently release its energy by spilling onto the beach. If the bottom rises sharply and the top layers are moving rapidly, waves may suddenly dump and hit the beach hard. Spilling waves can be fun to surf in your kayak, but dumping waves are bad news. For more on the surf zone, see pages 176–78.

Even if you're paddling well offshore, you'll want to keep an eye on your chart for any underwater obstructions like ledges or submerged rocks. These shallow areas may suddenly steepen a wave passing over them and cause it to break. Waves may also spend their energy as they strike steep headlands and cliffs that rise from deep water. These waves will often rebound, or reflect, and meet incom-

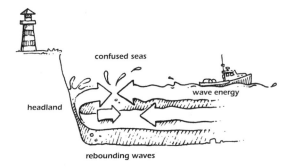

As waves strike an obstruction, like a steep headland, they rebound and meet incoming waves. Kayakers should avoid the very confused seas, or clapotis, that are created in these areas.

ing waves to create *clapotis*, which are choppy, confused seas created from this rebound effect. These conditions can cause confusing seas well off a steep shoreline, especially one with a long fetch, and should be given a wide berth as you paddle in these areas.

Waves not only rebound but may also bend as they begin to slow upon their approach to land. These refracting waves will often mirror the contour of the bottom they pass over. You can see this phenomenon at many beaches where waves have bent around a small point

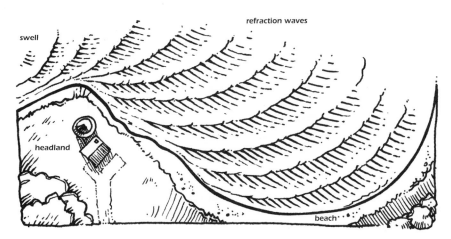

As waves encounter a point of land, they bend, or refract, around the land. These refraction waves often match the contour of the shoreline they approach and bend until their wave fronts are nearly parallel to the beach.

of land and match the contours of the shoreline they approach. You may also observe waves bending around an island. If the island is fairly circular, the waves will wrap around the island until they actually begin to overlap on its backside. As these waves bend, their wave fronts are nearly parallel to the beach, though the waves will be diminished the farther they bend from their original course.

Wave theory is not just an academic pursuit; it's part of the seascape we have chosen to explore in our small, responsive boats. Review a chart with an eye toward predicting some of these effects like rebound or refraction, and then try to observe these areas from your boat or land. You'll probably find that understanding some of these wave phenomena will make your trip planning more thorough and the resulting trip smoother.

THE SURF ZONE

The surf zone can be great fun, but only if you meant to be there! Kayak surfing is a study in its own right and offers hours of excitement that may range from wave playing on your sit-on-top to doing pirouettes off wave crests in a whitewater kayak. Generally, sea kayakers view the surf zone as part of a launching or landing process or as something to be avoided in loaded boats.

Landing or launching a loaded kayak requires you to be a bit more cautious and conservative than you might be with an unloaded boat. Your kayak may not respond as readily to leans and stern strokes and may want to wallow in a wave trough. Also, it will be even more dangerous when you're actually getting into and out of the boat if it's flung toward shore. You must not get caught between your boat and the shore—you could be seriously injured.

If at all possible, try to observe the waves that are breaking on the shoreline where you plan to land or launch. Look for areas where the wave break spills gently toward the shore. Avoid areas that may suddenly dump water or where waves seem to cross and create unruly turbulence that is hard to predict. Time the breaking of waves and try to look for patterns in their size. This information

Pick your way through the surf and don't be afraid to stall or even back-paddle for a better position during a surf landing. Try to time your landing to arrive on the back of a wave. Get out of your kayak quickly and pull it away from the water.

will come in handy when you actually land or launch.

Surf Landings

Choosing your landing site should have occurred during the trip planning phase before you left home. Using your chart, tide table, weather radio, and local knowledge to mark likely landing sites is every bit as important as successfully using your paddling skills once you're on the water.

To land in surf requires good timing and a certain quickness and agility when getting out of your boat. Observe the conditions from outside the surf zone, and then make your way to shore on the backs of the waves. You may have to do a lot of back-paddling to let waves pass underneath you and avoid getting surfed down their faces. If you begin to pick up too much speed, back-paddle and use the back face of the wave to slow your progress. Pick your way toward shore, trying to control your forward progress and staying aimed directly into the landing site.

Ideally, you want to land on the cushion of water that spills on shore, quickly get out of your boat, and haul it forward until it's out of reach of the next wave break. This step doesn't always go smoothly. You may broach and be thrown sideways onto the beach and begin to get sucked back into the surf as you exit the boat. Being ready to exit quickly helps; have your sprayskirt off and be ready to scramble out of the boat once it scrapes the shore. Normally, the strongest paddler lands first and uses agreed-upon signals (see pages 250, 251) to help others pick their way in to the beach. Having another person on shore to help get

the boat away from the water is handy and should make the subsequent landings easier.

Surf Launchings

Launching in surf requires the same skills you used to land successfully: close observation of the conditions, good timing, and a decisive move from the shore. You'll need to keep your boat pointed out and try to avoid broaching while you push away from the shore. If the

Be ready to go and scoot yourself toward the water to launch in surf. Keep the boat pointed perpendicular to the waves and paddle hard through the surf zone.

If a wave begins to break directly on you, stay low on your boat and keep the paddle alongside your boat. Avoid taking a wave hit directly on your torso or paddle face.

beach is soft and sloping, you may be able to enter your boat and get your sprayskirt attached and then use your hands to push toward the water until a breaking wave lifts you. Often this stage is foiled by a wave that hits while you're attaching your sprayskirt or before you're even seated in the boat. You may have several false starts, but keep trying until you're able to paddle away from shore.

Once you're launched, you'll need to paddle quickly and decisively forward. Time your paddling so that you don't get caught as a wave breaks, but instead paddle through until you're outside the surf. If a wave begins to break, get as much momentum as you can and try to punch through. Lower your body along the axis of the boat, and be sure your paddle is parallel to the boat and held low. You don't want to take the full force of a breaking wave on your torso or on an exposed face of a paddle blade. Once you're beyond the shore break, you can remove any water from the boat and check that any items on deck are still in place.

TIDES AND TIDAL CURRENTS

Several years ago, I was helping at a kayak demo day on Chesapeake Bay. At the end of the day I began my usual task of bringing gear well up the beach and above the reach of high tide for storage overnight. It was a habit ingrained from years of working these events on the coast of Maine. After stumbling through my third trip, I realized everyone else was watching with amusement. Finally someone pointed out that there was little chance of the tide on that beach rolling in and sweeping the gear away since it changed only by a few inches! Tides and tidal currents are quite specific to a given area, and this information is readily available and useful when planning a trip (or a demo day).

To make good use of resources such as tide tables and tidal current charts, you need to become familiar with tides and tidal currents terminology. Here are some of the most common terms.

- **tide:** the vertical movement of water that is governed by the gravitational forces of the sun and the moon.
- **current:** the horizontal movement of water. If this movement is caused by the rise and fall of the tide, it's called tidal current. Outside of the United States, the term *tidal stream* may be used in place of *tidal current*. This avoids confusion with ocean currents

(for example, the Gulf Stream or California Current), which are caused by thermal influences.

- **ebb:** the fall of the tide. When the tide goes out, it's said to be *ebbing*.
- **flood:** the rise of the tide. When the tide comes in, it's said to be *flooding*.
- **slack:** the period between flood and ebb tidal currents when there is little or no discernible flow. Also called *slack water*.
- **tidal height:** the vertical measurement between the surface of the water and the tidal datum, or reference plane. The reference plane will be noted on the chart, for example, mean lower low water.
- **tide table:** data, usually in tabular form, that show the height of the water at a particular location on a particular date. Annual tide tables are created by the National Ocean Service (NOS) and are the basic source of information on the time of high and low water, and their heights above the tidal datum.
- **tidal range:** the vertical distance between high and low water. Tidal ranges shift with the moon's position relative to the sun and according to orbital variations of the earth and moon.
- **spring tide:** the maximum tidal range for a given area, which occurs when the sun and the moon are in line. This has nothing to do with spring as a season.
- **neap tide:** the minimum tidal range for a given area, which occurs when the moon and the sun are at right angles.
- **set:** the direction of tidal current flow. If the tidal current flows from west to east, the set is given as "easterly," or as a compass direction (090 degrees). (Note that this is exactly opposite of how wind directions are given; a wind blowing from the west to east is considered a "westerly" wind.)
- **drift:** the speed of the tidal current, expressed in knots.
- **tidal race:** an area where velocity of the tidal flow is significantly increased by topographical features. These features may be entirely underwater. A kayaker rarely wins a race with a tidal race.
- **perigee:** when the moon is closest to earth and exerts the greatest lunar influence on the tides.
- **apogee:** when the moon is farthest from earth and exerts the least lunar influence on the tides.

Unless you always paddle on lakes and inland rivers, tides will be a factor whenever you go paddling. True, a small tidal range may mean that the tides in your area are relatively unimportant, but you're likely to encounter their effect somewhere along the line. Those of us in places with significant tidal ranges would never go paddling without some idea of what the tide is doing that day.

Tides originate in the open ocean and seas, but it's along our coastlines that we see the effects. Significant real estate will be covered and uncovered over the course of a day, and the power of the tide can stop even a large vessel in its tracks, not to mention a kayaker.

Tides result from the centrifugal and gravitational forces between the sun and the earth, and the earth and the moon. The moon, being closest to the earth, exerts the

Tidal ranges in some areas are huge and must be reckoned with. Strong tidal currents may occur and lots of real estate can be covered and then uncovered over the course of a tide's ebb and flow.

Understanding tides and the timing of their rise and fall could be critical in your trip planning. Misjudging low tide could leave you slogging through mud and across slippery rocks.

most influence on the tides. You can observe how the tide follows the moon over the course of a lunar cycle (about twenty-eight days). But the earth is rotating as well and must rotate slightly beyond one rotation to come beneath the moon once again. So the tidal, or lunar, day is 24 hours, 50 minutes. With two high tides and two low tides each day (semidiurnal), the time between a high and a low tide is about 6 hours, 12½ minutes; between two highs or two lows, it would be 12 hours, 25 minutes.

The illustration opposite shows how the presence of the moon creates a bulge of water that moves as the earth rotates underneath. A similar bulge of water is created on the opposite side of the earth with depressions between the two bulges. Since the sun can also create its own, though smaller, bulge of water on the earth's surface, the sun and moon can act to amplify or diminish one another. The greatest tidal range occurs when all three bodies (earth, sun, moon) are aligned. These occur at the new and full moon and are called *spring tides*. This can be further augmented when a spring tide falls

IT'S NOT A PERFECT WORLD

If the earth had good posture instead of slouching, and the moon would straighten up and fly right, things would be simple. We'd have two identical high and two identical low tides each day. But the earth tilts on its axis so that the moon travels north and south of the equatorial plane during the lunar month. The accompanying illustration shows the moon at its maximum north declination of 23 degrees. In a little more than seven days it will be over the equator, and seven-plus days after that it will be over latitude 23 degrees south. Whenever the moon is farthest north or south, the result in some places—including San Francisco and Seattle—is a mixed tide cycle, in which one of the daily highs is higher and one of the lows lower than the other. When this occurs, we speak of lower low or higher high water on a given day, and our tidal datum becomes mean lower low water.

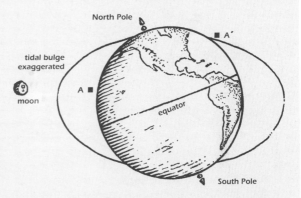

Here the moon is at its maximum north declination, and point A is beneath the fat part of the tidal bulge. But in 12 hours 25 minutes, the rotating earth will have carried point A to new position A', and the second high tide of the day in this highly simplified scenario will be a lot lower than the first.

When mixed tides are carried to their extreme, the result is a single high and low water each day—a diurnal tide—as along the Gulf Coast of the U.S. And yet, along the U.S. East Coast, "normal" semidiurnal tides predominate throughout the month. Why the differences? The configuration of the coastline, the shape and depth of a body of water, and the surrounding oceans and open seas all play a role. Rather than grapple with all these factors and try to predict the final outcome, we can simply look up the tidal information we need.

during the time the moon is closest to the earth (perigee). The moon is at perigee once a month, but this coincides with a spring tide only about twice a year. The height of the tide will be significantly greater during these times, which is a result of the moon's elliptical (rather than spherical) orbit.

For a sea kayaker, monitoring the tides and the position of the moon should be second nature. Ignoring them could lead to con-

sequences as minor as a muddy slog to the launch site or as major as being swept into a tidal race. It's simple enough to have a tide table handy in your paddling gear and make the needed corrections for paddling in your chosen area. You can usually find a tide table for a paddling area or one that has a correction factor for the tides in your area from a nearby reference station (documented location). Tide tables can be found

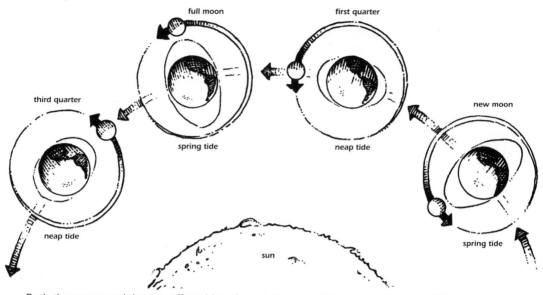

Both the moon and the sun affect tides, though the lunar influence is stronger. When the moon and sun work in concert (spring tide), the tidal range is greater; when they offset one another (neap tide), the tidal range is smaller.

in many forms, such as the small local versions handed out for free by a local outfitter or marine chandlery, and the annual publications by the NOS.

Tidal movement is continuous; it isn't being held in some giant vat only to be released at a particular hour and come rushing into your area. There will be lag times where water must move into and out of inland locations, and places where an incoming tide meets an outgoing tide to create turbulence and confusion. But in general, as water flows from high tide to low, or vice versa, it takes a bit more than six hours to complete its course. This rate of flow is not even. In most cases (exceptions often occur on rivers and estuaries), it's noticeably stronger in the middle two hours and gradually tapers on either side.

You must take into account that the bulk of the water is moving during the middle of a given tide. If you're using the current from a rising tide in your favor, paddle three to four hours after low tide for the best ride. By contrast, you'd want to avoid this timing if you were paddling against this tidal current, paddling instead during weaker flows or waiting until slack water. You should become comfortable checking your tide tables for the heights of a given tide and your tidal current tables (see pages 185–87) for information on the strength of the tidal current since these two factors may change at different times. One other thing to consider is that a strong river flow helps feed an ebbing tide, but not a flood tide. If you're paddling on tidal rivers or near the mouths of these rivers, keep this in mind, and be careful to study the tide table

MARCH

		Bar Harbor		Rockland		Boothbay Hbr.		Portland	
		am	pm	am	pm	am	pm	am	pm
MONDAY		6:03 HI	6:54	6:17 HI	7:08	6:19 HI	7:10	6:25 HI	7:16
	5	11.2 Height	10.0	10.4 Height	9.2	9.5 Height	8.3	9.7 Height	8.5
		— LO	12:43	— LO	12:52	12:01 LO	12:54	12:06 LO	12:59
		— Height	0.0	— Height	0.0	1.0 Height	0.0	1.0 Height	0.0
		5:56 Sun	5:19	5:59 Sun	5:22	6:02 Sun	5:25	6:12 Sun	5:35
TUESDAY		7:10 HI	7:58	7:24 HI	8:12	7:26 HI	8:14	7:32 HI	8:20
	6	11.6 Height	10.5	10.8 Height	9.7	9.9 Height	8.8	10.1 Height	9.0
		12:58 LO	1:48	1:07 LO	1:57	1:09 LO	1:59	1:14 LO	2:04
		0.6 Height	-0.5	0.6 Height	-0.5	0.6 Height	-0.5	0.6 Height	-0.5
		5:54 Sun	5:20	5:57 Sun	5:23	6:00 Sun	5:26	6:10 Sun	5:36
WEDNESDAY		8:14 HI	8:56	8:28 HI	9:10	8:30 HI	9:12	8:36 HI	9:18
	7	12.1 Height	11.1	11.3 Height	10.3	10.4 Height	9.4	10.6 Height	9.6
		2:02 LO	2:47	2:11 LO	2:56	2:13 LO	2:58	2:18 LO	3:03
		0.1 Height	-1.0	0.1 Height	-1.0	0.1 Height	-1.0	0.1 Height	-1.0
		5:52 Sun	5:21	5:55 Sun	5:24	5:58 Sun	5:27	6:08 Sun	5:37
THURSDAY		9:13 HI	9:50	9:27 HI	10:04	9:29 HI	10:06	9:35 HI	10:12
	8	12.5 Height	11.7	11.7 Height	10.9	10.8 Height	10.0	11.0 Height	10.2
		3:02 LO	3:41	3:11 LO	3:50	3:13 LO	3:52	3:18 LO	3:57
		-0.5 Height	-1.4	-0.5 Height	-1.4	-0.5 Height	-1.4	-0.5 Height	-1.4
		5:50 Sun	5:23	5:53 Sun	5:26	5:56 Sun	5:29	6:06 Sun	5:39
FRIDAY		10:07 HI	10:40	10:21 HI	10:54	10:23 HI	10:56	10:29 HI	11:02
○	**9**	12.8 Height	12.1	12.0 Height	11.3	11.1 Height	10.4	11.3 Height	10.6
		3:57 LO	4:32	4:06 LO	4:41	4:08 LO	4:43	4:13 LO	4:48
		-1.0 Height	-1.7	-1.0 Height	-1.7	-1.0 Height	-1.7	-1.0 Height	-1.7
		5:49 Sun	5:24	5:52 Sun	5:27	5:55 Sun	5:30	6:05 Sun	5:40
SATURDAY		11:00 HI	11:28	11:14 HI	11:42	11:16 HI	11:44	11:22 HI	11:50
	10	12.8 Height	12.4	12.0 Height	11.6	11.1 Height	10.7	11.3 Height	10.9
		4:50 LO	5:20	4:59 LO	5:29	5:01 LO	5:31	5:06 LO	5:36
		-1.3 Height	-1.7	-1.3 Height	-1.7	-1.3 Height	-1.7	-1.3 Height	-1.7
		5:47 Sun	5:25	5:50 Sun	5:28	5:53 Sun	5:31	6:03 Sun	5:41
SUNDAY		11:50 HI	—	— HI	12:04	— HI	12:06	— HI	12:12
	11	12.6 Height	—	— Height	11.8	— Height	10.9	— Height	11.1
		5:41 LO	6:08	5:50 LO	6:17	5:52 LO	6:19	5:57 LO	6:24
		-1.5 Height	-1.4	-1.5 Height	-1.4	-1.5 Height	-1.4	-1.5 Height	-1.4
		5:45 Sun	5:26	5:48 Sun	5:29	5:51 Sun	5:32	6:01 Sun	5:42

Get used to reading a tide table for your paddling area. Here, for instance, high tides on 6 March are at 7:24 A.M. and 8:12 P.M. in Rockland, Maine. If we were launching at 9 A.M., we would still have any tidal current in our favor as we paddle out of the harbor. As you can see from the table, the height of the tide changes dramatically from high to low (more than 10 ft./3 m).

and tidal current table for different points along the river's corridor where you may be paddling.

Topography and Tides

The shape of the land both above and below water can have a noticeable effect on how water moves through an area. Narrow, steeply pitched channels will funnel water and increase their rate of flow, while broad, shallow flats will spread the flow of water, slowing it down with the friction of it passing over land. You need to get used to reviewing your charts for areas where you would expect to see an increased flow of water. You don't have to be Inspector Clouseau to figure some of these out since their names are obvious clues: Flying Passage or The Gut. Look for

areas where there is a lot of water with only one place to go: river mouths or openings to basins or salt ponds. Check the chart for places where the flow is constricted: between two islands or where the river narrows.

You should also scope out the shape of the bottom in constricted areas. A large shelf of rock in the middle of one of these deep channels will create a sudden backup of water. Depending on the depth and rate of flow of the water, this might result in a terrifying boil at high tide and a classic whitewater drop at low tide.

Coastlines that are convoluted with narrow passages and fingers of land, or with numerous islands off their shores, will complicate the flow of water and make tidal current predictions difficult. Headlands and points of land must be given plenty of consideration.

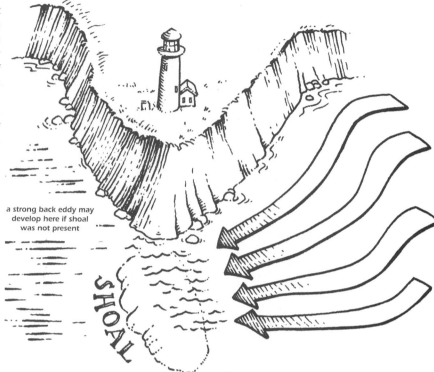

As strong tidal current flows encounter a headland, back eddies may build on the other side of the headland. If there are rocky shoals off this point of land, rough conditions can build as the flow of water crosses these shallow, rocky areas.

a strong back eddy may develop here if shoal was not present

SHOAL

Powerful back eddies may be created on one side of a headland; rough conditions may be created as water rounds a point of land and crosses any shoals off its shores.

A strong flood tide will often reverse a downriver current and create turbulence and standing waves. Smaller reversing falls are often favorite play spots for whitewater boaters; the larger reversing falls may draw huge crowds to view the raw power of these natural wonders.

Sea kayakers often face crossing a channel where tidal currents must be factored into trip plans. Typically a channel crossing will present paddlers with a tidal current at a right angle to the projected line of travel. The strength of this tidal current will usually be strongest in

Reversing falls occur when a strong tidal flow reverses the river's flow on a flood tide, creating standing waves. These conditions can range from playful to treacherous.

the middle of the channel where the water is deepest. Along the edges of the channel, the tidal current is usually weaker and eddies may actually develop if the topography lends a hand (see illustration). When crossing a channel, consider the strength of the tidal current and be sure that your crossing strategy minimizes the negative effects it can have on your progress and course. Tidal currents as well as wind and weather are discussed in more detail on pages 214–18.

Tidal current tables are published in a fashion similar to tide tables. There will be data given for reference stations and correc-

tion factors for other locations. Tidal current tables tell you the time and strengths of maximum flood and ebb currents, plus the times of slack water. The table will also note the direction of the flood and ebb tide. Tidal current tables are published in two volumes by the U.S. government or through commercial publications like *Eldridge Tide and Pilot Book*. You may also find smaller, local versions of tidal current tables available in your paddling area.

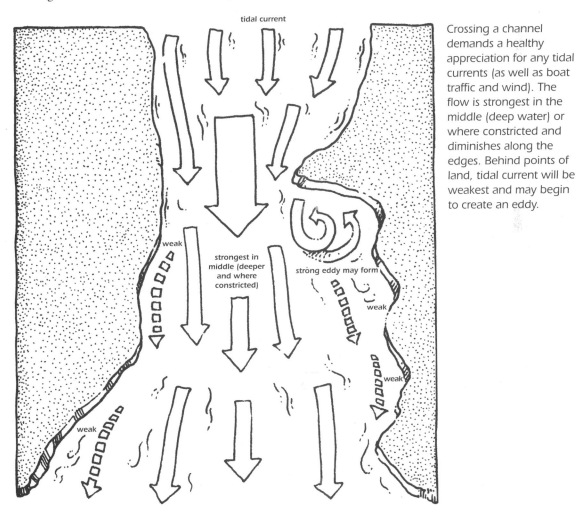

tidal current

weak

strongest in middle (deeper and where constricted)

strong eddy may form

weak

weak

weak

Crossing a channel demands a healthy appreciation for any tidal currents (as well as boat traffic and wind). The flow is strongest in the middle (deep water) or where constricted and diminishes along the edges. Behind points of land, tidal current will be weakest and may begin to create an eddy.

In addition to tidal current tables, there are tidal current charts published by the National Ocean Survey (NOS) for many areas. These charts show the direction and strength of the tidal currents at specific times in relation to the flood or ebb tide predicted at a reference station. The currents in a particular area are noted with arrows that show the direction and velocity. For kayakers, tidal current charts and diagrams give only a broad indication of conditions. Many times the nature of a tidal current only a short distance from a reference point can be dramatically different from the published data. Since we operate on

THE RACE, LONG ISLAND SOUND, 1983

F-Flood, Dir. 295° True E-Ebb, Dir. 100° True

DECEMBER

Day	Slack Water Time h.m.	Maximum Current Time h.m.	Vel. knots
1	0244	0539	3.6F
Th	0840	1203	4.3E
	1525	1816	3.4F
	2113		

A daily tidal current table shows the time and maximum velocity of the tidal current for each ebb and flood tide as well the time for slack water. The direction (true not magnetic) of the flood and ebb are also given. Daily tidal tables are normally published for areas with high boat traffic and/or significant tidal currents.

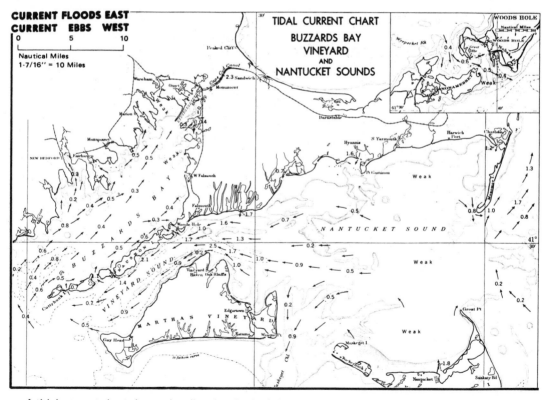

A tidal current chart shows the direction (set) of the current and its maximum velocity (in knots and at spring tide) at a particular time (in this example one hour after flood starts at Pollock Rip Channel). Note: directions are given as true, not magnetic.

A DANGEROUS SITUATION

The Kennebec River is a powerful flow of water that empties into the Gulf of Maine. On a pleasant summer's afternoon when you're lounging on the shore, it's tempting to put a boat in the water and drift with the tide. There's a wonderful beach just west of the river's mouth and several small, beautiful islands along this stretch of water. Seguin Island, with its picturesque lighthouse, sits only 2 miles (3 km) offshore. Yet several sea kayakers have had serious accidents, and one lost her life playing out just this scenario.

With the tide ebbing and a typical summer's onshore breeze blowing 15 to 20 knots by early afternoon, waves can steepen and shorten so that a kayaker cannot make headway and will struggle to remain upright. The bottom features at the river's mouth aggravate the problem, with a deep channel that funnels the water and increases the velocity of the tidal current and the presence of several treacherous shoals and bars. Once you're swept into this current, it's very difficult to make landfall until you're released from the grip of the river's power a mile or so offshore. In July, the water temperature is still a chilly 65°F (18°C) at best.

This scenario is not theoretical. It represents a real situation that can be predicted from an understanding of wind, waves, tidal currents, topography, and a healthy dollop of local knowledge.

such an intimate level with the water, these broad strokes of information may be only moderately useful. But combining the information shown on a tidal current chart along with local knowledge of your own and that gathered from other boaters will help you develop a thorough picture of what to expect in a given area at a particular time.

One of the best ways to get tidal current information is through local knowledge. Talk to other paddlers, people who fish in the area, and harbormasters if you have questions about paddling in an area unknown to you. Most of the popular paddling areas in North America have guidebooks with advice and descriptions of the paddling conditions you can expect.

Once you've scoped out where to expect strong tidal currents along your paddling route, you've got to factor in the wind direction in relation to these tidal currents. A strong wind opposing a swift tidal current can create standing waves that are steep and short. This situation can be disastrous for sea kayakers and should always be avoided. This is not uncommon; it could easily occur at the mouth of a large, powerful river during an ebbing tide with a strong onshore breeze (see sidebar).

WEATHER

Let's face it: weather can either make or break a kayak trip. We're at the mercy of its moods and its often fickle behavior. Even with an ear glued to a weather radio, I've been surprised by weather and could only minimize the effect of its passing. Though it may be tempting, don't throw up your hands and assume you can never be more than a passive participant. It's worth a try to learn how to predict the course of the weather and understand the signals you can observe from the cockpit of your boat. After all, some meteorologists are only right about half the time!

Weather is a fascinating study and a lifelong pursuit for the sea kayaker. If you haven't already, it's time to look skyward, sniff the breeze, and pay attention. Most folks who spend a lot of time outdoors develop an extra sense about weather. Developing this sensitivity takes years of experience and the willingness to systematically study cloud formations and light changes and relate them to the weather forecast and what actually happens out there.

First, study the clouds. Their formation and passing can give you a wealth of information about what weather is on the way. Don't just glance out the window on the morning you plan to paddle; get used to looking at clouds every day. This is a great chance to start a weather journal that notes your observation and then notes the actual weather. What did you see on Wednesday that might have been a clue to the actual weather on Friday? Jot down the cloud types and wind direction and estimated speed. Note your observations of how the air feels (fresh or stagnant), whether the morning grass was damp with dew, or whether your bum knee feels creakier than usual. Check weather maps online and then watch for the movement and behavior of clouds associated with what you see on the maps.

Pay particular attention to weather maps and forecasts several days before your paddling trip. Note any developing weather systems that move into your region and begin to develop forecasts for your trip dates. Once you're actually under way, you'll be monitoring a very small slice of the weather, only a mile or two in any direction. No radio broadcast or weather map will pinpoint this area for you. You'll need to depend on your own observations and understanding of the weather.

Clouds

Winds and temperatures can be felt, but only clouds are the visible signposts of weather. They're beautiful to observe in their own right, but it's their usefulness as weather indicators that makes them important to kayakers.

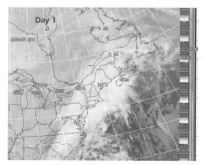 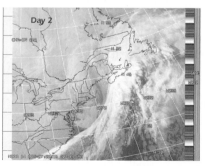

Review satellite weather images to spot developing patterns in the weather several days before your trip departure. The satellite images shown here represent two consecutive days of a weather front crossing New England in December.

WEATHER SAYINGS THAT JUST MIGHT HELP

One of the reasons that weather proverbs have survived the centuries is that many are more successful at predicting the weather than are local meteorologists! A proverb's scope might be limited, but its words are often wise and easy to remember. Here are some of my favorites.

- *"Red sky at morning, sailor take warning; red sky at night, sailor's delight."* When you see a red sunset, you're observing the sun's rays through suspended dust particles. If the suspended dust is dry, the sunset will appear red; if it's wet, the sunset will appear as a yellow or gray orb that is seen through the haze. Since most weather patterns move from west to east (especially storm systems), you're looking at tomorrow's weather. So a red sky at sunset predicts fair, dry conditions for the following day. A red sunrise, on the other hand, is lighting up the cirrus or cirrostratus clouds that are moving into an area. These clouds are the beginning of a weather pattern leading to thicker and lower clouds that could well turn wet over the course of the day, or at best, remain unsettled.

- *"When a halo rings the moon and sun, the rain will come upon the run."* There are many proverbs that use the presence of a halo around the moon or sun to predict the weather. When you observe a halo, you're seeing the development of clouds at higher altitudes. These cirrus and cirrostratus clouds are part of the same weather pattern described above and predict wet or unsettled weather within twenty-four hours.

- *"Wind that swings around the sun, and winds that bring the rain are one; winds that swing against the sun, keep the rainstorm on the run."* If the wind is moving from east to west, like the sun moves, skies will usually be clear. These veering winds (clockwise) often follow a cold front as they clear the air and bring a rise in barometric pressure. If the wind moves opposite the sun's path, or from west to east, wet or unsettled weather is generally in the offing. These backing (counterclockwise) winds usually are part of a warm front and a gradually falling barometer. Said another way, *"A backing wind says storms are nigh; a veering wind will clear the sky."*

When you observe conditions mentioned in a weather proverb, remember to make note of the weather that followed. It's the only way to know if you should put your faith in these old sayings.

Earth's lower atmosphere is in constant flux; the air is warming and cooling, rising and falling, and being set into general patterns by the earth's rotational direction. This air contains moisture that has evaporated from the oceans, lakes, and rivers. Warm, moist air rises and then begins to expand and eventually cool. When the relative humidity of this cooling air reaches 100 percent, moisture condenses into visible form as clouds. Clouds can be described by their altitude and general shape and color.

You'll notice a logic to the naming of clouds.

Cirrus clouds are high altitude with a wispy, thin appearance. The sun and moon may shine through these or at least create halos. Cirrus clouds often predict a change in weather a day or more away.

Cumulus clouds are puffy, dense, and billowing. They often tower and almost always block the sun when they pass. If they hang out at the middle altitudes, they pick up the prefix *alto*; if they thicken into rounded masses or roll at lower altitudes, they carry a *strato* prefix.

Stratus clouds are thick and usually solid sheets of dense clouds. This cloud sheet may appear at high altitudes (cirrostratus), middles altitudes (altostratus), and at lower altitudes as pure stratus clouds or combined as strato-

Cumulus clouds

cumulus or nimbostratus. The lower the altitude, the thicker and denser their appearance.

Nimbus clouds are the brewing, stormy clouds that are dark with ragged lower edges. They look like clouds ready to pick a fight. When they form thick layers as nimbostratus clouds, they'll block the sun and you'll often see rain falling from their lower reaches. *Cumulonimbus clouds* are the well-known anvil shapes of an approaching thunderhead with nimbus clouds forming the rolling edge.

Cirrus clouds

Stratus clouds

Cumulonimbus clouds

As you can see, cloud names swap prefixes and altitudes to fit their purpose. Becoming familiar with these cloud names will help you better understand weather forecasts. More important, observing the passage of different cloud types will help you develop your own forecasts.

In general, higher-altitude clouds (cirrus) signal weather development a day or so away. Their wispy streaks point to turbulence aloft and changing conditions. If the clouds thicken and appear lower over time, they carry more moisture and a chance of wet weather. If the cirrus clouds dissipate into blue skies, better weather is usually in the offing. If low, ragged clouds begin forming, you can expect unsettled conditions that could well turn nasty. Puffy white altocumulus clouds that are well separated are generally part of a pleasant weather pattern.

If you observe a cumulonimbus cloud heading your way, get off the water immediately since high winds and possibly lightning will accompany these thunderheads. The top of a cumulonimbus cloud will flatten and will spread into a plume, which gives this cloud its anvil shape. The plume will point in the wind's direction, and the lower edge of this cloud may roll ominously as the cloud moves rapidly forward. For more on lightning, see pages 193–94.

Weather Fronts

While clouds are the messengers of weather, it's the air masses and the boundaries, or fronts, between these air masses that actually create the conditions we experience. An air mass is a large volume of air (it may cover several hundred thousand square miles) where conditions of moisture and temperature are essentially the same in all directions. These air masses assume the basic characteristics of the surface beneath them (for example, polar, maritime, or continental). These air masses begin their dance with one another and bring their different styles of weather. When they interact, these fronts bring a change in weather, usually for the worst. Fronts may be characterized as warm, cold, stationary, or occluded.

Warm fronts occur when warm, moist air catches up to colder air and actually rides up over it. It can do this because warm air is lighter and can rise above colder, denser air. Warm fronts move more slowly than cold fronts, so their weather tends to stick around a bit longer until they're eventually overtaken by another cold front. Warm fronts generally bring low clouds and rain, but in moderation and over a longer period. The approach of a warm front is signaled by a slowly falling barometer as clouds build up, and it begins to drizzle and then rain. After a warm front passes, the barometer will gradually rise as cumulus clouds move in and the temperature rises, unless it was sent on its way by a strong cold front.

Cold fronts, which move more rapidly, will push under a warm air mass and force it upward. If it's a strong cold front, there may be a decisive shift in the weather with its passing. Cold fronts have the potential to do great harm to sea kayakers. They can create a squall line along their boundary with high winds and turbulent conditions. Squall lines will appear as a low wall of threatening clouds that approach swiftly. Heavy, though brief, rainfall may occur, so dense that visibility will be marginal. Or, the bottom of an advancing cold front may wedge underneath the warm air ahead of it. The warm, moist air will rapidly rise into towering cumulus clouds with a nimbostratus base. These thunderheads

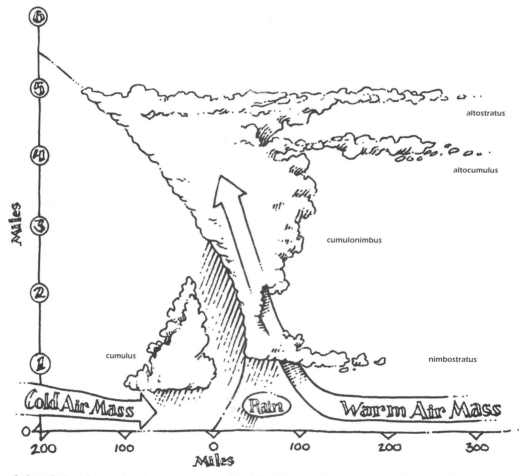

A thunderhead may develop as warm, moist air is driven up by an approaching cold front. Towering cumulus clouds form, and the front edge may appear as a rolling, ragged line of nimbostratus clouds.

can be exceptionally violent. The passing of either a squall line or a thunderhead is most impressive and will make you glad you're not on exposed waters where the winds from their passing can easily capsize a kayaker.

As the cold front approaches, you may detect a wind shift to the south and then southwest. This veering wind (clockwise) will be accompanied by a falling barometer (often rapid if the front is strong) as clouds lower and rain begins to fall. The wind will continue to veer and come from the west and then northwest as the front passes. After the cold front passes, these veering winds will clear the skies and the temperature will drop as winds come from the north and even northeast. While the passage of a cold front brings dry, clear weather, the accompanying winds may be quite strong.

A stationary front is what it sounds like— little or no forward movement as two air masses stall. The conditions will usually be rainy with low clouds like those of a warm front. An occluded front creates a low-pressure area with counterclockwise winds when a cold front overtakes and lifts a warm air mass off the ground. The cold front forms a wedge keeping the warmer air above it and may unsettle conditions until the stronger air mass prevails or another front moves in.

Storms

We've talked about how weather is created along the boundaries, or fronts, of cold and warm air masses. Storm systems are created the same way but are longer lived as areas of low pressure and counterclockwise rotation of winds occur that contain both cold and warm fronts. The most common storm systems across the United States develop and move eastward to north of east. Storms often take a day or more to develop and then several days to dissipate.

A thunderstorm is just an intense storm of short duration and is often part of a larger storm system's cold front. Thunderstorms are more common in summer months during late afternoons or early evening hours. The land must heat up over the course of the day to create a strong updraft of warm air laden with water vapor that reaches high altitude. If you see cumulus clouds start to build vertically, keep a close eye out, especially if there is an approaching cold front.

Lightning

Lightning occurs during a thunderstorm because there is a buildup of electrical charges within the towering cumulus cloud that may discharge within the cloud itself or between the cloud and the ground (the earth is normally negatively charged). Thunder is what we hear when the heat energy that a lightning strike releases creates sound waves. Lightning is extremely dangerous, especially for those on the water.

At the first hint of lightning, or thunder, get off the water. Determine if the storm is moving your way and try to time the difference (in seconds) between when you see the lightning and when you hear the thunder. If you're able to time the difference accurately, multiply this number of seconds by 0.2 (or divide by 5), which will give your approximate distance from the storm in statute miles. It may be difficult to pair the two

WHAT TO DO ABOUT LIGHTNING

Once you get off the water, try to look for low-lying areas with brushy growth and trees that are not the tallest in the area. Avoid open spaces like meadows or the high, bare ground of a headland bluff. Spread the group out (lightning can "splash" from its original target), and use your life vests as ground pads. Crouch low in a squat with your feet close together on your life vest and be sure any metal objects (paddle shafts, radios, and knives) are not close by. When you crouch on your life vest, keep both feet flat and avoid using your hands on the ground to balance yourself. You do not want to set up a path that allows lightning to travel across your body (especially the upper body).

occurrences and to time these accurately. Remember, too, that thunderheads have the potential to move very quickly.

Fog

Fog is simply a cloud that lies close to the land or water. As with any cloud, it's made up of tiny water droplets that are suspended. In this case, it obscures your view. You can feel and even see the amount of water suspended in fog; if you wear glasses, you'll get a double dose of poor visibility as these drops cling to your lenses. Foggy conditions occur when air with a lot of water vapor present begins to cool, condensing as tiny droplets.

Paddling in fog requires a keen eye and ear to your surroundings. Avoid crossings, exposed stretches of water, and high boat traffic areas if at all possible.

PADDLING IN FOG

Paddling in fog can humble the best of navigators and rattle the most confident among us. Fog is eerily stealthy as it creeps around to obscure your landmarks and even muffle nearby sounds. You are often left with only your chart and compass as you strain to see ahead and determine exactly where you might be.

If you paddle in areas where fog is prevalent, get used to noting your location throughout the day and mentally recording what is to each side and behind you every few minutes. It's easy to become disoriented as the fog rolls in. If you do, try to maintain your position by pointing into any wind (or tidal current if that's stronger), and sit still as you try to figure out your exact location. If you can see any land, consider heading toward it to ground out or land immediately. It's easier to think through things (not to mention maintain position) with the reassuring solidity of land beneath your hull.

Listen for sounds such as water lapping against rocks on a nearby shore, or traffic along a shoreline road. Watch the movement of the water. Can you observe any tidal current? Which way is it running? Are there any noteworthy bottom features that correspond to your chart? Gather as many pieces of the puzzle as you can using your observations, chart, compass, and tide table until you gain a better picture of your location.

When you navigate in the fog, be cautious. If you must make a crossing, do so by overcorrecting (or undercorrecting in certain conditions) for tidal current so any shoreline you hit is clearly above or below your intended point. In this way, you'll know which way to turn once you've crossed the channel. Always have your foghorn and whistle handy to signal your location if another vessel approaches your position. Keep an ear cocked for sounds of other vessels as you paddle.

This occurs next to the surface of the earth (land or water) that must be cooler than the damp air above it. As the damp air passes over a cooler surface, it begins to cool as do the successive layers above the surface.

Fog requires the presence of saturated air, which is simply air that cannot hold more water at that given temperature. There is more than one mechanism for creating saturated air. Unsaturated air may be cooled until the water vapor it contains is maximized, or unsaturated air may pass over wet areas (ocean, rivers, lakes) and pick up water vapor until it becomes saturated.

The fog that usually bothers kayakers most is the advection fog created in coastal areas. This type of fog is formed when warm, moist air is blown landward across the cold coastal waters. This is common on both the Pacific coast and the north Atlantic coast as well as larger inland lakes. This fog can produce a thick blanket that doesn't dissipate quickly. It takes a wind shift or increase in the wind's velocity to break up this fog and move it on its way.

You may also experience radiation fog, which is produced when cooler air drains into depressions like river valleys and low-

Wispy trails of sea smoke rise as cold air encounters warmer water. This phenomenon is common during an early cold snap in many paddling areas.

One final type of fog that you may experience as a sea kayaker is steam fog, or sea smoke. This form of fog occurs when cold air passes over warm water, which supplies the heat and water vapor that feeds the fog. This is common during autumn and winter and can be quite beautiful as wispy trails of fog rise from the water's surface. These conditions can be dense enough to affect visibility.

Knowing what conditions create fog can help you plan your strategy for dealing with it. In some popular paddling areas like the coasts of Maine and Washington, fog is a common occurrence during the height of the paddling season. You need solid navigational skills; you also need to carry sound signaling devices and monitor your VHF when you paddle in these conditions.

Fog can obscure sounds and make placing the sound of a motor very difficult; it could be an approaching motorboat or the sound from a road a few miles away. Becoming disoriented is very easy in fog when landmarks disappear, and even reading the movement of water becomes difficult. Although foggy conditions can occur during calm, peaceful paddling conditions, the anxiety of straining to listen for nearby vessels and keeping your eyes peeled for landmarks can be unsettling. You might do best to hug a shoreline or circumnavigate an island and save any crossings or exposed paddling for another day.

lands around lakes. The lake or river continues to feed water vapor to the cause as the air condenses over the area when it cools at night. Radiation fog is a more localized event than advection fog and usually burns off as the morning sun gains strength.

8

Finding Your Way:
Kayak Navigation

Navigating a kayak is both similar to and different from navigating other vessels. We use many of the same tools, and we depend on our observations and measurements of speed, distance, and time. But moving a 17-foot (5.2 m) boat that draws just a few inches of water is quite different from putting a large container vessel where you want it.

Kayakers rarely navigate far offshore on open seas. Instead, we're found along coastlines and near coastal islands where landmarks and other boat traffic abound. Our task is to pick safe routes from one place to another and be sure we're seen by other boaters. Our dangers are local and can almost always be avoided with thorough planning and a cautious regard for wind and weather. When under way, our navigational tools are simple: a chart, compass, and keen eyes.

CHARTS AND TOOLS

A chart is a map that emphasizes the characteristics of bodies of water and the land nearby. In contrast to a topographical map that features contour lines and vegetation, a chart shows water depths and the makeup of the bottom. Charts include the position and characteristics of aids to navigation (buoys, lights, and beacons, for example), as well as notable artificial features on land if they relate to boating traffic. The charts kayakers depend on the most are prepared by the National Ocean Service (NOS) of the National Oceanic and Atmospheric Administration (NOAA). Charts of Canadian waters are prepared by the Canadian Hydrographic Service and published by the Canadian Chart Distribution Office. Charts of other countries may be available from the U.S. National Imagery and Mapping Agency (NIMA).

Charts are available in a variety of scales. Most kayakers prefer charts of no less than a 1:40,000 scale, since we cover only a few miles per day and need the greater details provided on large-scale charts. The larger the scale, the smaller the area covered. A 1:40,000-scale chart means that every unit of measure on the chart (say, an inch or a

A nautical chart contains a wealth of information for the kayaker.

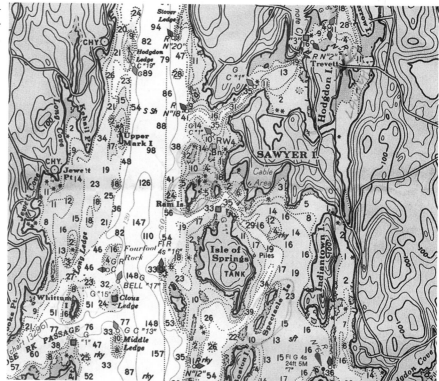

thumbnail) translates into 40,000 of those same units (inches or thumbnails) out on the water. Thus, a 1:80,000-scale chart is a smaller scale (the fraction ⅟₈₀,₀₀₀ is a smaller number than ⅟₄₀,₀₀₀) and covers a larger area.

The chart number and name are prominently displayed in the upper left corner of the chart. Just below this is the scale of the chart, the unit of measure for soundings, tidal datum, and other useful (and sometimes extraneous) information about the chart or navigation. Charts show longitude (along the top and bottom borders) and latitude (along the side borders) scales and distance scales (usually in both nautical miles and yards).

You can also find the chart's edition and most recent date of revision in the lower left corner of the chart. If your trip planning strategy depends heavily on the placement and identification of aids to navigation, it's wise to buy the most recent edition and check the *Notices to Mariners* and *Local Notices to Mariners* for any significant changes in this information. Published by the NOS, these notices are available from a retail sales agent or online (see the Resources chapter).

Charts will last for years if you take reasonable care of them. You're bound to fold them, and they often get soggy inside the chartcase. Spread them out to dry and try

SHOPPING FOR CHARTS

If you're looking for charts of your area, start by contacting a local paddlesports shop or outfitter. These folks not only have charts for sale but are usually able to offer advice and other product recommendations that might be of interest. If you're planning a trip outside your region or are unable to find a local outfitter or marine chandlery that sells charts, a bit of online cruising can provide access to a variety of chart and map products.

The NOAA website (www.noaa.gov) has links to chart information, or you can go directly to

- www.nauticalcharts.noaa.gov to view and order charts online or view a list of retail sales agents throughout the United States
- www.oceanservice.noaa.gov, a techier and more complete map and chart resource created through NOAA

Commercial sites abound, but two of the best are www.maptech.com and www.nauticalchartson line.com. Both offer a wide selection of updated charts and tables.

to keep the folds from permanently marring the information. Charts are best stored perfectly flat, but since they require so much room, rolling them loosely is the next best solution. Consider waterproofing your charts by coating them with a compound such as MapSeal. Or, purchase waterproof charts (available for most areas), though they're more expensive than regular NOAA charts. You may want to copy chart sections with your favorite paddling routes and laminate them to save your original chart from all the wear and tear.

Chart No. 1, which was formerly published by NIMA, is not a chart but a reference for all chart symbols, colors, and abbreviations used on nautical charts. It is a useful addition to any kayaker's library.

Also consider buying some basic navigational tools. Although you'll rarely pack

Parallel rulers can be used at home during trip planning. Use parallel rulers when plotting directions from the chart or for working with vectors (pages 218–21). Once under way, you'll have to use the edge of your hand to approximate the job of your parallel rulers.

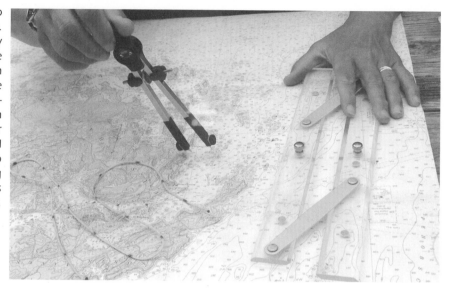

Dividers are used to determine distances. Since kayakers rarely travel in a straight line for very long, you can lock in a short measure of distance (for example, 0.5 nm) and then walk this along your route to get the overall distance. You can also use a piece of string with these increments marked on it.

these tools along on a trip, they're useful when plotting and measuring at home. Parallel rulers are two rulers hinged together that allow you to "walk" a straight edge across the chart while maintaining a particular orientation. This is invaluable for plotting directions from the chart (see photo on page 199).

Dividers allow you to measure distances by adjusting their length to stretch from one point to another or by locking in a small unit of distance like a half mile that can be "walked" along your route as you count the overall distance covered. When measuring distances on the chart, you can use the scales provided or use the latitude scale, with each minute of latitude equaling 1 nautical mile. A handy addition to any navigation kit is a piece of string with half-mile increments marked in ink. Be sure these marks match the scale on the chart you're using. This marked string is especially useful for determining mileage over winding or meandering routes.

LATITUDE AND LONGITUDE

Imagine the globe with a grid laid over its surface, each line representing a slice to the core. It would allow you to give an address of a location as the intersection of these lines; one line running along an axis between the north and south poles, and the other line running around the globe and parallel to the equator. Latitude tells you how far north or south you are from the equator. Longitude tells you how far east or west you are (up to 180 degrees either way) of the Greenwich meridian, the official zero-degree longitude line that intersects Greenwich, England. Latitude and longitude are given in degrees and minutes. One degree equals 60 minutes, and 1 minute equals 60 seconds. For example, a favorite paddling spot might be latitude 44°1′ North and longitude 69°4′ West. This is an exact location that can be located on a chart, plugged into a GPS (global position-

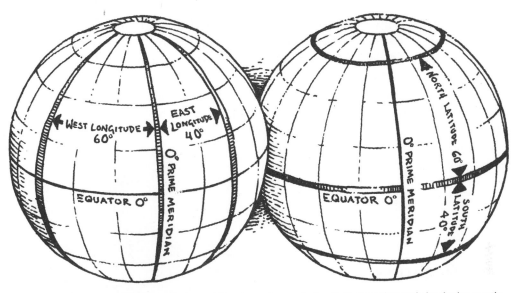

Left: Longitude lines (also called *meridians*) are large circles that pass through both the north and south poles. **Right:** Latitude lines (also called *parallels of latitude*) are smaller circles that are parallel to the plane of the equator.

ing system) receiver, or radioed to the coast guard in the event of an emergency.

A latitude scale can also be used as a measure of distance. The distance between two consecutive lines of latitude is equal anywhere on earth (for all practical purposes). One degree of latitude is 60 nautical miles; 1 minute of latitude is 1 nautical mile. A nautical mile is 6,076.12 feet and is pegged by international standards at 1,852 meters. In actuality, a geographical mile is 6,087.2 feet and is defined as the distance you must travel north or south from the equator to change your latitude by 1 minute. For our purposes, nautical miles work just fine. Notice that a nautical mile is slightly longer than a statute mile, which is commonly used on land and is equal to 5,280 feet (1,610.4 m). The latitude scale along the borders of a chart for measuring distance is useful. Most charts have

5-minute latitude lines drawn across their surface that may also provide a quick reference for distance.

Although you can use latitude lines for measuring distances, you cannot do the same for longitude lines. This is because longitude lines converge at the poles, and the distance between any two longitude lines changes as you move north or south of the equator. The higher the latitude, the greater the difference between 1 minute of longitude and 1 nautical mile. You can see this when reviewing different charts. The 5-minute grids are nearly square at low latitudes close to the equator, but become narrow rectangles at higher latitudes like the coast of Alaska.

Other than using the latitude scale for measuring distance, kayakers rarely make use of latitude-longitude readings. Instead, we use landmarks, buoys, and compass directions to and from a variety of locations that are easily noted on a chart. If you use a GPS unit, you might use latitude-longitude readings more often since a GPS receiver spits them out like ticker tape while under way. To take latitude-longitude readings from the chart requires a straightedge that can reach from the middle of the chart to the side and either the top or the bottom of the chart. As you can imagine, gathering these readings while under way is rarely feasible for kayakers.

AIDS TO NAVIGATION

Aids to navigation are all the objects used to determine your location or to assist in choosing a safe course along some waterway. These aids include buoys, beacons, fog signals, light signals, radio beacons, and even electronic systems like loran. The easiest way for a kayaker to determine a position on open water is to sight a buoy and then find that buoy on the chart. It's like standing under a road sign at an intersection. We'll discuss other ways to determine position, but making use of available aids to navigation is tremendously valuable.

Buoys and Beacons

Buoys float in the water and are anchored to the bottom, and they're distinguished by their color, shape, number, and presence of any light or sound signals. Buoys within a given paddling area will have unique combinations of these characteristics, and there is a system to their placement in the water

that can be determined from their color and number. More than twenty-five thousand buoys are maintained in U.S. waters alone.

Buoys may be cylindrical (called *cans*) or a cylinder topped with a cone (called *nuns*). These two shapes are easy to distinguish

Chart Symbol
GC "5A"

RN "2"

Buoys float in the water and are anchored to the bottom. These aids to navigation are distinguished by their color, shape, number, and the presence of any light or sound signals. **Top:** Green can buoys are cylindrical and always bear odd numbers. This one is marked on the chart as GC "5A." **Bottom:** Red nun buoys are conical and always bear even numbers. This one is marked on the chart as RN "2."

even when backlit and when colors cannot be discerned. Nuns are red and cans are green, though there are buoys that use horizontal or vertical striping of two colors to mark channel junctions and safe-water approaches, respectively. Cans, which always bear odd numbers, mark the left (port) side of a channel leading in from seaward; nun buoys are even-numbered and mark the right (starboard) side of a channel leading in from seaward (remember the saying, "red-right-returning"). On all buoys, numbers *decrease* as you head *seaward* (i.e., higher numbers are closer to harbor).

Buoys are clearly marked on charts as diamond shapes of either green or magenta and noted as "RN" for red nun or "GC" for green can. A buoy's number is printed in quotation marks to distinguish it from the numbers used for soundings. If the buoy also has a sound signal, this will be noted on the chart and the characteristics given. For example, a buoy may be marked as RN "2" bell or RN "8" whistle. If the buoy has light characteristics, the chart shows it with a magenta dot at its base, regardless of the actual light characteristics (see the illustration on page 205). Both nuns and cans can carry sound signals, light signals, or both.

Sometimes a buoy is designated by a number and letter or letters. This is often done if the buoy marks a well-known navigation hazard. For example, buoy "4HL" marks "Halibut Ledge," which sits at the edge of a channel used by many boaters. In general, the greater the marquee value of a buoy, the more it's trying to get your attention. So a large buoy with sound and light signals might be used to mark a hazard in a deep-water channel that is a thoroughfare for boats of all sizes. A word of warning: buoys can shift position as storms or strong tidal currents drag them about, and the U.S. Coast Guard may change the position or number of a buoy. You can find out these things by checking *Local Notices to Mariners* before starting your trip and monitoring announcements from the U.S. Coast Guard on channel 16 on a VHF radio while under way.

Day beacons are markers affixed to rocks, ledges, or structures onshore or in shallow water. They typically mark hazards and the edges of channels, and their system of identification corresponds to that used for buoys. Triangular day beacons are red, bordered by red reflective material, and use even num-

Chart Symbol

RG "46B"

Day beacons are markers affixed to rocks, ledges, or structures onshore or in shallow water. Their identification system corresponds to that of buoys.

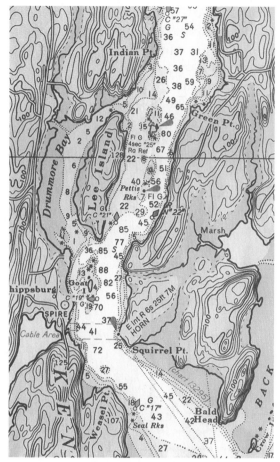

This section of a chart shows the many buoys marking a waterway. The IALA-B system of buoyage used in North America uses red buoys to starboard (to the right) when entering from seaward. Buoy numbers increase when moving from seaward.

bers; square day beacons are green, bordered by green reflective material, and use odd numbers. Day beacons may also carry lights and may use horizontal or vertical striping similar to can and nun buoys.

The United States adheres to the IALA (International Association of Lighthouse Authorities) B system of buoyage, as does the rest of North America, South America, Japan,

Korea, and the Philippines. This system uses red to starboard (right) when entering from seaward. The remainder of the world uses the A system, which uses red to port (left) when entering from seaward. Other buoyage systems may be used on inland waters, the Intracoastal Waterway (ICW), private moorings, and other special circumstances.

Light Characteristics

Lighthouses have long marked landfall for ships on the high seas, a welcome sight beaming from prominent ground. Today, buoys and beacons may carry light signals to mark hazards or channel entries as well. These lights have different characteristics so that they can be easily distinguished at night or in low-visibility conditions. The U.S. Coast Guard publishes several volumes of *Light Lists*, which describe all lighted aids to navigation.

Lights that are affixed to land or structures are shown as a magenta exclamation point on a chart. Thus, an active lighthouse is always noted in this manner, but not all magenta exclamation points note lighthouses. Some are simply lights affixed to small structures of granite or wood and may be disappointing to those hoping to see a traditional lighthouse (occasionally, a "LtHo" notation will be used).

The characteristics of the light are noted alongside the symbol in an abbreviated notation that's easy to read once you get the hang of it. This notation also includes the height of the light above mean higher high water, and the light's nominal range, which is the distance the light can be seen in clear weather and is an indication of its intensity. Your perspective from the seat of your kayak

Light Phase Characteristics

Light Pattern	Abbreviations and Meanings		
	Lights That Don't Change Color	Variations	Lights That Show Color Phase Description
	F. = Fixed	Alt. = Alternating	a continuous steady light
	F. Fl. = Fixed and flashing	Alt. F. Fl. = Alternating fixed and flashing	a fixed light varied at regular intervals by a flash of greater brilliance
	F. Gp. Fl. = Fixed and group and flashing	Alt. F. Gp. Fl. = Alternating fixed and group flashing	a fixed light varied at regular intervals by groups of 2 or more flashes of greater brilliance
	Fl. = Flashing	Alt. Fl. = Alternating flashing	showing a single flash at regular intervals, the duration of light always being less than the duration of darkness
	Gp. Fl. = Group flashing	Alt. Gp. Fl. = Alternating group flashing	showing at regular intervals groups of 2 or more flashes
	Gp. Fl. (1 + 2) = Composite group flashing	—	light flashes are combined in alternate groups of different numbers
	E. Int. = Equal interval	—	light with all durations of light and darkness equal
	Occ. = Occulting	Alt. Occ. = Alternating occulting	a light totally eclipsed at regular intervals, the duration of light always greater than the duration of darkness
	Gp. Occ. = Group occulting	—	a light with a group of 2 or more eclipses at regular intervals
	Gp. Occ. (2 + 3) = Composite group occulting	—	a light in which the occultations are combined in alternate groups of different numbers

Lights on navigation aids can be identified by their color and light rhythm. Varying the light and dark intervals produces distinctive patterns that may identify a particular light. One full cycle of changes is the light's period.

is somewhat limited, so you may not be able to see a light even under clear visibility at the nominal range stated on the chart. If you're paddling at night and will need to rely on particular lights and their range to help determine your location, it's best to adjust this range to take the earth's curvature and the height of your eye level into account, as well as the atmospheric visibility at the time. This can be calculated from various formulas and information provided by the *Light Lists*. Determining this is a rare exercise for most kayakers.

The illustration on page 205 shows common light characteristics and how they're noted on charts. It can be fun to pick out the different lights from your perch on an island shore at night, and eminently practical to use them when under way.

PLOTTING YOUR COURSE

Before you begin any trip, lay out your general course and note bailout points and backup plans (see chapter 9 for more discussion on this). Even if you plan to meander and explore whatever looks interesting along the way, lay out your general course and make note of directions and distances between points.

Examine the chart that covers your planned paddling area, marking the launching and landing sites you might use. Note other spots that might serve as rest stops or a place to picnic. Use your dividers to determine the distances between each of these locations and record these on an index card, waterproof notepad, or on the face of your

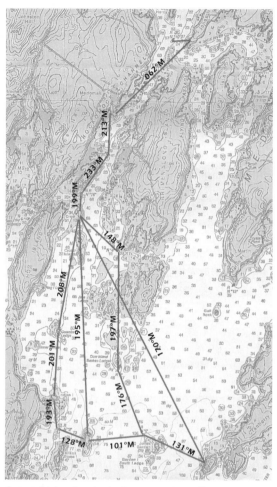

A good trip plan includes several contingency plans as well as primary routes. Mileage for each leg should also be noted and tide table information included.

chartcase in grease pencil. Knowing these distances will help you plan each leg of your trip and keep track of things when under way. Build in plenty of rest stops, even if you don't get out of your boat, and plan each leg of the trip for under an hour. After all, you can always choose to blow by a proposed stop, which is easier than trying to find a place to

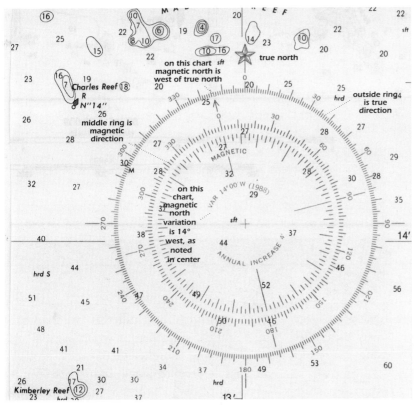

The compass rose provides both true and magnetic directions. The variation is noted in the center of the compass rose and can change across a single chart. Kayakers typically use magnetic directions because these correspond to their compass readings. The middle ring of the compass rose shows the magnetic directions.

duck into while under way. Longer crossings may require a long leg without a break, so note spots to pull into before and after the crossing.

Now that you have a general plan and know the distances to and from a variety of stops and checkpoints along the way, work out the directions to and from these same points. You'll need a set of parallel rulers or a course plotter (courser) for determining bearings, which are directions to and from different objects or landmarks. You can determine a variety of bearings before setting out that will help keep you oriented while under way. Record these magnetic bearings along with the distance between points

before your trip. It's far easier to fall back on this initial planning if visibility is reduced or you're simply tired or confused. While under way, take additional bearings and make note of your position and your speed of travel.

To take a bearing from your chart, you'll need to use the compass rose. Compass roses are the purple circles scattered across a chart that provide three scales for determining compass directions. The outer circle is oriented with north at the top of the chart and gives "true" directions that have not been corrected for variation. Variation is the difference between true north and magnetic north. The variation for a given area is at the center of the compass rose and may even vary

TRUE VERSUS MAGNETIC

It'd be much simpler if the magnetic fields of the earth flowed precisely north to a pinpoint location at the North Pole (along with Santa and the elves). But they don't. Instead, earth's magnetic fields flow along a line that runs roughly through northern Florida and Ohio to the magnetic north pole, which lies somewhere northwest of Baffin Island. Even this location is a slippery one, shifting slightly every year. If you used a compass at a position along this line, true north and magnetic north would be the same. Unfortunately, most of the waters that we paddle lie to the east or the west of this line. So we may paddle toward a point at the top of our chart but read our magnetic bearing by as much as 20 degrees west or east of true north, or 000 degrees.

There's no need to get too hung up on this discrepancy, since the corrections have been provided for you in the middle ring of the compass rose. But, like losing your faith in Santa Claus, it's best to be let down gently.

slightly from one compass rose to the next on the same chart. The change in variation over time is also given, though it's insignificant for our purposes (unless you're using a very old chart).

Since kayakers use their compasses while under way and rarely travel such long distances that they see significant changes in the variation over the course of a trip, we use the middle ring of the compass rose, which gives directions as magnetic bearings. When you use the middle ring of the compass rose, you won't have to correct for variation since this has been done and should correspond to what your compass reads when under way. The inner ring on the compass rose is also oriented magnetically and harks back to the days when compass directions were given as points instead of degrees. These compass points mark the cardinal (for example, north) and intercardinal (for example, north by east) directions and points in between. Each compass point is 11.25 degrees, with a total of 32 points (this gives 360 degrees).

Look at the first leg of your planned trip (let's be original and call this from point A to point B), and position your parallel rulers along that straight line of travel. Now, by alternately pressing and swinging the straight edges of the parallel rules over to the compass rose, you'll be able to see the actual magnetic bearing you'll need to paddle to get from point A to point B. Be sure to keep the parallel rulers oriented parallel with your line of travel, and then walk the straightedge over to the center of the compass rose and mark the position on the middle ring. This position on the compass rose is read in degrees and is your magnetic bearing. Check that you've read from the middle ring and in the direction of your travel, not in the opposite direction.

At first you'll feel clumsy with the parallel rulers, but you'll be comfortable walking them around a chart after a few practice sessions. It helps to have the chart spread on a flat surface and held firmly in place.

Whenever you determine a bearing, whether from a chart or while under way, be sure it passes the commonsense test. Look at the general direction of your bearing—is it north, south, northwest, southeast, or what? Now, does the number you've read as your bearing fall in that general direction? If you're traveling in a northwest direction, your bearing better fall somewhere between 270 degrees (west) and 360 degrees (north). It's easy to accidentally read a bearing in the opposite direction when the ruler runs across both sides of the compass rose or mark an edge of the ruler that doesn't pass through the center of the compass rose.

Get used to giving and recording bearings as three numbers, even if the first one or two are zeroes. When you relay a bearing to a paddling partner, say all three numbers and then "magnetic." If you yell to your paddling partner that a lighthouse has a bearing of "28," she might wonder if she missed a "1," "2," or "3" in front of the "28" or even a "-ty" at the end. Get in the habit of saying "zero"

Placed on a chart, a courser (course plotter) can be aligned along the north–south axis (true or magnetic). In this way you can take bearings and record directions without using parallel rulers.

for "0," not "oh." Since you're reading your bearings from a deck compass and the middle ring of a compass rose, they're magnetic and should be distinguished as such. If you had to

DOING A ONE-EIGHTY

When it's time to return home or backtrack along some route, your bearing is easy to determine. This return, or back, bearing is simply different from your original bearing by 180 degrees. Let's say you were paddling from your launch site toward your island destination at a bearing of 068 degrees magnetic. When it's time to return, you'd calculate your back bearing as 248 degrees magnetic, or 068 plus 180. If you look on the compass rose, you can see that these two bearings run in exactly opposite directions from each other.

When a bearing is greater than 180 degrees, simply subtract 180 degrees from it to get your back bearing. For example, if your original bearing is 312 degrees magnetic, subtract 180 degrees from it. This will give you a back bearing of 132 degrees magnetic.

Knowing the actual return bearing is useful, but it's also handy to know what things look like in that direction. As you paddle, you should look regularly over your shoulder to capture a visual reminder of how things look if you need to turn around. Keep an eye out for landmarks behind you that might come in handy when you head home or need to backtrack in fog.

RELATIVE BEARINGS

Sometimes it's helpful to view the world in relation to your kayak. Rather than note a magnetic bearing to an object, you could note at what angle that object sat off your bow. Imagine your bow as always being the zero mark, or 000 degrees. If a buoy sat directly off your starboard beam, it would have a relative bearing of 090 degrees. That bearing is only in relation to your position and direction and can always be found by using the equation

$$\text{actual bearing} - \text{kayak's heading} = \text{relative bearing}$$

Of course you can also use this equation to find any one of the factors that is unknown.

Relative bearings can be useful when you want to paddle a compass course and check off landmarks or navigational aids that you pass. Since you don't necessarily want to aim directly for one of these marks (which would be the actual bearing), you can note the relative bearing by noting its angle off your bow. This might be something as general as saying that "red nun 8" should be coming up off the starboard bow to a specific determination that "red nun 8" should lie at a relative bearing of 045 degrees. You can

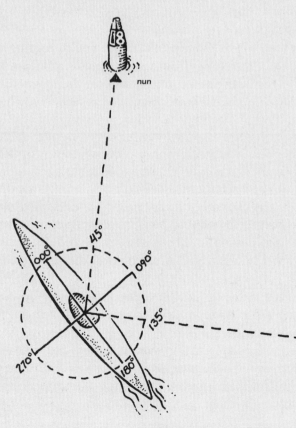

Relative bearings note the world in relation to your kayak, where your bow is always at 000 degrees. Something off the starboard bow would be at a relative bearing of 045 degrees, and off the stern quarter would be at 135 degrees.

estimate a bow angle by using your paddle shaft to point at the object or using your hand and finger widths. See the illustration on page 225 for information on estimating bow angles.

(Note: The actual bearing can be defined as true or magnetic, as can your kayak's heading. Don't mix and match true and magnetic. I'd suggest using only magnetic compass points since this is most useful for kayakers as we refer to our deck compasses, and it requires no correction.)

make an emergency call to give your location in relation to some landmark, this could be critical (for the U.S. Coast Guard, true bearings are the default setting).

When you fold your chart to fit into your chartcase, try to include a compass rose. If you cannot, mark the magnetic cardinal directions on the face of the chart piece so you'll have some sort of reference when you glance at the folded chart. Coursers—overlays that need only align with the north–south axis (either true or magnetic—we'll use magnetic)—allow you to take bearings without the use of parallel rulers.

When you're under way, it's simple to take a bearing. Point the bow of your kayak at an object and read the deck compass. This is your magnetic bearing. You may choose to use a handheld compass to take a bearing, but you'll need to stop paddling. Carrying a handheld compass in addition to your deck compass is a good idea, though. It can serve as a backup to your deck unit and as a check for compass deviation (see pages 88–89), and a handheld compass makes it easier to take bearings at right angles to your line of travel.

LINES OF POSITION (LOPs)

A line of position doesn't necessarily pinpoint your location, but it certainly narrows the possibilities since it places you somewhere along a particular line on your chart. If you point your bow at a lighthouse and read a bearing of 236 degrees magnetic, you know you're somewhere along the back bearing (056 degrees) from the lighthouse toward you. You could draw this line on your chart,

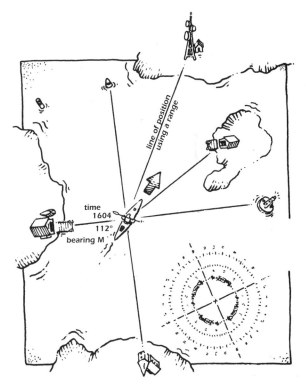

To create a line of position, take a bearing on a charted object; then, on your chart, draw the back bearing from that object toward your location. You're somewhere on the line.

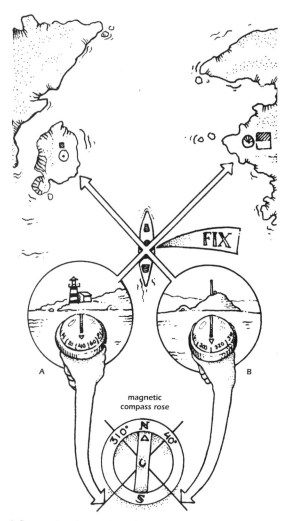

A fix can be determined from the intersection of two or more lines of position. Lines of position at right angles offer the best accuracy.

tion at a right angle to your first one. You can do this by taking a bearing to an object off your beam, or to the side. Use a handheld compass so you won't have to turn your boat around, and read this bearing (you can place it along your paddle shaft laid across the cockpit if you like). Now, if you drew this new line of position on your chart, you could pinpoint your location at the intersection of these two lines. You have a fix on your position.

Kayakers don't normally determine fixes while under way. Instead, we simply note landmarks or buoys as we pass and keep an eye to the side to mark our progress in relation to a shoreline. But understanding how to determine a fix is useful if you get disoriented or are unsure of your progress. It's also a great way to mark a spot on the water, say a favorite fishing hole, so you can return to it later.

RANGES

A range is an alignment of any two objects that's used to determine a line of position. Ranges are particularly useful because they also give you immediate feedback whenever you stray from this line of position. Kayakers can use a variety of ranges over the course of a day's paddling, discarding them along the way. Ranges can be natural or navigational ones marked on the chart. Most of the ranges marked on the chart guide large vessels along a stretch of water where navigational hazards or limited water depths don't allow for much tolerance in position. Think twice about using these ranges since they may put you into a channel with large boat traffic.

though doing this while under way isn't easy. In the absence of any other factors, you can advance along this line of position at your paddling speed in a very predictable manner.

If you want to pinpoint your position, you'll need more than one line of position. For the most accurate results, try to add a line of posi-

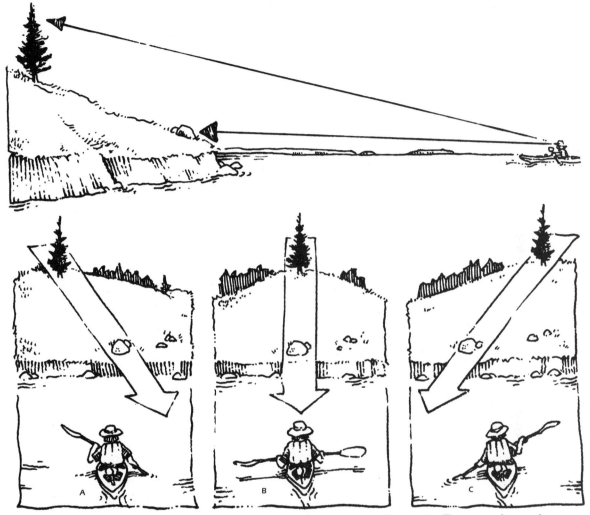

You can usually find numerous natural ranges along your paddling route. These may be used and discarded to help determine a line of position during different trip segments. If two objects aren't aligned, make adjustments to get back on course. In A, the paddler needs to move right to bring the range into alignment. In C, the paddler needs to move to the left.

Instead, pick out two stationary objects, one behind the other, that are some distance in front of you and along your line of travel (say, a smokestack and a large, distinctive rock). If you continue to keep these two objects aligned, you're on course. If the far-thest object in your range drifts to the right of the closer object, you're right of your course. Move your boat to the left until the objects realign. If the farthest object is to the left of the nearest object, move right to bring them back in line.

Ranges can provide invaluable feedback about conditions that may set you off course. Unlike paddling toward a single object, a range will keep you on a particular course and let you know when you've strayed from it. It's often easier to paddle using a range than monitoring a deck compass. Of course, ranges require good visibility and the proximity of objects or landmarks to align for use. Be creative about creating a range. You can align two buoys, a tree that splits a dip in a hillside, or rooftops and chimneys along a shoreline.

THINGS THAT CAN THROW YOU OFF

In chapter 7 we talked about "real-life paddling"—dealing with wind, tidal currents, and weather. All your efforts to plot a course and plan your travels must also take these factors into account. Navigation is a science, but it's also an art. Your ability to successfully blend these two aspects will allow you to relax and enjoy exploring an area. It certainly beats biting your nails and trying to quell that unsettled feeling in the pit of your stomach when you realize you're not all that sure of where you are.

Before setting out, you should be able to make reasonably accurate predictions about the effects of tidal currents and different wind directions during the different legs of your trip. You'll obviously want to minimize their effect or make good use of them whenever possible. Once you're under way, monitor their effect on your course and the time it takes to reach a destination or checkoff point.

Getting a handle on how wind and tidal currents may affect your paddling requires an understanding of these factors (see chapter 7) and how to quantify their effect. These factors may have an effect on both your course and your speed of travel.

SPEED OF TRAVEL

It may sound obvious, but you need to know how fast you travel in your kayak. Without knowing how long it takes you to cover a couple of miles, you can't very well plan an outing or know if you can even expect to get to your destination before nightfall. I'll give you a hint—your typical cruising speed probably falls somewhere between 2 to 4 knots (1 knot equals 1 nautical mile per hour). That's not to say that you can't kick into overdrive to reach a sprint speed of more than 5 knots, but you won't maintain this speed over a day of travel.

Determining your cruising speed over a measured distance can be handy. You may even be lucky enough to find a measured mile marked on your chart. If not, use your chart to measure a distance between two easily distinguished objects or landmarks, then time yourself as you paddle this distance. Remember that for trip planning purposes, you need to determine your cruising speed, which is how fast you paddle at an easy pace that you can maintain for at least an hour. Time your cruising speed several times and take the average of these speeds. Try to fix a memory of what paddling at this speed feels like in terms of exertion and cadence for future reference.

CLARIFYING SOME TERMS

It's important to understand the difference between heading, bearing, and course. These three terms get bandied about, often incorrectly, and can confuse those new to navigation. A *course* is where you want to go (or where you actually go). A *bearing* is a direction to some object. A *heading* is where the boat is pointing. In the absence of any factors like wind or tidal current, these three terms may describe the same thing at a given moment. You point your boat at an object, and that's your course as you paddle that bearing. But usually, these three terms end up being three different things. You may have a heading due west (270 degrees M), even though your course is to the northwest (maybe you're being pushed by a tidal current from the south) and you may take bearings to a buoy or landmark to mark your progress.

Heading, course, and bearing may note three different directions, and are distinct concepts. Understanding the differences between these terms is important. Here the paddlers have a heading different from the course (to compensate for wind or tidal conditions) and have taken a bearing to the buoy off their starboard beam.

A TRICK OF THE TRADE

Sometimes it's useful to get a handle on the speed of a particular current while under way. You can do this quickly by timing how long it takes your boat to drift with the current past a stationary point. Start your timing as your bow passes a point (like a dock piling), and end your timing as your stern passes that same point. Knowing the length of your boat and the time it took to pass a mark will tell you the speed you were moving. If your boat is 17 feet (5.2 m) long and you drifted past your mark in 5 seconds, then the current was moving you at 2.0 knots, since

$$\frac{17 \text{ ft.}}{5 \text{ sec.}} \times \left(\frac{1 \text{ nm}}{6{,}076 \text{ ft.}}\right) \times \left(\frac{3{,}600 \text{ sec.}}{1 \text{ hour}}\right) = \frac{2 \text{ nm}}{\text{hour}} \text{ (knots)}$$

You could do the same thing and come to the same conclusion by observing the drift of something like a piece of seaweed as it passes your stationary boat (hang on to the piling). Remember, the tidal current you observe in the shallows along a piece of shoreline will probably not be typical of the currents found in deep water during a crossing.

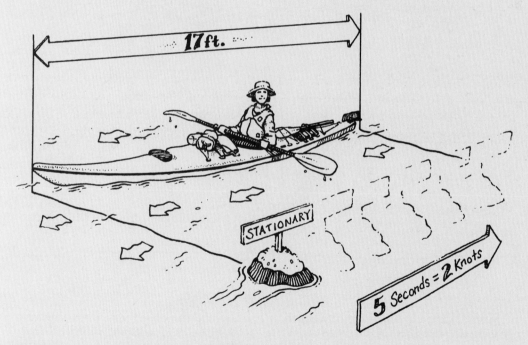

Knowing that a 17-foot (5.2 m) boat that drifts past a mark in 5 seconds is moving at 2.0 knots is a handy reference. You can use this to estimate your paddling speed or the velocity of a tidal current while under way.

Knowing your normal speed in the absence of wind and tidal currents will allow you to more accurately determine your speed made good, or net speed under real conditions. For example, if you know that your paddling speed is normally 2.5 knots, you'd expect to make a 1-mile crossing in 0.4 hours, or 24 minutes. Instead, you find that it takes a full hour for you to make this crossing; your speed made good was actually 1.0 knot. So the actual conditions of wind, tidal currents, or both affected your speed by 1.5 knots. This is useful information to record for future reference (we'll get to this later).

Knowing the speed of a tidal current before setting out will allow you to make calculations of what to expect for your speed made good for trip planning purposes. If you were directly bucking a known tidal current of 1.0 knot and your normal paddling speed was 2.5 knots, you could expect to have a speed made good of 1.5 knots. This speed will need to be used when determining the time required to make this crossing. On the other hand, you might be lucky enough to catch a free ride on a favorable current that moves at 1.0 knot. Your speed made good, assuming your same normal paddling speed, would be 3.5 knots, and it would take less time to reach your destination.

Both examples use a tidal current that's either directly opposing or supporting your line of travel; only your speed of travel is affected. Things get a bit more complex when tidal currents are on your beam (common when crossing a channel), but you can still make some calculations that will help your trip planning. By doing so, you can work out what course corrections to make and develop a strategy for paddling efficiently and wisely in these situations.

If the tidal current is running at a right angle to your course, you'll have to determine how much it will set you off course. The easiest way to do this is to divide the speed of the current by your paddling speed and multiply this by the distance of your crossing. This will tell you how far down you can expect to be set by the tidal current for this crossing. For example, if you're paddling a crossing of 1 nautical mile and you know from past experience or a tidal current table that the current in this crossing at this particular time of day is 1.5 knots and that you normally paddle at 2.5 knots, you can calculate that

1.5 knots (current speed) ÷ 2.5 knots (paddling speed) × 1.0 nautical mile (distance of crossing) = 0.6 nautical mile

This is the distance you'll be set over by the current when you make this crossing. You could certainly choose to make the crossing and then slog your way head-on into the current for another 0.6 mile to reach your destination. Or, you could point up into the current to a spot 0.6 mile above your intended destination and paddle toward that point. In theory, you would end up exactly at your intended destination as the effect of the tidal current balanced your course correction.

You might want to consider an "up-and-over" strategy for your crossing. First paddle along the shore to a point above your crossing slightly more than the distance you'll be set down current (0.6 nautical mile in our example). Then paddle straight across the channel to hit your mark or slightly above on the other side. You can then drift to your

You can calculate the distance of the tidal set if you know the speed (velocity) of the tidal current, your own paddling speed, and the crossing distance. Though these factors are assumed to be constant in calculations, this equation can help with trip planning and paddling strategy.

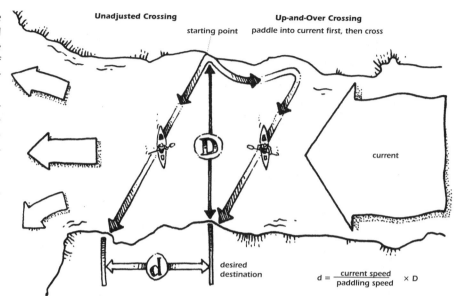

Unadjusted Crossing

starting point

Up-and-Over Crossing
paddle into current first, then cross

current

desired destination

$$d = \frac{current\ speed}{paddling\ speed} \times D$$

final destination. This makes sense if you'll also face strong winds on the way across or if reaching the far shore below your intended destination puts you in a dangerous position. The degree of padding you build into your strategy will reflect all the unique factors involved with your particular crossing.

Of course, the strength of the tidal current is not uniform over the width of the channel but is usually stronger in the deeper water at the center of the channel. During the amount of time it takes to make the crossing, the strength of the current may change as it moves through its cycle of ebb and flow. And, you still need to consider the effects of wind that you might encounter. Even with all these qualifiers, you still have a useful tool because you can plan your trip with these factors and their quantitative results in mind. Review several strategies for your crossing, and weigh the pros and cons of each before settling on the one that is safest and conserves your

energy. It's always best to choose a strategy that gets you to the far side of a crossing at a spot you know or at least are certain is slightly above or below your intended destination. You don't want to be left guessing which way you should turn to find your landing site.

VECTORS

Even if the thought of geometry makes you want to run away, you should try working with vectors. Vectors are simply directed quantities—lines that tell you how strong and at what angle some factor is working on your boat. They allow you to determine the result of these effects, or given the results, vectors can be used to determine the strength and the angle of a given effect.

Let's say you're planning to paddle to an island that sits at a bearing of 070 degrees magnetic. You know that you normally pad-

FERRYING

Ferrying is a common whitewater technique for crossing rivers without being pushed downstream. It's a handy technique that points the boat upstream and sets an angle so that as the boat is paddled forward, it's pushed across the river by the downstream current. All the paddler has to do in many cases is set a stern rudder stroke to keep the boat properly aligned.

It isn't quite as simple for sea kayakers since our crossings are rarely short sprints across fast river currents. Sea kayakers generally undertake crossings that are much longer, and our tidal currents aren't nearly as strong as most downriver currents whitewater paddlers use for ferrying (thank goodness). But the principle is still the same and can be used to make crossings more efficient. Setting a ferry angle will allow you to take the effects of any tidal current into account. By maintaining this angle from your intended line of travel directly across the current, you'll end up at your destination. You can set a ferry angle from experience and adjust it along the way, or you can use vectors to get a more precise determination.

Setting a ferry angle into the current for a channel crossing will result in more time being needed to make the crossing. Depending on the actual conditions like wind exposure, heavy boat traffic, and the dangers of being pushed down the channel, you'll need to decide how best to proceed.

dle at 2.5 knots. But you're concerned about the tidal current that is coming from due south (180 degrees M) at 2.0 knots. You wonder how much it will move you off course or slow your progress. You'd like some way to get a handle on how to correct for this effect on your boat. You can figure this out by using vectors. You'll need a ruler with something other than an inches scale (centimeters or any 10-unit scales are fine), parallel rules, and your chart (actually, just a compass rose).

Note: it doesn't matter whether you work in magnetic or true directions as long as you're consistent. The resulting answers will be the same. Examples are given in magnetic degrees since that's what we would typically use when paddling. If the set is taken from a tidal current table, it will be given as a true direction and converted to magnetic.

Use the compass rose closest to your paddling area and draw a line from the exact center of the rose that is 2.5 units long (centimeters, or whatever scale you wish to use) at 070 degrees magnetic. Now draw another line representing direction and velocity of the tidal current. This second line (with its head at the tail of the first) will be 2.0 units long and be drawn at 360 degrees magnetic, or the direction the tidal current is carrying you (its set). Now draw a third leg to close this triangle. This line will represent the results of paddling your bearing of 070 degrees magnetic at a speed of 2.5 knots while being affected by a tidal current of 2.0 knots from the south. Measure the length of this line using the chosen scale. This number represents your resulting speed, or speed made good. Determine the direction of this line using your parallel rules and the middle, or magnetic, ring of the compass rose. This directon represents your resulting course, or course made good. Your speed made good would be 3.7 knots and your course made good would be 039 degrees magnetic (see illustration). The current from the south has set you off course and actually increased your speed. (Remember, the direction in which a tidal current flows is called its set; its velocity is its drift.) It's important to understand that the set is the direction the current flows, thus a current from due south would have a set of 360 degrees magnetic.

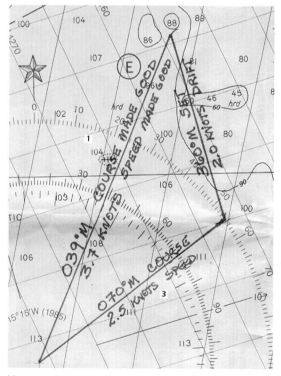

You can draw vectors on the chart. One line represents your course and speed, another represents the set and drift of the tidal current, and a third represents your course made good and speed made good. Remember to label each line.

Using vectors to determine the forces and their results makes it easier to visualize what's happening to your boat. It also makes it easier to catch a calculation error because you have a picture of the forces and the direction of their action. As when taking a bearing, be sure any calculation you do passes the "commonsense" test. If it doesn't, think through the problem again and find out where you might have gone wrong.

For our example, the course made good is in a direction that makes sense if you have a tidal current carrying you to the north. The increase in speed also makes sense as the tidal current is coming off the stern quarter of the boat and would give a helping hand to the kayak's speed (it would not, however, make this an easy course to paddle, see page 164).

Always label each line with the information it represents. You have two lines representing your kayak: one is your course and speed in the absence of the current, the other is your course and speed that result from the tidal current. The third line representing the direction and velocity of the tidal current should be labeled with the set and drift of that current.

Our original example showed us how our boat would be affected by the tidal current. A more useful exercise might be to determine what course we should paddle to take the tidal current into account so we end up at our desired location. We know we only want to paddle at 2.5 knots, and we know we want our course made good to be 070 degrees magnetic. We also know the drift (2.0 knots) and set (360 degrees M) of the current. See the illustration below for the resulting vectors. We can find the course we need to paddle, and we may also find our speed made good, which is helpful if you need to know your estimated time of arrival.

Looking back at the illustration opposite, it's tempting to simply take the difference between your original bearing of 070 degrees magnetic and the resulting course made good of 039 degrees magnetic, or 31 degrees, and make this the correction factor that would result in paddling a new course of 109 degrees magnetic to account for the set and drift. You'd be in the ballpark, but you wouldn't be entirely right! The force of the tidal current is acting at a slightly different

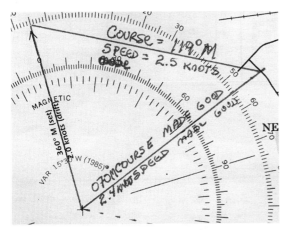

In this example, you want to know what course to paddle at 2.5 knots in order to make good a course of 070 degrees M. First draw a line for your course made good (070M). The final length of this vector line (speed made good) will be determined later. Now from the same starting point, draw a line for the set (360M) and drift (2 knots) of the tidal current. From the endpoint of this set-drift vector you need to draw a line 2.5 units long (your known speed) that intersects the course made good line and closes the triangle. You can now use your parrallel rulers to determine that your course is 119 degrees M. You can then measure the final length of your course made good line to determine that your speed made good is 2.4 knots.

angle on this (mistakenly) corrected course. You would have to change your paddling speed if you wanted to paddle this course and still end up at your destination.

Vector calculations serve a useful purpose, but they don't transfer to real life in a perfect way. You still must deal with the effects, if any, of wind and paddling in seas that may prove challenging. But vectors draw a picture of forces acting on your boat and can help you visualize what the results will be. Experience will allow you to forge a strategy for actually paddling under a given set of conditions.

THE EFFECTS OF WIND

In chapter 7 we discussed how wind affects your boat and builds seas. It's also useful to view wind as a force that affects your course and speed, much as a tidal current does. Getting a quantitative fix on this effect is not straightforward, but there have been attempts by David Burch (*Fundamentals of Kayak Navigation*) and John Dowd (*Sea Kayaking: A Manual for Long-Distance Touring*). Their resulting graphs tell us what we already knew or suspected but in a more scientific way! You'll begin to feel the forces produced by wind as it approaches 10 knots. When winds reach a velocity of 25 knots, you'll be slowed to a crawl if you paddle at your normal cruising effort, or you must work significantly harder to overcome the approximated 6 pounds of force acting on you and your boat in a headwind to maintain your speed.

As you spend time on the water, you'll get a good feel for how hard it is to paddle in different wind speeds. Other factors like whether your boat is loaded or empty, how long your exposure will be between rest stops, and what seas have been created by this wind will need to be considered as well.

You won't be able to calculate the effect of wind on your course and speed made good using vectors. But you should note the speed and direction of the wind and can even draw this on your chart as a vector line to help keep in mind its strength (drift) and what direction it's likely to push you (set). With this line of force in mind, you can make practical corrections for paddling in wind.

DEAD RECKONING

Though the term sounds ominous, *dead reckoning* is nothing more than keeping track of where you are by using your speed of travel over the direction you're paddling. Classic dead reckoning procedures don't take tidal currents or other factors into account, though many paddlers use this term more freely to include corrections for factors like tidal currents. A dead reckoning plot, called a DR track, begins from a known location and proceeds along your course at your paddling speed. From this DR track, you can plot what you think your path is through the water over time. The illustration opposite shows a typical DR track and the correct way of labeling information on this track. Note that the known location that begins the DR track is shown as a cross inside a circle (a dot may be used instead of the cross). The dead reckoning position along the track is shown as a line inside a half circle. This means of

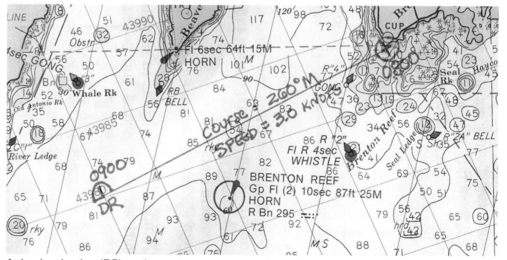

A dead reckoning (DR) track notes your course and speed and begins at a fix (known location) at a particular time. Knowing your speed, you can determine where you are along this track at a later time. A DR track does not take tidal currents or other conditions into account, and it assumes a constant speed. It simply notes where you would expect to be along your course track at a particular time given your speed. In this case you are 3 nautical miles along the track at 0900 hours, or one hour after starting.

labeling is an accepted standard and avoids confusing a dead reckoning position with a fix determined through radionavigation or other means.

Dead reckoning procedures simply formalize what you do, or should do, every time you go paddling—namely, keeping track of how long you've been paddling, how fast you've been paddling, and the direction you've been paddling. Since dead reckoning does not take landmarks or other aids into consideration, keeping track of time and how fast you're paddling is very important. Thus, dead reckoning relies on speed, time, and distance calculations. These quick calculations are easily done as long as you consistently note the units you're using. Speed should always be in knots (nautical miles per hour), distance in nautical miles, and time in hours. So speed (S) is clearly the distance (D) traveled over time (T):

$$S = D \div T$$

From there it's a simple matter to convert to minutes if you prefer since you know there are 60 minutes in an hour.

If you had paddled for a half hour at your normal cruising speed of 3.0 knots, you'd expect to have covered 1.5 nautical miles. Noting this spot on your DR track gives you an idea of where you are along your route. This is not as accurate as determining a fix, but it does tell you where you might be, and in the absence of landmarks, this information may be critical to staying found. The area of uncertainty may be large if you're unsure of your speed, have been sloppy about keeping track of time, or are paddling in wind and currents. The illustration shows how you might use a dead reckoning track and DST (distance-speed-time) calculations to keep track of yourself while under way.

In reality, you'll probably use a combination of piloting, or navigating by landmarks, and dead reckoning over the course of a day's paddling. You'll also use your knowledge and experience with tidal currents, wind, and sea conditions to make adjustments to your course and to determine the best strategy for completing each leg of your trip. Blending these procedures with your experience will give you the confidence to

TIME

It's a good idea to note time using a 24-hour scale. This allows you to drop the A.M. and P.M. designations and avoid any confusion when you record time on DR tracks or in a log. Thus, the thirteenth hour of the day, 1 P.M., is now 1300 hours, and 1:30 P.M. is 1330 hours. Using a 24-hour time scale keeps time notations simple and removes a lot of potential confusion. When stating time in this way, be sure to use four digits for each time (0300 hours for example is 3 A.M.) that you note. When calling out a time, it's typical to say "thirteen hundred hours" or "oh-three hundred hours" for 1 P.M. and 3 A.M., respectively. Note that this is different from the conventions used to say compass directions, where each number is stated. No one ever says "zero-three-zero-zero hours"!

explore farther afield in a broader range of conditions.

DISTANCE OFF

Occasionally you may need to know the distance to a landmark: you might use this to estimate your speed made good, or you might use the distance off along with a bearing to the landmark to determine a fix. There are several ways to determine distance off, some more useful than others to kayakers. Ideally, we don't want to relinquish our grip on the paddle for very long. Measurements need to be easy and done while under way.

One of the easiest ways to determine distance off is to use the method of doubling your bow angle (note that a bow angle isn't necessarily a relative bearing). The easiest bow angle to monitor is the one that doubles from 45 to 90 degrees (these angles are easy to visualize accurately). Imagine that you're paddling along a shoreline and would like to determine how far you are away from that shore. If you're able to pick out a specific point, say a chimney, you can time how long it takes for that chimney to pass from a point 45 degrees off your bow to a point 90 degrees off your bow. It's important to paddle this distance at a known rate of speed since you'll then use the time needed to double the bow angle to determine the distance you covered during that time. The distance you traveled along the shore during which the bow angle doubled is equal to the distance you are from your landmark (the chimney).

Distance off can also be determined by measuring horizontal and vertical angles.

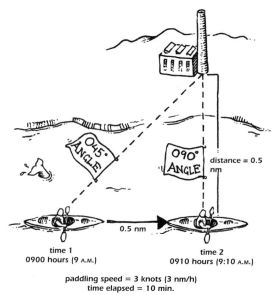

paddling speed = 3 knots (3 nm/h)
time elapsed = 10 min.

In this example, your bow angle doubled during 10 minutes of paddling at a speed of 3.0 knots. In those 10 minutes you covered 0.5 nautical mile: 3 nm per hour × 10 minutes × (1 hour ÷ 60 min.) = 0.5 nm, which is equal to your distance off.

But these are more difficult to monitor and will require that you stop paddling, if only for a short time, to make measurements. One method is a handy formula that uses the small triangle rule. This formula is useful only over angle measurements of less than 30 degrees, which is fine for most of our uses. The formula for finding the *distance off* (D, in nautical miles) from a horizontal *target angle* (A, in degrees) is

$$D = 60 \times (W \div A)$$

$$D = 60 \times \left(\frac{\text{target width in nm}}{\text{target angle}} \right)$$

where W is *target width*. *Note:* the unit of measure for distance off will be the unit of measure for your target width. On charts, this will usually be nautical miles.

Measure the target width from your chart (say the distance between two hills) and then determine the target angle. To find this angle, use your hand width or knuckles (see illustration) or take actual bearings, though this requires more time and maneuvering on your part. In the illustration, we found from our chart that the two hills are 0.5 nautical mile apart (this is our target width). Using our hand with our arms outstretched to estimate the angle, we found that the target angle was 15 degrees. Using our formula we can find the distance off as

$$60 \times (0.5 \text{ nm} \div 15 \text{ deg.}) = 2.0 \text{ nm}$$

So our two hills are 2.0 nautical miles away from our position. This provides a line of position. If we point our bow at one of these hills and note a bearing, we can create a second line of position. At the intersection of these two lines we have a fix on our location.

To avoid even having to lay down the paddle to make the angle measurement, some paddlers have etched lines on their paddle

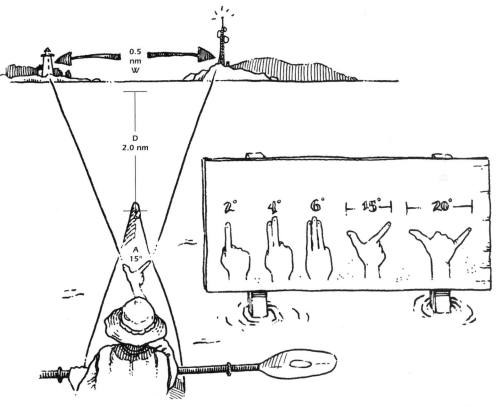

You can estimate a target angle (A) using your hands held at arm's length (in this case, 15 degrees). Your target width (W) can be determined from the chart (in our example, 0.5 nm). Therefore, your distance off (D) is 2.0 nm.

shaft that are calibrated to the angles measured with the hand and knuckle widths. Then, the paddle can be held up with outstretched arms and the angle determined from these calibrated lines.

To figure out the distance off from a vertical angle, you'll need to know the height of an object from your chart (a peak, lighthouse, or charted rock) and the target angle. The formula you use is basically the same, except now you use H, *target height*, rather than width. Distance off and target height are still in nautical miles, and target angle is in degrees. (*Note:* on a chart, the figure given in feet next to the lighthouse symbol is not the actual height of the lighthouse but rather the light's height above mean higher high water.)

$$D = 60 \times (H \div A)$$

Since most heights are given in feet and you know that there are approximately 6,000 feet in a nautical mile, you can change this equation to

$$D = H \text{ (in feet)} \div 100 \, A$$

(This same conversion to feet can be used for horizontal angles.) *Note:* if you're more than 2 nautical miles off, using a vertical angle becomes less accurate because of the earth's curvature and heights being measured from the true shoreline.

Measuring the target angle vertically can still be done with a hand or knuckle width on your outstretched arm. Since standing your paddle on end to use any calibrated marks you might have made for horizontal angles is not practical, you might consider using a kamal. A kamal is simply a plate with gradations marked on it that you can keep a fixed distance from your eye (this is a transverse scale); it can be a simple centimeter ruler about as long as your hand (15-cm rulers are most commonly used). Using some geometry that we won't get into here (if I haven't lost you already), you can make a kamal that is held 57 centimeters away from your eye using marks that are 1 centimeter apart and correspond to 1 degree in your target angle. Fifty-seven centimeters is a comfortable distance to hold the kamal from your eye (most adult arms can accommodate this distance). You can make that distance constant by holding

LEARN YOUR DISTANCES

Learn to recognize and gauge distances from your kayak. You might base your estimates on a standard distance you have fixed in your mind (a football field—100 yards—for instance). A lighthouse might look as if it's three football fields in the distance. Also take the time to view landmarks on shore from known distances and see how well you're able to distinguish details. Look for common details like distinguishing bricks from mortar on chimneys, making out the windows on a large house, or picking out people on shore—first as dots and then distinguishing arms and legs. Remembering at what distances you're able to pick out common details will help you determine an approximate distance off for quick reference while under way.

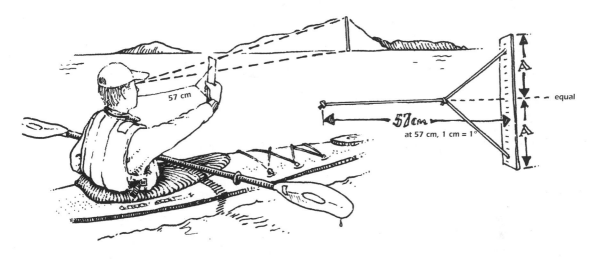

A kamal can be used to measure vertical angles.

a 57-centimeter-long string taut when using the kamal. To keep from tilting the kamal, attach the string as shown in the accompanying illustration, a suggestion made in Burch's *Fundamentals of Kayak Navigation*.

Many kayakers never use a kamal or formulas for determining distance off. For most of us, a quick glance at the chart and the shoreline or island in the distance is enough to stay found and mark our progress. But the more tools you have at your disposal, the less the chance of losing your way or even becoming momentarily disoriented. Also, the very act of working through these concepts creates a deeper understanding of navigation and makes us better mariners.

NAVIGATING WITH GPS

We have now covered navigation techniques and the simple tools you'll need to find your way on the water. While I am a strong proponent of preparedness and keeping things simple, we would be remiss to not discuss GPS (global positioning system) devices. In the past ten years these electronic units have become more sophisticated, more accurate, and considerably cheaper. For more information on GPS units, see pages 88–89.

When you use a GPS unit, you are calling on a system of satellites to triangulate your position (units typically have at least twelve channels to accomplish this). Triangulation is a trigonomic operation that can pinpoint a location when given its distance from two (or more) other points. The more satellites your unit "finds," the more accurate the triangulation and, thus, knowledge of your position. Generally, being on the water makes it easier for your GPS to locate satellites than if you were in the woods where topography and tall trees may obstruct the signal between the GPS unit and the satellites.

GPS devices can be used in a number of ways by kayakers: as a precise navigational tool that pinpoints your location; as a course plotter that records your position along a track; as a chart that is digitally displayed; as an electronic compass; as a trip-planning tool that allows rest stops, bailout points, and dangerous areas to be marked in advance; and as both a fitness and trip-planning tool that calculates your speed and headway against factors such as tidal currents and wind, and the time spent paddling during a given outing.

These GPS devices have the ability to store lots of data. This is often in the form of *waypoints*, or exact locations, noted and retained by the unit. Your GPS device will allow you to preload many waypoints and collect others over the course of your paddling. The greater the storage capacity of a given model, the more waypoints can be stored (the capability to store several thousand is not unusual). Many units also display charts on the screen that you can overlay with notations for your trip planning and even move data back and forth from your home computer or laptop.

It is quite reassuring to eye the planned route and your actual track as it unscrolls across the chart, accommodating your starts and stops and the effects of wind and tides. Some units can store tide tables and tidal current data and have an emergency button for sending your location to the U.S. Coast Guard. Other units combine with VHF radios, cell phones, and even MP3 players. Many kayakers have become as burdened with electronic devices as the average teenager!

You will want to carry your GPS device in a waterproof case. Even though many GPS units are waterproof (I highly recommend choosing one of these), you will still need the protection of a waterproof bag. Saltwater spray and the occasional wave dunking will eventually wear out waterproof gaskets and seals (this tends to happen after the warranty has run out). There are special dry bags made for GPS devices, or you can use one designed for cell phones or VHF radios. You can often operate the GPS through a clear window in the bag, which means the unit does not have to be removed and exposed to the elements. Units with large raised buttons on the front work well in this way. Avoid buttons on the side since you will probably have to remove the unit from its waterproof bag to press them. Large raised buttons are also easier to operate if your hands are cold and clumsy or clad in neoprene gloves. Also note that GPS units use batteries at an astonishing rate; make sure to pack plenty of spares.

Using Your GPS Receiver

When you get your new GPS unit, you will need to initialize it for your location. This process, which takes several minutes, allows the GPS to "find itself" the first time it is used. You can then begin loading waypoints and practicing with the features before actually taking the unit paddling.

A waypoint is an exact location that you have chosen to mark or let the unit mark for you. The GPS gathers information from any satellites available (the more the better) and then records the coordinates for this position. You will need to name all waypoints or let the unit assign a number to each. Even though it adds a step to the process, important waypoints should be named for easy use. It is much easier to remember "Bartlett Point" than "67" for the spot you marked and want to recall at a later date.

You may use your GPS to set a *route* you plan to travel or to *track* your actual course while paddling. To record a route in advance of your trip, you will need to regularly mark points along your intended line of travel. You can also add other notes for landmarks or areas of concern. Then, as you paddle, the GPS unit will display this route and any deviation from it as you travel from waypoint to waypoint along the route.

You may also use the GPS unit to track your progress and line of travel. In this mode, the GPS device marks regular waypoints as you paddle and stores them. You may then use this track to retrace your "steps" for a return leg, or use the information in the track to determine your average speed or your speed between each waypoint that has been recorded. This is very useful information. It will help with future trip planning since you will have an accurate record of your typical cruising speed under certain conditions and can even note where you may have varied significantly from this due to wind or tidal currents. (You must also make note of the given paddling conditions and the time in order to do this; for example, "15-knot wind out of the southwest, ebbing tide, 10:15 A.M.–11:45 A.M.")

If you are traveling in a group that may split into smaller pods, recording a common waypoint where you can rendezvous for lunch or a safety check is a smart use of GPS technology. The GPS unit then becomes a handy group management tool and ensures that everyone knows exactly where the rendezvous point is (or at least their GPS device does).

Limitations of GPS Units

In spite of the gee-whiz factor, GPS units don't really offer a great deal more than your basic navigation tools do. They allow an ongoing visual display as you paddle, but so does your chart, or the seascape around you. The best use of GPS devices is their ability to gather and then download information to your computer for review and future trip planning.

Many kayakers carry a GPS unit only as a backup or fun tool for their navigation. Some folks find it easier to read a chart folded on the deck (in a waterproof case) than the smaller screen of a GPS unit. There are larger screens and deck mounts for the GPS units that are typically combined with sonar and used as "fish finders," and these are quite easy to read. However, they are raised at an angle above deck level and are not feasible in many sea conditions, and they may also hinder certain rescue and reentry techniques.

I would encourage kayakers to carry a GPS because it is yet another tool and backup for finding and reassuring yourself about your position on the water. That said, a GPS can never replace thorough preparation, common sense, and good judgment.

RULES OF THE ROAD

As kayakers, we often bemoan the fact that we're not treated with respect by other boaters. They spray their wakes in our direction and shake their fists at us during channel crossings. While we have taken some unwarranted abuse, we've also gained a reputation as being ignorant of seamanship and common courtesies between vessels.

The laws and regulations that govern the interactions of all vessels on all waters are called the "Rules of the Road," or often just the "rules." These rules consist of requirements for navigation lights and day shapes; steering and sailing rules; sound signals for both good and restricted visibility; and distress signals. There are slight differences between the rules for inland and international waters, though inland rules must conform as closely as possible to international standards. Inland waters extend to exact demarcation lines agreed to by international treaty and don't refer to the waters of lakes, ponds, and nonnavigable rivers that are usually under individual state jurisdiction. Kayaks are vessels and are covered under these Rules of the Road, both inland and international. These rules are published by the U.S. Coast Guard and available from marine chandleries, U.S. Coast Guard stations, and online.

Often, the rules don't specifically note requirements for human-powered vessels (or we're included under "vessels of less than 12 meters"), but they do discuss vessels in general and what responsibilities and actions we're required to take under certain circumstances. If we as kayakers want the protection of these rules, then we must also understand and abide by these same rules. Remember, if you add a sail to your kayak, you'll be governed by rules for sailing vessels, which are different.

Light requirements for kayakers are simple. Between sunset and sunrise, we must have a white light aboard and available to show to prevent a collision (waters under state jurisdiction may have different rules). A flashlight is sufficient, and a wise kayaker would have one on board at all times. If you paddle after dark, become familiar with the lights shown by vessels common to your area. There are specific light requirements based on the size and activity of the vessel.

Sound signal requirements are also simple for kayakers. We must carry some "means of making an efficient sound signal." You'll have met this requirement by carrying a whistle attached to your life vest. If you paddle in areas where fog is common, consider carrying a foghorn. While not a requirement, a foghorn makes a more noticeable signal in restricted visibility than a whistle. In restricted visibility, kayakers are required to make "some other efficient sound signal" (that is, one not used by another class of vessel) at intervals not exceeding two minutes. This notifies other vessels of your presence and helps identify you.

The accompanying illustration shows all the distress signals that are officially recognized by both inland and international rules. A flashing white strobe light is recognized under the inland rules. Some of the distress signals shown are obviously more applicable to kayakers than others. But, you should be aware of all forms of distress signals in the event you observe one of these when paddling. Carrying a variety of distress signals is a smart choice. (Signaling equipment is discussed in more detail on pages 74–78 and 91–93.)

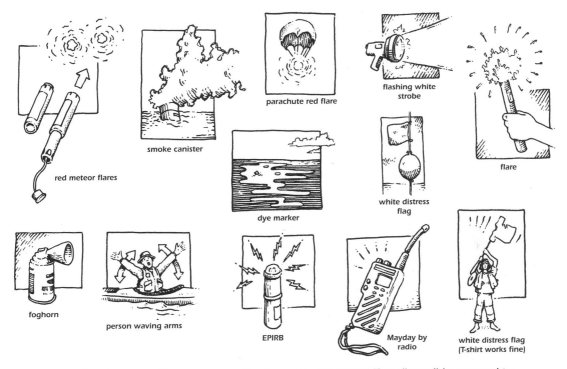

red meteor flares

smoke canister

parachute red flare

flashing white strobe

dye marker

white distress flag

flare

foghorn

person waving arms

EPIRB

Mayday by radio

white distress flag (T-shirt works fine)

Distress signals are used in emergency situations only. You must, if at all possible, respond to another's distress signal. (Discussion of individual distress signals is on pages 74–78 and 91–93.)

The rules on right-of-way don't specifically mention kayakers, but many of the general rules apply. The General Prudential Rule requires all vessels to consider the limitations of other vessels, which may render a departure from the rules when necessary to avoid immediate danger. Thus, other vessels must be aware of the limitations of a kayak, and you must be aware of the limitations of other vessels. All vessels must travel at a safe speed so that a collision can be avoided under the prevailing conditions of weather and traffic.

If you're approaching another vessel, or being approached head-on, both vessels must alter course to starboard so that you'll pass port to port. If you're being overtaken, or passed, by another vessel, you must maintain your speed and course until the other vessel has passed you. As a kayaker, you cannot impede larger vessels that can only navigate in certain parts of a channel or approaches to channels, called fairways. In areas where traffic lanes are present for large vessels, you should avoid paddling in these lanes and allow larger vessels unimpeded access to them. If you must cross these lanes, do so at a right angle and as quickly as possible—like dashing across a busy street. Too often, I've heard kayakers state that they always have the right-of-way because they're manually

Monitor the potential for collision by using a passing boat's angle off your bow. You can use your finger spread to estimate the angle and any change in it as you encounter boat traffic. If the angle remains the same as a boat approaches, take immediate and adequate evasive action.

powered. I say, if they persist in that knuckleheaded approach, let their heirs settle the issue in court.

It's often difficult to judge if you're on a collision course with another vessel. The easiest way to judge this is to use the angle off your bow where that vessel is sighted. For example, if you're paddling toward a small island in the distance and you notice a vessel approaching off your starboard bow (see illustration), you should note that angle off your bow. You can do this by laying a paddle shaft in line with the approaching vessel or using your hand width to measure its angle off your bow (see Distance Off on pages 224–27). As you continue on your course to the island, note whether that angle has changed over time. If that angle is closer to your bow, or moving forward, the

In busy harbors it's best to stay outside boat traffic lanes. Scan in every direction for other vessels, and be particularly wary of boats backing out of slipways or pulling away from docks.

other vessel will pass in front of you. If the angle falls off your bow, or moves backward, the vessel will pass behind you. If there is no change, you're on a collision course.

It's important to maintain your speed and heading when observing the bow angle of an approaching vessel. Continuing to point at a landmark or maintaining a compass course is the best way to do this. This method of observing an approaching vessel does not tell you whether it will be a close passing or not. In general, if you can see people on the other vessel clearly enough to make out their clothing, you want to be certain that vessel is passing and not still approaching!

Rules aside, you must always paddle defensively in traffic or in times of restricted visibility. Other boaters may not be aware of navigational rules, especially jet skiers, and you'll need to always be on the lookout for accidents waiting to happen. Other boaters might want to come close to your position so they can look at your kayak; we're often a curious sideshow! (Unfortunately, they often think it's funny to leave us bobbing in their wake.)

Try to plan your trip to avoid heavily congested areas and stay well to the side of channels and fairways whenever possible. Minimize your crossing times and pick your way from one safe spot (like some ledges) to another if you're paddling in open water with other boats. Make your actions obvious to other boaters who may be trying to guess your intentions. Remember, we can tuck into spots that other vessels cannot, so use this to your advantage.

9

Trip Logistics

Planning a kayak trip and then actually completing it safely and in style is satisfying. You not only have the reward of whatever sights you enjoyed along the way, but you also know you planned every step that formed the whole picture. It's very easy to make all kinds of mistakes when planning a trip, from packing, to navigation, to a poor understanding of your abilities or equipment. The more thorough the planning stage, the higher the probability of having a fun trip and getting what you want from the experience.

PLAYING THE "WHAT-IF" GAME

Some people assume they'll never be the ones we read about in the morning papers. You know, the stories about victims of stupidity or natural disasters, or both. I live in fear of being humiliated by such an incident, and my anxieties drive my trip planning skills. I not only have a plan B for every trip, I make sure to include a plan C, D, and E! I also go paddling to relax and experience the seascape and wildlife, and I can do that best if I don't have to worry about details while under way.

When you begin to plan a trip, spread the chart out for a bird's-eye view and mark all the spots that are accessible to you in the proposed paddling area. These would include public lands, private property where you have permission to land, or commercial establishments you want to visit. Note all launch sites and available parking. Now begin to lay out your trip, leg by leg, and note the mileage for each segment. Check the tide tables for each trip day, and be sure you have an easy launch and landing at each site or can make adjust-

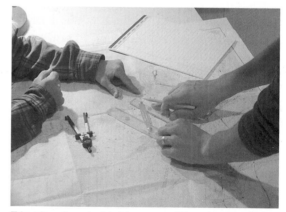

Trip planning starts at home well in advance of the actual trip dates. Begin laying out your trip legs and noting access points on your chart.

FLOAT PLANS

Before you paddle away from your launch site, leave a float plan with someone on shore. Doing this isn't meant to regiment your paddling plans but rather provides an outline of your plans as a safety measure. You can leave your float plan with a friend or family member. Many public and commercial launch sites require that you do this before launching, and some paddling clubs provide a float plan network that you can access by phone or computer.

Include the following information in your float plan.

- description of the boats and the names of everyone in your party
- when you plan to launch (day and hour) and where (include a description of your vehicle if needed)
- when you plan to return and where the area you'll be exploring for each day of your trip
- if it's a multiday trip, consider copying a piece of your chart and mark each of your planned stops and overnight locations
- note the day and time of any check-in calls you plan to make by cellular phone or VHF radio

> ### Float Plan
>
> Boat description: **Current Designs Solstice, bright yellow; Sisuitl (tandem), white; Sealution, teal** . . . .
>
> Members of party: **Shelley, Vaughan, Molly, Ken** . . . .
>
> Day, time, and location of launch: **Monday July 23, 7:00 am, Stonington (behind ferry)** . . . .
>
> Car/Cars license plate number, location, and description: **Jeep, 42kayak4, Sierra p/u, JL125U, Stonington boat launch (parking at Steve's garage)** . . . .
>
> Day, time, and location of return: **Wednesday July 25, 3pm, Stonington** . . . .
>
> VHF call sign . . . . Cell phone number **555-1234** . . . .
>
> Day: **July 23** . . . . . Planned locations: **Steve's I.—camp; Harbor I.—camp** . . . . Will call to check in: **8pm** . . . .
>
> Day: **July 24** . . . . . Planned locations: **Wheat I.—camp (explore Isle au Haut)** . . . . Will call to check in: **8pm** . . . .
>
> Day: **July 25** . . . . . Planned locations: **Return Stonington** . . . .
>
> Should arrive home or call to check in: **5pm** . . . .

Don't forget to close out your float plan when you return or if you cancel the trip.

ments for the expected water depths. You don't want to be surprised by a muddy slog at the end of the day or be held hostage by a low tide when you're antsy to get going in the morning. Along each leg of your trip, note spots where you can get protection from different wind directions or simply pull into a protected area to catch your breath.

Now record magnetic bearings to and from landmarks for each leg of the trip. You can write these on waterproof paper or index cards that you can slip into your chartcase. Some paddlers prefer to write in grease pencil directly on the chartcase cover. Write the mileage and estimated time to complete each leg. Be sure these mileages are reasonable for your skill and fitness level, and build rest stops into the plan.

Now look at the direction of travel for each leg. Is there a tidal current or predicted wind direction that will make things more difficult or require adjustments to your course? Can you make changes to your trip to make use of these factors rather than fight them? If not, how can you minimize the negative effects of any wind or tidal current? What water conditions can you expect in this area, given the tide and predicted or prevailing wind directions? What if a storm moves through the area or the wind is stronger than predicted or from a different direction? Where are your bailout points? What is your plan B?

You need to play this "what-if" game before you leave home. It's much easier to do this with a chart spread across your dining room table than on the water with a squall line approaching or fog bank looming nearby. You also need to play "what-if" for scenarios that include injuries or boat repairs. You can't and probably don't want to try to predict every little twist and turn that may only have a slim possibility of occurring. But, you need to consider the realities of weather conditions that can rapidly deteriorate, paddling partners who might be sick or injured, freshwater jugs that mysteriously drain, and where the next campsite might be if you arrive at an island crowded beyond

its carrying capacity. Then you can relax and enjoy your trip because you've already thought through these things and developed a strategy for dealing with them.

PACKING STRATEGIES

Loading your boat with gear and supplies for a long outing can end up producing an efficient, even elegant, system of storage. Or, you may have created the kayaking equivalent of Fibber McGee's closet. Regardless of your inclinations, packing your kayak deserves some thought and planning. It's never fun to paw your way through multiple dry bags trying to find the coffee by flashlight or have the rice smell like stove fuel. You'll also need to consider how packing your kayak affects the trim of your boat. Like trip planning, the time you spend on checking and packing your gear will reward you once you leave the launch site. And no matter how undisciplined you are, checking your safety gear before leaving is essential.

Repackage your food so any extraneous packaging can be jettisoned before leaving home, and clean and prep as many vegetables and fruits as possible to avoid creating your own compost during the trip. You can clip any directions or dietary information and slip them into a zippered plastic bag with the pancake mix or rice, along with any spices that might be part of the meal. If you're on a multiday trip, label each package with the day and meal and employ the "first in, last out" mode of packing. Entrées can be frozen and layered in soft coolers and used to cool perishables placed on top of them. Place

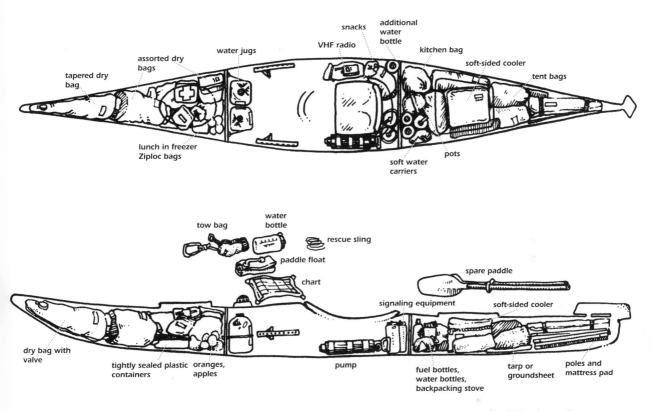

Packing in several small containers rather than one large one gives you more flexibility in packing your boat. Load heavy items first and place them close to the center and along the centerline of your boat. Secure all items in place.

coolers and bags with perishable food along the bottom of the boat, where it's coolest. For more on meal planning, see pages 240–42.

Consider a color-coded or labeled dry-bag system to separate safety gear from boat repair materials and personal gear. Be sure everyone knows which bag contains the first-aid kit and where it's stowed. To avoid confusion, it's helpful to be consistent about who carries which pieces of group gear. Everyone in the group should know how to place an emergency call on the VHF radio or cellular phone.

When it comes time to pack the boats, a little bit of thought goes a long way. It's amazing how much stuff you can pack into a 17-foot (5.2 m) kayak; it's equally amazing how long it takes to find something essential that's tucked up into the nose of the boat and blocked by something that doesn't need to be unpacked until day four. Packing will also affect the trim of your boat, so balance weight from side to side and end to end. Before you paddle away from the launch site, sit in your boat and have someone look at its position in the water. It shouldn't list to one side or be noticeably heavier in the stern or bow. Try to place the heaviest items along the midline of the boat and as close to the center point as possible. There may even be room between your feet and the bulkhead for a few items like water jugs, as long as they're secured in place. Be sure all heavy items are secured and cannot shift when you lean the boat on edge.

Even though most storage compartments are good at staying dry, don't assume that they're watertight. Anything that doesn't float or that would be ruined if wet should be stored in a dry bag. As your hatches begin to empty during a multiday trip, you can use empty dry bags to fill space and hold other gear in place.

Be careful about storing gear on the deck of your boat. Avoid heavy items or gear that presents a high profile to the wind. Be sure nothing blocks access to essential safety

An amazing array of gear can be carried in and on your kayak. **Top:** Sometimes it helps to first organize gear by category: safety and navigation gear (must be accessible), kitchen/food, clothing, camping gear, latrine gear. **Bottom:** When you're done packing, secure hatch covers and all gear carried on deck.

PACKING LIST

A well-organized trip always includes a packing list or two. I have a reusable version with essential gear and then another packing list for each particular trip. It's also handy to include a checklist for last-minute actions like hiding a spare vehicle key, filing your float plan, or loading camera film. Here is a list for essential gear (besides kayak, paddle, and life vest), which you may need to alter slightly for your particular paddling area. This list doesn't include your kitchen gear, provisions, camping gear, or personal clothing.

- bilge pump or bailer
- paddle float
- rescue sling
- signaling devices for day and night
- waterproof flashlight and extra batteries
- waterproof matches
- safety whistle (on life vest)
- spare paddle
- chart and chartcase
- navigation kit (string, pencil, dividers, course plotter, grease pencil, etc.)
- deck compass
- handheld compass
- extra coil of line
- cockpit cover
- sprayskirt
- plenty of dry bags
- repair kit (see page 301)
- first-aid kit
- water bottle, filled (more than one is a good idea)
- VHF radio and extra battery pack
- towline
- knife
- watch
- tide table
- toilet paper
- waste container
- moist towelettes
- trash bags
- sunscreen and lip balm
- sunglasses
- eyeglass repair kit and retainer strap
- spare clothes and hat
- boat sponge
- binoculars
- favorite snack or munchie

You might also consider the following items based on your own interests or the particulars of a given trip.

- sea anchor
- barometer
- anemometer
- EPIRB
- cellular phone
- stargazing guide
- flora and fauna ID books and guides
- camera and extra film
- snorkeling gear
- fishing gear
- sea wings (sponsons)
- Cyalume sticks (for night paddling)

equipment or hinders you when reentering your boat from the water. Also, none of the gear on deck should block access to the grab loop on your sprayskirt or its full release from the coaming.

Keep metal gear away from your compass. A compass will deviate from normal readings in the presence of nearby ferrous objects like other compasses, flashlights, battery packs, or a cast-iron skillet. Keep an eye on your compass during packing, and check it against other compasses in the group and your handheld version before setting out.

MEAL PLANNING AND COOKING

There's no more perfect end to a good day on the water than a great meal. But the last thing you probably want to do after a full day of paddling is to spend a lot of time preparing and cooking a meal and then be faced with a major cleanup effort. As much as I love to eat good food, I never let the menu have the upper hand. There's always a stash of energy bars and fruit in case the idea of preparing a meal seems overwhelming. That said, some of my favorite memories of kayaking trips are those of meals!

Small backpacking stoves are handy and may be all you need to prepare a meal for two. Pack along your stove's repair kit and consider carrying a backup stove for longer trips.

As I've said in other sections of this book, planning is key. Lay out a menu that takes into account answers to the following.

How many pots or skillets are required for this meal?

How many stove burners are needed simultaneously?

How long will the ingredients remain fresh (what are the expected air and water temperature ranges)?

Does anyone in the group have dietary restrictions?

Is there any way to store and use leftovers from this meal?

How much can be prepared in advance?

What tasks must be done just before mealtime?

How much cleanup does this meal demand?

Will cooking and cleaning tasks be shared?

Addressing these questions in advance will save you some headaches and make kayak trip mealtimes pleasurable instead of frustrating

GRAY-WATER DISPOSAL

Proper disposal of dishwater and other liquids that don't include human waste or trash varies by location. If the area surrounding your campsite has sufficient soil depth and organic material, gray water may be poured along a shallow trough and buried, as long as it's at least 100 yards (90 m) from any freshwater source. Gray water can also be poured within a fire pit ring.

If you don't use soap, disposing of gray water is simplified since soap is usually the strongest contaminant in gray water. Never dispose of gray water in a tidal pool or in a body of water where there is little water movement. Avoid areas where there are shellfish or other intertidal creatures that might be affected. It might be best to paddle away from shore to dispose of gray water in an active water column. Often, deep sand is a good surface for absorbing gray water. If there are any food scraps from dish rinsing, you should avoid disposing of the gray water close to the campsite since it may lure unwanted wildlife into the area. For other low-impact guidelines and advice, see pages 272–74.

Use a saltwater–sand–gravel scrub for meal cleanup to conserve your freshwater and to minimize the amount of gray water you dispose of. You may still want to use boiled salt water or freshwater for a final rinse. Dispose of all gray water below the high-tide line, and avoid tidal pools.

or wasteful. The perfect meal not only tastes great but uses only one pot (two is OK, but more than two is getting a bit demanding). Obviously, your group size and structure will dictate many things. Using a single burner to cook a pancake breakfast for twelve hungry adults could take you well into the lunch hour, but it's a breeze for four or fewer.

When planning meals, remember to increase the portion size over those used at home. After a day of paddling and fresh air, everyone's appetites will be astounding. One way to keep entrée portions under control is to serve appetizers during the hour before dinner. This will keep everybody calm and close to the camp kitchen so there'll be lots of help during meal preparation.

If you're planning on foraging, purchasing, or catching your dinner while under way, be realistic. There's a very good chance things won't go as planned, so you'll need a backup meal in the bag. This backup meal is also useful in case you're wind- or fogbound and must extend your trip by an extra day. (For information on freshwater needs, see Dehydration on pages 258–59.)

Kitchen Kit

Let's assume we're going on a four-day kayak trip with four people (none of whom have dietary restrictions). We'll plan meals for lunch on day 1 through lunch on day 4. We'll have to carry all our own freshwater, though we plan to use salt water for some cleanup and cooking (see sidebar page 268). The water temperature is a chilly 58 to 60°F (14–15°C), though air temperatures are expected to range from 70 to 85°F (21–29°C).

My kitchen kit (for two to six people) includes

4-quart pot
2-quart (small) pot
10-inch cast-iron skillet
coffeepot
spatula
large wooden spoon
paring knife
8-inch knife
pastry brush
whisk
dishes and cups for each group member
measuring cup
napkins
paper towels
aluminum foil
zippered plastic bags
trash bags
abrasive scrubby pad
Dr. Bronner's liquid castile soap
dry cotton rag
hot pad
oil cloth or plastic tablecloth
extra line for stringing a light or two
two-burner camp stove and fuel with
     funnel and repair kit
backpacking stove
matches (waterproof and strike-
     anywhere styles)
Parawing for weather protection
     during meals (this can also be used
     vertically as a windbreak)
spices (parsley flakes, thyme, rosemary,
     salt, cracked pepper, dry mustard,
     tarragon, paprika, cayenne pepper,
     dried shallots, basil, saffron threads;
     add or subtract as needed)

olive oil (in small plastic squeeze bottle with taped cap)

Menu Planner

Day 1

LUNCH

Italian subs made before leaving home without mayo, oil, or vinegar (being first out of the bag, you won't have to worry about them getting squashed, and saving the condiments for the lunch site will keep them from being soggy)

corn chips (in zippered plastic bag)

fat deli pickles (in Tupperware or zippered plastic bag)

veggie sticks (carrot, celery, zucchini, yellow squash, bell pepper—urge everyone to eat the squash sticks first)

assorted cookies (in zippered plastic bag)

juice, Tang, or lemonade (in reusable plastic jug)

hot tea and coffee, if needed

dry soup mixes, in case it turns wet and cold

DINNER

cheese and crackers, antipasto platter

salmon fillets in soy-mustard marinade (recipes for the fillets and other menu items begin on page 244)

saffron rice or yellow rice mix

tossed salad with herb dressing

crusty French bread

orange slices marinated in cognac (stored in Tupperware) and whipped cream with almond slivers

On day 1 dinner, you can pull out all the stops since everything is still fresh. The antipasto platter, salmon marinade, tossed salad, salad dressing, and marinated orange slices can all be prepared at home. Any leftover bread can be used for French toast the following morning, and the salad and antipasto items used in pocket sandwiches for lunch the next day.

Day 2

BREAKFAST

French toast with strawberries and maple syrup

bacon

fruit cup (melon, grapefruit, grapes)

juice and Tang

tea and coffee

LUNCH

pocket sandwiches with cheese, lettuce, veggies, and hummus (use any leftovers from dinner)

corn chips or crackers

apples and bananas

assorted cookies or fruit bars

juice and lemonade

tea, coffee, or soup, if needed

DINNER

salsa and chips, guacamole

chicken and veggie fajitas

tortillas

black beans

apple crisp
coffee, tea, juice

Day 3

BREAKFAST

omelets (cheese and anything you want
to throw in)
home fries or hash browns
sausage patties
juice and Tang
tea and coffee

LUNCH

peanut butter and jelly sandwiches
(using pita bread)
hummus, veggie sticks, and crackers
apples and oranges
trail mix
Tang or lemonade
tea, coffee, or soup, if needed

DINNER

Kalamata and cracked green olives,
pepperoncinis, cheese and crackers
shrimp jambalaya
roasted flatbread
cheesecake (no-bake mix) with kiwi
slices

Day 4

BREAKFAST

banana nut pancakes (by now the
bananas are soft and ready) and
maple syrup
sausage links

grapefruit sections
Tang
tea and coffee

LUNCH

pocket sandwiches (pull out something
special here like roasted peppers or
smoked salmon)
corn relish
leftovers!
lemonade
tea, coffee, or soup, if needed

None of these meals require more than
two stove burners for cooking, and the
meal preparation and cooking skills are not
demanding. Leftovers are easily rolled over
into the next day (if there are any at all), and
all but the salmon dinner can be adapted
for longer trips by using canned ingredients
(chicken or shrimp, for example) rather than
fresh.

Recipes and Tips

Salmon Fillets in Soy-Mustard Marinade

Prepare the marinade at home and store in a
reusable plastic bottle.

½ c. olive oil
1 T. Dijon mustard
2 T. soy sauce
2 T. balsamic vinegar
2 T. coarse cracked black pepper

Combine all ingredients and whisk to mix well
and store in refrigerator until trip departure.

The salmon fillets may be poached in a
large skillet using aluminum foil as a cover.

Since the thickness of the fillets may vary widely, cooking time may range from 15–40 minutes for a ½-pound fillet (a good serving size). Fifteen to 20 minutes before you begin cooking the fillets, brush them with the marinade. As they cook, continue to brush them with the marinade. If the fillets begin to stick, sprinkle with water or add some olive oil and more marinade. Keep the foil in place to hold in heat and cook over medium heat until the center of the fillet is flaky and opaque. (If you have the chance to grill over an open fire, go for it!)

Herb Salad Dressing

This classic dressing can be prepared at home and stored in a reusable plastic container. Since it's chunky, don't use a container with a narrow mouth. Drizzle any leftover dressing over pocket sandwiches or use as a bread dip.

2 T. shallots, minced
1 T. garlic, minced
2 T. red wine vinegar
2 T. fresh basil, minced
1 T. fresh tarragon, minced
2 T. fresh mint, minced
¼ t. sugar
½ t. salt
1 T. cracked black pepper
2 T. vegetable oil
⅓ c. extra-virgin olive oil
2 T. hot water

Mix all ingredients except for the vegetable and olive oils and the water and allow to sit for a few minutes. Then, while whisking rapidly (you can also use a food processor), add the vegetable oil and then the olive oil.

Add the hot water last and whisk well. Keep refrigerated until trip departure. *Note:* if you use dried herbs or shallots, cut their amounts in half. If you cannot find fresh mint, substitute fresh Italian parsley.

Saffron Rice

The dry ingredients for this rice may be measured, mixed, and stored in a zippered plastic bag.

2 T. butter
¼ t. saffron threads, minced
½ t. salt
1¼ c. white basmati rice
2½ c. water

Melt the butter and stir in the saffron threads and simmer for 1 minute. Stir in the rice and salt and then add water and bring to a boil. Lower the heat to a gentle simmer and cover. Cook for 15 to 20 minutes or until the rice is fluffy and the water is absorbed. *Note:* it's easy to hold steamed rice until the meal is ready by keeping covered with the pot well insulated (if it's hot weather, set it in the sun on a warm rock).

Marinated Oranges in Cognac

The night before leaving home, peel and slice four navel oranges into bite-size pieces and drench in cognac. Store in a tightly sealed Tupperware container until mealtime. Top off each serving with whipped cream and almond slivers (cut up whole ones for the best taste). Real whipped cream is a bit of a pain to prepare at a campsite, though I've done it on occasion. Your call—you can always use Cool Whip, which keeps better in hot weather.

Chicken and Veggie Fajitas

At home, skillet-brown or bake 4 chicken breasts and tear into bite-size pieces. Sprinkle these with water and seal in a zippered plastic bag and freeze or refrigerate, depending on which day you'll serve and how hot the air and water temperatures for your trip. Clean and cut vegetables into bite-size pieces and store in a zippered plastic bag. You can make the fajita sauce or purchase commercial bottled version.

    4 chicken breasts (boneless is easiest),
        cut into bite-size pieces (prepared at
        home)
    1 small carrot, chopped
    1 green pepper, chopped
    1 red pepper, chopped
    1 yellow pepper, chopped
    2 medium onions, chopped
    1 portobello mushroom, chopped
    2 T. vegetable oil
    ½ c. fajita sauce
    8–10 large tortillas
    3–5 scallions, chopped
    salsa
    1–2 cans of black beans, served on the
        side (heat if preferred)

Stir-fry chicken and vegetables in the oil. After 3–5 minutes, mix in ½ cup of fajita sauce and continue to stir occasionally until vegetables are slightly tender and chicken is entirely cooked. Wrap tortillas in aluminum foil and drape over a pot of boiling water (this could be salt water being readied for cleanup) while chicken and vegetables are cooking.

Scoop filling into tortillas, roll, and top with salsa and scallions. Serve with black beans.

French Toast

    4 eggs
    5-oz. can evaporated milk
    1 T. sugar
    1 t. cinnamon
    sprinkle of salt
    1 t. of vanilla
    bread

Mix everything but the eggs and bread and store in a reusable plastic bottle, or mix together all the ingredients except the bread just before the meal. Dip slices or pieces of bread into the mixture to coat thoroughly. Brown the bread in a pan, turning to cook both sides.

The kind of bread you use is up to you (in my humble opinion, it's hard to beat crusty sourdough), just be sure there aren't nuts or spices in the bread that are offensive to or risky for any group member.

Corn Relish

Corn relish can be prepared at home and refrigerated until departure. This is colorful and can be served cold for lunch or dinner.

    2 cans (14–15 oz.) yellow niblet corn,
        washed and drained (for the best
        relish, boil 8 fresh corn ears and cut
        from cob)
    2 T. red bell pepper, minced

½ c. fresh chives, minced
½ c. fresh Italian parsley, minced
½ small onion, minced

Mix vegetables and herbs together and then toss with ¼ cup of the herb dressing (see page 245) and refrigerate.

Apple Crisp

At home, peel and slice 5–6 apples, drizzle with fresh lemon juice, put in a zippered plastic bag, and store in refrigerator (don't worry if the apples get a bit brown—cooking will do this, anyway). In a separate zippered plastic bag, combine the dry ingredients.

  5–6 apples, sliced
  juice from 1 lemon
  1 ½ c. raw oats
  ½ c. walnuts
  ¼ c. sunflower seeds
  ½ c. flour
  1 t. cinnamon
  ¼ t. allspice
  ¼ t. salt
  ½ c. butter
  ¼ c. honey
  ⅓ c. orange juice (Tang works in a
    pinch)

Dot the bottom of a skillet with butter and then layer the apple slices. Mix the butter and honey and add to the dry ingredients. Spoon this mixture over the top of the apples. Pour orange juice over the top, cover, and cook over low to medium heat for about 30 minutes. The cooking is just to meld the flavors, so even a brief bubbling of the ingredients is sufficient if you're in a hurry. If the mixture begins sticking, stir regularly and lower heat; you may also sprinkle with water if it seems to be drying out.

Variations: use pears or peaches (or you can use canned). These will all shorten the cooking time. Add raisins or dried cranberries. Top with the leftover Cool Whip!

Shrimp Jambalaya

Take two boxes of Uncle Ben's Original Long Grain and Wild Rice mix, recycle the packaging, and mix in a zippered plastic bag before leaving home. Prep the onions, garlic, and peppers at home if you prefer and store in a zippered plastic bag. Peel and wash the raw shrimp and freeze in a zippered plastic bag.

  2 boxes Uncle Ben's Original Long
    Grain and Wild Rice
  2 chicken bouillon cubes
  3 ½ c. freshwater
  2 medium onions, chopped
  4 garlic cloves, minced (should yield
    about 2 T.)
  1 green pepper, coarsely chopped
  1 red pepper, coarsely chopped
  14–15 oz. can diced tomatoes
  14–15 oz. can whole unseasoned
    tomatoes (drained)
  1–1 ¼ pounds of shelled, raw shrimp
  1 T. cracked black pepper (or to taste)
  1 t. salt
  1 T. fresh thyme, minced (or a
    mounded teaspoon of dried; don't
    use powdered)

Sauté the vegetables in olive oil in large pot, add the dry rice mix, and stir for 1 minute.

Add water and bouillon cubes and simmer for about 10 minutes. Add both cans of tomatoes and continue to cook for another 5 minutes or so. Add shrimp and thyme and cook while stirring until shrimp is pink and just cooked through.

Banana Nut Pancakes

By day 3 or 4, the bananas are probably getting brown and mushy—perfect for pancakes!

> 2–3 soft bananas (cut out the really bad
>   spots)
> ½ c. chopped pecans or walnuts
> pancake mix or Bisquick (use a mix that
>   only needs water)

Mash the bananas and set aside. Mix pancake batter leaving out a couple of tablespoons of the water. Add the banana mix and chopped nuts. Mix with minimal stirring (too much stirring will ruin pancake batter). Cook pancakes on a griddle or skillet that's hot enough to make a drop of water dance on the surface (brush with butter or vegetable oil). Ladle in batter and cook until bubbles begin to form and then flip to cook on other side. Serve with butter and maple syrup (this can be warming by leaving on back of stove but not on a burner).

General Tips for Kayak Cookery

Every trip has its own demands; trying to fit your trip into a prescription found in any book may lead to disappointment. Food on a kayak trip should nourish and nurture; meals may serve merely to fill the empty stomach of a very tired paddler or can form the basis for a special gathering at the end of the day. Try to remain flexible and laugh at the foibles. If you feel overwhelmed, find ways to simplify the meal or bag it entirely and have the next day's lunch instead.

This sample menu does not make use of any special utensils like the Outback Oven, which makes baking much easier and more reliable (you can even use its prepackaged mixes). I've assumed that you won't be able to have a campfire and thus have avoided recipes that work only with a reflector oven or a Dutch oven.

The incredible range of trip needs and circumstances will dictate your own menu and cooking, but some general tips are worth considering.

- After two days in a kayak, nothing looks fresh and fluffy (that goes for you, too). For breads, select ones that are already flattened: flatbread, pita bread, tortillas, and crackers.
- Bring a variety of fruit and then eat it in the order of how quickly it bruises and perishes: bananas, peaches, grapes, pears, apples, mangoes, pomegranates, and oranges. Incorporate soft fruit into recipes, especially desserts.
- Have staples as backups for each meal: oatmeal for breakfast, peanut butter for lunch, and a rice mix (or pasta meal) for dinner.
- Adapt the menu and ingredients to hot weather: butter in a squirt bottle and meals that require less or no cooking.
- For hot weather or longer trips, use dry ice (wrap the slabs in waxed paper or thin cloth) in the coolers. Layer frozen entrées directly on the wrap-

Soft-sided coolers are perfect for sea kayakers. Place frozen foods on the bottom, and then layer perishables on top, based on when you'll use them. Label items clearly and minimize the time the cooler is open.

ped dry ice and then other perishables on top of these frozen items.

- Use high-quality soft-sided coolers. They're far easier to pack in a kayak hatch and can be compressed as you empty them.

- Use multiple small coolers and pack them in order of meals. The more a cooler is open, the less its contents are insulated from the outside air temperature. By marking the cooler to be used on the later days in your trip, you won't be tempted to open it until you need to retrieve the ingredients for those meals. Keep this cooler packed on the bottom of the stern hatch, and use other items to insulate around and above it.

10

Group Safety

Traveling in a group will mean coordinating all aspects of your kayak trip with others. This may be as simple as agreeing to the time and place of the put-in with your regular paddling partner or as complicated as copying packing lists and divvying up assignments among group members. Kayakers traveling together should make decisions about how they'll communicate on the water, what to do in case of emergencies or mishaps (injury, capsize, or broken equipment, for example), which kayaker has what piece of equipment (VHF radio, first-aid kit, GPS, or each day's food), and what kind of pace and formation will be used for covering the miles. These decisions must be made before setting out and should be clear to everyone in the group.

COMMUNICATION

Before you begin your trip, you need to work out a few simple signals for group communication while under way. It can be difficult to hear clearly on a windy day, and you need some means of communicating other than your voice. Ideally, everyone should be equipped with a safety whistle. A piercing whistle blow will carry farther and last longer than a voice in times of emergency. You can also use whistle signals for basic group communication.

A typical system of whistle signals might be one blast to get (nonemergency) attention (maybe you spotted a pod of dolphins in the distance), two blasts as a check-in or return call (in foggy conditions, counting whistle calls can be reassuring if someone has slipped out of sight), and repeated blasts for emergency signaling (someone needs help). Many groups use three blasts for emergency signaling, but it makes sense to blow repeatedly since the object is to get kayakers' attention and have them respond quickly.

In addition to whistle signals, consider using hand signals, especially in surf where hearing even a shrill whistle may be difficult. The illustration shows some common hand signals for communicating among group members. Part of the communication process will also be an understanding of how decisions are made while under way and what roles the various group members have.

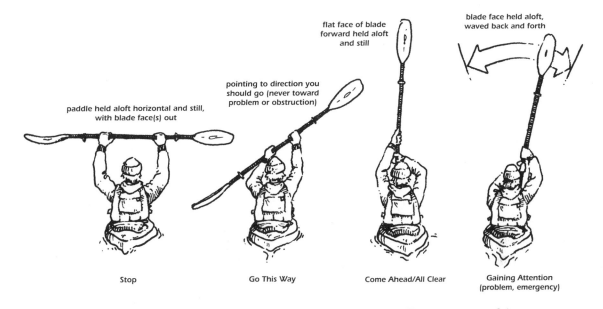

paddle held aloft horizontal and still, with blade face(s) out

pointing to direction you should go (never toward problem or obstruction)

flat face of blade forward held aloft and still

blade face held aloft, waved back and forth

Stop

Go This Way

Come Ahead/All Clear

Gaining Attention (problem, emergency)

Paddle signals are useful on open water and during surf landings. These are some of the most common ones.

TRAVELING IN A GROUP

Part of your trip planning must include the assignment of roles within the group. Group roles and leadership may be loose and informal among close friends and paddling partners or more formalized for paddling club outings or if new kayakers join you for a trip.

If your group is larger than four paddlers, you should form a traveling formation. If the seas are rough or visibility poor, how you position group members can be important. You may choose to set a lead and a sweep boat, capturing the remaining paddlers between those two positions. Or, you may set inside and outside positions that hold the group in between, especially if you're traveling along a shoreline with challenging condi-

Group members should paddle in agreed-upon formations and maintain visual contact at all times. Employing a buddy system works well.

tions or in heavy boat traffic. If the group is very large, you may want to split into smaller "pods" that have their own formation and responsibilities. Keeping the group close together will aid communications and visibility to other boaters and will allow quicker response times in an emergency situation.

Discuss in advance how you'll deal with capsizes or towing scenarios (for assisted reentry techniques see pages 141–51; for information on towing, see pages 254–56). The important thing is to have a plan and a well-understood means of communication. It's difficult to regroup and decide these things when conditions become rough, the visibility is poor, or multiple capsizes occur.

You should also discuss tactics for dealing with a lost paddler. The odds of this occurring may be slim at best, but it's a useful exercise to undertake. Keeping all group members in sight and employing a buddy system should prevent this scenario from happening, but having a plan in place to deal with the worst-case scenario is reassuring.

If someone is separated from the group, it may be best for her to point into the wind to minimize drift and sit quietly to listen for sound signals from the group. She should begin signaling the group with the agreed-upon signals. If land is nearby, it might be wise for the lost kayaker to land if possible or at least hold on to a piece of shoreline. Group members will need to have their search plan ready and coordinated.

Often, only the more experienced paddlers will undertake a search while the remaining group members raft up and maintain position or land on a nearby shore. The time and position last seen should be noted immediately, and a search that considers the expected drift and set from that position should be undertaken in a systematic fashion. Knowing that

SEASICKNESS

My own personal experience is that seasickness is not as likely in a kayak as other vessels, but it can still occur. The most common scenario for seasickness is when slow rollers cause the boat to wallow while you're sitting still or moving slowly. Try to look ahead to the horizon and avoid fixating on the bow or deck of your boat. Keep moving and even try to pick up your cadence and think about something other than that tightening knot and queasiness in your gut. Stay well hydrated, and consider splashing cool water on your face. Often, being given a short-term goal (like paddling to a nearby buoy) will keep seasickness at bay. Landing on a piece of shore will usually calm an unruly stomach.

Seasickness can be debilitating and will affect your balance. If you're seasick, let your paddling partner know immediately. Too often, seasick paddlers become quiet and aloof from the group, which exacerbates the problem. Having someone else help you through it will make things easier. You may need to be stabilized while you overcome some dizziness or vomit over the side.

Over-the-counter medications, taken before a paddling trip starts, can help control seasickness. Be sure you're aware of any side effects, like drowsiness, that might occur.

PADDLING AT NIGHT

Paddling under a full moon is magical. There is little boat traffic and generally calm conditions. If you're lucky enough to be in an area where bioluminescent organisms abound, you're in for a double treat! Each stroke creates a trail of sparkles through the water, and the thrill of rolling in these conditions is not to be underestimated.

Paddling at night, even under a full moon, requires that you be a bit more conservative in your plans (maybe rolling practice wasn't such a good idea, huh?) and group strategy. You'll want to be sure you and your paddling partners stay within visual contact of one another at all times since it's difficult to see other kayakers on the water at night. Cyalume sticks make great markers for paddlers in the group and can be placed on the back of a life vest or headgear for a quick count of group members. Reflective tape on life vests and boats will show up well at night when caught in the beam of a flashlight.

Navigating at night is challenging. It's more difficult to pick out the shapes of land and, unless a navigational aid is lighted, you might miss it entirely. You'll need a small light for reading your compass (you can mount two 3 in./7.6 cm Cyalume sticks on either side), and you should use a red lens on a small flashlight for reading your chart. Red light doesn't disrupt your night vision as a bright white light would.

If you'll need to make any crossings, you should become familiar with the lights displayed by different vessels that might be common in your area. Sometimes, the placement and color of lights will be the only way to tell if a boat is moving toward you or away from your position. Tugs and their tow will also display lights specific to their situation. Never paddle between a tug and the vessel it's towing, whether it's under way or not. The night can be a magical time to paddle, but only if you fully understand its language.

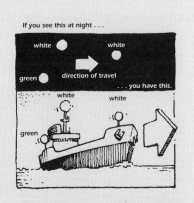

If you see this at night . . .
white   white
green   direction of travel
. . . you have this.
white   white
green

If you see this at night . . .
white
white   red
. . . you have this.
white
white   red

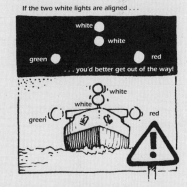

If the two white lights are aligned . . .
white
white
green   red
. . . you'd better get out of the way!
white
white   red
green

Night paddlers must be familiar with the running and anchor lights of different vessels. Sometimes these lights are the only way to tell a vessel's direction of travel. For example, power vessels 165 feet (50 m) and longer must display the running lights shown here.

the lost paddler would have been instructed to paddle to a nearby shore, or point into the wind and hold still, will make the search easier. Scenarios that may be likely for your paddling area should always be discussed before setting out.

TOWING

Experienced paddlers should always carry a towline and know how to use it. Towing scenarios can range from the seriousness of towing an injured paddler to providing a quick boost to combat fatigue. Towing doesn't have to be about emergencies. It's a useful way to pair paddlers of disparate ability for a long crossing or keep children connected to an adult's boat.

In most situations, you'll use a standard sea kayak towline. This style of towline is 20 to 50 feet (6–15 m) long to allow plenty of room for paddling in seas and to avoid having the towed kayak surf down a wave into the towing boat (for more on towlines, see pages 79–80). The simplest tow is the single straight-line

tow. The towing kayak is connected to the towed kayak at the bow toggle. A simple tow can be extended to include additional towing kayaks or towed boats in series, each needing its own towline. A series of towing boats will take the strain off a single paddler and saves the time of switching towing boats while under way. You might also employ a "husky tow," by which two paddlers are directly connected to the towed boat and pulling forward at an angle off the towed kayak's bow. This method can be a bit trickier in rough seas and is difficult if the towing kayaks don't have rudders. But the husky tow allows a quicker response than a serial tow.

If the towed paddler needs to be stabilized, another kayaker will need to paddle alongside. This paddler may position himself slightly astern of the towed paddler or may need to actually hold an injured or unconscious paddler upright during the tow. Each situation will require some thought as to which method works best. A paddle with paddle floats on either end or sponsons may be used to stabilize the towed paddler's boat if he's still able to sit upright.

series

husky

If two paddlers are towing, they may set up in series (top) or as a husky tow (bottom). The husky tow is quicker to set up but may be trickier to do in heavy seas.

Using inflated paddle floats on both blades will stabilize a towed paddler. Secure the paddle shaft under the deck rigging if the towed paddler is unable to hold the shaft in place.

Close-contact tows may be used when close to shore or in situations where there is only one other person to tow and stabilize a towed paddler. Close-contact tows put the towing kayaker in direct contact with the towed boat, usually slightly ahead to allow a full range of paddling motion. The towed paddler may need to be draped across the rear deck of the towing boat, depending on the circumstances. Many rescue or guide life vests include short towlines, often called *pigtails* (see also photo on page 79). It's wise to carry both a long sea towline and a close-contact towline to cover all needs.

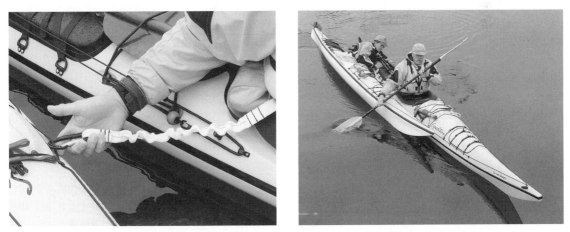

A close-contact tow can be used for short sprints to shore or when the towed paddler needs to be stabilized and observed closely. **Left:** Clip the short towline into the rigging or other hardware on the forward deck alongside the tower. **Right:** You can use a close-contact tow to tow a paddler stabilized on the back deck, where you can more easily monitor her. Strong winds or seas reduce the efficiency and practicality of the close-contact tow.

Place a towed swimmer immediately behind the paddler for the best boat control and stability. The swimmer should stay low and along the centerline of the boat.

You may find yourself in a situation where you need to tow a swimmer. The swimmer can crawl onto your stern deck and remain low while you continue paddling. She must keep a low center of gravity to avoid capsizing you. You can then paddle her to shore or reunite her with her kayak. Swimmers may choose to hang on to the bow of the towing boat for a short tow but will continue to be immersed, which is not the best choice in cold water.

FAMILY PADDLING

Sea kayaking can be a great family adventure. You'll need to make adjustments for all the family members involved in the trip, and be sure to have plenty of non-kayaking activities planned, especially if children under the age of ten are along. Short paddling hops interspersed with snacks, games, and the chance to burn off energy on land will help make the outing successful. Consider everyone's goals and preferences, not just yours as the experienced kayaker in the family!

Toddlers and very young children are best carried in a cockpit with a parent. Tandem kayaks make great family vehicles, much as a minivan fits the bill on land. Tandem kayaks are stable and can carry lots of extra "kid gear" and may even sport a large center hatch that can be used as a cockpit for young ones. Lining the cockpit with insulated pads is handy for padding and warmth. You'll definitely want to keep any kids' paddles tethered to the boat or you'll spend your time serving as a retriever. Sit-on-top kayaks make great family vehicles for short trips and a simple introduction to paddling.

Never venture onto the water without each child being outfitted with a properly fitted life vest that meets all U.S. Coast Guard and state requirements. Spend a few more dollars on a comfortable vest or one that shows their favorite cartoon character so your child will wear it. It's worth the extra investment to have them look forward to putting it on

Some doubles make great family vehicles. Here the child can ride in the center position and still be easily reached by either adult.

Adjust kids' life vests for a snug, comfortable fit. Vests for small children and infants have flotation behind the head with a grab handle and a crotch strap to keep the vest from slipping over the child's head when afloat.

instead of screaming bloody murder when you try to zip it in place. Usually, infant vests (up to 30 lb./13.6 kg) and most children's vests (30–50 lb./13.6–2.72 kg) have a flotation collar with grab loop and crotch strap. Some states require these vests to be type II vests, which provides flotation behind the head and increases the chances of floating an unconscious victim face up in the water (slightly different from the type III vests that most kayakers use). For the later years, youth vests (50–90 lb./22.7–40.8 kg) will more closely resemble adult vests and allow the child more freedom to paddle. Often these vests match adult models and provide pockets and a variety of adjustments for comfort.

Obviously a life vest is worthless unless it is worn. You can set a great example for your kids by always donning yours first and keeping it on at all times while paddling or when close to the water. Be sure your life vest and your child's vest are snugged down and zipped up at all times.

Introducing Your Child to Kayaking

Before ever putting your kayak in the water, let your child climb in and out of the boat and explore its depths while it sits in a stable spot on land. It's important that a child get used to the smell, feel, and the parts and pieces of this new plaything before you get into the water. It will be far easier to explain how things work and what is (and isn't) appropriate behavior while they're sitting comfortably on land where you are easily heard. You can reinforce the importance of remaining seated and not leaning out over the water without your help to balance the boat. And your child can pepper you with questions, which are more easily answered when sitting on the back lawn rather than under way.

Children should be shown how to hold the paddle properly. Small children may sit in your lap and hold on while you actually paddle. By doing this they will feel the resistance of the blade moving through the water and the motion of the paddle as you move from side to side. Your torso rotation may be limited, but this is not about fine paddling technique but rather a fun and reassuring introduction to paddling for your child. You will likely tire more easily because of the need to hold the paddle higher to avoid bonking your child on the head, so plan accordingly.

Older children should be encouraged to paddle even if it has little effect on your forward motion. Purchase your child a paddle with a smaller shaft diameter and reduced blade size (this will also help reduce its weight). It will need to be long enough to reach the water but not so long that it is unwieldy to use (paddle length formulas are of little use here). While it is unrealistic to expect a young child to paddle consistently the entire time you are on the water, let them know that their efforts are appreciated. When they pick up the paddle, you could say, "It really feels like we're going places now!"

When children become interested and able to paddle consistently, make sure they have sufficient back support and a comfortable seated position that allows them to contribute to the paddling. At some point, you'll need to decide when to let them venture out in their own boat. Obviously you'll want them tethered or within touching distance of you when you first try this. Many parents have been successful with tethering a children's kayak to their family double kayak. This allows the child to paddle as much as they like, but it also lets them have a free ride if they tire or become bored.

Many outfitters offer trips designed especially for family groups. Trying one of these trips might be the perfect introduction for your child if you do not want to take on the role of guide and instructor right away. The goal should always be to have fun, get a bit of exercise, and foster an appreciation for the natural world and our place on its waterways.

STAYING HEALTHY

Like any sport or outdoor activity, sea kayaking has its share of aches and itches, most of which are avoidable if you're willing to listen to your body and make adjustments. Paddling partners will need to keep an eye on one another for signs of dehydration, sunburn, hypothermia, and the like. Often, others will notice a problem before you're willing to voice your own concern and do something about the problem. Also keep a keen eye out for nature's offerings: critters, plants, and microbes that can bring your trip to a quick halt (for more, see pages 267–70).

Dehydration

Sea kayakers are notorious for getting dehydrated. We try to avoid the inconvenience of having to pee while under way (especially when wearing a dry suit) and end up with a splitting headache by midafternoon. Always keep a water bottle or two within easy reach and drain them at least every couple of hours while under way and even more frequently in hot, dry climates. You can refill them from a larger stash that's keeping cool in a hatch. If you detect the beginnings of a headache

Potable water constitutes the heaviest and bulkiest item you'll pack for a kayaking trip. Two paddlers on a two-day trip require 6 gal. (22.7 L)—which weighs about 50 lb. (22.7 kg). Unless you're sure you can reprovision along the way, never skimp on water.

coming on, you've probably gotten behind in your water intake and need to reach for the water bottle.

The effects of dehydration can make you slower to comprehend a problem or complete a navigational calculation, and make you unable to pick up the pace of paddling when needed. Staying hydrated will also help loosen sore muscles and has been shown to ease back and joint pain in most sufferers. I know I may sound like a snake oil salesman by declaring that drinking water will do everything from make you smarter to increase your stamina, but staying hydrated is a critical part of any outdoor activity.

Many sea kayak routes don't have access to freshwater, so pack your own supply; allow about 1½ gallons (5.7 L) per person per day. This seems like an enormous amount when it's time to pack the kayaks, but you'll need

it. Multiple collapsible water jugs or bags give you the most flexibility for your packing schemes.

Sunburn

Before setting out on a kayak outing in sunny or partly sunny conditions, you should slather yourself with a good waterproof sunscreen of SPF 30 or higher. Don't forget to protect tender areas like the tops of your ears, backs of your arms, and even under your chin where reflected sunlight reaches. You'll need to reapply sunscreen over the course of the day at least a couple of times, and more often if you're surfing or swimming.

If some patches of skin get toasted, gently swab them with a clean bandanna and water before applying aloe or a topical anesthetic like lidocaine. Drink extra water and be sure the affected areas are well protected from the sun if you're continuing your trip.

Barnacle and Shellfish Cuts

These little cuts and abrasions can be painful and continue to plague you throughout a multiday trip if you don't clean them properly. These cuts often occur on hands when paddlers reach for a rock or place their hands on a shallow bottom as they get into and out of their boats. They may look insignificant, but these nasty slices can flare into full-scale infections and prevent you from paddling if they're not treated quickly.

Clean the wounds with fresh, soapy water and then treat with hydrogen peroxide, making sure that no fragments are left on the skin. Apply an antibacterial ointment and put a clean bandage over the wound to protect it. You should repeat this treatment at the end of each paddling day until the wound is healed.

Saltwater Rashes

The bane of many sea kayakers, these rashes crop up where clothing seams and salt crystals work in concert to irritate the skin, or when entrapped sweat glands become inflamed. They can become very sensitive to the touch and make you quite miserable if you ignore them.

Wash the area with freshwater and dry with a soft material. Apply cortisone ointment (over-the-counter strength) to the area every six hours or so. If the rash is under the arm or around an ankle where a fabric seam will continue to rub, protect the skin with a soft piece of clothing. Continue to wash the area and treat with cortisone ointment until the rash disappears or you're able to seek medical help.

Wrist and Shoulder Aches

Many joint aches are caused by poor paddling technique. Many paddlers use a death grip on their paddles and inflame wrists sensitive to the repetitive motions of the forward stroke. Relax your grip and keep the back of your hand and wrist aligned with your forearm while paddling. This will avoid the side-to-side torque that will injure your wrist and leave you unable to paddle for any length of time.

Shoulder aches may also be a sign of poor technique. Many paddlers remain rigid in their upper body and square their shoulders with the front of the boat. If they make a stroke to the side or rear of the boat, this can put

Never put your shoulders or wrists in this vulnerable position. As you paddle, keep the paddle shaft out in front of you and squared with your shoulders. This will avoid awkward positions that may cause injury or strain.

their shoulders in a vulnerable position. Try to keep your upper body relaxed, and instead of squaring your shoulders with the boat, they should be squared with your paddle shaft. As the paddle shaft moves to the side, it should mirror your shoulder and torso movement. This is good paddling technique that should be employed regardless of any shoulder aches.

Sometimes, a shoulder, wrist, or elbow ache may be caused by using paddles that are extremely stiff. Carbon fiber paddle blades and shafts are often very stiff and rigid, which means that more of the stroke snap is absorbed by your joints. This is not a knock against carbon fiber paddles. The fact that carbon fiber paddles are so lightweight saves a lot of wear and tear on your body and will fatigue you less than a heavier paddle. But some carbon fiber paddle shafts are more resilient than others, so you may need to test-drive a few until you find one that works for you.

You may also make minor adaptations to your stroke, especially if you're faced with aching joints on a multiday trip or toward the end of a long day on the water. I think of it as wimping out at the catch of your forward stroke. As you plant the paddle blade during your forward stroke, let your torso slouch just as the paddle catches the water, then follow through with your normal torso rotation. This is not good paddling technique, but it lessens the jolt on your joints from a stiff paddle and has saved me in the past. In the long run, you'll need to make equipment changes to correct the problem.

Once you're off the water, ice or cool the aching joint and minimize making any movement that aggravates the problem. Many kayakers have found relief with the use of analgesic and anti-inflammatory creams such as Traumeel, BioFreeze, and Arnica. If you are prone to joint inflammation, you may want to consider packing some nonsteroidal anti-inflammatory drugs (NSAIDs) such as Motrin or Aleve, or their generic derivatives. Do slow stretches of the affected joint before you resume paddling the following morning, and start with a slower paddling cadence to ease into the day.

Numb Feet

Numb feet are a common complaint among kayakers and may never be avoided by some paddlers after long stretches in the boat. Occasionally, numb feet will escalate to affect the lower leg and even cause shooting pains up the back of the leg. Many times this is caused by forgetting to move your lower body while you're in the boat. This may sound silly, but I've seen paddlers appear to forget that they have a lower body when they're out on the water. Their feet never come off the foot braces and their knees never relax from a fully braced position against the thigh braces. This is a tough position to maintain without a break for several hours, so it's no wonder that feet go numb and lower backs begin to ache.

Although maintaining a secure paddling position (see page 95) is important, especially when the conditions turn dicey, there are usually times over the course of a day's paddling when things lighten up and you can relax. Remember to wiggle your toes, shake your feet, and even drum your toes on the underside of your kayak's deck. Drop the rudder and play around with it, pushing it fully from one side to the other. Pull your knees up into a cannonball position or even pop your sprayskirt and hang your legs over the side. If you're worried about stability, have a paddling partner raft up to stabilize you or use a paddle float as an outrigger for support. Although I'm a proponent of good posture and correct body alignment to support good paddling technique, there's also a time to relax and shake it out to avoid developing muscle kinks and things like numb feet.

If you find that your feet keep going numb, there may be other culprits at work. Often, a neoprene boot zipper or river sandal buckle is perfectly positioned to cut off blood supply to the foot and cause numbness. Also check your foot brace adjustment to be sure it's not set too short, forcing your ankle into an uncomfortable bend; if foot braces are too long, you'll stress your lower back as you have to straighten your legs to reach the pedals.

Check the seat base in your kayak. It's helpful to have a slight lift to the forward edge of the seat. This lift helps support the

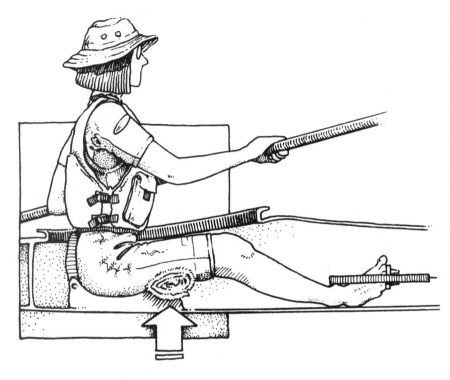

Numb feet are common and can often be avoided by tilting your seat lip up and supporting the backs of the thighs. Here, a rolled towel is placed under the thighs for support. Wiggle your toes and move your legs around over the course of the day. Too often, paddlers forget to stretch and move their lower body while paddling.

back of the leg, allows the pelvis to tilt forward, and positions your lower back and hips deeper into the seat where they may be better supported by the backrest. If you think your problems may be caused by a flat seat, you may create a higher seat lip by gluing some foam to the front seat edge or reinstalling your seat base and lifting its front edge by using foam blocking underneath. If you're in the field, you can used a rolled towel beneath your upper thighs or place an inflatable pad off the forward edge of your seat.

Hypothermia

In chapter 3, we discussed how to prevent hypothermia and the debilitating effects that it can have on kayakers. You may still be faced with a paddling partner (or you) becoming hypothermic during a kayak outing.

If someone in your paddling group shows symptoms of hypothermia—lethargy, uncontrolled shivering, blue lips, and general clumsiness—get that person dry and warm immediately. Provide him with a windbreak while he changes into dry clothes with lots of insulation and a windproof outer layer. Ply him with warm, sweet liquids like cocoa or sweetened gelatin, and be sure he's wearing a warm hat.

Most instances of hypothermia involve these early stages that can be remedied with the quick attention of paddling partners. Be conservative in your assessment of hypothermia. Don't let a group member shrug off help if you suspect he's cold. Often, a mildly hypo-

CONTACT LENSES

Sea kayaking can be rough on contact lenses. I've lost more than my share while under way and simply discarded a few after saltwater spray made them impossible to wear. You should always consider wearing a pair of sunglasses or goggles to protect your lenses when paddling if the weather or water is rough. Wind may fold a soft contact lens over in your eye and make it easy to lose. Add side protectors to your sunglasses to keep the wind from funneling across the surface of your eye and folding soft lenses and drying out your eyes.

Pack extra supplies of saline solution since your eyes will dry more quickly when you're spending time on the water or when it's windy. It's difficult to replace or clean lenses from your cockpit since your hands will probably be sticky from salt water. Wind can wreak havoc with lens handling, so pack along plenty of soothing drops to keep your eyes hydrated and to keep salt water from irritating them.

thermic person will refuse help and then slip into lethargy or become clumsy and end up capsizing.

If a hypothermic paddler doesn't begin to respond to treatments, he should be stripped and placed in a prewarmed sleeping bag or emergency blanket wrap on top of an insulated pad. Other group members may need to crawl in next to him and provide their own body heat for warming. If the person does not show signs of responding within minutes, you should contact emergency personnel and arrange evacuation. Rewarming an acutely hypothermic person can trigger shock and is best done in a controlled hospital setting.

Heat Exhaustion and Heatstroke

Heat exhaustion occurs when the body is not able to cool itself properly. If left untreated, this will lead to heatstroke, a serious emergency that is the complete breakdown of the body's heat regulation.

Keeping hydrated is the best defense against heat exhaustion. The first signs of overheating are a flushed appearance of the skin. Blood vessels close to the surface of the skin have dilated as they try to shed heat from the body. An overheated person is usually, but not always, sweating profusely. If she begins to feel dizzy or lightheaded, have her lie down and elevate her feet (no easy feat on the water). Be sure she consumes copious quantities of water, and place a wet, cool bandanna across the back of her neck. If possible, keep her out of direct sunlight and exposed to any cooling breezes.

If you're not seeing clear signs that the person is cooling down (return of normal color, more alert behavior), you must consider the potential for heatstroke. Heatstroke will result in the rapid rise of core temperature and loss of the ability to sweat. This needs to treated as a medical emergency since it can lead to unconsciousness and even death. Keep the person in the shade and continue to douse with water until you can get medical help.

11

Kayak Camping

One of the benefits of kayaking is that it can serve as a way to explore farther afield for several days, or even weeks, at a time. This usually means traveling in a self-sufficient fashion, carrying all your own food and water and providing your own shelter each night. Kayakers can make use of much of the same camping gear that backpackers use. We often can add more luxurious items such as camp chairs or special food items to our packing lists since we aren't as restricted for space as are land-trail travelers. But we often have to pack all the freshwater needed for the entire trip, and our clothing needs are often more demanding (think *immersion*) and more varied (swimsuits to dry suits).

CHOOSING AND SETTING UP A CAMPSITE

While your specific paddling area will play a major role in your choice of a campsite, there are several features that are universal to good campsites. You'll want to choose a campsite that is safe and pleasant.

Your site should be protected from heavy weather. Look at the lay of the land: does

it channel winds and cold air down to your campsite or protect you from them? If it's a warm-weather campsite, does it allow fresh breezes that will cool you and keep the bugs away? If at all possible, avoid camping beneath tall trees that might draw lightning strikes or be exposed to high winds. You don't need to lie awake and wonder if the next gust of wind will topple that spindly pine or bombard you with its broken branches.

Your campsite should be well away from any wildlife trails or feeding areas. Look for signs of wildlife around the campsite and its fringe: tracks, spoor, nests, and scratches or gnawed spots on nearby trees. If bears or raccoons are common in the area, have some means to protect your food, and store it away from the campsite and your kayaks. If careless campers before you have rewarded local wildlife visits to the site, then animals will most likely check out any possible food cache, including your tent and kayaks.

Check the ground for level spots suitable for your tent. Avoid any gullies or places that will collect water, and don't set up camp alongside streams or seasonal runs that may flood during a rainstorm. Don't trench around your tent site; it leaves an ugly scar on the land and is not needed with today's seam-sealed and coated tents. Be sure that there are no poisonous plants like poison ivy or oak close to the area.

If campfires are allowed and appropriate, check to see if there's sufficient deadwood in the area and an established (and permitted) fire ring. Or, plan to build your fire below the high tide line, and after letting it burn out, scatter any rocks that you used. Do *not* cut live branches or strip birch bark from nearby trees for fire materials. If you can't locate enough deadwood, save the fire for another night and spend the evening stargazing without any ambient light to lessen your views.

Obviously, be sure to site your camp above the highest high tide mark. If there's a full or new moon, or there's any storm surge, you'd do well to allow a significant margin of safety beyond the high tide line.

You might have other requirements for a perfect campsite: a quiet place to sit alone and watch the stars, a view across the water, or the presence of edible plants.

Setting Up Housekeeping

Once you've selected your campsite, you can begin to unload your gear and secure equipment for the night. Be sure the boats are

Designated campsites are created to absorb the compaction and wear of high use.
Do not clear vegetation to create additional sites.

A VIEW TO DISASTER

I once made a terribly poor choice of a campsite because it offered such a fine, bird's-eye view of a pocket cove and the Bay of Fundy. Around sunset, as I was finishing my evening meal, the winds began to build and funnel through a pass above the meadow where I had pitched my tent. By nightfall the winds began to roar, and they blasted against the side of the tent and lifted its stakes. I drove the stakes in deeper and piled rocks on top and lay spread-eagled on the floor of the tent, only to have it lift and roll me to the edge of the cliff that offered my beautiful view. I managed to escape and spent a miserable night hunkered behind a large log, but most of my camping gear was lost or shredded. I've never forgotten that lesson about wind and topography.

pulled up and battened down to protect them from any high winds. Stow paddles and strip the decks of any gear and store it inside the cockpit or hatches. A cockpit cover comes in handy (or you can use a sprayskirt and

You'll appreciate your camp kitchen being off the ground and organized.

cinch the waist tight), especially if there are sand fleas or other creatures that might like to explore your boat while you sleep. Be sure you have secured all kayak hatches. Consider your visual impact on others who might paddle by or have views of your campsite from a mainland shore. Avoid drying your colorful paddlewear by spreading it along a piece of shore or leaving gear strewn across the beach.

You'll probably want to establish your camp kitchen fairly close to your campsite in a spot well protected from the wind and without overhanging branches. For additional wind protection, rig a tarp between two trees as a windbreak. To capture the heat from a campfire, position a tarp that faces the fire and tapers to the ground on three sides, though avoid having the wind blowing smoke, or worse, embers directly toward the tarp. You'll probably want to position cooking surfaces and food prep areas above the ground, especially if the area is sandy. Your resulting meal will be less crunchy if you can spread out on a ledge, large log, or overturned kayak.

Before nightfall, check that rain gear, flashlights, and additional clothing are at the

Before calling it a night, make sure cockpit covers are in place and the boats are well above the high tide line and protected from strong winds. Store gear inside the boat and protect food from marauding wildlife.

campsite so you won't have to root around the boats at night. If needed, decide where you'll establish your latrine and be sure everyone is familiar with how to properly dispose of their waste. If there's a common latrine, hang a toilet paper roll or some other marker that can be taken when people are using the area and returned when they're finished. It's always nice to relax and know you have the place to yourself for a while!

BEWARE!

Every paddling site has its own pests and local dangers. The list provided here is merely a sampling of some of the more common prob-lems that exist in marine environments and the pests that frequent many coastal shores. While you can certainly encounter these problems during a day trip, an extended kayak camping trip may increase your chances of encountering these nasties, which can cut your trip short.

Red Tide

This is not what ebbs and flows in the Red Sea! Red tide is a bloom in the population of dinoflagellates, a single-celled organism, that can occur in the intertidal zone. These organisms are absorbed by other marine organisms like mussels and clams and can be toxic to humans as paralytic shellfish poison-

USING SALT WATER

Salt water may be useless as drinking water, but it can be used for cleaning, washing dishes, and certain cooking chores. If freshwater is precious, and it usually is on sea kayaking trips, you can do all the dishwashing and cleaning with salt water. Boil the salt water if you use it for rinsing. Often a good scrub with coarse sand and a rinse in boiled salt water is sufficient for most kitchen cleanup. If you prefer, you can follow this method with a quick freshwater rinse. If you need to use soap, use a biodegradable version like Dr. Bronner's, which can also be used to wash your hair and brush your teeth.

You can use salt water to cook anything that does not absorb the bulk of the water when cooking, but you must boil the salt water before doing so. Salt water works great when cooking shellfish, corn on the cob, and fresh beans and peas. Don't use salt water when cooking rice or in recipes with flour or meal—the resulting concoction may be inedible! If you have any concerns about the water quality in the area where you're paddling, don't chance using any salt water for cooking or cleaning. It's better to be conservative than to cut your trip short because of illness.

Launch sites may be posted with shellfish consumption warnings. You can also access information on marine weather radio channels.

ing (PSP). NOAA weather radio will broadcast red tide closings, and you should note these locations on your chart. Never forage for clams or mussels if you're unsure of the water quality or the presence of red tide. The paralytic shellfish poisoning that occurs from consuming these organisms can be fatal.

Even if you're confident that the shellfish you collected are free of these organisms, try rubbing a piece of the meat on your inner lip. If you experience any tingling, the meat may be suspect and you shouldn't eat it. Don't depend on this test in the absence of any other information about the presence of red tide in your paddling area, but use it only as a backup check.

Poisonous Plants

Poison ivy and poison oak thrive in many coastal areas, blanketing the ground and even weighing down large trees. Just paddling by

You should be able to reliably identify poisonous plants. Poison ivy (shown here) and poison oak are common in many popular paddling destinations.

these spots makes me feel itchy! Any wilderness traveler should know how to identify common poisonous plants in an area, because if you know they're around, you can avoid them.

Exposure to plants like poison ivy produces a reaction that's usually noticeable within a day or so after exposure. Small, red blisters may appear and be very itchy and sensitive to the touch. If you think you've touched a poisonous plant, clean the area well with warm, soapy water. If you're unaware of your exposure until blisters appear, then follow the cleaning with a treatment of cortisone ointment, and refrain from irritating the area by scratching. Other over-the-counter treatments like calamine lotion may help keep the itching to a minimum. If the blisters begin to weep and swell, or you're prone to severe reactions to these plants, *seek medical help.*

Local Pests

Many popular paddling areas have their own pests. These may range from biting insects and caterpillar infestations to alligators. Before you plan a paddling trip in a particular area, check with local outfitters and paddlesports shops for advice. Kayaking guidebooks are also a great source for this information, as are local paddling clubs. Before you set out, find out about any local species that bite, sting, or could wreak havoc on your trip.

Deer Ticks

Unlike their larger cousins, dog ticks, deer ticks are very difficult to detect. They may be no larger than a pinhead in their nymphal stage when they're most likely to transmit the spirochete that causes Lyme disease, a serious illness. Deer ticks may appear only as a small brown dot resembling a freckle or piece of dirt and go unnoticed for days. They're also fond of hiding in creases of skin and other hard-to-spot places.

It normally takes about thirty-six hours for the deer tick to transmit the disease to a human, so a daily inspection is important if you're traveling in areas where deer ticks are found. Your daily inspection should be thorough, and you'll need a hand mirror to check every crack and crevice (yes, every one). Even if you don't spot a deer tick, you'll need to check your skin for evidence of a deer tick bite. Usually, but not always, a deer tick bite that introduces the spirochete into your system will develop a telltale bull's-eye, or red halo, around the bite. If you find any sign of this, or if you were unable to remove all of the tick from the bite area, see a medical practitioner at once. Often an immediate treatment with antibiotics will destroy the spirochete. If there is a significant delay in responding, more extensive regimens of antibiotics may be required.

If you find a tick embedded in your skin, remove it carefully with tweezers. Try to pull the tick straight out without twisting or squeezing, and do not try to burn or remove it with the use of any substance. After removal, use antiseptic to swab the area and then wash your hands thoroughly. You may want to save the tick in a small vial to be given to medical personnel for testing if needed. Lyme disease is debilitating, so any deer tick bite must be taken seriously. For more information, talk to your medical practitioner or visit www .lymediseaseassociation.org.

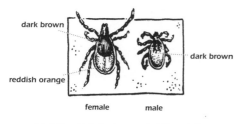

Adult Deer Tick *(Ixodes scapularis/dammini)*

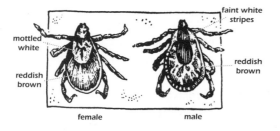

Adult Dog Tick

Smaller than dog ticks, deer ticks carry the spirochete that causes Lyme disease. Cover skin and band pant leg openings to keep them from finding a home on your body.

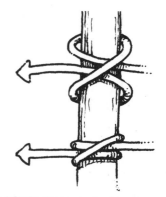

Clove hitch: these stacked loops can be used to make a line off to a post, rail, or small tree trunk.

Overhand knot: this is a simple knot often used to finish another knot or to keep a line from pulling through a hole.

Figure eight: this symmetrical knot can serve as a stopper knot at the end of a piece of line.

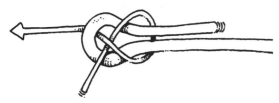

Sheet bend: use this knot for joining two lines of different diameters.

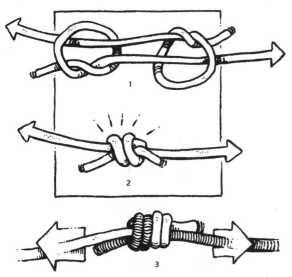

Fisherman's knot (1–2): this knot will join two ends to form a loop (for example, a rescue sling) or join two ropes of equal diameter. A double fisherman's knot (**3**) is stronger and adds another bite on either side. Use a double fisherman's knot on rescue slings.

Square knot: use this to tie off two ends of a line. One wrong move making this knot and you'll tie a granny knot instead, which will pull free easily.

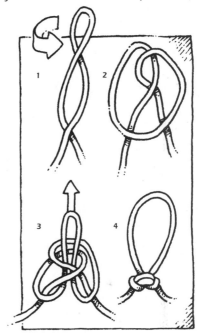

Butterfly knot: this is a great knot for creating a loop in line strung between two points. Use it to hang food bags between two trees.

Daisy chain: used to shorten any line and then quickly pull it free to the length you need. Towlines are often daisy-chained.

USEFUL KNOTS FOR CAMPING

Knowing your way around a piece of line or *warp* (short for *potwarp*), as we call it in Maine, is a handy talent indeed. Instead of looking puzzled and creating endless granny knots that fall free as soon as you turn your back, you'll be prized as a useful member of society. The illustrations on pages 270–71 show some handy knots for using around the campsite (see additional knots in chapter 4). You'll be able to hang gear, tie off tarps, secure boats, and string clotheslines with abandon!

LOW-IMPACT GUIDELINES

Sea kayakers should be as low impact as their craft. We leave no oil sheen or noise in our wake and should take care to leave the places we visit as untouched as we found them. Low-impact guidelines minimize the effect humans have on the land and seascapes they explore, so these unique places will be there time and again for us and others after us to

A good pair of binoculars is a must for viewing marine animals and sea birds from an unobtrusive distance that allows you to watch their natural behaviors rather than their response to your presence.

enjoy. There are many thoughtful ways you can travel in low-impact style in your sea kayak.

Each place you visit is fragile in its own way and must be taken care of in its own fashion. Some island soils cannot absorb the repeated impact of human feet or absorb the wastes left behind; others have nutrient-rich layers but may harbor unique flora. Learn

STRANDED ANIMALS

At some point you may come across what appears to be a stranded animal—a seal pup apparently left alone on a ledge or an osprey chick floundering along the shoreline. Do not approach the animals in these situations. Instead, move quietly from the area and try to observe the scene through your binoculars. Often, the mother may be close by but afraid to approach because of your presence.

If you're convinced that you're observing a stranded animal, make note of the exact location and contact local authorities. Typically, a university program, conservation organization, or aquarium may serve in this wildlife rescue and rehabilitation capacity. These are the folks who have the training to deal with stranded animals and increase the likelihood of their survival. Do not remove stranded animals yourself; call the proper authorities.

WATER TRAILS

In the past twenty years, water trails have become popular throughout the United States and Canada. These trails are intended for small boaters and may range from a short jaunt along a busy waterfront to several hundred miles of small-boat access points that can be explored for years. Kayakers have often played pivotal roles in developing and maintaining these water trails that protect the waterways and much of the land alongside them. Water trails will also protect access points that can often be difficult to find in this age of private property and no trespassing signs.

Water trails are often pieced together from both private and public land holdings. Kayakers may serve as volunteer stewards, donating time and energy to cleanup and maintenance projects, or in educational outreach programs in the community.

You won't find water trails marked on your chart. But some of the larger water trails organizations offer guidebooks for their members that detail camping sites, access points, route selection, and protected species along the trail. In return, you'll be asked to serve as a steward for trail sites and as the eyes and ears of the organization when you spend time on the trail. There will usually be low-impact guidelines specific to particular water trails that take the fragility of the land, waterway, and local wildlife into consideration. You'll be asked to abide by these low-impact guidelines and set an example for others to follow.

Find out if there's a water trail in your area or in an area you plan to visit. Local paddlesports shops, conservation organizations, and state parks departments are usually aware of their presence. If there's a water trail in your area, consider volunteering some time to help out. If there's not one, consider creating one. The process may be demanding and won't happen overnight. But if there's enough interest and dedication, it will happen. See the Resources section, pages 319–22, for more information on water trail organizations.

---

about the stress points for the areas you plan to explore and make adjustments to your behavior. It may require that you set up camp on the fringe above the high tide line and pack all wastes out, including your own, to be disposed of on the mainland.

One of the rewards of sea kayaking is being able to observe wildlife from the intimacy of eye level while you sit quietly in your kayak. Too often, kayakers observe only the flight and frightened behavior of disturbed wildlife as we venture too close. A good pair of waterproof binoculars is a must for sea kayakers. You'll be able to observe the natural behavior of the wildlife you encounter rather than their response to your presence. Be especially careful during nesting season or when mothers are rearing their young. This is an especially difficult time, and any additional stress placed on the mothers or their young can make the difference in the survival of that year's offspring. If you must pass close by wildlife, give them a wide berth and use low-angle strokes or try to quietly

Steves Island

Welcome to Steves Island. To ensure the island's ecological health, the quality of the visitor experience, and the future availability of all public islands for recreational use, we recommend that visitors follow these voluntary guidelines.

Length of Stay. Maximum: 2 nights
Island Capacity. Maximum: 12 overnight campers

The condition of the island and the visitor experience will be better protected if use levels are less than the recommended maximums. *Note: Circumstances may occur where it is not safe or practical to follow these guidelines. Please do not place yourself or others at risk on the water and please do not land on other islands where you do not have permission for access.*

Leave No Trace on Maine's Fragile Islands

PLAN AHEAD & PREPARE
Low-impact enjoyment of the islands begins before you leave home. When planning your next coastal trip, please familiarize yourself with the regulations, guidelines, hazards and use levels of the islands that you plan to visit. Plan carefully for safety, comfort and alternative destinations. Contact the Maine Island Trail Association for more information about island use guidelines.

TRAVEL & CAMP ON DURABLE SURFACES
We all need to work together to protect fragile soils and vegetation.
Walking. Please travel on sand, stone, resilient grass, and established trails. Avoid walking up dirt banks, in boggy areas, or on mosses and lichens.
Cooking. Please set up your camp kitchen on rugged surfaces below the high tide line. If the sites are already in use, squeeze into an existing site or bivouac on granite, sand or gravel. *Please do not cut or clear vegetation, trees or limbs -- dead or alive - for any purpose.*
Camping. Use existing campsites; do not expand established sites or clear new ones. If the sites are already in use, squeeze into an existing site or bivouac on granite, sand or gravel. *Please do not cut or clear vegetation, trees or limbs -- dead or alive - for any purpose.*

DISPOSE OF WASTE PROPERLY
Pack it in, pack it out. Please help keep the island clean.
Human Waste. Please carry off all solid human waste and toilet paper, and dispose of it properly on the mainland. Do not bury it or leave it in the intertidal zone. Human waste can be carried out in portable toilets, Tupperware containers or in a bucket with a tight-fitting lid.
Trash & Garbage. Pack out trash and food waste, both your own and any you find.

MINIMIZE CAMPFIRE IMPACTS
Fire hazards on islands and the shortage of available driftwood make campstoves the best choice for all of your cooking needs. ***MITA recommends no fires.*** If you must kindle a fire, a permit is required from the Maine Forest Service (800-750-9777). With permit in hand, build a small, safe fire below the high tide line, preferably in a fire pan or on sand. Fires on rocks leave permanent scars. Burn only driftwood or wood that you have brought from home.

RESPECT WILDLIFE
We are guests in this natural coastal habitat. Please give wide berth to those who call it home -- nesting seabirds, eagles, ospreys, rafting eiders, and seals. Please leave pets at home; an unleashed dog can wipe out a bird's brood for an entire year.

LEAVE WHAT YOU FIND
Allow others a sense of discovery by leaving rocks, plants, archaeological artifacts, and other objects where you found them.

BE CONSIDERATE OF OTHERS
The enjoyment of all visitors depends on a shared island ethic. Please be aware and considerate of other island users at all times. Those who live and work in the surrounding coastal area deserve our courtesy.

Organized Groups. Maine state law requires that individuals leading coastal boating or island camping trips for compensation must hold the appropriate license from the Maine Department of Inland Fisheries & Wildlife (207-287-2031).

This is your public land to protect and enjoy.
Many thanks for your cooperation!

Island Owner Maine Bureau of Parks & Lands 22 State House Station Augusta, ME 04333	**Island Manager** Maine Island Trail Association 41A Union Wharf Portland, ME 04101 207-761-8225

Most public lands have access information posted. This might include the carrying capacity and overnight stay limits. Use local sources (outfitters, water trail organizations, state agencies, etc.) to get this information in advance of your trip.

coast by to minimize your impact on them (though some argue that being noisy clearly identifies you as not being a predator). Keep your group close together and always be sure to offer animals an easy avenue of escape if you've inadvertently come too close. Learn and follow any governmental regulations for protection of animals, like the Marine Mammal Protection Act, which requires you to stay at least 100 yards (92 m) away and prohibits harassing any marine mammal.

Before setting out on any kayak trip, be sure you know

- the recommended practices for solid and liquid waste disposal
- whether and where campfires are appropriate
- whether any protected species reside in the area
- what restrictions apply to tent location and group size

These considerations should always be a part of your trip planning. Others following in your wake will be glad you made the effort.

12

Planning Your Dream Trip

Everyone has a dream trip in mind. It might be a misty fantasy of island shores and deserted beaches or a specific route traced on a chart and an airline reservation. My dream trip was always to return to explore all the nooks and crannies of Maine shorelines that I'd seen from the deck of the historic sailing vessel I worked on. I've been fitting these dream trips into every paddling season for over twenty years and still haven't run out of nooks and crannies to explore!

You can use your sea kayak to explore your choice of an incredible range of destinations.
Your dream trip may take you to remote Arctic waters or to a stretch of sandy beach in the tropics.

People yearn to explore new places and seascapes for many reasons. For some, negotiating a stretch of challenging coastline or reaching a remote island shore is an accomplishment that is deeply rewarding. For others, the escape to an exotic location brimming with odd creatures and a culture that stimulates the curiosity fuels the planning of their next kayaking adventure. Still others are happy to explore their local waters in greater depth and discover new views through studying the geology, cultural history, or marine biology by kayak. Every kayaker has a dream trip, however humble or exotic, challenging or restful. It's the follow-through that usually gets us!

Don't be tempted to choose a destination beyond your skill level; be realistic about gauging your skill level and those paddling with you. Find out what the worst possible conditions might be for a given destination and how probable they are.

MAKING A CHOICE

You may have no doubt about where your dream kayaking trip takes you and what you hope to see and accomplish. But some kayakers will need to narrow the choices, or at least prioritize them (after all, there can be several dream trips) before planning the nitty-gritty details that allow them to pull off a trip that is hassle-free and rewarding.

Skill Levels

There's no sense in attempting a trip that will put you or your fellow kayakers in danger. Challenge is stimulating, but lacking skills to deal with the expected conditions is foolhardy. Be realistic—if you're used to paddling 10 miles (16 km) a day and feel pushed to the limit if more than an hour of continuous paddling is called for, define your trip within those limits. If you think surf landings and launchings will be required to explore a given area, be sure you're comfortable with those skills before setting out. It sounds obvious, yet I've known of many cases where kayakers ignored the skill requirements for a particular trip with often disastrous results. Leave activities that are outside your skill level for a future dream trip.

Weather Preferences

Do you see yourself lounging on a sandy beach as the trees wave in the steady afternoon winds or staring in awe at an iceberg as the sunlight creates subtle shades of color? If you hate having weather throw you a curveball, you should stick with destinations that

THE HEBRIDES

The Outer Hebrides islands lie off the northwest coast of Scotland and are exposed to the often stormy North Atlantic waters. While spectacularly beautiful and steeped in history, these islands can only be explored by kayakers with advanced paddling and expeditions skills.

Most of the Hebridean weather comes off the ocean where low-pressure systems form with regularity and a certain fierceness. It's not unusual for a kayaking expedition to be windbound for several days, and the rocky coasts and shoals can stir water into a boiling froth that's simply impossible to traverse by kayak. Clearly, a dream trip of kayaking the Outer Hebrides should remain a dream for most paddlers and be attempted only by expert paddlers who have the skills to deal with these challenging conditions.

have predictable patterns and seasonal—not hourly—changes in the weather. If you revel in adapting to ever-changing weather patterns and feel a bit smug when Mother Nature kicks butt, then look to destinations that offer a potent mix of conditions that are stirred into often unpredictable patterns. Depending on your preferences, schedule your trip in the middle of a given season for predictability or on the edges of a season if

Destinations can be chosen for their climate predictability or their fickle weather, depending on your preferences. The shoulders of each season are usually attended by unsettled conditions, resulting in a wider range of weather.

CONSIDER THIS WEATHER

One of the most popular late-winter sea kayak destinations is the Sea of Cortés, or Gulf of California, a finger of water on the eastern side of Mexico's Baja peninsula. With daytime temperatures ranging from 75 to 90°F (23.9–32°C) during late February through mid-April, kayakers can be fairly confident about weather expectations. A typical day exploring the coves and fingers of rock south of the town of Loreto begins at sunrise when the air is cooler and calm. Paddling conditions are almost always ideal through the morning hours before the air has heated and winds begin to build. Afternoons usually bring dry, hot winds that blow hard and make kayaking a chore. Most kayakers choose to put in their miles before the heat of midday and use the afternoons for snorkeling, swimming, or dozing in the shade of a tarp. This semitropical weather and daily itinerary is generally predictable and relaxing.

The coast of Maine, on the other hand, can produce weather that is fickle and teasing. The old saying of "if you don't like the weather, wait five minutes" is a perfect fit for predicting the weather patterns off the Maine coast. I've experienced snow flurries in July and, several days later, felt stifled by muggy heat. Packing lists for kayaking in Maine need to include everything from heavy fleece and wool hats to swimsuits and sunscreen. Weather a few miles inland from the coast can be a poor indication of what you'll find when you actually poke your nose out of the protection of a harbor. Weather radios are useful for gathering information on the bigger patterns moving through the area, but often the small slice of water you're exploring creates its own microclimate, so a keen eye to observing cloud formations, humidity, and wind directions is a must. The best sailors in these waters will sniff the air and get a bemused look as they calculate where to find their wind and avoid the fog that plagues the area from mid-June through August (of course, even this general prediction is proved wrong time and time again somewhere along the coast every day!).

you prefer a mix of weather that can shift suddenly and frequently.

Timeline

How much time do you have for your dream trip, and how much of that time will be used for getting to and from your destination's point of access? A trip to the southern island of New Zealand will require some serious time off and several days to get to and from any access point if you live in North America. You must also decide how long the trip

needs to be for you to feel satisfied with the outcome. If your kayak trip is wedged into vacation plans that include a list of other sites and activities, then a simple overnight trip to a nearby coastal island shore may be just the ticket. It's often tricky to plan an outing that lasts long enough to satisfy your need to escape but not last so long that you can't wait for the last day to end so you can get a shower and restaurant meal. If you can, build an extra day into your plans to allow for more time on the water or some shoreside luxuries. This is also a good idea if you anticipate a

LEARNING BY KAYAK

Many colleges and adult enrichment programs have begun offering various courses that use sea kayaks as a vehicle for learning. College geology courses may cover a stretch of coastline and explore island shores where glacial activity and rock formations serve as a hands-on classroom for several weeks during a summer. The National Audubon Society (NAS) offers courses through its NAS Ecology Camp programs on subjects ranging from shorebirds to photography that use kayaks as the primary means of exploration.

If your dream trip includes learning more about a particular subject while kayaking, there may very well be a program available to you. Check adult education listings for your proposed paddling area, and ask local outfitters about such special offerings (many offer bird-watching or photography by kayak classes). Visit the Sierra Club, National Audubon Society, Nature Conservancy, and local conservation organization websites to request information about such course offerings. If you're unable to find a course to fit your needs, design your own and pack along a load of field guides, make notes about your observations, and shoot rolls of film to record what you saw. You can spend the off-season creating a journal that catalogs what you learned and that displays your images or field samples you collected. (Note: do not collect samples from shell middens, archaeological sites, or other sensitive areas.)

Keep a journal and record your observations or questions to research when you return home.

Sea kayaks make great vehicles for studying marine flora and fauna. Here, students and their instructor are identifiying marine organisms in a tidal pool.

wind- or fogbound day that might keep you landlocked.

Focus and Style

Is there a particular focus for your trip? Are you hoping to observe whales, visit a glacier, or find the remains of a coastal fishing village? If the success of your trip is contingent on certain things happening, then you must be sure to design the trip so that's your focus. All your paddling partners need to voice their goals and focus for the trip so everyone understands how the trip plan is structured. It can get ugly if you're intent on observing marine mammals for hours on end while your paddling partner is chafing to get going and cover the miles to visit some native ruins.

You also need to decide how basic or luxurious your trip will be. Will you create gourmet meals that dazzle or spend your energies on other aspects of the trip and feed your body's need for fuel with prepackaged meals? Having done both, I can assure you that both styles can work perfectly, depending on the needs of each particular trip. As a guide, I'm used

---

QUESTIONS FOR A LOCAL OUTFITTER

If you plan to use a local outfitting or guide service, there are certain questions you should ask, depending on whether you're simply renting gear or making reservations for a trip.

- What is the make, model, and material of the paddles and kayaks? If you're unfamiliar with the brands or models, ask for the manufacturer's catalog or visit its website to find out more about the gear you'll be using. If a gear upgrade is available, what is its cost? Often, you can pay more to get lighter paddles, composite boats, or even Gore-Tex dry suits instead of wet suits.
- Will the gear be properly sized for you? Often, outfitters use only one model of single kayaks for their fleet. That's fine if you're the average size and weight that model was designed to accommodate, but it can be tough if you're outside of those size ranges. Be sure there are other choices of sizes and styles of gear for a comfortable fit.
- What level of kayaking skill is expected? If you're a novice kayaker, will there be any instruction before the trip?
- What sort of meals are served? Ask for a sample menu or speak directly to the guide and get a description of a typical day of meals. If you have any dietary restrictions, can they be accommodated? Is there room for you to pack along a few of your favorite treats? If you're hoping to have a cocktail or wine with dinner, is this allowed?
- What personal gear is recommended? Almost all outfitters will provide a suggested packing list as well as a maximum amount of gear allowed per person (for example, two grocery bags full). Be clear about what is being provided by the outfitter (sleeping bag? tent? wet suit?) and what you need to bring. If certain gear is recommended but not provided, can you rent these items?

to impressing guests with elaborate meals and fresh ingredients—that's what they had been promised and had every right to expect. On my own, I'm often more than happy to snarf a couple of PowerBars and some juice before crashing for the evening after a long day of paddling in windy conditions.

Your trip plans may also include overnight stays that range from primitive camping conditions to decadent bed and breakfast pampering. Your style of travel will greatly affect your trip's budget, gear allocation, and need to resupply.

On Your Own or with an Outfitter?

Many of your concerns about skill levels, focus, and style can be put to rest by taking your dream trip with a personal guide or on a guided trip with others. Though some kayakers wouldn't dream of hiring a guide, for others it's a rational, and often safer, choice. An outfitting service will usually be quite clear about the skill level required for particular trips, what you should expect to see, and how far you'll travel per day and be able to provide sample menus in advance. You may have

- Will you be provided with a chart of the paddling area? If not, can you purchase one? Even on a guided trip, having a chart of your own is useful and leaves you with the perfect souvenir or future trip planner.
- What is the cancellation policy? Who makes that decision, and what is the deadline for that decision? If your trip requires air travel and other costly arrangements, consider obtaining trip insurance.
- What is the size of the group? What is the guide-to-client ratio? Are there other staff members (junior guides and cook, for example) along for the trip? If you're traveling alone, will you be paired with another client in a kayak or tent? Are there options if you're unwilling to do this?
- If you'll be camping, what are the campsites like? Is there freshwater for cleaning? Are there outhouses or must you pack out human wastes? It's important for some people to know these things, given the shock I have seen on faces when these details are discussed for kayaking in my home state of Maine.
- Where do you leave your car? If you're flying, is it possible to arrange transportation to and from the airport? Are there lodging recommendations for the area if you're arriving the night before or wish to extend your stay?
- What safety and communication gear does the guide carry? If needed, who should family members contact to reach you?
- What experience or certifications does your guide have? Many states require guide licensing, and some guides have instructor certifications (see pages 3–4) or wilderness medicine certifications as well.

a choice of traveling with others who have signed on for the trip or of designing a custom trip for your group. (See the sidebar on pages 280–81.)

You may also choose a trip that's resupplied by a local outfitter but that leaves you in control of your own itinerary (other than the resupply date and point). Local outfitters can also provide a wealth of knowledge about the local waters, weather patterns, wildlife, pests, and danger points. They can warn you about crowded areas to avoid and give you tips on local boating etiquette. Your trip plans may also require that you rent certain gear from a local outfitter. This may range from fully outfitting your group with all the kayaking gear and clothing to purchasing charts of your kayaking area. Even if you choose to go on your own and travel in a self-sufficient manner, a stop at the local outfitter or paddlesports shop is a good idea before beginning your trip.

GATHERING INFORMATION

Once you've settled on a trip destination (or at least narrowed your choices), you can begin gathering information on the area you've chosen to explore by kayak. There are numerous tools available to you, and most of your research can be done online. Check out popular outdoor destination websites, such as www.trails.com or www.gorp.com or the paddling-specific www.paddling.net. On these sites you can find descriptions of paddling conditions in certain regions, links to other websites that might provide information on the weather and water conditions, and a listing of local outfitters.

Visit websites of paddling magazines and search for your intended destination to find articles on kayaking trips to the region. Often these articles are the most helpful because they are written by kayakers familiar with a given area and include lots of paddling and outfitting tips for the area and information on possible safety concerns.

Do a Web search on the actual destination name. This will usually yield links to locally

An outfitter can provide the gear and its transport for your trip.

sponsored websites such as the chamber of commerce, lodging establishments, state or provincial tourism services, public parks, and retail establishments in the area. This is a good time to discover if any inoculations or travel visas are required for traveling in a particular area.

You can access local weather information through a variety of websites: www.weather .com, www.noaa.gov, or www.weather.gov (see Resources, pages 318–19). Go to your favorite local bookstore or online bookseller and search for guidebooks and field guides for those areas. Several series of kayaking guides are available, and you can often find local field guides for subjects of interest such as bird-watching, geology, marine mammals, or wildflowers. A kayaking guidebook will provide kayaking-specific information: weather and water conditions, tidal ranges, danger points, access points, wildlife, navigational aids, and actual trip routes.

You can also search for information on local history, industries (especially marine related), or even cookbooks (a great way to find out what sort of goodies are available and may show up on local menus). Find out if there are water trails in the area and if they require membership or other fees for access to campsites. *Sea Kayaker* magazine offers a clickable map for the United States and Canada that lists water trails in a given area (also see Resources, pages 319–22). Paddling magazines also provide extensive listings of outfitter and guide services in a given area.

You may need to contact a state or provincial agency if permits are required or if a float plan must be filed. A guidebook, water trail organization, or local outfitter should provide information on what permits are required and who to contact. Some permit reservation systems can be trying and require lots of advance planning. For instance, the Okefenokee Swamp in Georgia has several kayak and canoe trails with camping platforms scattered throughout this national wildlife refuge. You must make reservations for your trip that are specific to the trail and each overnight stop sixty or fewer days in advance of your trip dates. About all you can do is to begin calling the reservation number sixty days before your trip's start. You may spend a half hour or more punching the redial button until you hit the jackpot and make your reservations. (But it's worth it—this is a magical place to explore by kayak or canoe, and your reservation ensures that your group is the only one on a particular portion of the trail and at your campsite each night.)

LAYING OUT THE TRIP

Whether you're heading to Greenland or Chile, Washington State or Maine, there are a few steps you should always follow when planning a kayak trip. First, you must have a map of some sort. If you'll be paddling on the ocean or on the Great Lakes, you should get a nautical chart (see pages 197–200). This provides a lot of useful information about the proposed paddling area and the navigational aids available along your route. If you're exploring inland waters, a topographical map allows you to travel compass courses and recognize features along the immediate shoreline and surrounding land (a road map can even be used in a pinch).

Using your chart or map, mark all public access lands and campsites (or lodging establishments if you're including those in your itinerary), boat ramps, and public access points along the shore. This will mark where you can get out of your boat and where you may stay overnight. Note other areas that you hope to explore—a glacier, tidal river, island, or favorite orca feeding area. With these points of interest and access marked, begin laying out the legs of your trip and checking the mileage of each leg. Note possible lunch stops, snack and stretch breaks, and places to duck out of different wind directions. Note any tidal information that might affect your trip plans (see pages 234–36 for playing the "What-If" game).

Determine if your daily trip legs are of reasonable mileage and provide the best route given expected weather conditions (especially wind directions) and tidal currents. Avoid long stretches of exposed paddling if more protected routes, even if they are longer, are available. Start laying out backup plans and alternative routes for other weather conditions or trip factors (sick paddling partner, the need for a place to dry out, for example). Note places where you can reprovision or get freshwater if needed (I also note ice cream stands). Also mark spots where you can access roads or seek help in case of emergency. Review these plans with all your paddling partners and be sure everyone is in agreement about mileage and routes. This is also a good time to decide how you'll divvy up group tasks like food purchasing and prepping and cooking meals (see pages 240–42). Make a master list of who is responsible for each task or assignment and when it must

get done (reservations and permits might be first; disposing of trash and wastes at the end of the trip might be last).

Equipment

Your trip plans will dictate the type and quantity of equipment you carry and whether you're renting or using your own (for a general packing list, see page 239). For many destinations, folding kayaks will be invaluable. If rental programs at your destination are not what you'd like or are nonexistent, you can rent folding kayaks before leaving, which offers you the chance to get familiar with the equipment as well as be reassured of its quality.

If you're renting equipment at your destination, consider taking your own paddle and life vest, anyway. Often these two rental items can be laughably inadequate and leave renters yearning for their own equipment (I was once handed a museum relic horsecollar vest and a bent aluminum paddle with blades that weighed a good 2 pounds apiece). If you're out for an afternoon, it's no big deal to adapt, but a multiday trip could leave you miserable if you're battling inadequate equipment or a poor fit.

Details

You should plan to set up a date and time for checking in with someone on shore or back home. Checking in may not be easy if you're traveling in a remote location, but someone other than your paddling partners needs to know when and where you expect to return. If possible, leave a float plan with the folks back home and with a local contact (sometimes park rangers are willing to hold a float plan, and they often require one).

Remote locations may also make it difficult to purchase or prepare food for your trip. Depending on how flexible your digestive system is when it comes to handling new foods, you may want to pack along several freeze-dried or rice and noodle meals as a backup. I have heard more than one horror story of kayakers undertaking a trip with just the offerings at a local farmer's stand, only to become so sick and weak that they were unable to complete their trip. By the same token, I've known others that reveled in the notion of eating only local foods and what the sea and shoreline had to offer along the way. Whatever your preference, make it a planned one!

13

Taking Care of Your Stuff

Your kayaking equipment will last longer and look better if you treat it well and store it properly. Since I'm the world's worst about taking care of gear, I can attest to the bad things that happen when you don't take the time to put things away correctly. You'll also need to do occasional maintenance or repairs on some pieces of gear and give everything a good going-over at the beginning and end of each paddling season.

GEAR STORAGE AND MAINTENANCE

If you're lucky, you have a nice, big garage or barn with plenty of room to store your gear. If you don't, you'll have to be creative and even consider using your kayak and paddle as artwork in your living room! Any storage area should protect your gear from excessive ultraviolet (UV) exposure and be well away from any heat source. Cold storage is rarely a problem when storing kayak gear, though it may be an issue for some of the materials and solvents used for repairs.

Kayaks

Before storing your boat for the off-season, hose it down with water. Spray the rudder or skeg housing and foot braces to force any sand out of their workings, and allow everything to dry and the storage compartments to air. Leave hatch straps loose so that any hatch gaskets do not needlessly compress over long periods of time, and remove soft hatch covers. Coat the boat (polyethylene or composite) with a UV inhibitor like 303 Protectant. This can be applied with a soft rag and used throughout the season and before storage to prevent UV damage and color degradation. Check straps and lines for fraying, and make note of anything that will need replacing or tightening.

This is a good time to consider buffing and waxing your composite kayak (if so, you can skip the 303 Protectant for now). Buffing will remove all the little scratches and scrapes, and waxing will help protect the surfaces for the next season. You can use a very fine automotive rubbing compound and soft buffing wheel to help remove small mars and even out the color (it helps to remove deck rigging first). Then, a good-quality car wax can be applied and buffed to a shine to enhance the color and add protection from the sun.

For storage, your kayak will fare best if you can support it on its side or at its bulkheads. These are strong areas that can support the weight of your kayak over long periods without causing any damage or deformation of the boat. Don't suspend your kayak by the carrying toggles alone. These can break or pull out of the boat, and polyethylene models stored in this manner can actually sag to create a very long whitewater boat by spring.

Consider suspending pieces of 2-inch (50 mm) nylon webbing from rafters or ceiling joists to cradle your kayak overhead. This will keep it out of the way and out of the reach of many of the little creatures that might set up house in it during the off-season (use a cockpit cover to be sure).

You may choose to store your kayak on the ground on its side. If it's a polyethylene boat, check it regularly to be sure it isn't dimpling

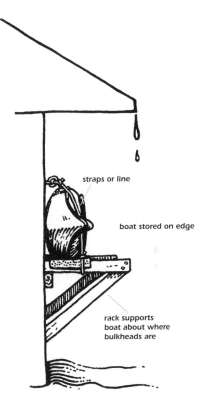

straps or line

boat stored on edge

rack supports boat about where bulkheads are

Kayaks can be stored on an outside rack attached to a building. Be sure your boat is protected from falling ice or snow and secured against high winds.

Support your boat as close to the bulkheads as possible. A set of webbing slings in a garage works well and may be useful for solo loading on your car.

or denting from sitting on an uneven piece of ground (think of these as bedsores on your boat). A pallet or some sort of platform under the boat keeps it from freezing to the ground in colder regions. Use a cockpit cover, or you'll end up sharing your cockpit in the spring with a variety of critters, or their leavings. If you store your kayak outside, either cover it (don't use a clear cover) or do something else to make sure it's well protected from the sun's rays. Don't store your kayak under cover in direct sunlight. Even on a winter's day, the

AGING BOATS

If you take good care of your kayak and protect it from the ravages of ultraviolet rays, it will last indefinitely. Composite boats may lose their luster, but the underlying boat can easily last for more than twenty years if cared for properly. Polyethylene boats may become brittle over time without protection but will last ten years or more when well cared for. Most polyethylene boats manufactured since the 1990s include UV inhibitors in their compounds. This and other advances in plastics manufacturing technology have increased the lifespan of polyethylene kayaks.

Any cracks or splits on your polyethylene kayak may point to a serious degradation of the boat material. Significant fading that leaves a chalky or cloudy color to the boat will also indicate that the material may be on its last legs. Be conservative when using a polyethylene boat that shows signs of advanced age. Surfing, rough-water paddling, or jarring landings have the potential to seriously damage old and brittle polyethylene. It might be wise to retire the old boat and look for a younger model.

heat and condensation that can be generated will damage a polyethylene boat and may create uneven color in the gelcoat of a composite boat. In heavy snow areas, don't place it below a roof slope where it might be bombarded with chunks of ice and snow.

For temporary storage during the paddling season, you can continue to show off your boat by leaving it on top of your car. If you do, check it regularly and tighten the straps and other attachments. Don't forget it's up there when you visit drive-through windows and low parking garages! Immediately after a rainfall, empty the boat of any water. Polyethylene boats can sag from heavy amounts of water in the cockpit, and a sudden jolt to a composite boat full of water can cause fractures.

Paddles

After using your paddle, hose it down with water, and if it's a two-piece version, take it apart before storing. A bottle brush works well to clean inside the joint and to brush sticky salt deposits from edges. Stand the two pieces with their blades up so any water trapped in the shaft or throat can drain. For long-term storage, they can be stashed inside the cockpit or hung overhead in their own webbing cradles.

Check any wooden paddles for chips or peels that will allow water under the finish. This might eventually delaminate the wood strips or bubble the fiberglass cloth wrap over the surface of the blades. And beware of porcupines, which are notorious destroyers of wooden (and other) kayak gear. They love the salt deposits, and salty wood is one of their favorite meals.

Paddlewear

Wash all your paddling clothing thoroughly after each use. Otherwise, accumulated salt crystals will rub you raw and itch like crazy.

Wet suits should receive a power wash with the hose nozzle to force particles from the closed-cell foam. Hang them inside out for drying on a large, stiff hanger (you can cut one out of plywood), and never store them if they're damp since mildew is quick to establish itself. For long-term storage, hang them up or store flat since wrinkles leave creases that eventually crack as the wet suit ages. Purchase wet suit shampoo, or use a small quantity of mild dishwater detergent.

The breathable membranes on Gore-Tex dry suits and paddling jackets should be washed well in water. It's every bit as important to wash the inside as well as the outside of these garments, since oil from your skin (or lotions spread on your skin) can eventually clog the membranes and lessen breathability. Gore-Tex doesn't clog as a result of exposure to salt water, and in fact, in the field you can use salt water to rinse it, if needed. But, a freshwater wash always results in a more pliable and comfortable garment. Keep sunscreen, insect repellent, and any solvents separate from your dry suit. These materials will disintegrate a latex gasket into a black sticky goo. Your dry suit should be dry before storing to avoid mildew, which can stain and clog the Gore-Tex membrane and degrade latex gaskets.

To store, roll the dry suit loosely with the zipper left open and place it in a mesh bag out of sunlight. Sunlight is as deadly to latex gaskets as the chemicals in sunscreen. You can help retard UV degradation of the gaskets by regularly treating them with 303 Protectant.

Over time, waterproof fabrics lose their ability to repel water. Instead of beading up and running off, water sits on top and gradually soaks through the outer layer. You can restore durable water repellency (DWR) by machine-drying the garment. Don't do this with a dry suit, since the latex gaskets will suffer (as will the inside of your dryer). Instead, you can iron the outer fabric on a medium-low setting. This will refurbish the water repellency to some extent, but only reconditioning with a DWR treatment will restore it.

THE PERILS OF DRY SUITS

It's easy to abuse the latex gaskets on your dry suit when you don or remove it after paddling. Wearing jewelry or a watch is one surefire way to rip latex; impatience is the other. I once tried to remove a dry top over my head and became trapped in the gasket because I forgot to remove my eyeglasses. In a claustrophobic panic I yanked the edge of the gasket, splitting it wide open (OK, it was pretty old).

Coat ankle, wrist, and neck gaskets with baby powder before you put on your dry suit to ease the process and keep saltwater rashes at bay. If you have trouble tugging a dry suit gasket over your wrists or ankles, slip a thin sock liner over the area before you pull the latex gasket into place. Then you can slip the liner out of the way. Don't forget to tuck sleeves and cuffs on undergarments inside the dry suit, or they'll wick water up to invade your dry space.

To restore the DWR, use a product like Nikwax TX-Direct, which is similar to the original treatment done by the manufacturers. This is dumped into the wash water so the garment is evenly coated with the treatment. Prewash the garment so the DWR can bond to the fabric. Before treating any garment, read the manufacturer's clothing care tags for additional information.

Life Vests

Life vests should be rinsed and dried to keep the fabric from stiffening with salt water. You can treat life vests with 303 Protectant to keep the colors true and increase the life span of the outer fabric. Once the fabric is torn, keep a close eye on the quality of the foam inside and plan on buying a new vest soon. When the foam is exposed to UV, it will rapidly degrade, and your life vest will not be able to float you properly. Test your life vest if you suspect that it's getting on in years or losing its flotation. You should float with your head well above the water when the vest is snugged into place. If you're being slapped in the face with each ripple, it's time to get a new life vest. Destroy your old one before disposal so no one is tempted to retrieve and use it (honest, I had that happen!).

Velcro Closures

Many pieces of paddlewear and footwear use Velcro closures that can become clogged with sand or mud. Use a spray hose and toothbrush to remove the grit to restore its stickiness.

REPAIRS: AT HOME AND IN THE FIELD

There's nothing more pleasing to the eye of an outdoor enthusiast than weathered gear that shows the scratches and dings of good times. Shiny, new gear is like a new cast-iron skillet—it needs seasoning and a lot of use before it glows with the rich patina of experience.

Over the years of kayaking, you'll probably be faced with a wide variety of minor repairs: small gelcoat fractures, blown gaskets, jammed rudders, and the like. A basic maintenance schedule may help you avoid many of these repairs, but eventually you'll be stricken. Consider it a merit badge. If your aptitude for fussing about with repairs and small bits of hardware is in the lowest percentile, arrange for repairs to be done at your local paddlesports shop or through a paddling club referral. If you'd like to tackle some of these repairs yourself, read on!

Gelcoat Damage

There's nothing as upsetting as hearing the nasty "crunch" of your first gelcoat damage. Don't despair, it can be fixed. You'll need to look both inside and outside to fully determine the level of damage to your composite kayak (fiberglass, Kevlar, or graphite). Cloth-and-resin layups are surprisingly tough, so you may have just created a deep gouge or scratch that you can fix at your leisure. If you can see daylight or a series of white spider-web fracture lines, then it's wise to make a repair before you plan your next kayak trip.

A puncture or serious fracture will require a fiberglass patch before gelcoat repair.

You'll probably want to match the gelcoat color on your kayak for the repair. Since this compound has a short shelf life, your local paddlesports shop may have to special-order it from the manufacturer. The catalytic hardener used with both gelcoat and the resin in fiberglass repair is best purchased locally since there are shipping restrictions that make its transport slow and expensive.

In addition to the gelcoat and hardener, you'll also need the following items.

- several pairs of latex gloves (or latex substitute)
- wooden paint stirrers
- large paper cups (for mixing the gelcoat and hardener)
- masking tape
- cotton swabs
- plastic wrap or waxed paper
- 320- and 600-grit wet-dry sandpaper

- acetone
- some soft, clean rags
- a respirator or dust mask
- eye protection
- fine-grit rubbing compound

Following are the basic steps of a gelcoat repair.

1. Protect yourself. Any use of acetone and the repair materials must be done in well-ventilated areas away from any open flames. Wear latex gloves, a respirator, and eye protection at all times.
2. Prep the damaged area. Before you begin a repair, apply masking tape to mask around the repair area to protect against scratching. Clean the wound with acetone, and if there are jagged edges, bevel them and smooth them out with 320-grit wet-dry sandpaper. Remove any loose bits of gelcoat.

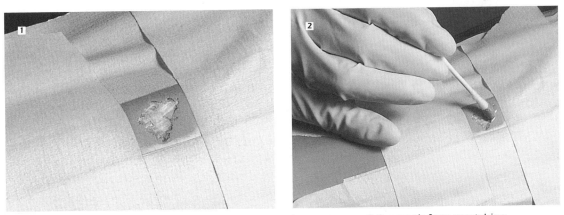

Gelcoat repair. **1.** Masking tape can protect the area around the repair from scratching and gelcoat drips. **2.** Once you've added the hardener to the gelcoat, smooth the repair quickly before the material hardens. (continued next page)

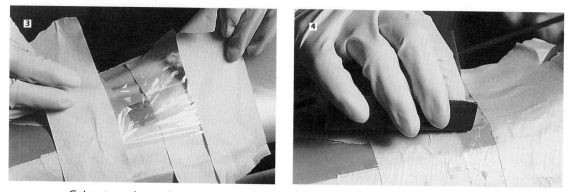

Gelcoat repair, continued. **3.** Cover the repair with plastic wrap or waxed paper and allow it to dry. **4.** Wet-sand with progressively finer paper to smooth the repair and blend it with the surrounding area.

3. Apply the gelcoat. Mix the gelcoat with a few drops of hardener (check the manufacturer's directions for specific instructions). Quickly work the gelcoat into place with the cotton swab and leave it just proud of (just above) the surface and smoothed out from the edges. Cover the patch with waxed paper or plastic wrap and clean around the outside of the patch with acetone to remove any gelcoat that slopped outside of the lines. The patch will need to set for several hours until it is completely hard (air temperatures must be above 50°F/10°C for proper curing).

4. The final steps. Remove the waxed paper and wet-sand the repair with 320-grit wet-dry sandpaper until the repaired area is almost level, or flush, with the surrounding area. Finish-sand the area with 600-grit wet-dry sandpaper using plenty of water. You can buff out any edge scratches with a fine-grit rubbing compound.

Making a gelcoat repair requires planning and organization. First, have all materials close at hand, and ensure you won't be interrupted. The repair material sets up quickly, so you must be ready to see it through to completion.

Structural repairs should be done before the gelcoat repair. A structural repair is more difficult than a gelcoat repair and may be something you prefer to have done by a local shop. Damage near or on a seam will require more expertise.

If you choose to undertake a composite kayak repair, heed the warnings in the repair instructions about protecting yourself. Fiberglass cloth may be used to repair both fiberglass and Kevlar boats. Kevlar cloth is more expensive and a bit more difficult to work with (it tends to "fuzz up" when sanded). If you need to make repairs to a graphite kayak, please consider having this done professionally. A quality repair to a graphite kayak is difficult.

Following are the basic steps for a cloth-and-resin repair.

1. Prep the damaged area. Before you begin the repair, dry-sand the entire area to facilitate bonding and remove any loose strands of cloth or gelcoat pieces. Clean well with acetone to remove impurities that will affect the resin.

2. Prepare the materials. Cut a piece of fiberglass cloth just large enough to cover the damaged area. Then cut another piece of cloth slightly larger than the first. Now cut a third piece of cloth slightly larger than the second. You can do this with household scissors. Mix the resin and hardener according to the manufacturer's instructions. You must be ready to begin work immediately since the resin will begin to set as soon as the hardener has been added.

3. Apply the resin. Use a clean piece of cardboard to saturate the pieces of fiberglass cloth with the prepared resin, using a small roller or brush. Lay each piece of cloth in place over the damaged area, starting with the smallest and finishing with the largest. Smooth out wrinkles and edges in each one before placing the next piece on top. Allow the repair to dry thoroughly (overnight is best). If the repair has been done to the inside of the boat, wet-sand with 320- and then 600-grit wet-dry sandpaper un-

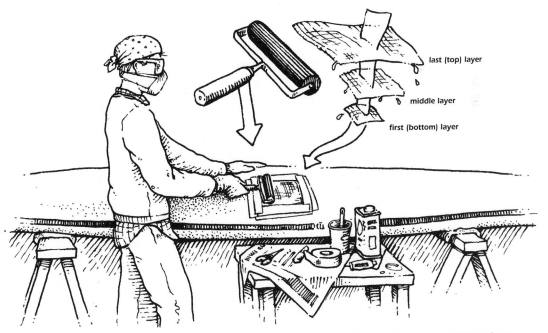

last (top) layer

middle layer

first (bottom) layer

Repairing damaged fiberglass requires layering pieces of resin-saturated patches. These pieces should get progressively larger and allowed to fully cure (usually overnight). Once smoothed, a gelcoat repair can be done to finish the job.

til the surface is smooth. If the repair is on the outside of the boat, dry-sand lightly to facilitate bonding to the gel-coat and clean the area with acetone.

Fiberglass patches can be used on either the inside or the outside of the boat (you may need a patch on both sides in the case of a puncture). Which side you choose is determined by the nature of the damage. If you use layered patches on the outside of the boat, you'll need to prep a larger area for the gelcoat repair. The added height of the fiberglass cloth requires a larger area to make the resulting finish less noticeable.

Thermoformed Boat Repair

Thermoformed kayaks can be cleaned with soapy water and a soft rag. If you have deeper stains, you can use isopropyl or denatured (ethyl) alcohol to rub them out. Never resort to strong solvents such as acetone or lacquer thinner, as these may damage the surface of the material.

Scratches and abrasions to the surface of a thermoformed boat can be removed with a polishing compound, which can be found at automotive or marine supply shops. Deeper scratches may require very light sanding with wet sanding paper (not wet sandpaper!) starting with 250 to 300 grit and working to a 600 grit before finishing with a polishing compound, as described above.

Cuts and gouges to thermoplastic boats can be repaired by filling with an adhesive such as methyl methacrylate, super glue, or a polyester resin (to the exterior only). Many repair putties used for acrylic spas and hot tubs also work well on thermoformed boats and may be used to fill grooves and gouges to the surface. Always check the manufacturer's specifications for repair materials.

Before applying an adhesive or filler, remove any chips or curls of material with a razor blade. Use just enough adhesive to fill the gouge or chip to the surface. Cover the wound with a piece of plastic wrap and let the adhesive cure until it has completely hardened (usually twenty-four hours). If needed, you can lightly wet-sand the wound with 400-grit paper and polish smooth with a buffing compound. Use a high-gloss acrylic spray paint if you want to match the boat color (contact the manufacturer for an exact match).

To repair a split or crack in thermoformed material, prepare the area as you did for the repair above and then drill a small hole, no bigger than $\frac{1}{16}$ inch, at either end of the crack to stop it from lengthening. You will need to close the crack using adhesive. Repair adhesives, commonly available in hardware, automotive, or marine supply stores, may have brand names such as Devcon, Permatex, or Plastic Welder, but all should say "methacrylate" and are typically two-part adhesives (refer to the manufacturer's specifications if available).

Once you have closed the crack with the repair adhesive, use strips of duct tape across the wound to hold the two edges together until this repair has hardened. Once it has hardened, you can remove the duct tape and then remove any excess adhesive with a soft rag and alcohol.

With the initial crack repair set, cut a piece of fiberglass cloth tape long enough to cover the entire wound and still leave about an inch at either end beyond the drilled holes. Saturate this tape with the adhesive, place it over the wound, and smooth it out, making sure to force out any air bubbles. If possible, do this repair from the inside of the kayak so the repair will be less obvious. If you must do a crack repair from the outside, you will need to lightly wet-sand the area and feather the edges of the repair so it is less noticeable. Then you may use high-gloss acrylic spray paint to help hide the repair and match the color of the boat.

The process of thermoforming kayaks and blending materials used in these composite sheets is constantly evolving. If you decide to undertake a repair on your thermoformed boat, check with the manufacturer for updates on materials and their use.

Polyethylene Repair

It's rare to damage a polyethylene boat so that a major repair is needed. Most repairs involve removing dents or dimples in the hull. These areas may be repaired by using gentle heat and pressure. Polyethylene is a material with "memory," and often a dimple or dent will pop back out by putting the boat in the sun with the area exposed. You can help the process by putting a tire inner tube inside the boat and inflating it. This helps push the area out from the inside.

Some dents demand more aggressive heat treatments, which can be done with an industrial hair dryer. You must be careful to continuously move the heat source and check to be sure the area isn't becoming soft by overheating. A hair dryer also works well on the little curls and edges that develop from

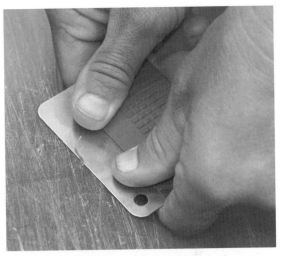

Small curls of plastic and sharp edges can be trimmed from your polyethylene boat using a ski wax scraper.

hull abuse. They can also be trimmed with a sharp putty knife or ski wax scraper.

Since industrial hair dryers aren't found on the average garage shelf, you can instead drape a folded towel over the dimple and pour very hot (just below boiling) water over the towel until the material is pliable enough for the dimple to pop out. As you pour, keep the stream of hot water moving across the surface of the towel as you saturate it and avoid any overspills directly onto surrounding plastic.

If your boat has cracked or been punctured, you must use plastic welding techniques to repair the area. Plastic welding isn't difficult to do, but it's tricky to do correctly without causing even more structural damage to the boat by overheating. Be extremely careful if you choose to undertake a plastic weld repair, and check the manufacturer's recommendations before doing so.

Plastic repairs can be made on linear polyethylene using plastic welding rods or P-Tex sticks. Be careful to heat only the repair material and not the boat (after initial warming).

You'll need some small pieces of plastic or plastic repair rods from the manufacturer to match the boat color. If you don't want to wait, you can use P-Tex, a ski base repair material that dries to a cloudy color.

The following are steps for a basic plastic weld repair.

1. Prepare the area. Use a soft cloth and alcohol, and remove any curls of plastic or dirt from around the wound.
2. Warm the area. Gently warm the area around the damage using a hair dryer. This warming readies the area to accept the repair material. The surface should not bubble or turn dark.
3. Prepare the repair material. Hold your matching color chip of polyethylene or P-Tex over the wound (wearing a pair of insulated gloves), and heat the chip until it's soft and ready to drip into the wound.
4. Apply the repair material. Hold the dripping repair material over the damaged area and drip or rub until the area is filled. It's extremely important that you heat only the repair material, not the boat material.
5. Smooth the repair. Use the back of a kitchen spoon or soft rubber scraper to smooth the area, and then let it set up.
6. Check your work. Be sure the repair is complete. You may need to add more repair material to finish the job.

Kayak Damage in the Field

Undertaking a major composite or polyethylene boat repair while under way is rarely practical. But a puncture or fracture severe enough to cause the boat to take on water will require immediate attention. You can use a two-part epoxy putty (like PC-7) that can be used under wet conditions. It will help if you can rough up the surfaces to facilitate bonding. This emergency patch may be difficult to remove once you get back home and want to properly repair your boat. It sets up to a rock-hard compound that can only be removed by grinding.

Duct tape can be used for a temporary field repair to gelcoat damage, and even some cloth damage. Round the edges before applying, and cross the duct tape over the wound. Monitor the repair, replacing daily or as needed.

Polyethylene boats will often not accept an epoxy putty repair. If the damage is small, you may be able to get by with a well-placed glob of Shoe-Goo or marine sealant. Sometimes driving a small screw with a rubber washer into place will seal a hole temporarily. You can then cover it with sealant for added protection until you return home.

If you've damaged your boat, but it's not taking on water, use duct tape to field repair the area. You'll need to get the damaged area dry and clean before wrapping with duct tape. Round the corners of the duct tape to keep the edges from peeling, and use multiple pieces that are crossed over one another. Completely wrapping the tape around the boat will help anchor the dressing. Duct tape may be used on composite or polyethylene boats and removed at home before a full repair. In fact, duct tape should be your first choice for most any boat repair in the field because it's simple and quickly reversible once you're home. If the duct tape is not sufficient, then use other materials like Shoe-Goo, sealants, and even screwed-in rubber washers to repair the wound, and finish off with a duct tape wrap for insurance (yes, I'm a big fan of duct tape).

Jammed Rudders and Skegs

As soon as you add moving parts to a kayak, you must face the inevitable—they will jam, break, or throw themselves overboard in deep water just to frustrate you. Rudders and skegs are prone to jamming since few of us actually take care to wash these areas on a regular basis. Sometimes, a spray wash will free up crusted mechanisms and flush sand and small pebbles from their hidey-holes. In the field, you can use a water bottle spout to force water into these areas. (But first check that you haven't simply jammed the lines by blocking them with gear stored in a hatch or on deck.)

If a simple wash doesn't save the day, dismantle the rudder or skeg for a full repair. Before you do this, be sure you have your repair kit handy (see page 301) with all the extra hardware and tools for this repair. Before beginning to dismantle anything, place a tarp under the boat so any loose parts will be caught. Sketch the correct orientation and placement of everything before you remove rudder cams or uphaul and downhaul lines. Reassembly isn't always obvious.

Often, the repair of a rudder or skeg isn't difficult, it's finding the problem. Check these potential culprits if you're experiencing problems (besides grit and small pebbles—always the first thing to check).

- rudder line that has jumped the track on a cam
- kinks in the skeg line
- downhaul or uphaul lines have frayed or broken or are misaligned
- a machine screw on the cam has fallen out or stripped, allowing cam to wobble
- the clevis pin or ring has fallen off the rudder pin
- the rudder base or attachment has cracked and loosened
- the skeg blade is loose or unattached from its cable
- a rudder cable screw has been lost
- a rudder cable swage or the cable itself has broken
- a sliding foot brace assembly is jammed or missing a retaining screw

Bulkhead Leaks

Your boat's seasonal checkup should include an examination of the bulkhead sealant. This material hardens over the years and may create small gaps or pull free of the bulkhead on both composite and polyethylene boats. Polyethylene boats are particularly prone to bulkhead sealant leaks because of their flexible nature and the differential contraction and expansion between the sealant, foam bulkhead, and the hull.

Before resealing a bulkhead, remove all the old sealant and clean well with alcohol. Work in a warm place out of direct sunlight, and wear latex gloves and eye protection. Apply a new bead of sealant on both sides of the bulkhead and smooth it in place with a small dowel or your finger. Let the repair air-dry overnight. It may be tacky to the touch for several days as it cures (you can use your boat but must not flood the cockpit or bump the bulkheads during this time). Use a marine sealant recommended by the manufacturer.

Take-Apart Paddles That Won't

If you don't regularly separate and clean your two-piece paddle, it will soon become a one-piece paddle. Salt deposits and grit will freeze the halves in place (I've seen a blade pulled from a shaft when a paddler tried to pull a particularly stubborn paddle apart). If you have a cantankerous two-piece paddle, clean the joint and then treat it with graphite powder (also used on frozen locks). A good scrubbing with a kitchen scrub pad and dusting with graphite powder will often do the trick (don't use WD-40, which attracts grit and will create problems). If you're still experiencing difficulties, you may need to do a little judicious sanding on the ferrule. This is irreversible, so don't overdo it and create a sloppy fit. You should also check the fit of the spring button since a poorly drilled hole that's too small or angled will also cause a paddle jam.

Paddlewear Repairs

Special attention should be given to wet suit and dry suit repairs since these are pieces of safety equipment, and often expensive ones. Most wet suits have a nylon skin. It protects the closed-cell material that serves as insulation. This exposed nylon surface is where most of the wear and tear occurs. If the damage is small, a glob of Aquaseal, a viscous sealant that is available in most paddlesports or camping shops, is sufficient. A tube of this stuff is almost as useful as duct tape and should reside in any repair kit.

If the tear has gone entirely through the wet suit material, you can use an iron-on neoprene patch like Iron Mend for a simple repair. In the field, you may need to hand sew the tear and then coat with Aquaseal. You may also use duct tape to cover this field repair but should remove it as soon as possible so glue residues do not affect the permanent repair with the Iron Mend patch.

Dry suit tears can be field repaired in the same way but will need to be returned to the manufacturer for a full repair. This will require a patch with tape-sealed seams, which is best done by professionals. The latex gaskets on dry suits are the most fragile component. Small tears or holes may be field repaired with a bicycle repair patch or a dab of Aquaseal with a piece of duct tape on either side.

A latex gasket replacement can be done at home using a kit from the manufacturer. The repair kit should contain the replacement gaskets and adhesive (Aquaseal glue is highly recommended). Leave the repair in a warm place for drying overnight. You'll also need the following in addition to the repair kit materials.

- waxed paper
- masking tape
- acetone or denatured alcohol
- coffee can
- sandpaper (may be included in kit)
- 303 Protectant
- knife or razor blade

With these items in place, follow these basic steps for your gasket replacement.

1. Clean the new gasket with acetone or denatured alcohol.
2. If the old gasket can be easily pulled from the garment, remove it; if the bond is strong, then cut the gasket back even with the edge of the fabric.
3. Using sandpaper, rough up the two surfaces to be glued: inside of the new gasket and the surface on the garment (plan on a 1 in./2.5 cm overlap).
4. Use a coffee can or small kitchen pot as a form (form size depends on the type of gasket being repaired) to stretch the gasket while drying. Wrap this form in waxed paper and slip it inside the garment opening. *Note:* you may also cut fiberboard rings to use as a form.
5. Stretch the new gasket onto the other end of the form so it overlaps by about 1 inch (2.5 cm).
6. Roll the new gasket back onto itself, exposing the sanded surface.
7. Apply a thin, even layer of Aquaseal glue to both sanded surfaces. Now gently roll the new gasket surface back down onto the fabric.
8. Using a spoon or your thumb, work out any air pockets or bubbles. Wrap the glued joint with waxed paper and use masking tape to hold in place.
9. Let the repair stand overnight in a warm place.
10. Before wearing the dry suit, treat the new gasket with 303 Protectant; do this regularly throughout the paddling season and before storage.

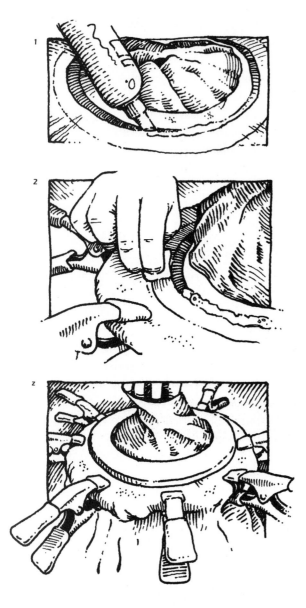

Latex gasket repair. **1.** After sanding both surfaces, apply a thin coat or layer of Aquaseal glue. **2.** Work out any air bubbles between the bonded surfaces. **3.** Allow the repair to dry overnight in a warm area. You may need to stretch the opening of the gasket before using.

It's tempting when trying on a dry suit to convince yourself that a gasket needs trimming (especially the neck gasket). It may, but you should give it a chance to stretch a bit before you begin any trimming. Leave a coffee can or large yogurt container (my favorite is a football) in place for a day or so to gradually stretch a new gasket, and then wear the dry suit before making a decision on trimming.

If you need to trim a gasket, use very sharp scissors or a razor to trim a small sliver at a time until you get a proper fit. Trim any rough or uneven edges. Remember, a dry suit gasket should be snug to keep all the water out.

A Repair Kit

A repair kit is nearly as essential as a first-aid kit. After all, if your boat isn't healthy, you're not going anywhere! Include the replacement parts and pieces specific to your boat, as well as those for general repairs. The items listed in the sidebar can be stored in a wide-mouth, 1-quart (1 L) Nalgene bottle and thrown into a hatch on every trip. Duct tape (never leave home without this) can be wrapped around the outside. That way, it doesn't take any additional space and is right there with your repair kit at all times.

HANDY SEA KAYAK REPAIR KIT

4-inch Vise-Grips pliers

stubby screwdrivers (flat and Phillips-head) or Leatherman tool

two-part epoxy putty

a tube of Aquaseal

a lighter for sealing ends of nylon line and bungee

stainless steel machine screws (in all sizes your equipment uses)

locknuts (in all sizes your equipment uses)

assorted rubber washers or rubber gasket sheet

an extra rudder or skeg cable

a handful of wire cable swages for crimping cables

several gear eyes or deck loops (the eyes on deck that the rigging is laced through)

rudder track screws with O-rings

replacement buckles and ladderlocks for hatch straps

wire ties in several sizes

shrink tubing

a small tube of contact cement

vinyl repair kit for dry bags, air mattresses, flotation bags

eyeglass repair kit

various pieces of small line

spring button for take-apart paddle

money for pay phone

Your repair kit should include all the bits and pieces needed to make field repairs on your boat and other gear. You can wrap duct tape around the outside of this container to save space.

Resources

BOOKS

You may find that some of these books are out of print, but if you can find them they are worth your while.

Instructional

Alderson, Doug. *Sea Kayakers Magazine's Handbook of Safety and Rescue.* Camden ME: Ragged Mountain Press, 2003.

———. *Sea Kayaker's Savvy Paddler: More Than 500 Tips for Better Kayaking.* Camden ME: Ragged Mountain Press, 2001.

———. *Sea Kayak Strokes: A Guide to Efficient Paddling Technique.* Salt Lake City: Rocky Mountain Books, 2007.

Brown, Gordon. *Sea Kayak: A Manual for Intermediate and Advanced Sea Kayakers.* Caernarfon UK: Pesda Press, 2006.

Díaz, Ralph. *Complete Folding Kayaker.* Camden ME: Ragged Mountain Press, 2003.

Dowd, John. *Sea Kayaking: A Manual for Long-Distance Touring.* Rev. ed. Seattle: University of Washington Press, 2004.

Dutky, Paul. *The Bombproof Roll and Beyond.* Birmingham AL: Menasha Ridge Press, 1993.

Foster, Nigel. *Nigel Foster's Sea Kayaking.* 2nd ed. Old Saybrook CT: Globe Pequot, 1997.

———. *Nigel Foster's Surf Kayaking.* Old Saybrook CT: Globe Pequot, 1998.

Gullion, Laurie. *Canoeing and Kayaking: Instruction Manual.* Newington VA: American Canoe Association, 1987.

Hanson, Jonathan. *Complete Sea Kayak Touring.* Camden ME: Ragged Mountain Press, 1998.

Harrison, David. *Hearst Marine Books: Kayak Camping.* New York: Hearst Marine Books, 1995.

———. *Hearst Marine Books: Sea Kayaking Basics.* New York: Hearst Marine Books, 1993.

Holtey, Tom. *Sit-on-Top Kayaking: A Beginner's Guide.* Honolulu: GeoOdyssey, 1998.

Hutchinson, Derek. *The Basic Book of Sea Kayaking.* Old Saybrook CT: Globe Pequot, 2007.

———. *The Complete Book of Sea Kayaking.* 4th ed. Old Saybrook CT: Globe Pequot, 2004.

———. *Derek C. Hutchinson's Guide to Expedition Kayaking: On Sea and Open Water.* 3rd ed. Old Saybrook CT: Globe Pequot, 1995.

———. *Eskimo Rolling.* 3rd ed. Old Saybrook CT: Globe Pequot, 1999.

Johnson, Shelley. *Sea Kayaker's Pocket Guide.* Camden ME: Ragged Mountain Press, 2002.

———. *Sea Kayaking: A Woman's Guide.* Camden ME: Ragged Mountain Press, 1998.

Knapp, Andy. *The Optimum Kayak: How to Choose, Maintain, Repair, and Customize the Right Boat for You.* Camden ME: Ragged Mountain Press, 2000.

Legg, Linda. *Nuts 'N Bolts: Touring in Your Sea Kayak.* Birmingham AL: Menasha Ridge Press, 1998.

Lessels, Bruce, and Karen Blom. *Paddling with Kids: AMC Essential Handbook for Fun and Safe Paddling.* Boston: Appalachian Mountain Club, 2002.

Loots, Johan. *Sea Kayaking*. Mechanicsburg PA: Stackpole Books, 2000.

Lull, John. *Sea Kayaking Safety and Rescue*. Berkeley: Wilderness Press, 2001.

Matthews, Alex. *Sea Kayaking: Rough Waters*. Petaluma CA: Heliconia Press, 2007.

Mattos, Bill. *Kayak Surfing*. Crystal Lake IL: Falcon Press, 2009.

McGuffin, Gary. *Paddle Your Own Kayak: An Illustrated Guide to the Art of Kayaking*. Erin ON: Boston Mills Press, 2008.

Robison, John. *Sea Kayaking Illustrated: A Visual Guide to Better Paddling*. Camden ME: Ragged Mountain Press, 2003.

Rowe, Ray, ed. *Canoeing Handbook*. 2nd ed. Nottingham England: British Canoe Union, 1989.

Schumann, Roger, and Jan Shriner. *Sea Kayak Rescue: The Definitive Guide to Modern Reentry and Recovery Techniques*. Guilford CT: Globe Pequot, 2001.

Seidman, David. *The Essential Sea Kayaker: The Complete Guide for the Open-Water Paddler*. 2nd ed. Camden ME: Ragged Mountain Press, 2001.

Soares, Eric, and Michael Powers. *Extreme Sea Kayaking*. Camden ME: Ragged Mountain Press, 1999.

Stuhaug, Dennis. *Kayaking Made Easy: A Manual for Beginners with Tips for the Experienced*. Crystal Lake IL: Falcon Press, 2006.

Washburne, Randel. *The Coastal Kayaker's Manual: A Complete Guide to Skills, Gear, and Sea Sense*. 3rd ed. Old Saybrook CT: Globe Pequot, 1998.

Webre, Anne Wortham. *Canoeing and Kayaking for Persons with Physical Disabilities: Instruction Manual*. Newington VA: American Canoe Association, 1990.

Seamanship, Weather, and the Ocean

Ashley, Clifford W., and Geoffrey Budsworth. *The Ashley Book of Knots*. New York: Doubleday, 1993.

Bascom, Willard. *Waves and Beaches*. 3rd ed. Flagstaff AZ: Best, 2000.

Broze, Matt, and George Gronseth. *Sea Kayaker's Deep Trouble: True Stories and Their Lessons from Sea Kayaker Magazine*. Camden ME: Ragged Mountain Press, 1997.

Burch, David. *Fundamentals of Kayak Navigation*. 3rd ed. Guilford CT: Globe Pequot, 1999.

Chapman, Charles F., and Elbert S. Maloney. *Chapman Piloting: Seamanship and Boat Handling*. 63rd ed. New York: Hearst Books, 1999.

Eyges, Leonard. *The Practical Pilot: Coastal Navigation Intuition and Common Sense*. Camden ME: International Marine, 1989.

Ferrero, Franco. *Sea Kayak Navigation*. Wales: Pesda, 1999.

Ifland, Peter. *Taking the Stars: Celestial Navigation from Argonauts to Astronauts*. Newport News VA: Krieger, 1998.

Killen, Ray. *A Sea Kayaker's Navigation Primer*. London: Katabasis, 2002.

———. *Simple Kayak Navigation: Practical Piloting for the Passionate Paddler*. Camden ME: Ragged Mountain Press, 2006.

Kotsch, William. *Weather for the Mariner*. 3rd ed. Annapolis: Naval Institute Press, 1983.

Moyer, Lee. *Sea Kayak Navigation Simplified*. Mukilteo WA: AlpenBooks, 2001.

Sobel, Dava, and William J. H. Andrews. *The Illustrated "Longitude."* New York: Walker, 1998.

U.S. Coast Guard. *Navigation Rules: International–Inland*. Washington DC: U.S. Government Printing Office, 1996.

Build-Your-Own Kayak

Brinck, Wolfgang. *The Aleutian Kayak: Origins, Construction, and Use of the Traditional Seagoing Baidarka*. Camden ME: Ragged Mountain Press, 1995.

Cunningham, Christopher. *Building the Greenland Kayak: A Manual for Its Construction and Use*. Camden ME: Ragged Mountain Press, 2002.

Kulczycki, Chris. *The Kayak Shop: Three Elegant Wooden Kayaks Anyone Can Build*. Camden ME: Ragged Mountain Press, 1993.

———. *The New Kayak Shop: More Elegant Wooden Kayaks Anyone Can Build*. Camden ME: Ragged Mountain Press, 2001.

Moores, Ted, and Greg Rossel. *Kayaks You Can Build: An Illustrated Guide to Plywood Construction.* Richmond Hill ON: Firefly Books, 2004.

Putz, George. *Wood and Canvas Kayak Building.* Camden ME: International Marine, 1990.

Schade, Nick. *The Strip-Built Sea Kayak: Three Rugged, Beautiful Boats You Can Build.* Camden ME: Ragged Mountain Press, 1998.

History and Traditional Design

Adney, Edwin Tappan, and Howard Chapelle. *The Bark Canoes and Skin Boats of North America.* Washington DC: Smithsonian Institute Press, 1983.

Brower, Kenneth. *The Starship and the Canoe.* New York: HarperCollins, 1983.

Dyson, George. *Baidarka.* Edmonds WA: Alaska Northwest, 1986.

Zimmerly, David W. *Qayaq: Kayaks of Alaska and Siberia.* Fairbanks: University of Alaska Press, 2000.

Travel and Adventure by Kayak

Bowermaster, Jon. *Aleutian Adventure: Kayaking in the Birthplace of the Winds.* Washington DC: National Geographic Society, 2001.

Coffey, Maria. *A Boat in Our Baggage: Around the World with a Kayak.* Camden ME: Ragged Mountain Press, 1995.

Duff, Chris. *On Celtic Tides: One Man's Journey Around Ireland by Sea Kayak.* New York: St. Martin's Press, 1999.

———. *Southern Exposure: A Solo Sea Kayaking Journey Around New Zealand South Island.* Crystal Lake IL: Falcon Press, 2003.

Fredston, Jill. *Rowing to Latitude.* Berkeley CA: North Point Press, 2001.

Jardine, Ray. *Siku Kayak: Paddling the Coast of Arctic Alaska.* Arizona City AZ: Adventurelore Press, 2005.

Jason, Victoria. *Kabloona in the Yellow Kayak: One Woman's Journey Through the Northwest Passage.* Winnipeg MA: Turnstone Press, 1999.

Lindemann, Hannes. *Alone at Sea.* Edited by Jozefa Stuart. New York: Random House, 1958.

Linnea, Ann. *Deep Water Passage: A Spiritual Journey at Midlife.* Boston: Little, Brown, 1995.

MacGregor, John. *A Thousand Miles in the Rob Roy Canoe on the Rivers and Lakes of Europe.* Murray UT: Dixon-Price, 2000.

Nordby, Will, ed. *Seekers of the Horizon: Sea Kayaking Voyages from Around the World.* Chester CT: Globe Pequot, 1989.

Rogers, Joel W. *The Hidden Coast: Coastal Adventures from Alaska to Mexico.* 2nd ed. Portland OR: WestWinds Press, 2000.

Stiller, Eric. *Keep Australia on Your Left: A True Story of an Attempt to Circumnavigate Australia by Kayak.* New York: Forge, 2000.

Streetly, Joanna. *Paddling Through Time: A Sea Kayaking Journey Through Clayquot Sound.* Vancouver BC: Raincoast Books, 2000.

Sutherland, Audrey. *Paddling My Own Canoe.* Honolulu: University of Hawaii Press, 1978.

Theroux, Paul. *The Happy Isles of Oceania: Paddling the Pacific.* New York: G. P. Putnam's Sons, 1992.

Waterman, Jonathan. *Arctic Crossing: A Journey through the Northwest Passage and Inuit Culture.* New York: Knopf, 2001.

———. *Kayaking the Vermilion Sea: Eight Hundred Miles Down the Baja.* New York: Simon & Schuster, 1995.

Guidebooks

Bannon, James. *Sea Kayaking Florida and Georgia Sea Islands.* Crystal Lake IL: Falcon Press, 1998.

Breining, Greg. *Wild Shore: Exploring Lake Superior by Kayak.* Minneapolis: University of Minnesota Press, 2000.

Bull, Shirley, and Fred Bull. *Paddling Cape Cod: A Coastal Explorer's Guide.* Woodstock VT: Backcountry Guides, 2000.

Bumsted, Lee. *Hot Showers!: Maine Coast Lodging for Kayakers and Sailors.* 2nd ed. Brunswick ME: Audenreed, 2000.

Cunningham, Scott. *Sea Kayaking in Nova Scotia: A Guide to Paddling Routes Along the Coast of Nova Scotia.* 2nd ed. Halifax NS: Nimbus, 2000.

Drope, Bodhi, and Dorothy Drope. *Paddling the Sunshine Coast.* Madeira Park BC: Harbour Publishing, 1997.

Dwyer, Ann. *Easy Waters of California—North.* Windsor CA: Ann Dwyer, 2000.

Evans, Lisa Gollin. *Sea Kayaking Coastal Massachusetts: From Newburyport to Buzzards Bay.* Boston: Appalachian Mountain Club, 2000.

Foster, Nigel. *Guide to Sea Kayaking in Southern Florida: The Best Day Trips and Tours from St. Petersburg to the Florida Keys.* Old Saybrook CT: Globe Pequot, 1999.

Garepis, Demece. *Sea Kayaking Northern California.* Camden ME: Ragged Mountain Press, 1999.

Gluckman, David. *Sea Kayaking in Florida.* Woodstock VT: Countryman Press, 2004.

Howard, Jim. *Guide to Sea Kayaking in Southeast Alaska: The Best Day Trips and Tours from Misty Fjords to Glacier Bay.* Old Saybrook CT: Globe Pequot, 1999.

Hughes, Alison Elizabeth. *Paddling in Paradise: Sea Kayaking Adventures in Atlantic Canada.* Fredericton NB: Goose Lane Editions, 2005.

Johnson, Shelley, and Vaughan Smith. *Guide to Sea Kayaking in Maine.* Guilford CT: Globe Pequot, 2001.

Malec, Pam. *Guide to Sea Kayaking in North Carolina: The Best Day Trips and Tours from Currituck to Cape Fear.* Guilford CT: Globe Pequot, 2001.

Miller, Dorcas S. *Kayaking the Maine Coast: A Paddler's Guide to Day Trips from Kittery to Cobscook.* Woodstock VT: Backcountry Guides, 2000.

Miller, Robert H. *Kayaking the Inside Passage: A Paddling Guide from Olympia, Washington, to Muir Glacier, Alaska.* Woodstock VT: Countryman Press, 2005.

Newman, Bill, Sarah Ohmann, and Don Dimond. *Guide to Sea Kayaking on Lakes Superior and Michigan: The Best Day Trips and Tours.* Old Saybrook CT: Globe Pequot, 1999.

Nolan, Andrea. *Sea Kayaking Virginia: A Paddler's Guide to Day Trips from Georgetown to Chincoteague.* Woodstock VT: Countryman Press, 2005.

Ohmann, Sarah, and Bill Newman. *Guide to Sea Kayaking on Lakes Huron, Erie and Ontario: The Best Day Trips and Tours.* Guilford CT: Globe Pequot, 1999.

Paigen, Jennifer. *The Sea Kayaker's Guide to Mount Desert Island.* Camden ME: Down East Books, 1997.

Reynolds, Jonathon, and Heather Smith. *Kayaking Georgian Bay.* Erin ON: Boston Mills Press, 1999.

Romano-Lax, Andromeda. *Sea Kayaking in Baja.* Berkeley CA: Wilderness Press, 1993.

Schumann, Roger, and Jan Shriner. *Guide to Sea Kayaking in Central and Northern California: The Best Day Trips and Tours from the Lost Coast to Morro Bay.* Old Saybrook CT: Globe Pequot, 1999.

Skillman, Don. *Adventure Kayaking: Trips in Glacier Bay.* Berkeley CA: Wilderness Press, 1998.

Snowden, Mary Ann. *Island Paddling: A Paddler's Guide to the Gulf Islands and Barkley Sound.* Custer WA: Orca Book, 1997.

Venn, Tamsin. *Sea Kayaking Along the Mid-Atlantic Coast: Coastal Paddling Adventures from New York to Chesapeake Bay.* Boston: Appalachian Mountain Club, 1994.

———. *Sea Kayaking Along the New England Coast.* Boston: Appalachian Mountain Club, 1991.

Wachob, Bruce. *Sea Kayaking in the Florida Keys.* Sarasota FL: Pineapple Press, 1997.

Washburne, Randel. *Kayaking Puget Sound, the San Juans, and Gulf Islands: 50 Trips on the Northwest's Inland Waters.* 2nd ed. Seattle: Mountaineers, 1999.

Williams, Scott. *On Island Time: Kayaking the Caribbean.* Jackson MS: University Press of Mississippi, 2005.

Cooking

Daniel, Linda. *Kayak Cookery: A Handbook of Provisions and Recipes.* Seattle: Pacific Search Press, 1986.

Jacobson, Donald. *The One Pan Gourmet: Fresh Food on the Trail.* Camden ME: Ragged Mountain Press, 1993.

Kesselheim, Alan S. *Trail Food: Drying and Cooking for Backpacking and Paddling.* Camden ME: Ragged Mountain Press, 1998.

Miller, Dorcas S. *Good Food for Camp and Trail: All-Natural Recipes for Delicious Meals Outdoors.* Boulder CO: Pruett, 1993.

Spangenberg, Jean, and Samuel Spangenberg. *The Portable Baker: Baking on Boat and Trail.* Camden ME: Ragged Mountain Press, 1997.

Wilderness Medicine

Forgey, William W. *The Basic Essentials of Hypothermia*. Merrillville IN: ICS Books, 1991.

Gill, Paul G., Jr. *The Onboard Medical Handbook: First Aid and Emergency Medicine Afloat*. Camden ME: International Marine, 1997.

———. *Wilderness First Aid: A Pocket Guide*. Camden ME: Ragged Mountain Press, 2002.

Hampton, Bruce, and David Cole. *NOLS Soft Paths: How to Enjoy the Wilderness Without Harming It*. Mechanicsburg PA: Stackpole Books, 2003.

Isaac, Jeff, and Peter Goth. *The Outward Bound Wilderness First-Aid Handbook*. New York: Lyons & Burford, 1991.

Schimelpfing, Tod, and Joan Safford. *NOLS First Aid*. Mechanicsburg PA: Stackpole Books, 2006.

Tilton, Buck, and Frank Hubbell. *Medicine for the Backcountry: A Practical Guide to Wilderness First Aid*. 3rd ed. Guilford CT: Globe Pequot, 1999.

Low-Impact Guidelines

Leave No Trace: Outdoor Skills and Ethics: Temperate Coastal Zones. Lander WY: National Outdoor Leadership School.

Meyer, Kathleen. *How to Shit in the Woods: An Environmentally Sound Approach to a Lost Art*. 2nd rev. ed. Berkeley: Ten Speed Press, 1994.

Waterman, Laura, and Guy Waterman. *Backwood Ethics: Environmental Issues for Hikers and Campers*. 2nd ed. rev. Woodstock VT: Countryman Press, 1993.

Repair and Maintenance

Getchell, Annie, and Dave Getchell, Jr. *The Essential Outdoor Gear Manual: Equipment Care, Repair, and Selection*. 2nd ed. Camden ME: Ragged Mountain Press, 2000.

MAGAZINES

As the lines blur between hard-copy magazines and online-only versions, it becomes challenging to form a list such as this. Numerous "online magazines" are not regularly updated and do not have a breadth of articles from known experts in the field. Although they may offer a dynamic blog or forum, they were not included in this list. The list below is tried and true, but many more listings can be found through online searches if that is your wish.

Adventure Kayak Magazine, Palmer Rapids ON, www.adventurekayakmag.com, 613-758-2042.

Atlantic Coastal Kayaker, Ipswich MA, www.atlantic coastalkayaker.com, 978-356-6112.

Canoe and Kayak, Kirkland WA, www.canoekayak .com, 1-800-MYCANOE.

Explore, Toronto ON, www.explore-mag.com, 416-599-2000.

Kanawa, Kingston ON, www.paddlingcanada.com, 888-252-6292.

Paddler, Steamboat Springs CO, www.paddlermag azine.com, 970-879-1450.

Paddling Life (e-zine), Steamboat Springs CO, www .paddlinglife.net, 970-870-0880.

Sea Kayaker, Seattle, WA, www.seakayakermagazine .com, 206-789-1326.

Wavelength Paddling Magazine, Nanaimo BC, www .wavelengthmagazine.com, 250-244-6437.

WetDawg (online magazine), Seattle WA, info@wet dawg.com.

VIDEOS

All About Kayaking, Kent Ford, 2005.

Amphibious Man, Ivar Sills, 1999.

Brent Reitz Forward Stroke Clinic, Brent Reitz, 2000.

Birthplace of the Winds, Jon Bowermaster, 2007.

The Essentials of Sea Kayaking with Ben, Ben Lawry, 2010.

Grace Under Pressure, Nantahala Outdoor Center, 1993.

Nigel Foster's Sea Kayaking Series (Volumes 1–6).

Paddler's Personal Trainer, Waterworks and Bonesteel, 2000.

Performance Sea Kayaking: The Basics and Beyond, Kent Ford, Performance Video and Instruction, 1994.

Practical Kayaking, Dolphin's Eye Productions, 2003.

Recreational Kayaking: The Essential Skills and Safety, Ken and Nicole Whiting, 2007.
Rolling a Kayak, Ken Whiting, 2008.
Rolling with Maligiaq, John Heath, 2000.
Sea Kayak Adventures: Exploring the World from the Sea, Jon Bowermaster, 2009.
Sea Kayaking: Beyond the Basics, Larry Lee Holman, Moving Pictures, 2000.
Sea Kayaking: Fundamentals, Show Me How Videos, Peter Casson, 2007.
Sea Kayaking: Getting Started, Larry Lee Holman, Moving Pictures, 1998.
Sea Kayaking: Intermediate Skills, Show Me How Videos, Peter Casson, 2007.
Sea Kayaking Safety, Rock and Sea Productions, 2000.
Sea Kayaking: The Ultimate Guide, Ken Whiting, 2005.
Seamanship for Kayakers: Getting Started, John Dowd, 2003.
Seamanship for Kayakers: Navigation, John Dowd, 2004.
Surf Kayaking Fundamentals, by John Lull, 1998.
University of Sea Kayaking (USK) Video Series (www.useakayak.org). Vol. 1, *Capsize Recoveries*, and vol. 2, *Rescue Procedures*, Wayne Horodowich, 2001.
What Now? Sea Kayak Rescue Techniques, Vaughan Smith and Shelley Johnson, 1992.

PADDLING CLUBS

Some paddling clubs have been active for many years, whereas others come and go, so it's difficult to keep an up-to-date list of clubs. Local outdoor or paddlesports stores are the best source of current information, but the list below will give you a good starting point. Online lists at www.seakayer magazine.com and www.paddling.net are regularly updated and helpful.

Alabama

Mobile Bay Canoe & Kayak Club
www.baykayaker.blogspot.com

Alaska

Juneau Kayak Club
P.O. Box 021865
Juneau AK 99802-2865

Arizona

Desert Paddlers Club
Tempe AZ
www.desertpaddlers.com

Desert Paddling Association
620 E. 19th St., Ste. 110
Tucson AZ 85719

Southern Arizona Paddlers Club
P.O. Box 41443
Tucson AZ 85713
www.SoAzPaddlers.org

California

California Kayak Friends (CKF)
2419 E. Harbor Blvd., #96
Ventura CA 93001
www.ckf.org

Explore North Coast
P.O. Box 4712
Arcata CA 95518
www.explorenorthcoast.net
info@explorenorthcoast.net

Miramar Beach Kayak Club
Number 1 Mirada Rd.
Half Moon Bay CA 94019

Penguin Paddlers
4381 Granite Dr. Suite A
Rocklin CA 95677
www.penguinpaddlers.com

San Diego Kayak Club
14244 Primrose Court
Ponway CA 92064
www.sdkc.org

San Diego Paddling Club
1829 Chalcedony St.
San Diego CA 92109

San Francisco Bay Area Sea Kayakers (BASK)
229 Courtright Rd.
San Rafael CA 94901
www.baskers.org

Shared Adventures
90 Grandview St., #B101
Santa Cruz CA 95060
www.sharedadventures.com

Valley Wide Kayak Club
24923 Barito St.
Hemet CA 92544
951-927-5951
www.valleywidekayakclub.org

Western Sea Kayakers
P.O. Box 1531
Mountain View CA 94042-1531
www.westernseakayakers.org

Colorado

Rocky Mountain Sea Kayak Club
P.O. Box 100643
Denver CO 80210
www.rmskc.org

Connecticut

ConnYak
P.O. Box 571
Plantsville CT 06279
www.connyak.org

Delaware

Delmarva Paddlers
www.groups.yahoo.com/groups/delmarvapaddlers
Don's Delaware Kayak Club
Box 266a, Church Rd.
Milford DE 19963

Storm Paddlers
www.stormpaddle.com

Florida

Coconut Kayakers
P.O. Box 3646
Tequesta FL 33469

Emerald Coast Paddlers
P.O. Box 2424
Ft. Walton Beach FL 32549

Palm Beach Water Yaks
Palm Beach FL 33480
meetup.com/palm-beach-water-yaks

Paradise Coast Paddlers Club
Naples/Marco Island area and southwest Florida
www.paradisecoastpaddlers.com

Paradise Paddlers and Pedalers Club
Florida Keys Overseas Heritage Trail
c/o Office of Greenways and Trails
3 La Croix Court
Key Largo, FL 33037
www.kayakfloridakeys.com

Seminole Canoe & Kayak Club
4619 Ortega Farms Circle
Jacksonville FL 32210
www.flsckc.com

South Florida Bush Paddlers
Miami FL website only
www.bushpaddlers.org

Southwest Florida Paddling Club
20991 S. Tamiami Trail
Estero FL 33928
www.swfloridapaddlingclub

Tampa Bay Sea Kayakers
P.O. Box 7104
Seminole FL 33775
www.clubkayak.com/

Georgia

University of West Georgia Kayak Club
Carrollton GA 30118

Hawaii

Hawaii Island Kayak Club
74-425 Keal a Kehe Parkway
Kailua-Kana HI 96740

Hui Wa'a Kaukahi
P.O. Box 11588
Honolulu HI 96828
www.huiwaa.org

Kanaka Ikaika Racing Club
P.O. Box 438
Kaneohe HI 96744

Maui Outing Club
P.O. Box 277-330
Kihei, Maui HI 96753

Idaho

Lake Pend Oreille SeaKayakers Association
Sandpoint ID 83864
www.lposka.7ich.com

Illinois

Chicago Area Sea Kayakers Association
Blog: CASKAblog
www.caska.org

Chicago Kayak Club
2738 Noyes St.
Evanston IL 60201
www.chicagokayak.org

Saukenuk Paddlers Canoe and Kayak Club
Moline IL 61265

Indiana

Northwest Indiana Paddling Association
11645 West 50 N
Westville IN 46391
www.nwipa.org

Louisiana

Pelican Paddlers
Sulphur LA 70664
www.pelicanpaddlers.com

Maine

Maine Island Trail Association
P.O. Box C
Rockland ME 04841-0735
www.mita.org

MDI Paddlers
c/o The Alternative
16 Mt. Desert St.
Bar Harbor ME 04609

Southern Maine Sea Kayaking Network
P.O. Box 4794, DTS
Portland ME 04112
www.smskn.org

Maryland

Chesapeake Paddlers Association
P.O. Box 341
Greenbelt MD 20768
www.cpakayaker.com

Massachusetts

Boston Sea Kayak Club
191 Allerton Rd.
Newton MA 02461
www.bskc.org

Martha's Vineyard Oar & Paddle
P.O. Box 840
West Tisbury MA 02575

North Shore Paddlers Network
P.O. Box 50
Marblehead MA 01945
www.nspn.org

Michigan

Lansing Oar and Paddle Club
P.O. Box 26254
Lansing MI 48909
www.loapc.org

Traverse Area Paddle Club
P.O. Box 803
Traverse City MI 49685
www.traverseareapaddleclub.org

West Michigan Coastal Kayakers
Grand Rapids MI 49507
www.wmcka.org

Minnesota

Inland Sea Kayakers
P.O. Box 80331
Minneapolis MN 55408
www.inlandseakayakers.org

Superior Kayak and Outdoor Adventure Club
   (SKOAC)
P.O. Box 581792
Minneapolis MN 55458-2792
www.skoac.org

Mississippi

Bayou Haystackers Paddling Club
Southern Louisiana & Mississippi
www.bayouhaystackers.com

Gulf Area Water Trails Society, Inc.
P.O. Box 473
Pearlington MS 39572-0473

Mississippi Canoe and Kayak Club
P.O. Box 246
Jackson MS 39205

Missouri

Great River Paddle Touring Society
334 S. Marguerite Ave.
St. Louis MO 63135

St. Louis Canoe & Kayak Club
www.groups/yahoo.com/group/stlouiscanoekayak
   club

Nebraska

Missouri River Valley Paddlers
Omaha NE
www.mrvp.informe.com

Nevada

Southern Nevada Paddling Club
P.O. Box 370392
Las Vegas NV 89137
www.kayaknevada.org

New Jersey

Jersey Shore Sea Kayaking Association
c/o Sam Mikhail
7-11 South Ave.
Garwood NJ 07027
www.jsska.org

New York

Adirondack Mountain Club
Genesee Valley Chapter
P.O. Box 18558
Rochester NY 14618

CNY Kayak Club
4661 Antoinette Dr.
Marcellus NY 13108
www.cnykayakclub.com

Cold Spring Kayak Club
P.O. Box 81
Cold Spring NY 10516
www.cskc.org

Finger Lakes Ontario Watershed Paddler's Club
   (FLOW)
43 Whelehan Dr.
Rochester NY 14616
www.flowpaddlers.org

Hudson River Watertrail Association
Box 110
245 Eighth Ave.
New York NY 10011
www.hrwa.org/index.html

Huntington Kayak Klub
51 Central Parkway
Huntington NY 11743-4308

Latino Kayakers of America
Alicio Valle, President
P.O. Box 491
Vails Gate NY 12584
www.latinokayakersofamerica.com

Long Island Paddlers
P.O. Box 115
West Sayville NY 11796
www.lipaddlers.org

Metropolitan Association of Sea Kayakers
195 Prince St. Basement
New York NY 10012

Metropolitan Canoe and Kayak Club
P.O. Box 021868
Brooklyn NY 11202-0040

North Atlantic Canoe and Kayak, Inc. (Long
   Island)
P.O. Box 124
Wantagh NY 11793
www.getthenack.org

Sebago Canoe Club
Paerdegat Basin, Foot of Ave N
Brooklyn NY 11236
www.sebagocanoeclub.org

Shelter Island Paddler Club
Shelter Island NY 11964
www.sipaddlerclub.com

Skaneateles Kayak Club
2825 West Lake Rd.
Skaneateles NY 13152

Storm Paddlers
www.stormpaddle.com

Touring Kayak Club
205 Beach St.
City Island, Bronx NY 10464
www.touringkayakclub.org

North Carolina

Cape Fears Paddling Association
Wilmington NC website only
www.capefearpaddlers.org

Carolina Kayak Club
Central North Carolina
www.carolinakayakclub.org

Crystal Coast Canoe and Kayak Club
P.O. Box 671
Morehead City NC 28557
www.ccckc.org

Ohio

Bradstreet Sea Kayakers
Bay Village OH 44140
www.seakayaker.org

Columbus Area Kayak Association
Worthington OH 43085

Oregon

Oregon Ocean Paddling Society (OOPS)
P.O. Box 69641
Portland OR 97201
www.oopskayak.org

OutKayaking Northwest
P.O. Box 4761
Portland OR 97208
www.outkayaking.org

Southern Oregon Paddlers
P.O. Box 2111
Bandon OR 97411

Pennsylvania

Pittsburgh Council AYH
6300 Fifth Ave.
Pittsburgh PA 15232

Three Rivers Rowing
300 Waterfront Dr.
Pittsburgh PA 15222
412-231-8772
www.threeriversrowing.org

Rhode Island

Rhode Island Canoe/Kayak Association (RICKA)
P.O. Box 163
Wood River Junction RI 02894
www.ricka.org

South Carolina

Long Bay Paddlers
Myrtle Beach SC
www.longbaypaddlers.com

LowCountry Paddlers
P.O. Box 13242
Charleston SC 29422
www.lowcountrypaddlers.net

Palmetto Paddlers
P.O. Box 984
Columbia SC 29202
www.palmettopaddlers.org

Sea Island Sea Kayakers
Hilton Head Island SC 29925
marshgrassproductionsinc@yahoo.com

SeaYacker Paddle Club
525 Longbranch Rd.
Gilbert SC 29054

Tennessee

Bluff City Canoe Club of Memphis
P.O. Box 40523
Memphis TN 38104
www.bluffcitycanoeclub.org

Texas

DFW Paddlers
Dallas-Fort Worth area
www.groups.yahoo.com/group/DFWpaddlers

Houston Association of Sea Kayakers
12601 Boheme Dr.
Houston TX 77024
www.hask.org

Houston Canoe Club
P.O. Box 925516
Houston TX 77292
www.houstoncanoeclub.org

Vermont

Champlain Kayak Club
89 Caroline St.
Burlington VT 05401
www.ckayak.com

Virginia

Pirates of Lynnhaven Kayak Fishing Club
P.O. Box 61005
Virginia Beach VA 23466
www.piratesoflynnhaven.org

Washington

Baidarka Historical Society
P.O. Box 5454
Bellingham WA 98227

Boeing Sea Kayak Club (Boeing employees)
P.O. Box 3707, M/S 7M-HC
Seattle WA 98124
www.bewet.org

Desert Kayak and Canoe Club (DKCC)
Tri-Cities and eastern Washington
www.dkcc.org

Hole in the Wall Paddling Club
Anacortes WA 98221
www.holeinthewallpaddlingclub.org

Lesbian and Gay Sea Kayakers
1122 E. Pike, #896
Seattle WA 98122-3934

Matelot Sea Kayak Touring Club
Tacoma WA
www.matelotkayakclub.blogspot.com

The Mountaineers
700 Sand Point Way NE
Seattle WA 98115
www.mountaineers.org

North Sound Sea Kayaking Association (NSSKA)
P.O. Box 1523
Everett WA 98206
www.nsseakayaker.homestead.com

Olympic Kayak Club
Port Gamble WA 98364
www.olympickayakclub.com

Olympic Peninsula Paddlers
P.O. Box 83
Port Angeles WA 98362
info@olympicpeninsulapaddlers.com
www.olympicpeninsulapaddlers.com

Port Orchard Paddle Club
2398 Jefferson Ave. SE
Port Orchard WA 98366

Puget Sound Paddle Club
P.O. Box 112361
Tacoma WA 98411-2361

Sea Kayak Club of WA
Bicton WA 6157
www.seakayakwa.org.au

Seattle Sea Kayak Club
7173 State Rt. 9
Sedro Woolley WA 98284
www.seattlekayak.org

Sound Rowers Open Water Rowing &
Paddling Club
www.soundrowers.org

South Sound Area Kayakers
www.ssak.hctc.com

Washington Kayak Club
P.O. Box 24264
Seattle WA 98124
www.washingtonkayakclub.org

Washington Water Trails Association
The Good Shepard Center
4649 Sunnyside Ave. N, #305
Seattle WA 98103
www.wwta.org

Whatcom Association of Kayak Enthusiasts
(WAKE)
P.O. Box 1952
Bellingham WA 98227
www.wakekayak.org

Yakima Kayak Club
P.O. Box 11147
Yakima WA 98909

Wisconsin

Badger State Boating Society
www.bsbs.org

Mad City Paddlers
Madison WI 53703
www.geocities.com/

Wyoming

Grand Tetons Paddling Club
Snake River Kayak & Canoe
365 N. Cache St.
Jackson Hole WY 83001

International

Argentina

Mar Del Plata Kayak Club
c/o Adrian Pol
Ayacucho 3108
7600 Mar Del Plata

Australia

Investigator Canoe Club
c/o 28 Rowells Rd.
Lockleys 5032

NSW Sea Kayak Club
P.O. Box 691
Turramurra, NSW 2074
www.nswseakayaker.asn.au

Queensland Sea Kayak Club
c/o 19 Easter Crescent
Pacific Pines QLD 4211
www.qldseakayak.canoe.org.au/

Tarwin River Canoe Club
P.O. Box 65
Tarwin Lower
Victoria 3956

Victorian Sea Kayak Club
P.O. Box 426
Seaford, Victoria 3198
www.vskc.org.au

Brazil

Turma do Remo dos Sete Mares do Sangava
Fernão dias, 12 apto 1504
11055-220 Santos, São Paulo
gil@santosdata.com.br
www.turmadoremo.com.br

Canada

Alliance of British Columbia Sea Kayak Guides
221 Ferntree Place
Nanaimo BC V9R 5M1

Atlantic Kayak Association
atlantic_kayak_association@hotmail.com

Big Lake Kayak Touring Club
c/o Tony Kinal
162 Whitley Dr.
Winnipeg MB R2N 1M8

Campbell River Paddlers
Campbell River BC
www.crpaddlers.com

Chinook Club de Kayak Mer de Montreal
www.chinook-kayak.com

ClubLocarno
1300 Discovery St.
Vancouver BC V6R 4L9
www.clublocarno.com

Cowichan Kayak and Canoe Club
2881 Mountain Rd., RR #7
Duncan BC V9L4W4

Creative Options for Recreational Kayakers
(C.O.R.K.)
P.O. Box 32073
Langley BC V1M 2M3

Great Lakes Sea Kayaking Association
P.O. Box 22082
45 Overlea Blvd.
Toronto ON M4H 1N9
www.glskafreehostia.com/

Kayak Newfoundland & Labrador
P.O. Box 2, Stn. C, St. John's
Newfoundland A1C 5H4
www.kayakers.nf.ca

Komoux Valley Paddlers Club
Box 10045
2064 Comox Ave.
Comox BC V9M 3S5

North Island Paddle Association
Box 703
Port Hardy BC V0N 2P0

Ocean Kayak Association of British Columbia
106 Payne Rd., Box 15
Saturna Island BC V0N 2Y0

Pacific International Kayak Association (P.I.K.A.)
P.O. Box 32073
Langley BC V1M 2M3

Royal Bamfield Kayak & Yacht Club
Box 32
Bamfield BC V0R 1B0

Sea Kayak Association of British Columbia
Box 751, Postal Station A
Vancouver BC V6C 2NC
www.skabc.org

South Island Sea Kayaking Association
SISKA
Victoria BC
www.siska.ca

Touring Kayakers of Ottawa
www.touringkayakersottawa

Victoria Sea Kayakers' Network
752 Victoria Ave.
Victoria BC V8S 4N3

Chile

Club de Kayak Sur Extremo
Santiago
www.ecodeporte.cl/kayakdemar

Finland

Helsingin Kanoottiklubi
P.O. Box 72
00251 Helsinki

Helsingin Melojat
Käpyläntie 1 C 42
00610

Melaveikot r.y.
c/o Matti Seppanen
Maistraatinkatu 6 C 15
00240, Helsinki

Sipoon Kanoottiklubi - Sibbo Kanotklubb
Talmankuja
04240 Talma, Sipoo
www.sipoonkanoottiklubi.net/

France

Calvados Kayak Mer
Calvados & Normandy Coasts
www.calvadoskayakmer.asso1901.com

CK/mer
8 rue de Portail
35-132 Vezin-le-Coquet
www.ckmer.org

Neree chez SZLAPKA
Chemin de Galance
84120 La Bastidonne
www.neree.org

Germany

Kanu-Verein Unterweser Bremerhaven
c/o Wolfgang Bisle
Tidemanstr. 37, D-28759 Bremen
www.kvu.der-norden.de

Salzwasser Union
c/o Bernhard Hillejan, Karl-Arnold-Strasse 10
D-51109 Köln
www.salzwasserunion.de

Great Britain

International Sea Kayaking Association
5 Osprey Ave.
The Hoskers, Westhoughton
Bolton, Lancs, BL5 2SL

Jersey Canoe Club
c/o Kevin Mansell
177 Quennejais Pk.
St. Brelade, Jersey, JE3 8JU

Paddlers International
8 Wiltshire Ave.
Hornchurch, Essex, RM11 3DX

Pentland Canoe Club
c/o Ken Nicol
Downton Cottage, Crescent St., Halkirk
Caithness, Scotland KW12 6XN

Sea Kayak Group UK
c/o John Fiszman
54, St. Clare's Close
Littleover, Derby, DE22 3JF

Shetland Canoe Club
c/o Bridge-end Outdoor Centre
Bridge-end, Burra Isle, ZE2 9LE

Tower Hamlets Canoe Club
3-4 Shadwell Pierhead
Glamis Rd.
London E1W 3TD
www.towerhamletscanoeclub.co.uk

Greenland

Qaannat Kattuffiat
Grønlands Kajak Forbund
National Kayak League
P.O. Box 345, DK-3911 Sisimiut

Peqatigiiffik Qajaq Nuuk
Foreningen Kajak Nuuk
Nuuk Kayak Club
P.O. Box 557
DK-3900 Nuuk

Iceland

Kayakklúbburinn KAJ
East Iceland
c/o Ari Benediktsson
Blomsturvellir 46.740 Nordfjördur
kayakklubburinn@gmail.com
Kajakklúbburinn Kaj - Heim

Ireland

Causeway Coast Kayak Association
12 Glenvale Ave.
Portrush, Co. Antrim, BT56 8HL

East Coast Sea Kayaking Association
c/o Des Keaney
Barchuillia Commons
Kilmacanogue, Co. Wicklow

Irish Sea Kayaking Association
c/o Des Keaney
Barchuillia Commons
Kilmacanogue, Co. Wicklow

Israel

Dor-Kayak Club
in the Dor/Habonim nature reserve
www.dor-kayak.co.il

Terra Santa Kayak Expeditions
The Club
24 Menora St.
Menora, 73134
www.seakayak.co.il/

Italy

Canoa Kayak Friuli
Via Dante, 17
33051 Aquileia (Udine)
www.canoafriuli.com

Il Kayak da Mare
c/o Sergio Cadoni
Viale Colombo 118
09045 Quartu S., Elena, Cagliari

Inuit People Group
c/o Stefano De Florio
Via Morosini 16, 21100 Varese

Japan

Sasebo Sea Kayaking Club
3-8 Motomachi Sasebo City
Nagasaki Prefecture, 857

Sea Walkers
Iso 4-18-2
c/o PO Katsura
Urasoe City, Okinawa 901-21

Netherlands

Peddelpraat
p/a Ine Dost
Duivenkamp 726
NL-3607 VD Maarssen

New Zealand

Canterbury Sea Kayakers Network
14 Birdling Place
Halswell, Christchurch 8025
kayakamf@gmail.com

Kiwi Association of Sea Kayakers
c/o Paul Caffyn
RD 1
Runanga, West Coast
www.kask.co.nz

New Zealand Recreational Canoeing Association
www.rivers.org.nz

Sea Kayak Operators Association
P.O. Box 195
Picton

Wellington Sea Kayak Network
wskn.wellington.net.nz

The Yakity Yak Kayak Club
Auckland

Norway

Grenland Havpadleklubb-Telemark Coast
c/o S. Hansen
Skaugaards gt. 31
N-3970 Langesund

Lillehammer Ro-og Kajakklubb
c/o Kai Gjessing
postbooks 422
N-2603 Lillehammer
www.lrkk.no

Stavanger Kajakklubb
c/o Kjell Hauge
Smavollen 4
4017 Stavanger
www.stavangerkajakk.no

Portugal

Amigos da Pagaia
www.amigosdapagaia.com

Spain

Pagaia Club de Caiac Cap de Creus
Apartat de Correus 140
17490 Llanca-Girona
info@pagaia.com
www.pagaia.com

Sweden

Brunnsvikens Kanotklubb
Frescati Hagväg 5
S-104 05 Stockholm
www.bkk.se

Ornsbergs Kanotsallskap
Box 9240
10273 Stockholm
www.oks.nu

Tjorn Kayak Club
c/o Jens Marklund
Elvkvarnsliden 8472 31 Svanesund

Tasmania

Maatsuyker Canoe Club
Tasmania
jennings@vision.net.au
www.maatsuykercc

Tasmanian Sea Canoeing Club
P.O. Box 599F
Hobart, Tasmania 7001

Turkey

BoDeKa
Bogazici Deniz Kayakcilari
Istanbul
www.bodeka.com

Venezuela

Kayak Club Venezuela
info@kayakclubvenezuela.com
www.kayakclubvenezuela.com

ORGANIZATIONS AND ASSOCIATIONS

American Canoe Association, www.americancanoe .org. Comprehensive list of ACA-sponsored events and instructional clinics, information on membership benefits, and coverage of many environmental issues affecting paddlers.

British Canoe Union, www.bcu.org.uk. Information on membership, skills, instructor training and certifications, and numerous paddling links.

British Canoe Union (North America), www.bcuna .com. Information on BCU programs and coaches in North America. Instructional and assessment programs are provided for all sites in North America as well as BCU information on membership and guidelines for training.

Canadian Recreational Canoe Association, www .crca.ca. Paddling events and membership and subscription information for *Kanawa* magazine, as well as reading lists by and for its members.

Leave No Trace, www.lnt.org. Low-impact techniques for traveling in the wilderness.

National Audubon Society, www.audubon.org. Information on NAS programs and travel as well as ornithology news.

The Nature Conservancy, www.tnc.org. Information on TNC preserves and programs.

Paddle Smart, www.paddlesmart.com. Safety information for small boaters, events calendar, and hypothermia data.

General Information and Some Useful Links

Doing an Internet search for "sea kayaking" yields thousands of sites ranging from the generally informative to the commercially specific to the completely unrelated. The list I've included here takes you to some of the general sites with lists of great links that are updated regularly. I have not included sites specific to any one outfitter or store, though some of these sites do sell gear.

California Kayak Friends, www.ckf.com. California Kayak Friends has served as a respected voice in the paddling community for many years.

Gorp.com, www.gorp.com. This site provides a wealth of links for all outdoor sports.

Outdoorplay.com, www.outdoorplay.com. This is a large commercial site, but it provides some helpful features like interviews, book excerpts, and advice from the experts.

Paddling.net, www.paddling.net. This is a good site for gear updates, press releases on paddling topics, and active discussion groups.

See Kayak, www.seekayak.com. Somewhat biased toward the Northeast, this site is sponsored by Guillemot Kayaks and provides a wealth of information through its many links.

Weather and Tides

National Oceanic and Atmospheric Administration, www.noaa.gov

National Oceanographic Data Center, www.nodc .noaa.gov

National Weather Service, www.weather.gov

The Weather Channel, www.weather.com

Tide and Current Predictor, www.tbone.biol.sc .edu/tide/sitesel.html

Odds and Ends

Coastal Kayak Fishing, www.kayakfishing.com

Disabled Paddlers, www.disabledadventures.com, www.adaptivekayaking.com

Kayak Diving, www.kayakdiving.com

Kayaking singles: www.fitness-singles.com

Surf and swell information: www.surfline.com

Build-Your-Own Schools

Aleut Wood and Skin Kayaks (Bruce Lemon), Jacksonville NY, 607-367-8000

Berkshire Boat Building School, www.berkshireboatbuildingschool.org, Sheffield MA

Skin Boat School (Corey Freeman), www.skinboats.org, Anacortes WA, 360-299-0804

Superior Kayaks (Mark and Celeste Rogers), www.superiorkayaks.com, Whitelaw WI, 920-732-3784

Wooden Boat School, www.thewoodenboatschool.com, Brooklin ME, 207-359-4651

WATER TRAILS

Water trail networks have grown significantly over the last ten years, and the links and contact information are often compiled and posted on commercial sites. The best of these offer extensive listings by state and province as well as useful information for planning a trip in a particular area. Here are some of my favorites:

www.americantrails.org
www.outdooradventurescanada.com
www.seakayakermagazine.com
www.trails.com
www.watertrailslocator.com

Canada
Alberta Water Trails
Alberta TrailNet
www.albertatrailnet.com
www.tpr.alberta.ca/recreation/trails

Alexander Mackenzie Voyageur Route
Alexander Mackenzie Voyageur Route Association
www.amvr.org
museum@peaceriver.net

B.C. Marine Trail
B.C. Marine Trail Association
www.bcmarinetrails.org

Canadian Heritage Rivers System
Parks Canada
www.chrs.ca
These designated rivers total some 8,000 kilometers in length and represent outstanding rivers across all the Canadian provinces. This site has many water trail links through provincial sites and other resources.

Ontario Water Trails
www.ontariotrails.on.ca

Sanguenay Fjord
Parc du Saguenay
www.outdooradventurescanada.com

South Saskatchewan River Trail
www.meewasin.com

United States
Alabama
www.alabamascenicrivertrail.com
www.outdooralabama.com

Alaska
This site links to several state-regulated trails:
www.dnr.alaska.gov/parks/aktrails

Cross Admiralty Island Canoe Route
www.fs.fed.us/r10/chatham.anm

Honker Divide Canoe Route
www.fs.fed.us/r10/ketchikan/tnb/thorne

Kenai National Wildlife Refuge
www.r7.fws.gov/nwr/kenai/canoe

Sarkar Lakes Canoe Route
www.fs.fed.us/r10/ketchikan/tnb/thorne

Shuyak Island Marine Trail
www.dnr.alaska.gov/parks/aktrails

Tongass National Forest
www.fs.fed.us/r10/tongass

Wood-Tikchik State Park
www.dnr.state.ak.us/parks/units/woodtik.htm

California
Clear Lake Water Trail
www.konoctitrails.com

Lake Tahoe
www.laketahoewatertrail.org

San Francisco Bay
www.bayaccess.org

Connecticut
Connecticut River Estuary Regional Planning
   Agency
www.crjc.org

Connecticut Rivers Alliance
www.connecticutwatertrails.org

Connecticut Water Trails Association
www.connecticutwatertrails.com

Florida
Calusa
www.calusablueway.com

Everglades
www.evergladeswildwtrway.org

Florida Paddling Trails Association
www.floridapaddlingtrails.com

Florida Saltwater Paddling
www.dep.state.fl.us/gwt

Illinois
Northeastern Illinois Water Trails
Chicago's Lakefront Water Trails
www.openlands.org/watertrails

Indiana
Indiana Water Trails
www.in.gov/dnr/outdoor

Kansas
Kansas Canoe and Kayak Association
www.kansas.net/~tjhittle/

Louisiana
www.bayoutrails.org
www.cajuncoastpaddle.com

Maine
Allagash Wilderness Waterway
www.maine.gov/cgi-bin/doc/parks

Maine Island Trail
Maine Island Trail Association
www.mita.org

Northern Forest Canoe Trail
www.northernforestcanoetrail.org

Maryland
www.baygateways.net
www.dnr.state.md/us/greenways

Potomac Water Trail
www.potomactrail.org

Massachusetts
Connecticut River Water Trail
www.byways.org/explore/byways/

Michigan
www.michigan.gov.dnr

Hiawatha Water Trail
www.hiawathawatertrail.org

Keweenaw Water Trail Association
www.kwta.org

Michigan Heritage Water Trails
www.wmich.edu/glcms/watertrails

Tip of the Thumb Water Trail
www.thumbtrails.com

Minnesota
www.dnr.state.mn.us

Boundary Waters Canoe Area Wilderness
www.bwca.com

Lake Superior Water Trail
www.lswta.org

Missouri
Lewis and Clark Water Trail
www.missouririverwatertrail.org

New Hampshire
Northern Forest Canoe Trail
www.northernforestcanoetrail.org

Upper Connecticut River Valley Trail
www.crjc.org

New York
Adirondack Canoe Routes
www.adirondacks.com/canoe

Department of Environmental Conservation
www.dec.ny.gov

Hudson River Watertrail Association
www.hrwa.org

New York Seaway Trail
www.newyorkseawaytrail.com

Northern Forest Canoe Trail
www.northernforestcanoetrail.org

North Carolina
Albemarle Sound Canoe and Small Boat Trails
    System
www.albemarle-nc.com
www.coastalguide.com
www.pamlico.com
www.canoenc.com

North Carolina Coastal Plains Paddling Trail
www.ncsu.edu/paddletrails

Ohio
Ohio Water Trails
www.ohiodnr.com

Oregon
Coos Bay Estuary Water Trails
www.coostrails.com

Lewis and Clark Columbia River Water Trail
www.columbiawatertrail.org

Northeast Discovery Water Trail
www.wwta.org/trails

Siuslaw Estuary Water Trail
www.siuslawwatertrail.com

Tillamook County Water Trail
www.tbnep.org

Pennsylvania
www.fish.state.pa.us/watertrails

Juniata River Trail
www.fish.state.pa.us/watertrails/juniata

Lehigh River Water Trail
www.fish.state.pa.us/watertrails/lehigh

Susquehanna River Trail
www.susquehannarivertrail.org

Rhode Island
Rhode Island Blueways
www.exploreri.org

South Carolina
Beaufort Blueways
www.beaufortblueway.info

Berkeley County Blueways
www.berkeleycountyblueways.com

South Carolina Parks, Recreation, and Tourism
    Department
www.sctrails.net

Tennessee
French Broad River
www.knoxcounty.org/frenchbroad

Pellissipi Blueway
www.cs.utk.edu~dunigan/blueway

Texas
Inland and Coastal Paddling Trail
www.tpwd.state.tx.us/fishboat/boat/paddlingtrails

Vermont
Lake Champlain Paddlers Trail
www.lakechamplaincommittee.org/lake/paddlers

Northern Forest Canoe Trail
www.northernforestcanoetrail.org

Virginia
Upper James River Water Trail
www.upperjamesriverwatertrail.com

Washington
Lower Columbia Water Trail
www.columbiawatertrail.org

Washington Water Trails Association
Cascadia Marine Trail
Lake to Locks Water Trail
Northwest Discovery Water Trail
Willapa Bay Water Trail
www.wwta.org

Wisconsin
Apostle Islands National Lakeshore
www.nps.gov/apis

Index

Italicized numbers refer to pages with illustrations.